DOROTHY ROGERS

*State University
of New York
at Oswego*

THE
ADULT
YEARS

An
Introduction
to Aging

Prentice-Hall, Inc.
Englewood Cliffs, New Jersey
07632

Library of Congress Cataloging in Publication Data

ROGERS, DOROTHY
  The adult years.

  Bibliography: p. 436
  Includes index.
  1. Adulthood. 2. Middle age—Psychological aspects.
3. Aged—Psychology. 4. Aging—Psychological aspects.
I. Title.
BF724.5.R57   155.6   78-31352
ISBN 0-13-008987-7

For Betty

Printed in the United States of America

10 9 8 7 6 5 4 3 2 1

Prentice-Hall International, Inc., *London*
Prentice-Hall of Australia Pty. Limited, *Sydney*
Prentice-Hall of Canada, Ltd., *Toronto*
Prentice-Hall of India Private Limited, *New Delhi*
Prentice-Hall of Japan, Inc., *Tokyo*
Prentice-Hall of Southeast Asia Pte. Ltd., *Singapore*
Whitehall Books Limited, *Wellington, New Zealand*

ACKNOWLEDGMENTS

Permission to reprint the following copyrighted materials in this book is gratefully acknowledged:

Quote, p. 136, reprinted from *The American Scholar*, Volume 45, November 2, Spring, 1976. Copyright © 1976 by the United Chapters of Phi Beta Kappa. By permission of the publishers.

Quotes, pp. 4, 6, 7, 14, 149, 258, 409, 410, 427, reprinted by permission of *Daedalus*, Journal of the American Academy of Arts and Sciences, Boston, Massachusetts.

Quote, p. 380, permission granted by The Gerontologist Society.

Quote, p. 330, copyrighted 1971 by the National Council on Family Relations. Reprinted by permission.

Quote, p. 176, copyrighted 1973 by the National Council on Family Relations. Reprinted by permission.

Quotes, pp. 72, 76, 175, 193, 194, 207, 208, 209, 219, 222, 236, 240, 260, copyrighted 1974 by the National Council on Family Relations. Reprinted by permission.

Quotes, pp. 103, 104, 193, 205, 208, 215, 273, copyrighted 1975 by the National Council on Family Relations. Reprinted by permission.

Quotes, pp. 123, 152, 221, 349, copyrighted 1976 by the National Council on Family Relations. Reprinted by permission.

Quote, p. 218, copyrighted 1977 by the National Council on Family Relations. Reprinted by permission.

Quote, p. 251, reprinted by permission of New Woman, Inc. Copyright © 1971 by *New Woman* Magazine. "The Case Against Marriage" first appeared in the September 1971 issue of *New Woman*.

Chapter 2: Abriged from Dorothy Rogers, *Psychology of Adolescence*, 3rd ed. (Englewood Cliffs, N.J.: Prentice-Hall, Inc., 1977), pp. 477–498, with permission.

Quote, p. 361, © 1977 by The New York Times Company. Reprinted by permission.

Photos, pp. 99, 158, 241, Frank M. Gaines, III.

Photos, pp. 48, 109, 135, 271, 425, courtesy of Community Relations Office, State University of New York at Oswego.

CONTENTS

9
CHAPTER   Alternative Life Styles   226

10
CHAPTER   Work and Leisure   257

14
CHAPTER   Policies and Programs   367

15
CHAPTER   Death   392

PREFACE

This book is designed as a textbook for courses in adult psychology. It deals with adults in general as well as adults at three life stages: early, middle, and later adulthood. The fact that certain topics are dealt with on all three levels produces an illusion of redundancy. Nevertheless, this approach reveals the significance of certain matters at successive age levels. All adults share certain aspects of life content as well as those distinctive at particular stages.

A comprehensive, developmental view of adulthood is built into the book's organization. Part I introduces the reader to the study of adulthood, in terms of current theories and research emphases. Part II relates to young adults, including their passage into adulthood, their main tasks and life styles. Part III deals mainly with middle-aged adults—their characteristics, life styles and activities. Much of the material presented in this section might well apply to adults generally. In Part IV older adults are described in much the same way, in terms of characteristics and life styles. In addition, special focus is placed on their problems and crises, including death, and on programs designed to help them. Finally, in Part V an attempt is made to integrate concepts and conclusions about adulthood, and to suggest projections about the future.

Certain features add to the book's desirability and usefulness as a classroom text. A summary of the salient points of each chapter underscores the basic principles of adult psychology and provides convenient review. A glossary explains terms which may be unfamiliar to the student and serves as a useful reference tool. Supplementary study material is suggested in annotated reading lists compiled from a wide range of scholarly journals and books.

The text is written in a simple, lucid style, yet without sacrifice of intellectual depth. Concepts are carefully explained and often are clarified by anecdotal illustrations. Where no source is given for quoted passages and illustrations, these materials are from the author's own files and are the results of her own research.

In terms of content, stress has been placed on relevance, special issues, up-to-dateness, and human interest. An effort has been made to sift out purely esoteric material and to retain that which is of genuine concern to adults today. Since students who use this volume—whether adults already or adults-in-the-becoming—will become involved in, and identify best with, personalized material, a human-interest approach has been used. Adults are discussed regarding many significant issues, often relating to such controversial topics as marriage therapy, group marriage, nursing homes, and sustaining life by machines. Throughout the book the concept of pluralism is recognized, that adults have infinitely varied personalities and fall into complexly differing categories. Such content, however, is integrated with up-to-date theory and research. Most of the sources used date within the past five years. Attention is also given to "anticipatory" material—that is, an effort is made to sense issues-in-the-making, and what may lie ahead. The idea is to show that the status of adults is not static but fluid, with its roots in the past and reaching into the future.

I wish to thank Kitty Woringer for the superb quality of her assistance in editing the book and to my ever faithful typists, Ann Hoefer and Cherie Blanchard. I also wish to acknowledge the assistance of Sue McDougall, Betty Bartkowiak, Amelia Carpenter, Maria Ricketson, John Wilson and Tim Hammond for helping gather the anecdotal material used in this book.

I
PART

Introducing the Psychology of Adulthood

1 CHAPTER

Introduction

What are the
BASIC CONCEPTS ?
Why is there
Interest in Adulthood ?

What is
A recent phenomenon. Only recently has adulthood begun to come into its own. Children were studied in the 17th century, adolescents in the early 20th century, and the aged a few decades later. A variety of writers, social reformers, medical personnel, and psychologists focused on the physical and mental limitations of later years in the wake of the industrial revolution. However not until the 1940s was gerontology, the study of the elderly, recognized as a new medical field, and only about midcentury did social scientists decide that old age was a significant problem. It was later still, in the 1970s, before the first real interest was shown in the early and middle adult years. Even in 1968 there was no article on adulthood in the *International Encyclopedia of the Social Sciences* (Jordan, 1976). But now social scientists have become concerned about it, and more research is being done and more books written on the subject. While publications are still few in comparison to those about children and adolescents, the interest being paid adults dwarfs what has been shown them before. It is just possible, surmises Graubard (1976), that we are entering "the century of the adult, at least in America."

Why is there
Interest in old age. There are various plausible reasons why interest in adulthood has grown. Concern was first felt about the elderly because of their dramatic increase in numbers and the ever-growing burden on society for their care. Because of the steadily decreasing birthrate and medical advances that have permitted vastly greater numbers to grow old, the elderly have become far more visible than in former years. Though still a minority, they are the fastest-growing age group. During the first seven decades of this century the total population of the United States increased in size almost three times, but during the same period the older population mushroomed almost sevenfold and is still growing. In the 1960s alone, older Americans grew in numbers by approximately 18% compared with a 13% growth in the general population (Lowy, 1975).

The problem was further enhanced by the rapid transition in America from the extended family to the nuclear family, which required helping oldsters to make it on their own. In the extended family, which

4

included the parents, the children, and perhaps other relatives (usually grandparents), older people blended unobtrusively into the society. However, industrialization and technological society made the extended family unwieldy and the stripped-down nuclear family, which was capable of moving about the country with relative ease, the vogue. Hence the task of caring for the old, cast loose from extended family moorings, raised the question, what are older people like and what are their needs? The answer was a growing interest in gerontology, the study of old age, and geriatrics, the science of treating and healing its illnesses and disorders. Gerontology is especially concerned with "differences in aging: how some people may age successfully, how others may experience increasing difficulties, how one person may continue learning and growing while another gets stuck, lost in the past" (Zarit, 1977, p. 11). Gerontology is not concerned merely with problems, but also with the possibility of continuing growth in older people. Overall it is the study of "the whole person" and the aging process as "reflected in all aspects of life functioning" (Zarit, 1977, p. 12).

Interest in entire adult span. Why did a psychology of all the adult years develop? Perhaps partly it was a belated recognition that this stage was all that was left of the life cycle to study, a matter of closure, or a need for completion. Also certain samplings of children who had been studied over a span of years (in what is called longitudinal research) had grown up. Naturally researchers became interested in what might happen to these people in decades ahead. For another thing, for the first time in history adults in modern Western society have become sufficiently affluent and have enough free time to think about their personal development. In former times their energies were largely absorbed by the sheer business of survival and childrearing. In addition, the possibility of limiting family size has made it possible for parents to stake out their own claims to "personhood," and to make childrearing fit their own life patterns, instead of the reverse.

What is an Adult?

Definition. Just what is an adult? The term "adult" evokes all sorts of associations in our minds. When we were children adults seemed all-powerful and adulthood itself terribly remote; to be adult was to pay more to go to the movies, or to drive cars, or to smoke cigars.

Even among adults the term "adult" has no definite meaning. Does anyone know for sure when he or she becomes an adult? The following replies from young adults are illustrative of the quite varied ages when people first feel like adults and of their reasons for doing so.

At age 20 when I first moved out of my parents' home into my own.

I still don't feel like an adult, but more like a young adult. When I took off a semester from school to live in Europe I felt I was on the road to adulthood.

At age 18 as a result of paying for my education and working to support myself.

At age 21, when it became legal to do anything I wanted in any state.

At age 18 when I had my first apartment.

At age 21 when people finally began treating me as an adult.

At age 14 when I held my first job and worked from 20 to 40 hours a week.

At age 17 when family problems placed heavy responsibilities on my shoulders.

At age 14 when my mother was hospitalized and I had to take care of my younger brothers and sisters.

About age 12 or 13 because both my parents worked and I had to take care of myself.

It should be added that a number of the young adults questioned said they still didn't feel like full-fledged adults.

Even social scientists seldom raise the question, what is adulthood? It doesn't have the kinds of associations for us that the words childhood or adolescence do. Instead it "seems almost a catch-all category for everything that happens to the individual human being after a specific chronological age—whether 18, 21, or some other" (Graubard, 1976, p. v).

Indeed the adult has been "a pretty casual fellow," taken for granted in cultures around the world. After all, didn't adults know what adults were like? A conscientious concern for "what it means to be an adult is a specifically American phenomenon, and a rather recent one at that. No precise equivalent of the Anglo-American term adulthood—that is, denoting a distinct stage in the life cycle—exists in any other European language" (Malia, 1976, pp. 169–170). Instead the Europeans typically speak of maturity in the sense of ripeness as applicable to any living thing. True, they do have terms meaning grown up or "major"—that is, of legal age, and in a sense they carry the connotations of "responsible" or "adult." Nevertheless neither these countries nor their languages consciously identify adulthood as a distinct stage in human development (Rudolph & Rudolph, 1976).

The same has been true through the ages and around the world. The term "adult" itself comes from the Latin "adolescere," to grow up.

Though Americans accept adulthood as a stage, they have no set image of what an adult is like.

It suggests a process rather than the more final attainment of a specific status (Bouwsma, 1976). Similarly, Confucianism interprets adult maturity not as a state of attainment, but as a process of becoming. The paths for self-realization are varied, and the life of Confucius is not the only standard. Confucius himself never taught his students simply to model themselves after him. Instead he insisted that they realize humanity or adulthood within themselves (Tu Wei-Ming, 1976).

What are the

Images. While Americans tacitly acknowledge adulthood as a stage, they hold no consistent image of what adults are like. A random selection of views on the subject proves this to be the case. According to Erik Erikson (1976), "to be grown up, in any language and vision, has a particular quality of standing tall, so proudly and yet so precariously, that there is a universal need to attest and to protest that one knows where one stands, and that one has some status in the center of a vision of a new, or, at any rate, forever renewed, human type" (p. 18). Stegner (1976) suggests that qualities of adults include "sanity, normality, rationality, continuity, sobriety, responsibility, wisdom, conduct as opposed to mere behavior, [and] the good of the family or group or species as distinct from the desires of the individual. . . . " (p. 39). Adulthood in its highest form is symbolized in the lives of wise men, saints, and

7

culture heroes. In our pluralistic society there are so many kinds of ideal figures that they are not always easily reconcilable with each other. Indeed if the present trend toward increased ethnicity and diversity persists we may not have an identifiable American adult, but instead diverse and inconsistent life styles and values representing the various subcultures (Stegner, 1976).

The term adult may also suggest less flattering descriptions such as stodgy, settled, or more practical than idealistic. Growth is perceived by some as proceeding until adulthood when a certain dormancy sets in, and the dreams of youth go down the drain. And the older the adult, the truer this image becomes. In old age, some people believe, adults are at the lowest point of their lives: they are inflexibly set in their ways.

Most images of adulthood relate to the middle years. We have no clear picture of the young adult, and that of the aged is distinct from that of the middle years. It was not always so—the aged as a human tragedy is a fairly recent phenomenon. In the late nineteenth century American society moved from acknowledging growing old as a natural process to perceiving it as a separate period of life accompanied by weakness, decline, and obsolescence (Hareven, 1976). Advanced years, formerly respected and regarded as evidence of strength and an ability to survive, were later deplored as indicative of deterioration and dependence.

THE AGING PROCESS *What is* ?

Factors in Aging *What are the* ?

Maturational factors. *What are the* In many people's minds the term "aging" suggests growing old; however, gerontologists sometimes point out that aging begins at the moment of conception. As a result of aging the organism proceeds through stages of immaturity, maturity, and deterioration. Progressively, as people grow older, incoming stimuli are processed more slowly, the rate of biological interaction in the body decreases, and metabolic processes slow down. In fact, "there may even be various pacemakers built in to predetermine some of these changes which, with age, ultimately lead to a type of shut off or, as Freud suggested, an intrinsic death force or built-in pattern leading to an inorganic state" (Cath, 1975, p. 207). In the biological sense aging is often fatalistically viewed as the ticking away of an uncontrollable time clock that dooms us to a continuous process of decline and ultimate demise. Despite its inevitability, it is not altogether beyond our control.

The morale factor. The aging process is not solely a matter of genetic destiny, for all the stresses that the body has experienced during a lifetime are involved. Every period of stress, especially those which involve frustration and lack of success, leave actual scars which contribute to tissue aging (Selye, 1974). By contrast successful activity, even if intense, leaves apparently little scar. In fact it provides exhilaration, leaving one feeling youthful even to advanced old age. For example, Hans Selye tells of entering medical school at age 18 and becoming so fascinated with research about disease and life that he would get up at four in the morning and study in the garden until six in the evening. His wife would warn him that he could not endure such long hours without ultimately experiencing a nervous breakdown. However even now, in his late 60s, he still gets up at 4 or 5 A.M. and works until late at night with few interruptions and is in perfectly good health. All he does to fight aging and senility is to swim for an hour or ride his bicycle when he wakes up. The trick, declares Selye, is to determine those jobs that one can do, the one that one can do best, and that which he himself and others can best appreciate.

It is a matter of common observation that life satisfaction appears to retard aging. Kalish (1975) observes that "the commonly noted signs of aging may be significantly altered by a warm human relationship, by ability to find new meaning in life, or by involvement in some activity" (p. 24). On the other hand, severe trauma can seemingly transform the middle-aged into the aged within a short span of time.

Physical factors. There is also plentiful evidence that healthful living and preventive medicine can retard the effects of aging and increase longevity. People in the Western world now have a life expectancy of 70 years, a figure which will probably increase to 80 by the end of the century. By contrast, life expectancy in ancient Rome was 22 years, and in classical Greece, 18. While much of this difference derives from the decline in infant mortality rates, it is also a fact that far more people are living longer today than ever before (Katchadourian, 1976).

In recent years growing attention has been paid to the effects retarding diet, exercise, and activity have on aging. Cath (1975) concludes that if there is one significant physiological finding of the last two decades regarding the prevention of aging, it is the advice to remain active, to exercise to whatever degree is tolerable, and to remain busy. When people are no longer active the prognosis for a long and healthy life is poor and "atrophy from disuse is almost as certain as night following day" (p. 206).

Environmental factors. In recent years much attention has been paid to the quality of the physical environment—including pollutants, tobacco, and pesticides, as well as housing or neighborhoods—which may influence health directly or indirectly. Another factor is diet, since persons who eat improperly almost certainly die earlier. For example, too much animal fat probably relates to a high mortality rate, although the evidence is not conclusive.

Among areas of the world where many people live a century or more and retain all their faculties are the tiny village of Vilcabamba in the Andean mountains of Ecuador, the Abkhazian district in the Caucasus mountains of the USSR, and the province of Hunza in the Karakoram mountains, a part of Pakistan-controlled Kashmir. While heredity appears to play a part in longevity in all three places, other factors—even the simple expectation of long life—seemed of more importance. When asked how long they expected to live, young people in the Caucasus generally replied, "to a hundred."

Another important factor is a region's typical diet. The Vilcabamba people in Ecuador raise their own vegetables and grain, and are almost completely vegetarian. Their average daily caloric intake is low, approximately 1200 calories. In Hunza, another agricultural community, the people grow fruits, nuts, vegetables, and grain; their caloric intake too is very low. While the people in the Caucasus eat more than the Hunzans, around 1800 calories, that amount is still 600 calories less than the current recommendation of the United States National Research Council. Moreover their intake of fat is less than half as great as ours. Thus in all three areas the people maintain a low calorie intake while avoiding animal and saturated fats.

Another striking feature of all three areas is the high level of physical activity and fitness required by their mountainside existence, which keeps the inhabitants of these regions in fine physical shape. Dr. Leaf (1974) concludes that these peoples' hearts are in excellent condition because they are engaged in so much physical activity, which is the best way to supply the heart with blood. Very few of these people have heart attacks. In addition, if one artery gets pinched off because it has hardened, there is sufficient circulation to the heart that its affected muscles will not atrophy.

Dr. Leaf also concluded that psychological factors are quite important in cases of extreme longevity. In all three places mentioned, social status is largely dependent upon age, and the older people are the higher they are regarded both by their contemporaries and by younger people. Nor is there any retirement in such agrarian economies. The older people, even the very old, continue to work and take part in both the economy and social life. Hence they have a feeling of purpose in life. In addition these people have strong feelings about the sanctity of marriage, and Dr. Leaf observed couples who had been married 80 years or more. Moreover when one partner survived, remarriage up to age 100 was common. It appears, therefore, that both a happy marriage and a prolonged active sex life contribute to longevity. Oddly enough, too, women with many children lived longer than those who had none, at least in the Caucasus.

What are the

Pathogenic factors. By contrast, other factors accelerate rather than retard the aging process. Certain pathogenic (disease-producing) elements—for example, cigarette smoking and excessive exposure to the sun—relate to having skin wrinkles. Air pollution to some as yet undetermined extent may also contribute to aging. It is well known that people who experience long-term malnutrition and/or work in such environments as coal mines and unhealthful factories age earlier than people in more fortunate circumstances.

Why is

Aging: A Complex Individual Process ?

It becomes apparent that aging is not a simple process, but concerns the impact of time on all aspects of an individual's being and behavior (Zarit, 1977). We can have several different ages at the same time—biological, social, psychological, and chronological. Not all humans age in exactly the same way. They differ greatly in the rate and processes of aging. While genetic factors, as well as life style, undoubtedly play a part, just how all these factors mesh together is not well understood.

What are the

Frames of Reference ?

What is

The chronological model. Because of the varied factors involved in aging, various frames of reference are employed in approaching the topic. Ordinarily people employ the chronological model—they use calendar years—with regard to aging. According to Lowy (1975), "gerontologic research has divided aging into three stages: middle age, later maturity, and old age. Middle age would extend chronologically from 45 or 50 to about 65. Later maturity would begin around 65 and would stretch approximately to 75. Old age would begin at age 75" (p. 139). The chronological approach is simple, precise, and easily explained. Yet it also has significant drawbacks. One of them is that changes that occur with age are not necessarily caused by change in age. For example, 40-year-old men are often far more conservative regarding youthful sexuality than are 25-year-old men. But is this greater conservatism a function of age? The 40-year-olds are more often parents, and the so-called parenting effect may be operating. That is, as parents they become concerned about the potential effect of youthful sex practices on their own children for whom they are responsible. The 25-year-olds are not yet married and think only in terms of themselves (Kimmel, 1974).

In a sense chronological age becomes less important as people grow older simply because people are more variable as they age (Dibner, 1975). Indeed "some 40-year-olds are biologically older than some 80-year-olds, and any individual might 'age' much more or less during one discrete time period in his life than in another" (p. 67).

Chronological age is also an inadequate yardstick for aging because an individual doesn't age all at once. One can be at quite different ages in physical health, mental capacity, endurance, creativity, or other functions (Butler, 1975a). In the process of writing the centennial history of my college, I sought out and interviewed many of the oldest living faculty members and graduates. One woman still lived by herself at the age of 90. She hobbled about and had arthritis; but she had a sparkling personality and her mind was entirely clear. Another woman, age 88, had had the reputation for being a fireball in her earlier years as a teacher in the school. Now she was remarkably well preserved physically but she was emotionally bland and mentally senile. The 90-year-old by all odds seemed a decade or so younger.

What is

The legal model. The law often employs chronological age as a criterion for legal responsibility (Goldstein, 1976). Being an adult in the eyes of the law is not the same as being adult in one's own eyes or in those of others, nor in terms of culture, religion, science, philosophy, or any other source of definition. Being adult in the law is to be not a child, and to be a child is to be below the age of majority and dependent on adults. Legally to become an adult is simply to reach the age of majority as defined by the law. The age of majority varies over time and from one state to another. Since World War II the trend has been toward a lower age of majority; this trend culminated in the 1971 amendment which lowered the federal voting age from 21 to 18 (Goldstein, 1976).

The concept of legal adulthood carries certain implications. When persons are declared adult, their parents are no longer required by law to support them. On the other hand, adults are no longer subject to the authority of their parents. They are presumed to be able to make binding contracts, purchase or dispose of property, marry, and vote. They are supposed to be able to take care of themselves and are held responsible for their own acts. In using chronological age as the basis of adulthood the law impersonally recognizes the right of all persons to become adults. While this approach may seem simplistic, people differ so greatly that no other mark of adulthood would be legally workable.

What is

The biological model. In another approach, concepts of age and aging are related to human biology. The concept of biological aging generally considers those physical changes in the organism which have been found in general to be associated with aging. These changes may be in cell structures, organ systems, or their functioning (Dibner, 1975). In the biological sense the stages of life might be distinguished by such events as birth, puberty, and menopause. By contrast with the psychological model, which focuses on the development of the individual, the biological model stresses the characteristics and preservation of the species (Troll, 1975).

What is

The sociocultural approach. In another sense adulthood is a social concept, for in some ways aging is socially and culturally determined. In other words, people don't determine for themselves whether they are adult; rather they are perceived by others to be (Stegner, 1976). A 70-year-old may declare that he's a 50-year-old at heart and that he feels not a day older than he did then. But if he looks like a 50-year-old, his self-concept is socially meaningless (Rosow, 1974). Society perceives him as age 70 and treats him accordingly. How adults are perceived also varies from one era or society to another (Hareven, 1976). The 80-year-old who is revered in China might be considered an old fogy or over the hill in the United States.

For better perspective, cross-cultural comparisons are certainly useful. Aging processes in different cultures are profoundly different, and researchers are discovering why (Kessler, 1976). They are also studying relationships between generations in different cultures in order better to understand the dynamics of age-group interaction.

"Social age" also refers to socially assigned roles that a person fills, roles that then determine what his social behavior should be. The role of grandmother, retired person, or old man are examples of socially ascribed roles for the aged (Dibner, 1975, p. 69). These roles, too, vary greatly from one era or culture to another.

What is

The developmental frame of reference. Psychologists most strongly favor the life-span developmental approach, in which each phase of adulthood is viewed in terms of both what has gone before, and what is yet to come. In this "life-span framework human development is perceived as a life-long process and life stages in terms of their antecedents and consequences" (Elder, 1975, p. 1). The developmental approach is concerned with both psychological and biological changes. For example, an institution using this approach would take into account people's socioeconomic roles. It also takes into account what has been found out about the processes of aging—for example, that the notion that people deteriorate or that their abilities decrease is "unduly pessimistic" and not necessarily consistent with fact (Hareven, 1976, p. 65).

The developmental model also focuses on life at any stage as a changing, growing process, even throughout the adult years. In the static world of earlier centuries life stages might have been pretty stable; however, to borrow Henri Gergeson's words, life now suggests that "to exist is to change; to change is to mature; to mature is to create oneself endlessly" (Anthony, 1972). More specifically, life involves the "continuous process of change, sequential development and continuity from birth to death" (Kimmel, 1974, p. 2). In other words, in modern culture adulthood has moved from simply being to becoming (Jordan, 1976). As a result the aim of the psychologist is to identify the regularities in human life and to explain variations in usual patterns.

Finally the developmental approach involves studying individuals as they relate to, or interact with, their interpersonal and nonpersonal environments. In fact Hareven (1976) prefers to use the term "life course" rather than "life cycle" because life course considers people not merely as individuals but in terms of the basic institutions such as the family, of which they are a part. That is, people are not treated as though they dwell in a vacuum but in complex ever-changing environments to which they must continuously adapt.

Functional age. A related concept is that of functional age. According to this concept individuals are viewed as aging at different rates in different functions, and an individual's functional age can be estimated very much the same way as the mental age concept. Thus functional age might become relevant to programs of variable retirement in which people may retire at varying ages (Schaie & Gribben, 1975). Functional age should be distinguished from chronological age. While chronological age refers to years lived, functional age refers to the changing effectiveness of behavior across the years. As an example, "a finely operating Model A Ford may function better than an over-burdened pollution-curtailed modern automobile monster in all respects except perhaps speed" (Bischof, 1976, p. 81). Functional age is a more valid measure than calendar age because it considers what a person is capable of doing and not simply the number of years that he or she has lived.

While functional age is important, it is extremely difficult to determine. For several years an interdisciplinary team at the Boston Veterans Administration Hospital has been trying to figure out how to measure functional age (Fozard, Nuttal, & Waugh, 1972). By studying 600 healthy men, ages 20 to 80, the team has identified certain preliminary aspects of functional age: blood serum and urine; auditory functioning; anthropometric descriptions; verbal, perceptual, and motor abilities;

personality; and sociological factors. Their goal is to derive a functional age for each man that will indicate how far along the life span he is. It now appears that the distance from death may be a more significant measure of an adult's developmental status than the distance from birth. For example, a woman of 60 may have 10 more years to live while another woman of 60 may have 30 more. Of course such measurements are difficult to determine. To date, at least, the single measure which correlates most closely with chronological age is grayness of hair, although certain individuals gray quite early and others never do. Nevertheless this measure neither indicates peoples' functional age nor how they feel.

Kastenbaum and his associates (1972) have tackled the issue of functional age in a different way by asking individuals to estimate how old they feel, act, think, and look—that is, what their personal ages are. Older individuals say that they feel, think, and look younger than their calendar age. Nevertheless the age they give for their looks is closest to their chronological age. The personal ages of older persons who were around 60, varied from their actual chronological age more than did those who were about 20. Most people, however, believe that they look their age.

What is the

Personal age. The concept of personal aging refers to the way an individual relates his or her own experience to the aging process. It is well known that people of the same chronological age differ widely in how old they actually feel. Such perceptions of self with regard to age are probably derived from personal experience and social stereotypes. Even those individuals who are unusually young physiologically see themselves somewhat in terms of the way others view them. No matter how vigorous and robust individuals may feel, if they live in a society that attaches strongly negative stereotypes to aging they will have difficulty escaping a deteriorating self-image as they age. In such cases much depends upon attitudes toward the self that an individual carries across the years, for they tend to resist changing external situations.

Any individual's "internalized judgment of behavior" depends on a variety of factors (Craig, 1976). "Socioeconomic status, rural or urban setting, ethnic background, historical periods, wars, financial depression, or other life events—all may strongly influence the definitions, expectations, and pressures of adulthood. . . . If a man is dependent upon physical labor for his livelihood, he may feel that he has reached his prime at age 30 and old age by the time he is 50. A business or professional man, on the other hand, may judge himself—and is usually judged by others—according to his experience, mature judgment and self-confidence; recognition and financial success may not come to him until he is in his

40s or early 50s, and his productivity may well continue into his late 60s" (Craig, 1976, p. 415). Thus an individual's "age clock" is determined in part by social class; and the higher one's status the longer it takes to judge oneself or be judged as belonging to the next higher age stage.

What is the
STAGE THEORY ?
What is the
Concept of Stage Theory ?

In various contexts we have already referred to stages of life, each with its own characteristics. While these stages follow no fixed chronological schedule, they are presumed to occur in all persons at roughly the same period in development. They are also hierarchical; that is, each new stage is dependent on those that have gone before.

Stage theory is no recent arrival on the psychological scene but is rooted deep in the past. However, the way the life cycle is broken up varies with the times and is somewhat arbitrary. Certain critics doubt that any way of presenting aging "or even . . . the general idea of life cycle linearity, can be proved, so variable are individual makeups; so accidental, culture bound, and intermittent are experiences producing human stress; so persistent the psychological manifestations of idiosyncratic childhood or even genetic factors" (Bailey, 1976, p. 35).

Bischof (1976) recalls certain vivid observations regarding stages of life. Disraeli is presumed to have said that "youth is a blunder, manhood a struggle, old age a regret." Gracian observed that "at 20 the will reigns, at 30 the intellect, and at 40 the judgment." According to a certain Greek proverb "childhood ends at 12, youth at 18, love at 20, faith at 30, hope at 40, and desire at 50." In *As You Like It* Shakespeare portrays life as involving seven stages

> The infant mewling and puking . . .
> The whining school boy . . .
> The lover, sighing like a furnace . . .
> A soldier, full of strange oaths . . .
> The justice, in fair round belly . . .
> The sixth age shifts . . . with spectacles on nose . . . his shrunk shank . . . voice turning again toward childish treble . . .
> Second childishness . . . sans teeth, sans eyes, sans taste, sans everything . . ." (Act II, Sc. 7)

A Sampling of Stage Theories

Hall's recaputulation theory. G. Stanley Hall played an important part in the history of developmental psychology and the conception that life involves relatively discrete or separate stages. He stressed that ontogeny recapitulates phylogeny; that is, the individual human growth pattern parallels evolution, and succeeding phases in life demonstrate characteristics relevant to the chief evolutionary (phylogenetic) advances. During the period of youth, which Hall designated as the years 8 to 12, children pass through the early history of man: cruel and savage, yet moving toward higher human aspirations. The adolescent period becomes the stage which lifts children above the anthropoids but nevertheless can involve backsliding (Grinder, 1969).

Shortly before his death Hall's voluminous book on old age, *Senescence: The last half of life*, (1922), appeared. On the basis of questionnaire data and his own observations, he concluded that the critical transition into later years varies widely from one individual to another, so that "one man's norm would be another man's disaster" (p. 393). While asserting that "man remains essentially juvenile" (p. 411), he believed that senescence requires that one "construct a new self just as we had to do at adolescence, a self that both adds to and subtracts much from the old personality of our prime."

He portrayed growing old as "walking over a bridge" which "slowly tapers to a log, then a tightrope, and finally to a thread. But we must go on till it breaks or we lose balance. Some keep a level head and go further than others but all will go down sooner or later" (p. 437). Thus Hall's conception of aging was quite pessimistic, contrary to the upbeat version of later years coming in vogue today. While Hall's recapitulation theory currently has few if any adherents, it did lay a foundation for understanding human development in terms of progressively higher levels of developmental function. His theories were built upon and broadened by such persons as John Dewey, Henry Goddard, Arnold Gesell, and Lewis Terman.

C. G. Jung's theory. Jung defined youth as the period between post-pubescence and adulthood, a time of moving away from childhood preoccupations toward a general expansion of life perspective. Later, between the ages of 35 and 40, certain childhood traits may emerge again. Personality changes evolve, and interests and motivations change. Attitudes stabilize so that by age 50 an individual has become relatively rigid and intolerant.

Jung focused a great deal of attention on old age, which he perceived as marked by further in-depth psychic reorganization. Older men often become more feminine and women more masculine. The main task at this time is dealing with death instead of holding onto the past or competing with youth. An individual must come to view death as a personally meaningful event rather than a source of peril, for "... an old man who cannot bid farewell to life appears as feeble and sickly as a young man who is unable to embrace it" (Jung, 1960).

Havighurst's developmental tasks. *What are* Robert Havighurst proposed the possibility that we have a series of developmental "tasks" appropriate to the various life stages. A developmental task "is [one] which arises at or about a certain period of the life of the individual, successful achievement of which leads to his happiness and to success with later tasks, while failure leads to unhappiness in the individual, disapproval by the society, and difficulty with later tasks" (Havighurst, 1972, p. 2). The tasks proposed by Havighurst for earlier adulthood (ages 18 to 30) include selecting a mate, learning to live with the marriage partner, beginning a family, rearing children, managing the home, embarking on an occupation, assuming civic responsibility, and finding congenial social groups. The tasks of middle age (ages 30 to 55) include achieving adult social and civic responsibility, establishing and maintaining an appropriate standard of living, helping teenage children to become happy and responsible adults, developing worthwhile adult leisure activities, relating adequately to the spouse as a person, accepting and adapting to physiological changes of middle age, and adjusting to aging parents. In later maturity (ages 55 and over) the tasks include adjusting to declining physical health and strength, adapting to the death of a spouse, adjusting to reduced income and retirement, establishing relationships with one's age group, and fulfilling civic and social obligations.

Havighurst's theory has both strong and weak points. It helps to place adulthood in perspective and underscores the importance of the teachable moment. That is, it is wise to define purposes of education at different age levels so that people may achieve the developmental tasks appropriate for each stage. On the other hand, people can omit some of the steps proposed by Havighurst. For example, many persons never marry yet live satisfactory lives. Finally, developmental tasks as defined by Havighurst relate to life in this culture. Tasks to be mastered at particular life stages vary considerably according to the time in history and the type of culture or society, whether primitive or modern, technological or agricultural, communist or democratic, affluent or poor.

Erikson's stage-task theory. *What is* Perhaps the best-known concept of the life cycle is that of Erik Erikson (1959), who divides the life cycle into eight phases or ages. Each stage involves a task specific to that phase, and the stages follow a general chronology, although they do not involve arbitrary, rigid age limits. The first four phases relate to childhood, the fifth to adolescence, and the last three to adulthood. Life tasks belong to particular stages only in that they arrive at critical points of resolution during those stages. Otherwise they are prepared for in previous stages and elaborated in those that follow. Thus at successive stages, components of all the eight major tasks are present, either as "precursors," "derivates," or "crises." In this sense adolescence does not mark the end of childhood or the beginning of adulthood. Instead adulthood is anticipated in childhood, and the child exists in the adult.

In order to be ready for adulthood the adolescent, in stage five, must achieve a sense of ego identity. Only after having defined one's sense of self is an individual ready to establish intimacy with another. This is the first phase-specific task of adulthood (stage six in the total life span). This intimacy involves relationships with oneself, with the opposite sex, and with others of both sexes. Meantime isolation, which is the converse of intimacy, is demonstrated by one's tendency to withdraw from or destroy those forces in people that one perceives as unfriendly to oneself. Thus Erikson defines each phase-specific task in terms of opposites which are either successfully resolved on the one hand or fail on the other.

Yet apparently negative outcomes may sometimes have a certain utilitarian value, for given the condition of the world, individuals without any ability to protect themselves would soon be destroyed. Thus the tasks relating to a particular stage do not involve either alternative exclusively, because pure forms would be maladaptive.

The next phase of adulthood, stage seven, is concerned with either generating or stagnating, the phase-specific task here being the establishment of the next generation through producing and caring for children. Those who do not become parents may achieve "generativity" through creative and unselfish behavior. The biological status of parenthood does not necessarily constitute genuine generativity. The failure of generativity results in stagnation, which may assume the guise of obsessive pseudo-intimacy or narcissistic self-indulgence whereby an individual may treat himself as though he were his one and only child.

The last phase of adult life involves the issue of integrity versus despair and disgust. Integrity (a sense of wholeness) represents the "fruit of the seven stages," and is the result of having successfully accomplished the tasks of all the former ages, including taking care of others, adjusting to oneself, and generating ideas. It suggests having adapted to one's own life cycle, an essential task of life. If one does not accept the reality of one's own life cycle, the outcome is despair because there is no opportunity for new beginnings. This despair in turn produces a disgust with the world and the self.

Other stage theories. *What are* Others have attempted to let research speak for itself. Instead of assuming a theoretical position and then seeking to support it, they analyze the data to determine where significant groupings occur. Gould and his associates had 524 white middle-class people fill out questionnaires. These people fell into seven distinguishable phases grouped by age: 16 to 17, 18 to 21, 22 to 28, 29 to 36, 37 to 43, 44 to 50, and 51 to 60 (Gould, 1975, p. 76). For most of the questions asked, responses stabilized or remained essentially the same between ages 22 and 29 and continued stable from then on. However, certain questions evoked distinctive responses even from adjacent age groupings, and these questions were used to identify the phases of adult life. In general, responses of the 16- and 17-year-olds closely resembled the stable patterns of response of the 22- to 29-year-olds. Like the older groups, the adolescents lived in a family (though it was the one of origin) and thought of themselves more as members of the family than as individuals. By contrast the next older group, the 18- to 22-year-olds, gave replies quite distinctive from the just younger or just older group. People in this middle age-grouping had their own individual psychologies and private worlds. They were especially open to new ideas, but when they again joined the "mainstream" of adult society, after age 22, their responses became typical of the rest of the population.

Rhona and Robert Rapoport (1975) divided the life cycle into main stages according to peoples' main (focal) preoccupation. For young adults the focal preoccupation is identification with social institutions; for the establishment (middle-age) phase it is life investments (concern with productivity, performance, and evaluation); and for later years (the retirement phase) it is personal and social integration.

While most stage theorists acknowledge at least a rough division of adulthood into young adult, middle age, and later years, a minority go further and carve out additional stages of life, including the young old and the old old. We do not yet know whether these further subdivisions will be useful (Hareven, 1976). Nor do we know what new categories may emerge in the future.

What is a Critique of Stage Theory ?

The significance of stages. *What are* Society's organization of life tasks and roles by stages has certain implications. For one thing, society assigns people age and role identities that have a strong influence on their behavior.

In fact age identity "is no less [strong] than in influencing the behavior of children" . . . People accept the social sanctions related to age norms. (Neugarten, 1968, p. 144). For example, it is easier for the person with a middle-age identity to be viewed as sufficiently responsible, as well as vigorous enough, to be considered for the presidency of the U.S. than for younger or older adults. Age-role identity also produces age segregation in American society. For example, certain clubs and housing developments which cater to young adults would subtly discourage the presence of middle-aged persons.

What is the
Perspective on stage theory. Certain other observations will help place stage theory in better perspective. Passages from one stage to another vary "in their desirability, their inevitability, their reversibility, and their repeatability" (Goodman & Feldman, 1975, p. 166). They also vary in terms of their clarity and emphasis. Much emphasis is placed on old age, and little on young adulthood. The boundary between middle and older adulthood is clearer than between younger and middle adulthood. Old age, unlike other adult stages, has a formal beginning, age 65—at least as far as work life is concerned. Moving into it is institutionalized by retirement and the beginning of social security benefits (Hareven, 1976). Hence adulthood as a stage should always be related to adulthood as a process.

Finally, changes associated with the passing of time are not limited to individuals. Aspects of the environment are also changing, including nations, societies, cultures, and institutions. Concepts of development and decline may be applied to the institutions of society just as they are to the life history of an individual. Thus we have changing individuals relating to a changing society; and the effect of such events will vary with the life cycle. Certainly such social events as economic depressions or wars would affect young people differently from older persons who are already retired, no longer draftable, or even employable (Bengtson & Starr, 1975).

Traditionally the field of human development has involved concepts that were primarily either psychological or sociological. Still other ideas come out of interdisciplinary studies in which both psychologists and sociologists participate (Lowenthal, 1977). Such concepts are based on (1) longitudinal and cross-sectional data regarding how people "at various stages of the life course perceive and affectively respond to individuals, networks and institutions . . . and (2) study of the networks themselves as they encompass, respond to, or reject individuals at various stages of the life course." The foregoing theories are called psychosociological because the self is perceived as proceeding through developmental stages within a sociocultural framework.

What is
The Concept of Generations ?

People in the same age grouping who experience the same problems at any particular time belong to the same generation. The time during which generations live limits their range of experience, which in turn modifies their values, thoughts, and behavior. Those cohorts, or groups within the same generation, who utilize their common experiences in distinct ways are said to constitute generational units. Such units share a common destiny in history and time. In other words membership in a particular cohort alone will not directly determine generational behavior; however, chronological age combined with psychological awareness and exposure to specific sociocultural and historical factors explains generation units (Braungart, 1975). Consider this illustration. In the late 1960s college students and their parents constituted different generations. The college students, by their common involvement in the antiwar protests and civil rights movement, attained a certain distinctiveness or identity. That is, they became a generation unit.

In other words the cultural and historical experiences that we live through leave their mark upon us. And they have a different effect on people of different ages. People who were young adults at the outbreak of World War I were affected more by that war than were the young children of those years. Thus we have the so-called generations effect, in which successive age cohorts are different not merely because of age differences but because they have experienced particular historical events differently. The resultant differences between generations are said to constitute a generation gap. Therefore it becomes apparent that developmental progression through the life cycle relates to points in historical time. For example, persons aged 65 in 1968 who were young adults during the depression may even yet feel undue anxieties over money. It would be easy to ascribe their economic conservatism to their older years, when in fact it arose from their own young adult experiences with financial stress.

Generations also differ somewhat in power and status, and hence take on certain aspects of higher or lower social class. The distribution of power, too, is a function of place and time. For example, in rapidly changing times successive waves of life style and thought rapidly become obsolete. In such a situation even middle-aged persons may be considered out of date, and the young become more significant. As a case in point, when Jimmy Carter embarked upon his administration he chose mostly young adults as his aides.

The generational process itself is a function of the times—that is, the generational process is not constant. Instead periods of rapid change may result in generation gaps in families just as historical episodes, such as cold spells or droughts, can be noted in the rings of a tree (Kimmel, 1974). For example, there has been a significant generational shift away from earlier traditional values, from those of the current grandparent generation to those of the present parent middle-aged generation. One reason is that the current middle-aged and young adults have had more education than the present older generation. In turn the diminished gap between the present middle-aged and younger generations suggests the stabilization of a less conventional culture.

THE STUDY OF ADULTHOOD ?

What is

Methods ?

What are the

What are

Cross-sectional and longitudinal research designs. The most common approach to studying adulthood is cross-sectional, in which comparisons are made of behavior at different ages. Sheehy (1976) employed the cross-sectional method in seeking to pinpoint personality characteristics and life styles of adults in their 20s, 30s, and 40s, among the group that sets the pace in America, the middle class. Such studies are carried out with different age groups at the same period in time. For example, at the same time early, middle-aged, and older adults may be given tests which measure their capacities for creativity. The differences that are found might be assumed to be strictly a result of age. However education is far more common today than it was when present-day older people were young. Hence whatever differences may be found are at least partly a function of differences in education as well as changes in health care, nutrition, and density of population—that is, the differential influence of historical events (Troll, 1975).

More effective than cross-sectional studies is longitudinal research, in which the same subjects are studied periodically over a length of time, sometimes even a lifetime. The results are then compared for successive testings, and attempts made to account for observed changes. Longitudinal studies help to determine the causes of particular age changes, because these studies include such variables as past experience, family history, or medical history. They help not only to identify continuities across the life span but also to explain breaks or discontinuities, for one has as much significance as the other. For example it might be determined that a securely attached infant will normally mature into a well-adjusted adult, but if such an infant becomes a neurotic adult the question of what happened arises. That is, it is important to develop systematic methods for uncovering both discontinuities and continuities in order to determine their cause and help an individual's progress through life (Antonucci, 1976).

A fascinating book, *Whatever Happened to the Class of '65?*, suggests just how difficult it is to predict what direction individual lives will take. The 30 students interviewed were by no means a random sampling of Americans, nor were they selected on any other basis than that they were members of that class. Among the 30 individuals the all-American quarterback became a reverend in a moderately bizarre religious cult while earning a livelihood as a masseur. The most popular boy in the class killed himself, while the gang leader of the Saracens erected a million-dollar business empire. The head cheerleader and homecoming queen became a history professor at Princeton; and an idealistic brilliant loner emerged as an egomaniac and a John Bircher. More predictable individuals who simply embarked upon uneventful, pleasant lives proved to be few and far between. Certainly the contrast between what the students had expected would become of each other and the reality of what did happen was extreme (Medved & Wallechinsky, 1976).

Unfortunately longitudinal studies pose certain problems. For one thing, they require long periods of time and large funds. Or a study may outlive the original investigators. Another problem is that certain subjects may die or drop out of the sample, and the dropouts may be relevant to the variables under investigation. Still another difficulty is that changes occurring in individuals over the life span may be ascribed to their age when they may actually have been due to the times in which they lived. The best way to overcome the deficiencies inherent in both longitudinal and cross-sectional approaches is to combine the two. It is essential to study individuals as they proceed through their individual life spans, but it is also important to compare people at selected points in their lives or at different ages at the same point in historical time (Neugarten & Datan, 1973).

Various methods are being designed for untangling confusing variables. In a study by Woodruff and Birren (1972) a group originally tested in college was retested 25 years later, and at the same time a current group of college students was tested. The results indicated that cohort differences were larger than aging differences; also consistency instead of change was characteristic of the follow-up (older) group. In a more complex effort to separate effects of age and cohort, Schaie (1970) employs two or more longitudinal studies of different cohorts. In addition, he has developed a three-part developmental model which uses statistical analysis to determine approximately how much variance may be attributed to age, cohort, or time-of-measurement effects. As greater numbers of researchers employ these new research designs the knowledge of aging processes will come to rest on a far more secure empirical base.

What are

Life histories. Any particular study, regardless of overall approach, may employ several techniques. In Vaillant's (1977) study of midlife males, which he originally began during their college careers, a complete record was compiled about each man based on in-depth interviews and psychological tests. A staff member prepared histories of their families, and after graduation every individual submitted a questionnaire each year until 1955. Thereafter a questionnaire was completed every two years. A social anthropologist visited each man between 1950 and 1952, and in 1967 Vaillant interviewed 94 survivors of the original 268, whom he randomly selected from the larger sample (Muson, 1977).

What are

Other techniques. Another method involves measuring such characteristics as intelligence, dexterity, or memory. Tests may also be of the projective type, the two most common being the Thematic Apperception Test and the Rorschach Inkblot Test. For measuring physiological factors various physiological and organic measuring devices are employed, such as the electrocardiograph for heartbeat and the electroencephalograph for measuring brain waves.

What is an Appraisal of Research ?

What are the

Weaknesses. Research regarding adulthood, like that about other subjects, is subject to biases that distort conclusions. Adult development is being studied at Harvard, Berkeley, Chicago, and UCLA, all of which are highly respected institutions. However most of this research is done by male researchers who are studying other men. Separating the sexes in that way is unrealistic because the way each sex lives affects the other; and how one sex develops cannot be understood without understanding the life styles of the other. Social scientists also reflect both the biases of people who are influential in their fields and their own values—which influence the way they structure their research and the interpretation they place on their findings. Hence, advises Dragastin (1975), researchers must remain aware of their own values and point of view and they should make them "explicit, at least for themselves" (p. 292).

Distortions also arise from limitations on the topics being investigated. Often researchers work on problems which are simple and easily quantifiable because they are short of time and money. Or they may hesitate to investigate certain questions, such as sex relations among the aged, because of ethical problems. Recently there has been a "crisis of integrity" created by certain experimental procedures employed in psychological and medical experiments (Goethals, 1975, p. 59). As a result new standards of ethics have been adopted; some experimenters have despairingly concluded that the new regulations make it difficult to carry out any worthwhile research. Nevertheless Goethals quotes a friend as expressing a directly opposite view. Carefully defined standards would compel the professions to move forward, not backward; and introducing integrity into experimentation would compel the sciences to review their whole method of inquiry. In the process, "we [might] get less of the truth, but . . . we would have to get the truth in more truthful ways" (p. 59).

A problem inherent in all developmental and personality research is determining the various meanings that individuals may attach to behavior. Because of the infinite variation and complexity of human behavior, individual differences are easily obscured and distorted whenever subjects are thrown into categories for purposes of measurement, no matter how carefully the categories may be defined. It is important to consider individual differences in assessing the meaning of social behavior. For example, an older person might have only a single confidant. For the individual who is somewhat quiet in terms of the active-quiet dimension, just one friend may be enough. Persons on the other end of this continuum might feel better satisfied with several confidants, or would at least expect intense contact with the single confidant. When people find themselves in situations uncongenial to their natural tendencies—whether the situation is too active or too dull—they feel there is too much or too little "input" (p. 138). Such a situation would arise when a "quiet" individual is placed in an "active involved community or institution, or conversely, an active person is placed in a quiet, relatively isolated type of environment" (Antonucci, 1976, p. 138).

An additional example is found in much of the aging research, which shows that people generally remain the same throughout their lives with regard to attaching themselves to others, or the reverse. Formerly disengagement or distance from others was associated with the aging (Havighurst, Neugarten, & Tobin, 1968). Now it is better understood that disengaged people, whether aging or otherwise, exist across the life span. The use of this typology by researchers varies in appropriateness at different ages. For example, depending on the stage in life, the "rocking chair type described as extremely passive, and disliking responsibility, may represent [either] a perfectly 'disengaged' retired person—a role considered appropriate in this society, or a lazy bum—since passivity and 'shirking of responsibility' are behaviors considered inappropriate, if not abnormal, in a young person" (Antonucci, 1976, p. 138).

2/hat is the

Status of research.? The study of adulthood from the developmental point of view is in its infancy, except in the field of gerontology. As Sheehy (1976) points out, it is a great deal easier to do research on adolescents and older people because those groups are captive research subjects in schools and rest homes. Meantime the middle aged are out in the world, working and trying to grasp the complexities and ambiguities of life. Once having applied what they know about personality to their children as they grow up, they deposit their offspring on the edge of adulthood to fend for themselves.

Nevertheless new trends in research are apparent, one being a concern for all life stages as they relate to each other. Only through studying the total life span, including old age, can one fully understand the complete significance of any earlier period. As Charlotte Bühler observed in a letter to Robert Havighurst: "My interest was in the whole of human life. . . . after some years, I decided that life as a whole could be better understood from its end than from its beginning" (Havighurst, 1974, p. 398). Hence she and her students studied biographies which were sufficiently well documented to provide detail so that lives could be followed to their very end. Interest is also being shown in the more optimistic healthful aspects of aging as distinct from the former almost total concern for its problems. Unfortunately we still lack firm answers regarding the nitty-gritty question of how to translate such studies into trustworthy empirical data.

What are the

Special needs.? Looking ahead it is hoped that certain significant deficiencies will be remedied. For one thing, more research should be done regarding the early adult years from about 21 to 35. By comparison with other age stages, little research has been done concerning this period. More studies should also be made of older people who are not institutionalized and who have aged successfully. Unfortunately medical and behavioral scientists have simply succumbed to society's negative stereotyping of the aged and have associated later life with inevitable decline. In consequence research concerning the elderly is completely inadequate, and such research as has been done has focused chiefly on the minority of the elderly who are in institutions. Meantime the few studies of the healthy elderly who live in the community are providing completely new insights into this age group. Such studies should be greatly expanded, always taking into account the particular life conditions in which successive cohorts have lived. For example those elderly who were born in the early 1900s lived through the depression as adults, often losing their homes, savings, and morale (Butler, 1975).

A second need is to study adults not as a homogeneous grouping, but as subtypes, according to cultures and social class. Sheehy (1976) chose to study in depth the group that sets the pace in America—healthy, motivated people, the middle class. The subjects ranged in age from 18 to 55 and included both housewives and professionals of many varieties and of both sexes. Similar studies should be made of upper and lower classes. It is also important that we study group relationships from the life-span point of view so that the data revealed "may open up vistas for human attachment that we cannot even imagine now. Longer lives may be accompanied, not by stagnation or deprivation of love and friendship, but by transformations of old patterns into richer new ones" (Troll, 1975, p. 144). There should also be replication of research so that policies and programs will not be implemented in terms of studies which lack adequate substantiation or have become out of date. Finally there should be more anticipatory research; that is, there ought to be attempts to gauge the future in order better to prepare for it. While such research admittedly lacks the definiteness of that which already is, the alternative is sheer guesswork about what lies ahead.

Another need is to direct more animal research specifically toward matters of aging. In general, research regarding adulthood is still too thin in almost all areas. We are a long way from having the substantial body of research concerning adults that has accumulated regarding children and adolescents. Even that which has been done must be replicated from time to time because of rapidly changing conditions. Only as studies in this field grow and proliferate will we become sophisticated in techniques of researching adulthood, and capable of integrating data into meaningful theories.

What is the PLAN OF THE BOOK ?

The chapters that follow this introduction will be concerned with adulthood in the United States, on three successive age levels. Part II relates to young adults, including their transition into adulthood, their main tasks, and their life styles. Part III focuses on middle-aged adults—their characteristics, life styles, and activities. Some of the material in this section could be said to apply to adults generally. In Part IV older adults are treated similarly, in terms of characteristics, life styles, problems, and finally death. Certain of the same topics are employed in order more clearly to demonstrate the transitions that occur with age. Topics that relate more specifically to each stage are also covered.

While adulthood conceivably could be subdivided somewhat differently, adult age roles are ordinarily defined in America as young, middle-aged, or old. As treated here, young adulthood will be interpreted as embracing the period from the first assumption of an adult role until the late 30s, when the exploring, getting-ahead-in-the-world phase yields to a more stable settled stage. Middle-age is perceived as lasting until retirement, or age 65, chiefly because old age is commonly presumed to begin then. Because of the vast difference between people in their sixties and seventies, and those in their eighties and nineties, it might be more accurate to think of the young-old and the old-old. However, it should be clear from the text which of these two levels is concerned.

Finally the last chapter is designed to tie together the preceding chapters and briefly to forecast the future. Because of deficiencies in research thus far as well as the continuously evolving status of adults in modern society, generalizations are necessarily tentative. However if we are ever to develop a useful psychology of adulthood, it is essential to seek the meaning and significance of such data as we have, and to make whatever conjectures appear justified.

What is the SUMMARY?

In recent years for the first time interest has developed in the psychology of adulthood. The growing numbers of old people, the logical extension of already existing longitudinal studies of children, and the increasing amount of free time in adulthood, are among the reasons for this interest. But just what adults are like is still unclear; and various images of adults exist.

(3) Reasons for recent interest in adulthood

Aging, or the process which accounts for the successive stages of life, is modified by several factors. In the biological sense it involves certain "pacemakers" that establish a general time frame for life stages. However people are not wholly the victims of genetic destiny, for life satisfaction and healthful living can retard aging. Conversely lack of activity, cigarette smoking, and a polluted environment can hasten it. Aging itself is a complex process concerning the impact of time on all aspects of an individual's behavior.

(2) Modifications of aging process

Of the several models of aging, the chronological approach treats the life process in terms of calendar years. The legal model involves such matters as age of majority and the acquisition at that time of certain rights and responsibilities. The biological model relates aging to physical changes over time, in the organism; while social age refers to socially ascribed roles at successive life stages. The developmental model focuses on life as a changing, growing process from conception until death; functional age suggests that people age at different rates in

(7) Models of aging

different functions. Finally personal age refers to the way individuals relate their own experience to the aging process.

Life cycle involves stages

The life cycle itself is portrayed as involving stages which, according to stage theory, occur in all persons at roughly the same period in development. This concept has been variously interpreted by Jung, Havighurst, Erikson, and others. According to one view, people in

Ex: generation

the same age grouping who experience the same historical problems at any particular time constitute the same generation. The historical period in which a generation lives limits its experience, and consequently its values and behaviors. The generational process itself is not constant, but varies according to the speed and nature of change.

(3) Methods of study

The most common methods employed for studying adults are the longitudinal and cross-sectional, while life histories may involve a variety of techniques. All have their strengths and weaknesses, but the longitudinal and life history approaches are proving especially fruitful. Such research where adults are concerned is still in an exploratory stage, but it is rapidly gaining momentum. Looking ahead it appears that exciting new insights will certainly emerge, as was the case in the earlier phases of child and youth research.

SUGGESTED READINGS

Back, K. W. Personal characteristics and social behavior: Theory and method. In Binstock, R. H. & Shanas, E. (Eds.) *Handbook of Aging and the Social Sciences*. New York: Van Nostrand Reinhold Co., 1976, 403–431. A theoretical frame of reference is provided for studying and attaining appropriate perspective on personality and social behavior across the life span.

Bengston, V. L. & Cutler, N. E. Generations and intergenerational relations: Perspectives on age groups and social change. In Binstock, R. H. & Shanas, E. (Eds.) *Handbook of Aging and the Social Sciences*. New York: Van Nostrand Reinhold Co., 1976, 130–159. The concept of generations is defined and related to matters of time, age grouping, and social structure. Also discussed are intergenerational differences in attitudes and opinions, interaction between generations, and emerging generation events of the elderly.

Bronfenbrenner, U. Toward an experimental ecology of human development. *American Psychologist*, 1977, 32 (7), 513–531. A broad concept of human development is suggested that stresses progressive accommodation throughout life between humans and their changing environments.

Dworkin, R. H. and others, A longitudinal study of the genetics of personality. *Journal of Personality and Social Psychology*, 1976, 34

(3), 510–518. A longitudinal twin study was designed to determine whether personality traits which could have been inherited in adolescence continue to do so in adulthood. Certain of the personality traits were significant in either adolescence or adulthood; others, at both ages. Several personality traits involved in the change from adolescence to adulthood were found to be genetically influenced.

Haan, N. "...change and sameness..." reconsidered, *International Journal of Aging and Human Development*, 1976, 7 (1), 59–65. In the response to Block's critique of her study of consistency in personality development Haan discusses the problems in working with numerous complex variables and reanalyzes the original data.

McCall, R. B. Challenges to a science of developmental psychology. *Child Development*, 1977, 48 (2), 333–344. In this exploration of methodological and conceptual issues in developmental psychology, it is concluded that at present we lack an adequate science of natural developmental processes because there has not been enough research in natural settings.

Maddox, G. L. & Wiley, J. Scope, concepts and methods in the study of aging. In Binstock, R. H. & Shanas, E. (Eds.) *Handbook of Aging and the Social Sciences*. New York: Van Nostrand Reinhold Co., 1976, 3–34. Study of the aging is treated in terms of the disciplines, themes, and issues involved. Questions of methodology are also discussed.

Neugarten, B. L. & Hagestad, G. O. Age and the life course. In Binstock, R. H. & Shanas, E. (Eds.) *Handbook of Aging and the Social Sciences*. New York: Van Nostrand Reinhold Co., 1976, 35–55. This chapter is concerned with the social and psychological age organization of society. Among the topics considered are age grading in modern societies, age and social interaction, age norms, historical and projected future trends in age grading, and multiple time tables (group, sex, individual).

Riley, M. W. Age strata in social systems. In Binstock, R. H. & Shanas, E. (Eds.) *Handbook of Aging and the Social Sciences*. New York: Van Nostrand Reinhold Co., 1976, 189–217. In this somewhat theoretical but plentifully researched chapter, the author outlines a conceptual model in which people and social roles are divided into strata according to age.

Rosow, I. Status and role change through the life span. In Binstock, R. H. & Shanas, E. (Eds.) *Handbook of Aging and the Social Sciences*. New York: Van Nostrand Reinhold Co., 1976, 457–482. An inclusive taxonomy of status and role types is designed to clarify ambiguities in popular concepts of role change through the life cycle. This statement is viewed as tentative, and is intended to stimulate further research and theory.

Sears, R. R. Sources of life satisfactions of the Terman gifted men. *American Psychologist*, 1977, *32* (2), 119–128. A follow-up of L. M. Terman's study of gifted men (who were studied at intervals beginning in 1922) whose average age was 66, which disclosed factors predictive of vocational, family, and life satisfaction. This article also provides insight into the nature and benefits of longitudinal research.

Sheehy, G. *Passages: The predictable crises of adult life.* New York: E. P. Dutton & Co., Inc., 1976. On the basis of many case histories of young and middle-class adults, Sheehy constructs a blueprint of adulthood, indicating the major characteristics of each stage and how certain crises and circumstances mark the passage from one stage to another.

Streib, G. F. Social stratification and aging. In Binstock, R. H. & Shanas, E. (Eds.) *Handbook of Aging and the Social Sciences.* New York: Van Nostrand Reinhold Co., 1976, 160–185. Social stratification is shown to vary according to social class, status, power, age, and ethnic background. These variables in turn have a somewhat different impact on stratification within different cultures and countries of the world.

PART II

The Young Adult

2
CHAPTER

Induction
Into
Adulthood

COMING OF AGE IN SIMPLE SOCIETIES

All societies make clear distinctions between the status of child and that of adult. Most simple societies have a simple formula for inducting their youth into adulthood. The youth undergoes certain rituals, or *rites de passage*, which vary in amount of stress produced and after which—abracadabra—the youth is an adult (Muuss, 1970).

Pubertal rites for the sexes always differ, but they do so in varying manner and degree. Rites may be for one sex only, or they may be more elaborate for one sex than for the other. They may be quite different for both sexes or, in a few cases, much the same. Among the Sepiks in New Guinea, for example, boys can become men only by ritualizing birth and taking over as a group the function that women perform naturally (Mead, 1950). Societies generally pay more attention to the rites for males, perhaps because the man's role in most societies is more dominating and desirable. Besides, the boy undergoes no specific physical event that in itself signals the onset of puberty. His pubertal changes occur slowly, and no developmental events give him an immediate right to say, "I am now a man."

COMING OF AGE IN MODERN SOCIETY

Pubertal Rites: Western Style

It would seem that primitive youth, whose status is more clearly defined, have a better deal than more civilized young people. Do they? Kilpatrick (1974) believes that modern youth experience a prolonged period of crisis, which costs the high prices of stress and alienation. By contrast, since primitive youth do not have a prolonged identity confusion, they do not suffer these neuroses. On the other hand, this lack of crisis may be responsible for primitive societies' failure to reach higher cultural levels. Therefore, concludes Kilpatrick, "take your choice between communal solidarity or creative crises. Unfortunately, we seem to have arrived at some inbetween stage where we neither get the advantages of the one nor the benefits of the other. We live in a transitional society which seems to allow for neither noble savages nor aristocratic adolescents. We get the anxiety without the autonomy, the

confusion without the creativeness, the chaos without the character—
in short, we get the crisis without achieving identity" (p. 408).

In this impasse many youth have felt that the answer was in neo-
primitivism; hence, they have sponsored such ideals as "simplicity, community, and the return to nature." We have had "flower children in the
west and Woodstock in the east. The global village, it seemed, was at
hand. But it was all too soon, and too easy, and too soon gone. Dis-
sention, drugs and distrusts began to split the tribes apart. One commune after another failed, and with the passage of events the
Woodstock occurrence began to take on the quality of a mythic happening occurring in the dawn of time sometime before the fall, but still
within the memory of the tribal elders" (p. 409). These failures, concludes Kilpatrick, simply indicate that Americans are still highly individualistic and that it was the "spirit of Thoreau rather than the spirit
of the kibbutz which prompted many of the young to head for the
communal woods, even when they adopt the organization of the latter"
(p. 409).

The problem is that the culture is seeking an identity at the same
time that youths are. Since the old culture is dying and the new one is
yet to be fully born, youth have nothing firm against which to cast
themselves. Moreover, today's youth has a double identity crisis. It lives
in two contrasting cultures, and neither has a firm identity of its own.
The old culture at least had some consistency, and when anyone opposed it he or she had some ground on which to stand. However, the
ground today has grown "mushy," and the youth's moratorium produces not "autonomy and self awareness" but "alienation and confusion" (Kilpatrick, 1974, p. 410).

Obstacles to Establishing Maturity

A major obstacle to maturing is the lack of association between age
groups. The adolescent group is often set off by itself, and teenagers
spend their time in teen herds. Since they are also not allowed to exercise true responsibility or directly identify with adults, they never get a
true apprenticeship for adulthood. Another obstacle to such an apprenticeship is the parent who refuses to acknowledge that his or her child
(usually the girl) is growing up. Mothers especially may not know how
to retire from parenthood, and their children cannot become independent without feeling guilty and making their mothers very unhappy.

In addition, the youth's role consistently differs from that of adult.
In fact, growing up is an open-ended affair that discourages children
from growing toward adulthood in a precise way. Hence, much that our

children learn in early life has practically no relevance for adulthood. They must change from being submissive in early years to being independent and even aggressive later on. Fun and irresponsibility must give way to serious concerns. Even schools, supposed to train students for the business of life, teach subjects that have little to do with students' lives. That is, they do not integrate the curriculum with life outside the school. Youth think of graduation as crossing the threshold into real life, as though in the years up to that time they had been waiting to be born.

Adults also encourage immaturity by imitating youth and rejecting age. According to Harvey Cox (1973), Americans are able to be parents or children, but they have a difficult time being adults. One of their strategies to avoid maturity is to worship a simple child God. Cox suggests that perhaps "people get the Gods they deserve," and America, a youth-worshiping, age-despising culture, has finally been granted its fondest hope, an adolescent deity. Cox mentions especially, the conversions to the 15-year-old Guru Maharaj Ji of the Divine Light Mission. In the Western world, we love the divine child in the manger and the familiar pictures of Jesus, the boy, "confounding the wise men in the temple, and the recently pooh-poohed legend of St. Christopher, in which he carried a small child across a stream and then discovered that the child was, in fact, Christ himself" (Cox, 1973, p. 17).

Strangely enough, prolonged adolescence, which some people say is necessary because life in modern culture requires a long training, may also make it harder for people to become mature. The period is so long that the characteristics of the adolescent personality become set. Indeed, some individuals never grow up. Examples are the middle-aged mother who likes to be the belle of the ball and the paunchy college graduate who returns to his alma mater every year to be one of the boys. Those adults who attempt reruns of adolescence provide comic relief, but they may also do some harm. Such individuals may serve to "reinforce the incompetent amateurism and the self-indulgent or self-pitying protective cults by which young people so often counteract adult expectations" (Jencks & Riesman, 1967, p. 5). At any rate, they are probably better than aloof adults who wash their hands of the "now" generation and pay them as much attention as fourth-class mail.

Differing Criteria of Maturity

Another problem of maturing in modern societies is the lack of any standard for determining when an adolescent has become an adult, largely because people reach maturity in different areas at different ages.

For example, achievement of maturity varies with social class and culture. Children of the lower class are turned loose earlier and become heads of families and wage earners immediately after high school. Apparently, black youth find adults of more significance than do white youth, so they model after them more and attain adulthood earlier (Schwartz & Baden, 1973). Also, despite their later age of puberty, males are considered to be adults earlier than females. College males are often referred to as men, whereas females of the same age are commonly called girls. Nor does the girl's status improve very much as she approaches womanhood, for the female's adult role holds little prestige. As a result she considers maturity less attractive than a boy does (Lyell, 1973).

Marital and job status also make a difference. If the youth has a wife and family, he is considered a man, but a single male of the same age is still a boy. Two-thirds of our states permit 18-year-old females to marry without their parents' consent; in the same states, full financial and legal responsibility is denied the unmarried 18-year-old girl who still lives with her parents (Vincent, 1972). However, the married girl's advantage is more apparent than real; for her status as an adult depends upon her marital status. Economically, psychologically, and socially she is considered dependent on her husband. And although this situation is changing now, many of the worst things about it are still true.

Contributing further to the confusion are society's capricious standards of responsibility. One teenager is locked up for a crime and held accountable as if he were a man; another of precisely the same age and convicted of an even more serious crime may be let go because of his youth. When society is unpredictable, young people are even more uncertain about themselves. They cannot be sure just what privileges they are entitled to or when they will be held accountable.

FACTORS THAT HASTEN MATURITY

Some things speed up youth's progress toward adulthood. One of these is the constant pressure on high-school students to perform well so that they will be admitted to good colleges. For another, at an early age many students feel that they are on their own and cannot depend on their parents for help. This problem may be caused by economic forces (the parents being unable to continue to support the child) or by misunderstanding between the generations. One result of this is that youth feel little obligation either to maintain close ties with their parents or to follow their parents' standards. As early as the age of 12 or 13, some young people relate almost exclusively to their peers. In short, many

A youth's first job is one of several factors which hastens maturity in modern society.

adolescents have simply gone underground and developed life styles of their own.

Once it begins, the transition from adolescence to adulthood is almost always swift for boys, often less so for girls. One day the youth is carefree and protected; the next day, the problems of being an adult are dumped in his lap. Within the span of a few brief months he may have to play the serious adult roles of wage-earner, husband, provider, and citizen.

Students show how complicated it is to be recognized as an adult by their answers to the question, "At what age do you expect to consider yourself an adult and why?"

I'll be an adult by age 26, because by then I'll have had experiences as a teacher and as a housewife. I'll have a burden of responsibility and a position of respect.

40

I had so many responsibilities during my teens that I feel I was an adult long before I entered college. As to stating a specific age, that's impossible.

I am young in spirit and will probably not feel like I'm an adult until I am 30.

I already feel like an adult. I began feeling like one about age 18 and certainly by 21. Why? I first lived away from home and learned what sex was (in theory). Above all, college gave me a personal insight into self.

ATTITUDES TOWARD GROWING UP

Adults' Attitudes

Among factors that either help or hinder youth as they enter into adulthood are the attitudes of adults themselves. Some parents, unconsciously, or otherwise, resist their children's growing up. It is difficult to change ideas we have held for a long time. Besides, if parents acknowledge that their children are growing up, they must concede that they themselves are aging. Other adults may accept their children's changing status, possibly because they assume they are expected to, or perhaps because they look forward to escaping the responsibilities of being a parent. On the other hand, if adults view young people as adults-in-the-becoming and train them from childhood to make positive contributions to society—as is true in socialist societies—becoming an adult is a smooth and orderly process. However, in our own capitalist society youth and their elders do not share the same goals (Baumrind, 1974).

Youth's Anticipation of Adulthood

Attitudes toward growing up. Nobody knows for sure how today's youth, as a generation, feel about growing up. According to Keniston (1975), youth "view adulthood with all of the enthusiasm of a condemned man for the guillotine. Far from seeking the adult prerogatives of their parents, they vehemently demand a virtually indefinite prolongation of their non-adult state" (p. 8). In fact, teenagers think adolescence is more attractive than adulthood and more attractive than childhood. Adults, on the other hand, find childhood and adulthood attractive and adolescence unattractive (Bamber, 1973). Youth today are also more enthusiastic about their future than were their counterparts of the 1950s (Kleiber & Manaster, 1972).

Nevertheless, individual reactions vary widely. Some adolescents eagerly look ahead; others have mixed feelings; and still others cast a wary eye on approaching adulthood as though it were like flying into the eye of a hurricane. Less than enthusiastic adolescents note that adults are often stodgy, dull, and paunchy. They sympathize with the wit who said, "Adulthood is a time when one stops growing at the ends and starts growing in the middle." Adulthood is the time to settle down; fun seeking as a way of life is over. A 15-year-old boy, when asked by his mother to tend the store one afternoon, made this plea: "Remember, Mother, I have only one childhood when I can play. The time will come soon enough when I have to shoulder responsibilities and my carefree days will be over."

Youth's goals for adulthood. The life-styles most youth would prefer as adults are somewhat traditional, though in some respects they reflect the times. According to one nationwide survey of young people, ages 14 to 25, the great majority (82%) approved marriage, although they believed that the form of the family might change. Almost half would delay childbearing at least 3 years after marriage, and almost 90% said they accept the idea of planned childless marriage, although a mere 5% expected to remain childless themselves ("Youth's Attitudes," 1975).

By comparison with youth of the 1950s, today's young people want fewer children (Simon, Berger, & Gagnon, 1972). Since sex attitudes and practices reflect the times, it is important to remain abreast of recent research. In one study (Scarlett, 1972), which involved undergraduate students, almost all (96%) agreed on the desirability of limiting their families. Eighty-one percent indicated they wanted two children (64%) or fewer (17%), while only 18% wanted three children (11.5%) or more (6.5%). In a second study, which involved college students, 41% preferred having two children, 31% three, and 25% four or more. Only 3% favored having only one child ("How Many Children?", 1972). Such figures reflect current conditions; we can't be sure that present trends will continue.

Youth also have clear-cut preferences about where they will live, and generally they don't like cities. In one sampling ("How Many Children?", 1972), the majority chose a small town or rural area; 19% preferred the suburbs; and only 14% chose a city. Sixty-seven percent chose a small town or rural area.

The nationwide survey cited above also shed light on youth's values regarding their future. When asked about their most important life goals, 45% named "the opportunity to develop as an individual," and 42% cited "a happy family life" as most important. Nine percent chose "a fulfilling career," and only 5% listed "making a lot of money." In addition, 35% of the men and 30% of the women would choose a traditional way of life: "A successful executive or professional job, a family, and a home in a good neighborhood, compared with 30% and 26%, respectively, who would choose such a life in 1970" ("Youth's Attitudes," 1975, p. 14).

Of 12 items to be ranked as necessities of life, "owning own home" was named first by 59%, followed by "pension plan" (57%), and "a savings account of at least $5,000" (54%). Only 38% named "college education" as a necessity; "a master's degree" ranked near the bottom of the list of necessities, the same (12%) as "a color TV," but less necessary than "a new car," "an air conditioned home," and "an opportunity to travel abroad" (p. 15).

For their part, young women no longer look on housewivery, motherhood, and conventional feminine behavior as the be-all and end-all of women's existence. On the other hand, neither will they go to the opposite extreme of attempting to assume careers identical with those of men. Rather, they seem to plan for flexibility in their careers, with brief interruptions for motherhood or for cutting down on a career when their children are young. On one hand, they intend to maintain intellectual activities and interests outside the home; on the other, they anticipate achieving real happiness from their home and the family. They do not feel that all their satisfactions will come from outside activity, but they also refuse to be confined wholly to the home.

Preferred Life Style of College Sampling

In previously unpublished research (1976) by the author (Table 2–1), undergraduates at the State University College Oswego, New York, indicated the type of life styles they would prefer as adults. Only 3% would remain single, while two-thirds (67%) would marry and also have children. The preferred places to live were suburb (32%), small city (24%), and rural area (25%). A mere 2% would choose a large city. Only one student wanted to work alone on the job, whereas 44% preferred working with others, and 53% indicated a preference for a combination of working alone and with others. In terms of chief concern in a future career, "doing something interesting" won out easily (44%), followed by job and financial status (19%), chance to be creative (18%), and a chance to serve others (15%). Only one student named job status as his chief goal.

Here are several typical replies regarding future plans and goals:

After college
Male, age 22: I would like to marry and have children, but that is largely due to my involvement with my girl friend. If I lost her, I wouldn't be so sure of my answer.

Table 2–1 Adulthood Plans of College Students

Topic	TYPES OF STUDENTS		
	Females (N = 60)	Males (N = 60)	Total (N = 120)
	%	%	%
PREFERENCE REGARDING MARITAL STATUS			
Remain single	3	3	3
Marry, have children	68	66	67
Marry, have no children	3	6	5
Cohabit, without marriage	3	5	4
Other, or don't know	20	16	18
PREFERRED PLACE TO LIVE			
Large city	3	1	2
Small city	23	25	24
Suburb	33	31	32
Small town	13	13	13
Rural area	25	25	25
WHAT MATTERS IN FUTURE VOCATION			
Job status	1	1	1
Chance to serve others	18	13	15
Chance to be creative	20	16	18
Job and financial security	10	28	19
Doing something interesting	48	40	44
PREFER JOB INVOLVING			
Working alone	1	1	1
Working with others	56	31	44
50/50, alone and with others	40	66	53

Male, age 21: I would prefer to wait until about 5–10 years after school, probably when I'm about 30, to get married, or possibly just live with someone, and then I would like to have a few children.

Female, age 21: My choice would be to get married eventually and have children. Right now I'm not sure that I really want to have children. I don't think it is fair to the child to be put into a world that is as problem-oriented as ours. I would like to adopt a child who needs a home. Society should care for the people already living rather than just producing more.

Female, age 21: I do want to get married eventually, but I am not the type of person to rush into it for marriage sake. I am very disturbed by the number of divorces that have occurred among my friends and my cousins. I want to be sure when I get married. Sometimes I do feel that perhaps living with someone and not becoming formally married may in fact be a good idea. But I think we are all too oriented toward the security most marriages bring.

Where to live after college

Male, age 21: I think a city about the size of Syracuse where there are things going on, yet it is not as over-crowded as, say New York.

Male, age 21: Ideally, I would like to live in a small town. I like the easy going pace, but realize that most job opportunities are highly lacking in small towns. I have to draw a balance between my ideal living conditions and my ideal career aspirations (although I don't even know what they are yet).

Female, age 19: I was raised in a rural area and found it very rewarding because I was able to take the responsibility of having pets, as many as I wanted, and always had a place to get away from it all.

Male, age 20: I grew up in a rural-suburb area. In the future I plan on living in the same type area. I like being somewhat to myself but with people being around.

Future vocation

Female: I am looking for a job I can be secure in (both financially and job wise) and a place where I can be creative. I am more of a doer than a sitter and feel that both of these two parts have to go together for me to function well.

Male: I know of a job in which I could have both job and financial security but I will only do it as a last resort because it has nothing at all to do with my interests.

Female, age 21: I want most to help others but also to be happy in what I'm doing. I would have to feel that I'm accomplishing something.

Male, age 21: In my after college years I would like to get a good paying job. After I have established myself financially I would like to get married and have a family. I'd prefer to live in a suburb and work in a city. I would like to work with a few people not like in a factory. I would prefer a law enforcement job which you mainly work alone or with a partner.

Male, age 21: In my years after college I plan to become a policeman or federal agent. I would like to get married and have at least three children. However, I want to have good financial status when I do get married. I want my children to go to school, and even go to college. My sons, I want to be fair, honest, and athletic; my daughters, fair, honest, healthy. I want to live in the country. I want my family to feel like a family, not like a cardboard structure of a family found in suburbs and cities.

CRITERIA FOR MATURITY

Measuring Maturity in Terms of Developmental Tasks

Progress toward adulthood is sometimes measured in terms of developmental tasks. That is, an individual must have particular attitudes, habits, and skills if he or she is to function effectively as an adult. Already lurking just around the corner, adulthood often sneaks up on adolescents, catching them unprepared.

Various listings of developmental tasks exist. Generally, they do not conflict but stress different points. The points below, derived from several of these lists, have been expressed or implied already, but for clarity's sake we will summarize them here.

1. A basic criterion of maturity is that the normal tasks of adolescence will have been completed. In other words, young adults must have firm preadult underpinnings; otherwise, energies still required for fighting childhood battles and healing old wounds cannot be set free for solving adult problems.

2. Youths who are ready for maturity have found healthy channels for expressing emotions but cannot yet control them as much as they should. They have learned to inhibit external expressions of emotion, as well as to ignore many of the stimuli that caused stress in their early years. This is not to say that they remain emotionally insulated from their environments. On the contrary, they make heavy emotional investments, but they are capable of quick comebacks after disappointments. They are resilient, capable of taking in stride the inevitable frustrations and disappointments of life.

3. Young adults accept the principle that they can best meet long-term needs by facing the realities of life, the good along with the bad. They are optimistic enough to permit a zest for living but not so optimistic that they are blind to unpleasant truths that should be changed. They see themselves, their families, their associates, and the various other forces in their environments in their true perspective. They have abandoned certain prejudices and preconceived ideas that obstruct the capacity for clear thinking. They understand and accept their own limitations but recognize and capitalize on their strengths.

4. Facing reality, in turn, calls for adjusting in a satisfactory way—organizing all those factors in a person's physical and social environment over which one has control in ways that allow both personal fulfillment and long-range social welfare. Obviously, such adjustment requires a satisfactory balance between concerns for themselves and for others; mature individuals enjoy their inner lives but are not self-centered. They use their environment to the fullest, taking advantage of whatever it has to offer. They relate meaningfully to the world with a sense of commitment and of belonging to the "human enterprise." On the other hand, they manage to maintain personal independence and freedom from undue control by others. They have acquired the self-confidence, skills, and values that permit self-direction. Young children have to rely on many decisions being made for them, but grownups need considerable self-determination. Likewise, adults should be capable

of making wise decisions and adjusting to a constantly changing world. They must be flexible enough to adjust to a constantly shifting environment.

5. Mature individuals can maintain their autonomy more easily if they have established a sense of identity and a way of life consistent with their own potential. They are aware of self, not in a self-conscious way but in a manner that allows them to act with self-respect. That is, freedom to act is reinforced by the self-understanding, skills, and inclinations needed to act intelligently. Mature individuals make use of the things they do well, capitalizing especially on unusual talents even if the result is an apparently lopsided manner of life.

6. Another developmental task of attaining adulthood is to retain the best of one's earlier stages, while dispensing with the rest. Certainly, it is good for adults to preserve the sort of energy, idealism, and *joie de vivre* characteristic of youth. On the other hand, other aspects of adolescence, if they persist, can become a stumbling block to later adjustment. A case in point is the pressure on American adults to remain pegged at an adolescent stage of development. Indeed, Americans lose much marital satisfaction and happiness in society because adults are expected to perform at 40 or 50 as they did at 20 to 25.

7. Mature individuals have come of age. They have established themselves as adults and developed genuine self-determination on their own outside their childhood homes. They have abandoned earlier concepts of themselves as sons or daughters, little or big brothers or sisters, or as students, all of which limit their freedom because they make people feel young and dependent; or they have integrated their old concepts into fresh versions of self more appropriate to the current situation. They are now also able, without undue stress, to hold ideas different from those of their parents about fundamental matters.

8. They have learned to play mature roles successfully in the areas of sex, vocation, and social groups. They have established satisfactory relationships with their own and the other sex. They have developed a parental sense, or interest in establishing the next generation, implying a faith in life and in one's place in the total scheme of things. They are prepared to decide when (or whether) to become a parent and what sort of parent to be.

On the other hand, "there are people who, from misfortune, or because of special and genuine gifts in other directions, do not apply this gift to offspring but to other forms of altruistic concern and creativity which may absorb their kind of parental responsibility" (Gutmann, 1973, p. 153). Certainly, this concept involves more than taking care of children. It includes many kinds of generation, including all the ways of creating and nurturing new persons, new products, new

Individuals who function well as adults have learned to play mature roles in the area of vocation.

institutions, and new life styles through periods of their origin and early existence and early "vulnerability." This kind of caring requires "not only warmth and good intentions; it requires a disciplined capacity to surrender personal claims—for comfort, for security, for self expression—in the name of whatever new thing is being created" (Gutmann, 1973, p. 153).

Parenting thus involves giving up some of one's own goals and controlling one's own reactions. Note that ". . . a creative artist cannot see in paint or stone only a vehicle for his own self expression; if he is really good, then he must see himself as the vehicle whereby paint or stone or clay finds its best possible form. The medium is not there to release him; he is there to release his medium" (Gutmann, 1973, p. 153).

9. Mature individuals have successfully begun a career that permits self-actualization and a reasonably adequate standard of living. They have established effective relations with others and know-how in group situations. They have good friends but are not slavishly loyal to them. They can maintain effective business and social relations even with those of whom they disapprove. They have found a place in society and have made satisfactory adjustments to the major social institutions, both on the local and the larger scene.

10. In defining one's relationship to the world, the mature indi-

vidual has developed a rational moral code and a philosophy of life. This philosophy provides the individual with a satisfying concept of the universe and his or her place in it, and the moral code serves as a measuring stick for one's actions. The code must also be flexible, designed to effect its basic purpose—to insure the greatest ultimate good of all concerned. A person's moral code leads him or her to choose patterns of conduct, not because one is afraid of criticism or punishment but because those patterns are consistent with his or her philosophy. Since people must operate in a social setting, they recognize that they must also adjust to society's standards, but they do not accept them without question.

The young adult must also be sufficiently tough, resourceful, and flexible to cope with giant-sized problems. We can prophesy with some degree of certainty that today's young people will ultimately be required to cope with awesome issues, including problems of population, pollution, the bomb, interracial tension, and perhaps, interplanetary relationships. Toward such issues young adults must be critical but constructive. According to Eisenberg (1973), the adolescent who "insists upon a critical re-examination of conventional wisdom is making himself into an adult. And the adult whose concerns extend beyond family, and beyond nation to mankind, has become fully human" (p. 222).

11. Young adults must continue exploratory activities they have already begun—a matter of life-styles on trial in a wider arena. One does not find oneself all at once; making final decisions, at this age-stage, is neither immediately necessary nor desirable. Adjustments too hastily made are rarely as satisfying as more carefully considered decisions. Nevertheless, a youth cannot cling too long to adolescence, Some individuals simply never clear the hurdle into adulthood and become examples of developmental arrest.

In short, looking around must be combined with moving ahead. Every adult must develop time sense. These are life's peak years. In *A Roving Commission: My Early Life,* Winston Churchill sounded a challenge: "Come on now, all you young men, all over the world, you are needed more than ever now. . . . You have not an hour to lose. . . . Twenty to twenty-five! These are the years! Don't be content with things as they are. Enter upon your inheritance; accept your responsibilities!"

Perspective on Criteria for Maturity

We can make certain generalizations about all the lists of criteria for maturity. First, the estimates are largely subjective in nature. Writers are inclined to use themselves as points of reference, accepting their own value systems as the measures of maturity. Maturity is also commonly thought of as achieved once and for all. Actually, an individual develops faster in some areas than others. Furthermore, there is something of the uncompleted work of adolescence in every adult. In fact, regressions are normal, but they are relatively infrequent and less serious in the mature individual. It may even be good to retain certain characteristics of earlier age-stages, including freshness of outlook, vigor, hope, and trust. Finally, maturity cannot be identified with any fixed level of achievement. Where adjustment is concerned, to stand still is to move backward. The essence of true maturity is continued growth.

Readiness for Adulthood is not an All-or-None Concept

Research on the topic of youth's readiness for adulthood is inadequate. What there is indicates progress in some areas and continued immaturity in others, with the general trend in the right direction. Regressions, however, are normal, and youth sometimes have trouble looking ahead because they are looking behind. Nor is there a single road to maturity; there are many paths to adulthood and many styles of life called adulthood (Dreeben, 1974). In the Oakland Growth and Guidance Studies, which so far have followed the same individuals from childhood until middle adulthood, the main conclusion has been that people differ very much from each other and that they move from adolescence to adulthood in very different ways (Haan, 1972).

HELPING YOUTH TO GROW UP

Although most youngsters manage to muddle through to maturity reasonably well, some of them, like the youths quoted here, may become confused. They should be helped to trim their sails and set their compasses more accurately:

Female: On the whole, I am only allowed to make unimportant decisions about my life. Most of our decisions are guided by what other people think.

Male: My perception of the future is mixed. I have trouble striving in college and sometimes I get discouraged. I am really afraid of life in a way. I have always concentrated on happiness, but in my childhood I was always unhappy and my adolescence is the same. Sometimes I have to stop work in the summer and have a good time to sort of regain my childhood. I am interested in humanities, philosophy, and social science. I want to work eventually as a clinical psychologist or teacher. I perceive the college adult world with disdain but when I look at our own generation I am not happy. The world of the businessman I don't like nor the world of competition.

Anyone trying to help such youths should remember the following points:

1. First, youth should not be forced into maturity too soon. If we make people grow up too fast they fail to retain aspects of youth, such as hope and enthusiasm, that should be preserved. Besides, writes Bauer (1965), we rob adolescents of their youth by organizing them and structuring their society by adult rules and standards. We even try to make something productive of children's play. He recalls a conversation between two six-year-olds, one of whom had spent the day playing house, playing school, fighting with a girl friend, skipping rope, and blowing bubbles. Her companion had just returned from a summer day-school and listened to the first youngster's recitation of what she had done. Then his expression changed as he recalled his purpose in life and he inquired seriously, "But what did you do that was productive?"

2. Similarly, the adolescent years may be preserved as a psychological and social moratorium during which individuals remain relatively free from adult pressures. They need time to engage in identity play and other forms of experimentation to determine who they really are.

3. To lessen youth's confusion, society should clarify ambiguous standards of responsibility and maturity. "As it stands now," point out Kelly and Baer (1971), "no one really knows what the criteria for adulthood are in this country. Is it the driver's license? The high school diploma? The vote? The army? Marriage? Child raising? The achievement of economic independence? And even if one passes all these plateaus there can be, and often are, nagging doubts about one's identity. Killing a lion with a spear at least has the advantage of being clear cut. When it's over, it's over" (p. 411). Certain types of rites of passage would contribute more toward identity formation than a lengthy and confusing moratorium, which achieves nothing. Note, for example, the success of the outward bound program in rehabilitating juvenile offenders (Kelly & Baer, 1971).

Perhaps our society should institute a rite of passage, a series of tests an adolescent must pass to be considered an adult. Such a rite of passage should meet certain criteria. It should involve real rather than simulated experience—for example, not simply studying about aircraft but taking a solo flight in which knowledge and skills are demonstrated. It should challenge students' abilities to stretch their capacities through transcending barriers within themselves and tackling goals not readily obtainable. One would not simply learn to play an instrument he already plays somewhat better, but he would choose a goal requiring a great extension of his talent, such as trying out for a chair in a junior symphony. In addition, the challenge should be genuinely one's own, because youth in our culture must make decisions from among a vast array of alternatives in work, life-style, and relationships. Unfortunately, in our culture students have little training in decision making or chances for assessment and reassessment of what they do. The trials should also constitute a significant learning experience within themselves, involving not merely a chance for the student to demonstrate knowledge and skills, but providing a meaningful confrontation with oneself, making one self-aware, aware of what he or she is capable of doing. Moreover, this trial or ceremony should not simply test what has gone before in one's schooling. It should test one's capacity to make the transition to to life that follows.

In sum, the students' culmination of education should meet five basic challenges: (1) adventure, including a demonstration of endurance, skills, and daring in an unfamiliar environment; (2) creativity, or expression of imagination in some meaningful or aesthetic form; (3) service through identifying and supplying some human need; (4) some practical skill, including exploration of some useful activity and production of something useful; and (5) logical inquiry, or some challenge to explore one's own curiosity, formulate problems, and pursue solutions systematically and by investigation.

Each category would involve relevant behaviors. In the adventure catgory, the student might live alone off the land, participate in some rock-climbing expeditions, explore underground caves, or take a month-long expedition along some trail. In the service category, students might do volunteer work with the old, the infirm, or the retarded, provide sports programs for the handicapped, instruct on playgrounds, clean up eyesores in the community, or survey community needs. In the creativity category, youth might fashion their own creations in making sculpture, jewelry, or leather; in writing poetry, magazines, and plays; in drawing cartoons; in preparing gourmet foods; in organizing a rock group or string quartet. In the practical category, they might demonstrate fine secretarial skills, analyze stock market trends, row a boat they have designed and built for sale, develop a travel guide book for high-school students, construct a telescope with hand-ground lenses and develop photographs taken through it. In the logical inquiry area, they might show how they have answered such questions as: How does a star fish regenerate a lost arm? What do people experience while meditating that they don't experience just sitting with their eyes closed? What are the best techniques for teaching dogs obedience? Does faith healing work, and if so, how?

In order to prepare for these tests, "experience weeks" would be arranged for the activities. Big brothers and sisters would be provided to help younger students prepare for competence in these areas. Finally, before graduation, students would tell invited friends and relatives about their experiences, perhaps using slides, movies, or other audio-visual aids.

Responses to this idea have been favorable, with some exceptions. Even its advocates believe it is important first to establish well thought out and financially supported pilot projects in selected communities, and then to disseminate the data. Opponents argue that such rites of passage would involve many special hazards, including unusual financial costs, danger of accidents and suits in cases of the school's liability, and difficulties in organization and implementation. Some critics also fear turning large numbers of students loose on the community (Gill, 1974).

4. To be appreciated, adulthood should be earned. Easy induction into adulthood is not necessarily the same as a good adjustment to it. According to Baumrind (1974), adults who excessively indulge young people prevent them from understanding that only through becoming competent do they attain true freedom. That is, they cannot feel that they have a future or that they can make a place in the world without appropriate understandings, skills, and attitudes. Adults, in attempting to be kind, may confuse and hurt young people by providing options that are inappropriate at their stage of life. Instead, adolescents must come to grips with the reality principle. They must learn that they cannot, through drugs or even overinvolvement in work, forever protect themselves from fears of failure, loneliness, and anxiety. Therefore, they must learn how to "tolerate delay, control rage and sexual desire, sublimate, think rationally, act responsibly, endure suffering, adjust to that which cannot be altered and serve the community" (p. 82).

When young people are deluded into believing that their opportunities are greater than they are, they cannot adapt to environmental problems and imperfections. Also they must gain meaning from their experience, but instead, "they demand meaning, as though one generation can deliver meaning to another on a silver platter" (Baumrind, 1974, p. 82). Such meaning must be gained through becoming responsible within a frame of reference of reality. To this end, it would help to provide for youth, from age sixteen on, chances for participating in public service (Baumrind, 1974). In working with people of various ages and backgrounds, they can experiment with different social and vocational roles, without committing themselves to any one. For example, in one program, high-school juniors and seniors in twelve cities work and intern in industry and government, receiving full school

credit. Society should also make it easier for a youth to reenter school
if he wants to hold a job now but return to school later on. Youth should
be encouraged, says Baumrind, to look on themselves as "experimenters" instead of "dropouts."

In substance, Coleman and his panel on youth agree (Behn et al.,
1974), recommending that youth be trained for adult roles, to provide
an outlet for youth's "idealistic creative and constructive impulses."
Nevertheless, argues Behn, the panel's plan involves many assumptions
with little factual support. Nor does it prove that young people are not
adequately socialized for their adult roles.

On the other hand, youths must be accorded mature status as
rapidly as possible. According to Stone and Church (1973), the sooner
people begin to take the young person's adulthood for granted, the
sooner and more easily he or she assumes the role and the easier it is
for others to react to him or her as an adult. That is, we can best help
adolescents into adulthood by treating them, at least in public, as much
as possible like adults. We must not, however, throw them so completely on their own that they are overwhelmed by anxiety. Adolescents
themselves, for all their straining for acceptance, usually pass into adulthood without immediately being aware of it. At some point, but they
do not know when, they no longer expect people to challenge their
adulthood. They know then that they have crossed the threshold, although it is probably not until a considerable while after the fact.

5. Training during adolescence should involve a realistic discussion of problems to be faced in the period that follows. Fledgling adults
would benefit from answers to questions like these: Should a couple
delay having children until family finances are in good shape? How old
should young children be before a wife returns to work? According to
Kagan (1973), in the education process adolescents should be exposed
to different theories about children's development and encouraged to
develop their own. In addition, they might be introduced to some of the
most controversial issues in human development; for example, should
children grow toward some universally acceptable goal or select from
legitimate alternatives in their own development?

6. Youth should learn not only how to resolve adult problems but
how to enjoy adulthood. Unfortunately, maturity is rarely pictured as
satisfying. Instead, in most television programming the primary emphasis is on problems of romantic love involving young, good-looking subjects in fictional situations. Hence, youth have fuzzy ideas about the
most productive and satisfying aspects of adulthood.

7. Youth must expect to discuss their own life styles within the
adult world they join. They must realize that their elders command the
resources and the skills involved. Although youth may help reform the

system, if they become too impatient, their efforts may be doomed. In other words, the young Don Quixote, though tilting at windmills, is unlikely to bring the adult empire toppling down. For this reason, the generations must understand each other and stop becoming snarled in constant fruitless arguments.

8. To be effective in their leadership, adults must become engaged in common activities with youth. How this goal should be achieved is the question. The Coleman II Report (Coleman, 1974) also recommends that different ages interact so that youth may learn directly from adult models those values, knowledges, and skills appropriate to entering adulthood. Moreover, they feel that this integration should take place within the world of work. Meantime, adults would gain from exposure to youth's enthusiasm and idealism.

In making this suggestion, the Coleman committee has failed to take into account the basic differences and interests between age groups. They made the assumption that when people of different ages are brought together, simply becoming members of the same community will make people agree on values and goals, and that youth and their elders will automatically adapt to each other and become sensitive to each others feelings.

The panel also thinks separation contributes to "irrational and unreasonable anti-adult and anti-establishment norms" (p. 131). However, this reasoning suggests that youth's causes have no merit of their own, that their questioning of adults' competitiveness and materialism is caused by resentment, since they are outsiders. A not too subtle implication, concludes Hall (1974), is that adults should use age-integrated settings to assume their rightful authority over young people. Coleman fails to realize that youths' outside position may help them to gain a better and more objective perspective on their society. It is like having a grandstand seat at a ballgame, where you can perhaps see the total picture better than the players themselves can.

9. Adults earn youth's disrespect, partly, by giving up their own convictions too easily. Some impatient youngsters champ at the bit; they can already taste the power of running a world. Hence, adults cannot shirk their responsibility of debating issues with the young. It isn't a case of choosing to be a hawk instead of a dove. It is just that adults must not simply give up the authority and the self-confidence that come from experience (Wireman, 1970). Instead, all too many adults have become self-doubting and intimidated by the aggressiveness, impatience, and impulsiveness of the young and refuse to engage them in the sort of vigorous debate on substantive issues that youth so greatly need. This tragedy, says Wireman, is a "cop-out" because "it tends to perpetuate in the minds of the young a mistaken belief, indeed a cruel

hoax, that they alone can solve the issues of our time" (p. 19). This crisis can only be solved by "thoughtful citizens of all ages working together" (pp. 19–20).

Perhaps those adults who can best assist youth toward maturity are persons only a little older than themselves. Under conditions of rapid change, young persons must assume responsibility for, and be anchormen in, the destiny of still younger persons in ways impossible for older people and least of all for parents to perform. If society would institutionalize this responsibility of the young for the younger, writes Erikson (1970), it would produce different images for both young and young adulthood. Youth would then be capable of continuing the work already begun on a variety of frontiers by pioneering youth groups in the last few decades. Then adults would be able to contribute their knowledge and experience without having to maintain an authority that goes beyond their actual competence.

10. Adolescents' own efforts to help themselves should be recognized and encouraged. Only in a culture in a state of rapid and continuous change, says Spindler (1970), does each generation manufacture its own new culture. Although each new generation finally changes to a position roughly resembling that of the preceding generation, in the transition each generation invents its own culture, which nudges the whole society in an unanticipated and slightly altered direction. Thus, the generation gap becomes a means to change, if not always to progress.

11. Any program for helping youth grow up must be continuously related to current difficulties in achieving maturity. A group of young adults reported such difficulties as "adjustment from civilian to army life and back again" and "trying to adjust to living with my in-laws while I completed my college education." Especially in recent times, youths need a sense of the cosmic and the cataclysmic, lest they fear being engulfed by forces too big to handle. Certainly, this aim is utopian, and perhaps we cannot reach it; nevertheless, it can help to establish guidelines for youth's education.

SUMMARY

All societies recognize differences between the status of child and that of adult, and all have informal ways of inducting youths into adulthood. In modern societies, there is no initiation ritual or pubertal rite. Perhaps the requirements of a swiftly changing, complex society would make rigid formulas for growing up impractical.

The training received in childhood does not prepare children for the responsibilities expected of adults in modern Western culture. Much that is learned in early years has almost no relevance for adulthood. Adolescents do not get a true apprenticeship for their responsible role in society. Other obstacles to maturity are the lack of association between adolescent and adult age groups and the refusal of some parents to acknowledge that their children are growing up.

Both adults and youth hold characteristic attitudes about youth's growing up. Adults' attitudes may serve either to help or to obstruct their youngsters' induction into adulthood. Parents, in particular, may accept their children's changing status because some of them no longer want the responsibilities of being parents, or they may resist recognizing their children's increasing maturity because to do so would acknowledge their own aging status. For their part, youths also hold somewhat ambivalent attitudes about growing up. They may look ahead eagerly, desiring the privileges adults customarily have, or they may cling to adolescence because it is more carefree, romantic, and pleasant. Some individuals—among them, college athletes—have a greater stake in prolonging adolescence than others.

Youth's readiness for maturity may be defined in various ways— for example, in terms of developmental tasks or the acquisition of those attitudes, habits, and skills required to function effectively as an adult. The youth's progress toward maturity may also be defined according to how one's own progress corresponds with that of others of the same age. No one criterion is adequate; a composite of measures might best be used. We must remember, too, that estimates are subjective in nature, depending upon value judgments of the individuals who devise them, as well as the culture or subculture concerned.

It is generally agreed that certain measures may help youths in their progress toward maturity. They should not be forced into maturity too soon; they should be permitted some time to test the ground rules of their society. They also need clearcut standards of responsibility so they will be able to define their own adult roles. Perhaps certain customs or rites of passage might ease the transition. Certainly, youth must not simply be presented adulthood as a gift; they should earn it if they are to discharge their mature roles adequately. In addition, the adult society should be made more attractive so that youths are not reluctant to join the ranks of their elders. Adults must present worthy models for youth to trust their leadership and respect the ranks of those they must ultimately join.

The foregoing points call for an objective approach based on adequate, continuously revised research. Topics that have been neglected should be investigated, and their scope should be broadened to include youths of all sorts in all countries and subcultures. The research effort should extend backward into the past and forward into the future, projecting what may lie ahead.

SUGGESTED READINGS

Cosby, A. G., Thomas, J. K., & Falk, W. W. Patterns of early adult status attainment and attitudes in the nonmetropolitan South. *Sociology of Work & Occupations*, 1976, *3* (4), 411–428. A study among youth in the Deep South indicated that youth's aspirations for future employment are unrealistic in terms of available opportunities and only marginally related to current attainments. Both white and black students were unduly optimistic and unrealistic about future opportunities.

Devine, H. F. & Loesch, L. C. In loco parentis and the new age of majority: The views of freshmen and their parents. *Journal of College Student Personnel*, 1976, *17* (5), 420–425. Despite the increasing recognition of age 18 as the beginning of legal adulthood, parents want the university to exercise considerably more control over their college-age children than the young people themselves are willing to accept.

Fein, R. A. Men's entrance to parenthood. *Family Coordinator*, 1976, *25* (4), 341–348. Interviews of 30 husbands who attended childbirth preparation classes before and after the birth of their first child suggest the need for more adequate research regarding men's preparation for parenting, their involvement in the birth process, and ways they can participate more effectively in family life.

Jackson, R. M. & Meara, N. M. Father identification, achievement, and occupational behavior of rural youth: 5-year follow-up. *Journal of Vocational Behavior*, 1977, *10* (1), 82–91. Rural economically deprived adolescent males, previously surveyed as high school seniors and again a year after graduation about their post-high school plans, were questioned 5 years after their graduation about their current occupational status and aspirations, their current job satisfaction, their evaluation of their high school preparation with regard to their present jobs, and their hopes for the future.

Lowenthal, M. F. & Weiss, L. Intimacy and crises in adulthood. *Counseling Psychologist*, 1976, *6* (1), 10–15. It is hypothesized that aside from overwhelming external challenge, most persons are motivated to live satisfying autonomous lives only within the framework of one or more mutually intimate relationships involving two people. While Erik Erikson recognized the importance of interpersonal intimacy, Lowenthal and Weiss propose a theoretical framework for studying psychosocial changes in adulthood. The framework would focus on areas of commitment, which they suggest is a more flexible life stage theory than Erikson's.

Mahoney, J. Age and values: The generation non-gap. *Psychological Reports*, 1976, *39* (1), 62. A reanalysis by age of M. Rokeach's (1973) national sample of 1,489 adult Americans suggests a core of intergenerational agreement concerning personal life goals but less agreement on role-appropriate values. Apparently social change effects role-appropriate behavior more than it does life goals.

Modell, J., Furstenberg, F. F., Jr., & Hershberg, T. Social change and transitions to adulthood in historical perspective. *Family History*, 1976, *1* (1), 7–32. This comparison of patterns of transitions to adulthood across the past century indicates their significance for the life course and their relationship to the time. It also points up major differences between the youth of the 19th century and those of today.

Spanier, G. B. Sexualization and premarital sexual behavior. *Family Coordinator*, 1975, *24* (1), 33–40. An interview study of 1,177 college students disclosed a complex social-psychological pattern of variables that influenced premarital sexual behaviors. The relative impact of these variables—including parental influence, religion, current situation, and peer impact—was analyzed, and the author's version of how the process proceeds is explained.

3

CHAPTER

The
Tasks
of
Young
Adulthood

OVERALL TASKS

According to developmental task theory, progress through the life span involves constantly learning and mastering the new tasks that are appropriate to each new age stage. At each stage an individual must attain particular attitudes, habits, and skills if the tasks of the next stage are to be taken care of adequately. In chapter 1 we discussed Erik Erikson's portrayal of young adulthood as the time when individuals must attain intimacy as opposed to isolation. They must learn to relate unselfishly on a deeply intimate level to another person, as is required in a wholesome marriage relationship. And they must achieve generativity, becoming creative or parental. This means being ready to commit themselves consciously and willingly to guide new generations. In Eriksonian terms, the issue is between generativity (going beyond selfish concerns to make contributions of lasting value) or stagnation, which is characterized by boredom, bodily preoccupation, and self indulgence. The resolution of this issue affords people a sense of personal integrity and purpose.

Gould (1975) was able to delineate adult tasks by studying 500 middle-class subjects ages 16 to 60. He divided their lives into phases. The first was that of youth before the break from the family of origin. In phase two, ages 18 to 21, changes take place so that by phase three, ages 21 to 28, independent adult behaviors and attitudes have become stable.

Living now and building for the future. Sheehy based her concepts of young adult tasks on her interviews with young couples. Early on these adults have to make hard decisions. Will they take a trip to Europe now or salt the money away for Junior's college education? Should they spend evenings in the office getting a jump on the competition, or should they join other couples at bowling? Thus on the one hand, among Roger Gould's group-therapy patients at UCLA the 22- to 28-year-olds perceived themselves as what has been called the now generation. They felt that the time to live was now, but that they should also be preparing for the future (Sheehy, 1976). On the other hand, the 20s involve the question of how to gain a foothold in the adult world. At this time, people spend less time thinking about questions that were vital to them during their late adolescence, such as problems of identity, and become primarily concerned with how to achieve their goals. This preoccupation produces a certain sense of urgency from the mid-30s to the mid-40s.

Contrasting needs: To secure and to explore. Sheehy sees among young adults two conflicting aspects of self, one of which she calls the merger self and the other the seeker self; they can push and pull against each other. The first suggests the wish to be attached to other people, to seek the ultimate security. By contrast the seeker self is motivated to become separate and independent. This involves the attempt to determine and master one's own destiny. If the merger self is allowed to dominate, then an individual's life style can become narrow and locked in. However if the seeker self completely covers up the merger self, an individual may take on a completely self-centered life style in which interpersonal relations play no part. Such persons may pursue their goals so strenuously that they become emotionally exhausted and their warmer, more expressive, urges are completely subdued.

Until recently, observes Sheehy, boys have done most of the seeking and girls, the merging. Girls might excel academically just as long as it did not hurt their popularity. They might develop their talents so long as they did not turn out to be truly gifted, in which case they might be faced with making a difficult choice between marriage and career. Meantime boys learned the skills of competition and team work on the athletic field that would help them in their political and business lives.

The Tasks of the Thirties

A period of reflection. Gould (1975) divides the 30s into two phases. The first is from ages 29 to 36, and concerns the beginning of deep personal involvement and self-reflection. The next phase, from 36 to 43, involves feelings of personal and marital unrest and decreased financial problems. After investing tremendous energies to developing an adult life style and becoming increasingly aware of the all-too-rapid passage of time, a nagging question begins persistently to assert itself: Am I doing what I should best be doing, and am I on time in progressing toward my goals?

The need for appraisal of progress. Like Gould, Sheehy (1976) perceives the 30s as a time for reflection and the evaluation of one's life to date. After spending their 20s considering what they should be doing, both men and women must pause and look around as they approach age 30. While their choices to date may have seemed appropriate, now they feel differently about them. They are concerned about satisfying their inner needs, a task that involves making new commitments, or strengthening existing ones. All these tasks involve tremendous personal change, and may also cause crises in people's lives. Some individuals feel simultaneously elated and depressed (Sheehy, 1976). A typical reaction is simply to tear apart the pattern that the 20s were dedicated to establishing. A married couple may decide to call it quits, and either resume their single lives or take new partners. A single person may decide that it's time to get married and have a child. The woman who formerly was content to stay at home and rear babies now feels a restlessness to re-enter the world.

Settling down. The 30s are also devoted to putting down roots (Sheehy, 1976). The life style makes more sense as these roots are sent down. Men settle down seriously to making a go of it in their career. Often a couple is less satisfied with their marriage than they were during their 20s. The wife ordinarily focuses on rearing the children, sometimes holding an outside job at the same time. Social life is somewhat neglected. Whether the wife acts on the basis of her life reassessment at this time depends on many factors, and often some "marker event" will determine her future. For instance, her husband may fall ill, or she may obtain a divorce, or she may be offered a job she feels she cannot easily pass up.

Men often react to their wives' crises, and their need to break out of their shells, with considerable alarm. After all, aren't wives supposed to be their husbands' support system? Some husbands are unselfish and perceptive and help their wives to jump over the hurdles. Others force their wives back into their shells so that they continue their earlier monotonous existence. Still others, who fail to be supportive, may make their wives that much more determined to "do their own thing," with or without their husbands' approval.

Beyond such broad objectives there has been little effort to identify the tasks of young adulthood more specifically and to explore their significance. Therefore in this chapter we shall supplement the scanty research on the topic with a sampling of young adults' views. Unless otherwise identified, these people are in their 20s.

TASKS RELATING TO PERSONALITY DEVELOPMENT

Attainment of Autonomy

Basic to the achievement of other adult tasks is the achievement of autonomy—that is, young adults must launch themselves and establish their distinctiveness as persons from their families of origin. A minority do not establish independence, but continue to accept their parents' authority, partly because society tacitly condones it, at least for daughters. Ordinarily young adults need their families' emotional and financial support in order to establish a base for their own lives. However, as they move through their 20s they become less dependent and have fewer contacts with their parents. Typically the first step is physically to remove themselves to school or college, or to a job in another city, or perhaps to get married and have their own homes. When they strongly disagree with their parents over such matters as the people they date or their life style, they sometimes lessen or break off contacts with their parents (Stein, 1976).

It should be added that autonomy is not exclusively a matter of becoming free of excessive parental authority. Sometimes a spouse, usually the wife, merely transfers dependency on the parent to a somewhat childish reliance on the mate. This situation is more common when one partner is considerably more dominant than the other.

The Search for an Identity

The establishment of autonomy is simply one aspect of the continuing search for, and refinement of, identity. This process continues throughout life, in different ways at each age level. For example it is often in young adulthood that adoptees seek their natural parents because of a critical need to know what sort of biological characteristics they may transmit to their children. Also they may be concerned about generational continuity, both for themselves and their children, especially when the first child arrives. Practically all young adult adoptees who succeed in finding out who their parents are believe the search to have been worthwhile. For instance, one young woman said that she had found out she was Scotch Irish, and that both sides of her family were quite healthy (Baran, Sorosky, & Panor, 1975).

Young adults also try to achieve an identity by patterning themselves after people they admire, who function as role models for their own personal and vocational careers. Such models are plentiful enough for young men, although any particular male may have difficulty finding one appropriate to him. For women the problem is more serious. In one study only 44% of the undergraduate women questioned reported that they had found a female faculty member with whom they could identify. Women need such models, not only in the university but later as they establish themselves as adults, so that they can have encouragement from people who are significant to them, and support in resolving conflicts between traditional femininity and a desire to achieve ("Where are the role models?" 1977).

Not always, or even usually, does a young adult discover a single adequate role model. There may be different models for different roles. A young male high school teacher may be especially inspired by some outstanding instructor he once had. In his role as a father he may unconsciously model himself after his own father. Or his models may be composites derived from various people whom he has strongly admired.

Establishment of Emotional Stability

During their 20s young adults must somehow settle down so that their energies are not tied up in emotional problems that should have been resolved by now. Whatever degree of emotional stability or health they have achieved by age 30 tends to persist, even into later years. In research by Maas and Kuypers at the University of California at Berkeley the two personality characteristics prized most by successful persons of all ages were dependability and capability or productivity (Casady, 1975a). On the other hand, healthy individuals learn to adapt their values and personalities to changing situations through the life cycle.

Of course the stability of generations varies somewhat, according to tensions of the times. Currently some of the young people who matured during the 60s, and are now approaching age 30 have adjusted well to adulthood, while others are "now adrift, and suffering from anxiety and self doubt" ("Depression and disillusionment," 1976). Among the latter there is an increasing incidence of suicide and alcoholism, and a growing preoccupation with astrology, religious cults, yoga and "pop psychology, packaged as TM, EST, primal therapy, and encounter groups, all means by which they are seeking to discover themselves" (p. 13). While many young adults have good jobs, they nevertheless find life meaningless. In the 1960s they attempted to get close to each other, to be intimate, to be authentic, to "let it all hang out," but somehow it did not all hang together. Now they are lonely, rootless, and still seeking new values. In addition they seem unable to shape their future. They feel helpless and purposeless. Professionals attribute these problems to this age group's disillusionment following Watergate, the disorientation that resulted from using drugs, the new sexual freedom, and the failure of their free-swinging way of life to meet their expectations.

This picture may be unduly gloomy. Most graduates of this era are proving to be responsible young adults with more realistic ideals than mere contentment. Perhaps they will achieve more meaningful goals than young people who grew up in more stable eras. As Colin Campbell points out, emotional maturity should not become equated with happiness. He believes that people too actively pursue happiness and that the direct search for happiness is a sure way to unhappiness. Instead one's ideals should be directed toward fulfilling duty, not pleasure (Tavris, 1975).

Development of Guideposts for Behavior

Values. An especially significant task of young adults is the establishment of those values which will serve as a compass for steering their way through life. Many middle-aged people believe that they were in pursuit of the wrong goals when they were in their 20s and 30s. Men in their 40s wish that they had not been so consumed by ambition in their 20s, thus depriving themselves of important experiences with their families. They feel that they were not aware of what was really important in their lives. In general, values in young adulthood shift toward greater self-tolerance, and understanding and appreciation of the complexities of other people and the world in which they live. Still, there is much that can slow down or block that understanding (Gould, 1975).

It is often theorized that young people today live in so changing a world, one subject to such conflicting pressures, that they become hopelessly confused and prone to develop shallow value systems that they do not integrate well into their lives. On the other hand, many of them have found it a constructive experience to grow up in a generation in which the old value systems were being sloughed off and new ones developed. Many of them are now successful, open, realistic, confident, and more aware sexually and emotionally than earlier generations. Apparently some individuals rise to the challenge when moving over uncharted terrain while others simply fall by the wayside. The challenge for researchers is to determine what accounted for the relative success or failure of different types.

At any rate, eventually most adults feel reasonably content that their own values are adequate guides for their lives. In research by Norma Haan, middle-aged adults portrayed themselves as "interesting, objective persons with high intellectual aspirations." They were verbally fluent, socially poised, and interested in a wide variety of subjects and activities. They also valued themselves as "dependable, productive, likable and straightforward" (Casady, 1975a, p. 138).

Goals. Although goals are less abstract than values, the latter are nevertheless vital in determining goals. In fact peoples' values are often apparent in their statements of goals. In one study, when asked about their most important life goals, 45% of the young people in their early 20s named "the opportunity to develop as an individual," and 41%

cited a happy family life. Nine percent selected a fulfilling career, while only 5% named making a lot of money. In the mid-1970s 35% of the young men and 30% of the young women chose a traditional way of life—a successful executive or professional job, a family, and a home in a good neighborhood—compared with 30% and 26% respectively in 1970 ("Youth's attitudes," 1975, p. 14).

Because they are uncertain to what extent their lives will be devoted to family or vocation, some young women's goals are not clearly defined. Upon returning to her alma mater, Radcliffe, which she attended in the 1920s, and talking to many of the present-day students, Diana Trilling concluded that young women are too vague about their goals. Many of them idealistically claim that they want to affect others' lives in a positive manner, but they have no clear-cut idea of how they will do so. Even high-ranking colleges like Radcliffe are failing, declares Trilling, and if such outstanding institutions do no more than encourage such vague idealism, what is the likelihood of these and other young women working successfully toward full equality for women? (Trilling, 1977).

As will be apparent from the statements below, young adults' goals are, for the most part, relatively simple and somewhat traditional. They are not seeking dramatically different experiences or unusual successes. Their goals are moderate, and involve the need for good, solid, satisfying jobs, a loving family, and contentment. Few are thinking of performing some great mission or service to society. Rather, they want a satisfying, reasonably comfortable life.

> Having always been a rather noncompetitive person, I have tried to make my goals simple and attainable, but worthwhile to me. After having lived for some years completely on my own I now have confidence in myself and my abilities not to fear the terrible outside world. I have simple goals, mostly trying to surround myself with things that will make me content. The only unusual thing is that I require more freedom than most. (*Male*)

> Travel is of utmost importance, as well as success in the business world. I hope to be able to keep my idealistic views, no matter what job or place in society my life affords me. During my twenties I want to take courses that will enrich my mind, both with regard to my vocation and anything else that interests me. I want to maintain my individuality, but also to interact with people. (*Male*)

> I hope to achieve a moderate amount of success, as well as to find a woman whom I love and who loves me, as a source of security. (*Male*)

> My goals for my twenties are ones of exploration and higher education. I want to travel before going to graduate school. I would

also like to have some stability by the time I'm thirty, location and ability-wise. I'd like to try various jobs, but one that would enable me to be financially secure. (*Female*)

Basically I want to grow these next few years. I want to be in new situations, to learn, and to enjoy all that the world has to offer me. (*Female*)

My goals are to have a job, marry and work for a while, and have children. Then I expect to quit work until the children are in school, and then go to work again. (*Female*)

My goals for my twenties and thirties encompass a vast array of things. Travel is one of them. There is so much to see, and new people to meet. In my thirties I see myself as more of a realist, a person who must be responsible to a family, have a steady job, and make money. (*Female*)

My goals are to rear my young sons to be healthy and well-adjusted, and to find all the good things in life. I need to be happy and at peace, and to understand myself better and to learn my limitations. (*Female, age 34*)

INTERPERSONAL RELATIONSHIPS

Establishment of Intimacy

As we stated earlier, Erik Erikson named the establishment of intimacy as a basic task of young adulthood. Intimacy might apply to a variety of human relationships, whether or not it involves sexual feelings. Such intimacy "includes the ability to experience an open, supportive, tender relationship with another person, without fear of losing one's own identity in the process of growing close" (Newman & Newman, 1975, p. 270). As creating intimacy follows the establishment of personal identity, the potential for achieving such intimacy is related to each of the marital partners' concept of self as competent and significant. Intimacy suggests the capacity for "mutual empathy" and adaptation of needs and life styles. Each party must be able to give and receive, and while intimacy is ordinarily "established within the context of the marriage relationship, marriage itself does not, by definition, produce intimacy" (p. 270).

One problem is that men and women may attach different significance to intimacy and have different ideas about how to establish it. Males have often been taught to deny their dependency needs and to restrain their emotionality, while females have been rewarded for nurturant, supportive, and expressive behaviors. Hence it may take a while for young men to establish true intimacy, if they ever do, chiefly because they learned to resist very close relationships. Often it is only in middle age that men finally relax sufficiently to acknowledge their dependency needs.

In one respect young women today have a much easier task than their counterparts of other eras in establishing intimacy, and that is with regard to sex. In other years they may have felt at ease with outer expressions of affection and gentle caresses, while being unprepared for more intimate sexuality. More recently young women have come to accept their own sexual needs and to relate on a more equal basis with men.

One crisis often undergone by young adults is isolation. For some individuals the intimate, dependent relationships of marriage weaken their sense of self. They feel a "blurring of the boundaries of their own identity" (p. 273) and unconsciously "erect barriers" in order to maintain an intact sense of identity. Such people must somehow learn that achieving a sense of intimacy can actually strengthen their feelings of identity.

Marriage

Why young people marry. For most young adults the most vital outcome of interpersonal relationships is marriage. In fact most women have traditionally taken it for granted that they will get married and bear and raise children. As children they themselves played at being married and keeping house. In the early 1970s Blake (1972) concluded that "marriage and parenthood ... are not really chosen, they happen to people. ..." (p. 19). Sheehy (1976) agrees, observing that the idea that people marry for love is largely a myth. First, marriages happen chiefly because people feel they should—it is simply the thing to do. Second, people marry for security, in order to have dependency needs satisfied; this is true for men as well as women. Adults have never gotten over their childhood needs to be taken care of by their parents and to return for security to the safety of the family. A third reason for marriage is to compensate for some inadequacy within oneself. Or a man to whom his career is very important may marry a wife who will make a satisfactory showpiece. Still another motive is to get away from home, in some cases to escape responsibilities. An individual may marry someone with unusually high status or a considerable amount of money. At any rate, in Sheehy's study, "not a single man interviewed, over age 30, indicated that he had married for love. While couples may, early on, think of themselves as being in love, they may be driven by other emotions, possibly the need for others' approval, a desire for security, or a strong sex drive. On the other hand, love may develop across the years, especially after couples get used to the fact that each of them has idiosyncrasies which nevertheless may be indulged. Marriage is still popular and not about to become extinct" (Dreyer, 1975, p. 195).

Certainly almost all young adults today expect to get married, usually in their late 20s, and only after they have had their fling. Still, a very small but growing minority expects to remain single or to live with a member of the opposite sex without getting married for an indefinite period, perhaps always. Here are several young adults' views on the subject.

> I live with my fiance whom I am marrying in two months. I hope to have a good marriage, a full social life, and a career. These things take precedence over a family. We are in the process of planning a large home in the country with lots of land and woods. Many young families and couples live there. They still have the fun of kids, but with the responsibility of adults. They are very friendly, casual, warm, and accepting. Older people also mesh in, with young attitudes and acceptance. It is diversified but harmonious. (*Female*)

> I want to get married some day, but I'm not in a hurry. I lived with a man for two years and I enjoyed it, but I also enjoy being on my own. I'm very independent and selective, so it may be difficult to find a suitable partner. (*Female*)

> I believe I will remain single, free of responsibilities, at least through young adulthood. If you don't get all the adventure out of your system, you'll be frustrated the rest of your life. (*Male*)

> I cannot foresee marriage for a few years. I have to get my own head together and I don't want to put someone else's together also. (*Male*)

Age at marriage. A small minority of couples marry during their teens for a variety of reasons, the chief one being to escape an unsatisfactory home situation. Sixty-one of one hundred young people who had married early reported their parents were alcoholics, separated, divorced, or mentally ill (Reiner & Edwards, 1974). On the other hand, the choice of marriage partners was not casual. In only 12 of the 100 cases had the pair dated less than a year, and many had gone together several years. Often there was a strong identification between them. Nevertheless after marriage the couples experienced serious and widely varied problems. Often they lacked the economic or personal resources for dealing with their problems. In many cases the husband lacked the training to hold meaningful jobs. Often they had sexual problems which were masked by an assumed sophistication. Wives who did not work often lived in unfamiliar neighborhoods; and if they did work, day-care resources were often inadequate or missing altogether. During such times as the couple had off they could find few recreational resources that did not cost more money than they could afford.

The majority of young people marry in their 20s, and later than in the past. For this reason there are more young adult singles than ever before, although almost everyone eventually marries at least once. Several factors account for the delay, one being that many couples no longer perceive marriage as a prerequisite for sex. Indeed couples who have known each other for some time are more likely to engage in premarital sex than ever (Hunt, 1973). In addition, with the increased availability of and knowledge about birth control and greater ease in obtaining abortions, fewer persons feel compelled to marry. Finally the women's liberation movement has shown women that married life is not their only viable life style (Lasswell, 1974).

We might ask, is there a best age for marriage (Lasswell, 1974)? Certainly the teens are the worst time to marry in terms of marital stability and satisfaction. Couples who marry before the age of 21 double their probability of divorce within 20 years, and it is doubled again if the husband earns less than $8,000 a year (Reiner & Edwards, 1974). Statistically marriages are most stable for men who marry between the ages of 27 and 31 and women at about 25. Women who marry at 28 or even later, and men who marry between 28 and 30, are the most satisfied. Of course the best age of marriage depends much on the style of life desired by each party to the marriage, both singly and as a couple. For example if both parties want a career they may prefer to marry after going to graduate school and establishing a base in their profession.

Having Children

Motivations for becoming parents. Generativity in the form of having children is closely related to getting married and the establishment of intimacy. Yet young couples do not automatically proceed to have a series of children as their forebearers did. Kenneth Terhune, psychologist at SUNY at Buffalo, polled 600 women regarding the number of children they wanted. Women with over one child spoke of children in somewhat negative terms, saying they didn't want any more. They talked about the expense, fighting among the children, their own desire for privacy, and problems of overpopulation (Fleming, 1975). Indeed the notion of opposition to "automatic motherhood" has touched all social classes. According to a 1973 survey only 35% of college and

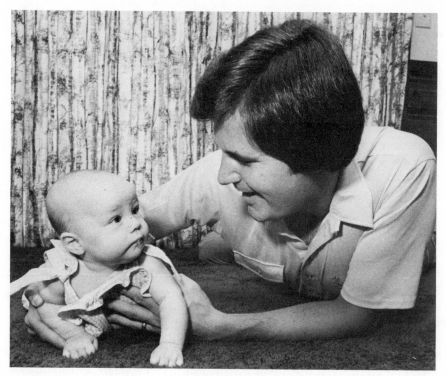

Parenthood presents some problems but many feel that its compensations are greater.

50% of non-college women agreed that "having children is a very important value." On the other hand career counselors find that while young women may be aware that motherhood is no longer necessarily a lifetime career, they still may want that career. (Yankelovich, 1974b).

Motivations for becoming a parent are complex and often difficult to unravel. Perhaps one of the most effective reasons is social pressure which, though often subtle, is nevertheless real (Blake, 1973). For example, childlessness has traditionally been associated with "irresponsibility, unnaturalness, immaturity, emotional instability, marital unhappiness, divorce, illness, psychological maladjustment, and generally unsatisfactory mental health . . . " (Veevers, 1974, p. 399). While childbearing is not necessarily perceived as a solution to all marital problems it is commonly believed to help with adjustment problems, including everything from loneliness to frigidity to marital unhappiness. Parenthood is also encouraged by such social policies as baby bonuses or preferential tax treatment for parents.

The right to become a parent. In general people believe it an inalienable right to become parents. However the existence of a variety of hereditary disorders may suggest that it is an individual's obligation to determine whether he or she is capable of transmitting a sound biological heritage. Increasingly, as the data regarding genetics accumulate and genetic counseling becomes available, young couples must decide for themselves whether they can give their children a good or even adequate biological heritage, and whether they should have children at all. For example, a woman in a family of hemophiliacs will transmit the malady to her sons, for hemophilia is sex-linked. This woman's daughters will be just like the mother, carriers of hemophilia, passing fully developed hemophilia to half of their sons. While only half the sons will have hemophilia, parents must decide whether or not they should take that chance (Restak, 1975).

One might also ask, do people who lack proper training for this significant task have a right to become parents? Few young adults know much about what it is to be a good parent. Neither sex, upon arriving at adulthood, has firm information in such important areas as prenatal care, birth control, social and emotional development of children, or good childbearing practices in general. Although young women know a great deal more about these subjects than young men, they still are far from sophisticated about them. In one study over half the youth questioned believed it was all right to spank a one-year-old for throwing things. Fewer than a third (only 21% of the males) realized that lack of love during the first year of life can be psychologically damaging. Certainly the mere act of getting married and having children does not convert such youth into knowledgeable parents. The result is that otherwise well-informed, young adults often engage in parental behavior that research has proved is damaging. Perhaps the answer is education for parenthood, both among teenagers and adults, in a combination of formal instruction and practical experience (Horn, 1975). It would involve learning not only the skills required for effective parenting but a sensitivity to the serious, often burdensome, responsibilities involved.

In other words, many of those who decide to have children fail to comprehend the responsibilities involved. Nor are they prepared to make the sacrifices or to modify their life style in order to insure their children's healthy development. The idealized image of devotion to a child "bears little resemblance to . . . [the] social reality: that most children are born simply because sex is pleasurable; that the crying, the mess, and the safety surveillances of early childhood are . . . for many parents (especially mothers) a relentless burden; that the condition of a child's sound growth may mean adult sacrifices—confinements, foregone pleasures, and marital tensions that, for many, can be all but unbearable. . . . " (Bailey, 1976, p. 36).

While becoming a father presents some problems, many men find its compensations even greater. The problems involved include financial strain, loss of sleep, adapting to new routines, interruption of sex, and marital readjustment (Russell, 1974). Nevertheless a sampling of men ranging in age from 21 to 37 believed that their babies had strengthened their marriage and given them and their wives a common concern. Those who had received training for their infants' childbirth said that watching their children being delivered was an experience they would not have missed for anything. Yet they were not prepared for the parenting that followed.

Preparation for parenthood. One usually neglected task of young adults is the acquisition of parenting skills. Certainly such skills should be learned by both sexes, on successively more sophisticated levels, in childhood, adolescence, and early adulthood. Young adults should update their parenting skills and continually refine them as their children grow up.

In one of the few studies of this topic, Russell (1974) has reported that preparation for parenthood by attending classes, reading books, and caring for other children contribute to men's but not women's satisfaction with parenthood. In a study of couples during and after the birth of their first child (Fein, 1976) those men who had the clearest concepts of themselves either as bread winners or as nontraditional fathers adjusted best during the postpartum period. The breadwinners saw themselves as responsible for providing for the family while the wife cared for the children. They were proud of their children and wives, and concerned about the finances involved, but helped little with the baby's care. For their part, the wives typically enjoyed being fulltime mothers. By contrast men in the nontraditional role became deeply involved in their baby's care, which they divided with their wives. Moreover they attempted to arrange their schedules so that they could spend as much time as possible at home after the baby was born. In such cases the mothers generally combined mothering with work, and both parents perceived pregnancy, birth, and childrearing as an experience that both parties shared. Those who made the poorest adjustment were ambivalent, uncertain what their roles should be, and wavered somewhat between nontraditional and breadwinner roles (Fein, 1976). Those fathers who helped with the infants did not feel that it hurt their masculinity in any way. Instead it appeared to reduce their anxiety and to give them considerable satisfaction.

The couples expressed satisfaction both with studies that prepared them for the birth process and being together during that time. They seemed better prepared for the birth itself than for the period that followed. The factors that contributed most positively to the young fathers' postpartum adjustment were the baby's health, a clear understanding between the couple concerning child care, family support, and work support. Couples had more difficulty when the child was colicky, slept fitfully, or cried a lot. Their problems were also reduced when, prior to the birth, the couples had negotiated between them a division of labor in child care, especially when both parties worked. Also important was support from their families, including help with daily homemaking tasks and respect for their wishes regarding the babies. Unfortunately, few of the men received any real support from their place of work. While they might receive good wishes from their fellow employees, they received no institutional help such as flexible hours or paternity leave.

Size of family. The birth rate has steadily declined so that the current average number of children per family is only two and a fraction. This is primarily due to better birth control methods and changing values attached to children. In the past children have been valued for what they could contribute to the family welfare in terms of performing chores. And formerly most families grew much of their own food, which made feeding extra mouths inexpensive. However, labor-saving devices, urbanization, and changed living patterns have made children an expensive luxury. They no longer pay their way. Parents can no longer count on their children to support them in later years. Meantime changes in marital roles have reduced the number of children desired, when considered in "reward-cost terms." The modern marital relationship tends to be more individualistic and democratic than formerly, and these factors modify views about family size (Scanzoni, 1976).

The best age for having children. If parents decide to have children, when is the best time? The worst time is when parents are in their teens. Most very young parents have yet to achieve emotional and financial stability and may be still in need of parenting themselves. Besides, before the age of 20, young women have usually not matured physically and have more than average trouble delivering a normal child. For such women the incidence of still births, birth defects, and infant mortality is high (Lasswell, 1974).

On the other hand problems may arise from delaying parenthood too long. A parent who is almost 40 may lack sufficient energy and patience to cope with a 2-year-old. In addition it is conjectured that the aging of the woman's egg cells may increase the possibility of birth defects. In particular mongolism has been linked to aged eggs which produce chromosome defects. In physiological terms the best age for women to give birth is between 21 and 35. On the other hand, older couples have an advantage financially, and often they are more stable psychologically.

In conclusion, observes Lasswell, it seems that women should wait until they are 25 to marry, and should have two children, at ages 28 and 30. By this time they normally have been married for three years, and the marriage should be stable both emotionally and financially. Assuming that he follows the popular societal notion that he should be two years older than his wife, the man should marry at 28 and father his children at ages 30 and 32. On the other hand this custom may not be good since women outlive men by several years and may be widowed longer than they would be if women did not marry men older than themselves.

The childless marriage. An increasingly popular option, the childless marriage, was formerly frowned upon by society. Veevers (1974) tells of a woman, age 21, who asked to have her tubes tied. The intern concerned went

> scurrying out. He came back in with a female gynecologist who had three children of her own and proceeded to tell me all about how it is possible to work and have children and how they fulfill your life. . . . I said, 'Yes, but I don't want two children. I just don't want to have them'; so they went and got the head gynecologist who called me a silly, idiotic female and told me to shut up. I didn't know what I was talking about, and I didn't know what I would want . . . (Veevers, 1974, p. 403).

Of course taking measures forever to prevent childlessness is irreversible. It is often assumed that young couples do not know whether they might desire children later on. On the other hand the matter of having a child is irreversible too (LeMasters, 1973, p. 59). In any case it seems likely that many reluctant parents would reject their children, at least on the unconscious level.

Still, the vast majority of couples intends ultimately to have children, although a growing minority expects to remain childless. Perhaps one reason is that the younger generation has come to accept the childless marriage as a viable option. Another reason is the threat of overpopulation, and while some experts believe that such a "diffuse objective" is hardly relevant, some couples do insist that the population problem is a factor. Certainly it becomes a legitimate reason for accepting a childless marriage. A third reason is the great expense of child-rearing; it could cost from $80,000 to $150,000 to send two children through college in the early 1970s ("High cost of kids," 1972). In addition having children is a considerable gamble, perhaps the biggest of a lifetime. Parents cannot know in advance the characteristics of their child-to-be. Even if the child is mentally and physically healthy the child's personality may be unacceptable to one or both parents. Furthermore some parents doubt their aptitude, skills, or other qualifications for parenting. In such a case, instead of being selfish, they may simply be saving the "unsuspecting child" from the strains of being brought up by unqualified parents (Veevers, 1974). Yet other couples may prefer to remain childless because of the greater freedom that childlessness affords (Veevers, 1974). Not only do childless couples maintain more flexible schedules; they also have greater latitude with regard to their behavior, language, and the hours keep. Of course in any individual couple the motivations for childlessness are complex and to a certain extent may be ill-defined and even unconscious.

Young adult testimony. To sum up, the vast majority of young adults plan eventually to get married; and almost, but not quite, all those who marry expect to have children. The great majority want two or three, although rare ones want more. Those who do not want children generally perceive them as an obstacle to their own life goals. Young adults today do not have children simply because it is the thing to do or from a sense of obligation. Instead they perceive parenthood as a unique, challenging experience, and as one way of enriching their own lives. Here are several representative views.

I would like to have children, partly because of wanting an extension of myself. (*Male*)

I plan to have two or three children after age 28 to 30, depending upon my spouse, finances, and the care and affection levels that I can handle. (*Female*)

I want children, basically because it would be a tremendous accomplishment to help develop and shape someone's life. (*Female*)

I definitely want a family of my own—two of my own and four or five adopted children. Why two of my own? No special reason. As for the adopted children, I'd like to give them a good home where they can become able to live with a positive outlook. (*Male*)

I want children in order to fulfill myself as a woman—and also I enjoy children. I grew up in a family of nine children, and watching them grow up was quite an experience. It would be even more of an experience if they were my own children. (*Female*)

I want no more than three children but not less than two, because it is important for a child to have a brother or sister. I would not have too many children because of the potential population explosion. (*Male*)

I would feel as if I'd missed something in life if I didn't have children.

Besides, I like children. I want two children—I'm afraid I'd spoil the child if I had only one. (*Male*)

I don't know if I want to get married or have a family. I certainly hope I find alternatives to this mode of self-fulfillment. (*Male*)

I'm getting married in June, and we do not plan to have children right away. If we do decide to raise a family it won't be for six or seven years, as we both want to pursue our careers. We also want as much time together as possible, and having children right away would interrupt what *we* want to do. (*Female*)

Establishing Friendships

Almost all young adults, both married and single, establish a supportive network of friendships within the context of their newly defined lives. Often their paths or new interests have taken them away from friends of earlier years. They must form friendships with people whose personalities and life styles are congenial to their own at this stage of life. Thus, maintaining older friends is part of the integration process of later adulthood, while establishing new friendships is part of the expansion process of youth and earlier adulthood (Jones, 1974). Besides, it is easier to change or substitute friends in earlier life.

For young adults, a task related to that of making new friends is articulating their own family life with their life outside the family. Philippe Ariès, France's great historian of the family, feels that young adults nowadays turn inward and become too demanding of each other, and that the parent-child relationship has become unbearably confining. In such a situation parents focus on the child and demand the child's entire affection. The obligation is no less real simply because it is implicit—that the child owes everything to the parents. Ariès sanctions a more open family instead of the current family, which is too often a prison of love. Fortunately the woman's movement is inducing many young women to rebel against their erstwhile imprisonment within the confines of the family (Mousseau, 1975).

Opposite-sex friendships. An almost ignored phenomenon in American society is the lack of friendship between members of the opposite sex, one of whom is married (Lamp, 1976). The lack of this socially defined role stems from several reasons, one being that traditional marriage has idealized its exclusivity. A second reason is that women have traditionally been looked upon as sex objects rather than individuals, and so any interest in them is interpreted as having sexual overtones. The third reason is the fear that opposite-sex relations outside marriage may endanger the marriage itself. As a result married women generally limit themselves to women friends just as married men have chiefly male friends.

If this hitherto nondefined role became socially accepted, believes Lamp, the long-term effects would be profound. It would enrich individual lives and interpersonal development as well as strengthen marriage bonds. Positive effects would stem from broader interpersonal contacts and the potential for satisfying emotional needs and desires that are not fulfilled by one's spouse. Since there would be less obligation on a spouse to become all things to one's mate, marriage might become less emotionally demanding and threatening.

THE ORGANIZATION OF LIFE TASKS

Type and Place of Residence

Housing. Life also involves its more mundane practical aspects, such as choosing a place to live. In a mobile society such as ours, this decision must often be made several times. Looking for a house becomes a matter of attempting to find surroundings that will support one's life style. For example, two young college professors who got married shopped for a three-bedroom house, not because they expected to fill it with children but because each spouse wanted a private study (Donnelly, 1976).

Most couples, certainly most of those with children, can hardly be so specific in their requirements. Since the number of households has been growing by one and a half million a year in the late 1970s, compared to a million a year in the early 1960s, and construction costs are also sharply rising, it will be increasingly difficult for young adults to buy their own single-family dwellings. Hence many couples will settle for smaller units such as apartments, townhouses, mobile homes and no-frills houses (Donnelly, 1976).

Despite such realities the vast majority of young adults today share a common dream, with minor variations. They expect to delay marriage for several years while they establish their career, travel, and have varied experiences. During this time, while they are single, they are content to live in apartments; however, once they have a family they want their own home, a good-sized one, in a small town or rural area, not too far from a city. They are seeking such ideals as freedom, simplicity, privacy and quiet—yet they want to be close enough to a city to avail themselves of its advantages. A small minority who expect to remain single, or who differ in other respects from the large majority,

With rising construction costs many young couples are settling for smaller living units such as no-frills houses.

express correspondingly varied preferences for living arrangements. Obviously young adults believe housing and environment to be fundamental in supporting their preferred life style. They express little doubt that they will ultimately attain their goal despite the expense of single-family dwellings.

> During my twenties I want to remain single to pursue my career, a goal very important to me: then I want to marry and have two children. While I'm single I'd like to live in an apartment complex with other young people. Later, with my own family, I want to live in an apartment complex or a medium-sized town. I'll continue my career, too, taking classes from time to time to keep up to date. (*Female*)

> After I get married in my late twenties and have two children, I want to live in a one-family dwelling in a large enough community so that everyone does not know everyone else's business. (*Female*)

> During my twenties I'll stay single and live in diverse community settings. I want to spend some time in a major city like New York, but my heart belongs in the country. In my thirties I plan to marry, or live with someone on that level, and settle there. I want one child, and to adopt another two or three. (*Male*)

> I prefer to raise my family in the country—not on a farm but in a home with a few acres of land. If that's not possible I'd like some place outside the city and suburbia so there's not lots of traffic, noise, crime,

and door-to-door salesmen. Why? Because I'd be happier and freer raising my family in such a setting. (*Female*)

With my wife and three children I'd like to live in a community near a big city that combines privacy and my need for a fast pace and entertainment. (*Male*)

I intend to remain single and have a cottage on a lake near a city where I work. Later, after I retire, I want to join with other singles in establishing a sort of commune in the north woods of Minnesota. (Female)

The community and neighborhood. Many young adults have no firm preferences about where they might best live, but they generally do not favor cities. In one sampling, young adults in their early 20s preferred a small town or rural area; 19% liked the suburbs; and only 14% preferred the city. About two-thirds mentioned a small town or rural area ("How many children?" 1972).

Perhaps most young people have inadequate information about the communities to which they move, or the characteristics of the neighborhood they choose for their home. According to one categorization, neighborhoods can be classified into six different types. In the *parochial neighborhood* people interact frequently and feel very much part of the area, but they are isolated from the larger community. They merely take care of their own, and have their own network of neighborhood groups. That is, they face inward instead of outward. By contrast the *integral neighborhood* is like a large radar network. Residents have good jobs and links with many community groups. They are active both inside and outside the neighborhood. In the *diffuse neighborhood* people rely more on their families than on their neighbors. They identify with the community but interact little with each other, feeling little connection with the larger community. They identify with the neighborhood merely because they find it a pleasant place to live. They get together little with neighbors and do not depend on the neighborhood for shaping their life style. The *stepping-stone neighborhood* is similar to the integral neighborhood. Young adults, perhaps young executives, may move into the neighborhood and then out again when they get their next job. Such neighborhoods often have formal mechanisms for integrating newcomers very quickly—for example, welcoming committees greet them and invite them to join neighborhood groups. Nevertheless the residents continue to be more involved in outside than in local groups. Neighbors are open and friendly, but transient—hence they do not feel strong connections. In the *transitory neighborhood*, where the population turnover is even greater, neighbors have little in common and avoid any local entanglements. Finally, in the *anomic neighborhood* the more affluent may be isolated in their condominiums, and content with their anonymity. People in poorer anomic neighborhoods do little to help each other solve their problems. They are distrustful of outside groups yet receive little help from their own groups. Such people may spend much time watching TV. Some simply don't like other people nosing into their business (Warren & Warren, 1975).

Money Management

A task of special importance for young people is money management, for people give priority to whatever they deem the necessities of life. In a study conducted in the mid-1970s, among 12 items ranked as necessities adults named owning their own home first (59%), followed by the need for pension plan (57%), and a savings account of at least $5,000 (54%). Only 38% mentioned college education as a requirement, while a master's degree ranked close to the bottom of the list of necessities, the same (12%) as a colored TV, but was considered less necessary than a new car, an air-conditioned home, or an opportunity to travel abroad ("Youth's attitudes," 1975, p. 15).

Even in today's economic climate most young people have made no significant reduction in their material wants. In another survey, which involved 1,247 families, a substantial minority (37%) felt that their standard of living was worse than the year before and 45% thought that things might not improve in the future. In consequence some young people are making adaptations. For example they spend more free time at home nowadays than they used to. Thus changing economic realities are affecting modifications in life style (Campbell, 1975b). However a majority still looks upon colored television, eating out, going to movies, and owning a car as necessities, not luxuries.

Of course individuals vary widely in their patterns of money management. One young married woman, age 27, who analyzes budgets and programs in the Community Services Division of the Washington State Department of Social and Health Service tells how she handles her own budget. She spends $100 a month on food, eating TV dinners supplemented with a daily vitamin pill. For breakfast she takes a thermos of coffee to work and brown-bags her lunches, using the same hardware-store paper bag every day. She makes about six sandwiches from a single can of tuna fish. She only buys steak or lamb chops when she has been working considerable overtime. Even at work she sometimes wears rumpled slacks and worn sneakers, and spends little on her wardrobe. On the other hand, after much looking she purchased a two-bedroom frame house, somewhat rundown but in a pleasant neighborhood, for $14,000. With satisfaction she explains, "I like having a place in the world that belongs to me." She uses a newly purchased circular saw, jig saw, and electric drill for doing her own household repairs. She describes herself as a workaholic; but with her new home feels that her life has become more balanced (Tarrant, 1976).

Other young people may be more impulsive and less frugal. Tom and Mary have modest incomes but a strong appetite for the good life. They have purchased a car, a house, furnishings, and appliances on the installment plan. They have no savings and Tom carries only a small life insurance policy. They live from one pay check to another. With their combined checks they have managed to stay afloat, but if one of them should become unemployed, or if Mary should become pregnant, they would have to call on their parents for help. While they have discussed the need for a more conservative life, they never quite get around to it.

LAUNCHING A CAREER

New Attitudes toward Work

It is generally assumed that young adults, even females, will pursue some vocation. Young people today are willing to work, but they expect their work to be meaningful, and they "reject a nose-to-the-grindstone philosophy of life" (Yankelovich, 1974b, p. 85). What they are concerned about is actively pursuing work as an avenue to self-fulfillment, "with money, security and possessions included in the over-all scheme, partly taken for granted, partly demanded as a matter of right" (p. 85). Their chief aim is to pursue the life style most appropriate for expressing and realizing their own personal and psychological potential and to convert the ideals of youth into reality, perhaps through their vocational choice. For example, one former civil rights activist became a union executive and organizer working for the welfare of farm laborers. Another young activist became a psychiatrist at Harvard, and is also heavily involved in the woman's movement (Casady, 1975b).

Prospects for Youth Today

High-school versus college graduates. While high-school graduates must often take what work they can, growing numbers of college students are preparing themselves for managerial, technical, and professional jobs, which are among the most rapidly growing occupations in our post-industrial society (Yankelovich, 1974b). One half the freshmen who entered Yale University in 1974 selected premedical studies. In other Ivy League schools students are choosing medicine, law, clinical psychology, and professions which offer a combination of monetary rewards, personal fulfillment, and autonomy. Ultimately, because of shifts in the work picture, there may be enough rewarding types of jobs available to them.

Nevertheless, in times of economic instability, such as the middle and later 1970s, even college graduates may find the job market a rough place where ambition is dulled and hopes and aspirations broken ("When college graduates . . ." 1977). In desperation some young people switch to a different career, which they sometimes enjoy more. One 27-year-old woman who lost her job as an elementary school teacher became a factory supervisor and prefers this work. Other young college graduates who are unable to find jobs in their own fields make do with such jobs as being secretaries, receptionists, or typists. Yet they are often turned down for such jobs and told they are over-qualified. Still others go into business for themselves, undertaking anything from making belts to selling house plants. Graduates with a liberal arts education may have special trouble finding work. They are trained for nothing in particular and lose out to applicants with more specific qualifications. Whatever work they do find may fail to satisfy them because their liberal education makes them desire the relatively rare creative jobs.

The picture for the seven out of ten young people who will receive little or no college education is even less rosy. Like college youth, they want meaningful, interesting work. They too want to be upwardly mobile, but they may be giving up chances for mobility in starting work earlier. Yet they know that they can hardly move out of their jobs if they do not have more education. Meantime opportunities for skilled workers in industry are decreasing, while the lower-status service jobs are of the dead-end type.

Thus the divergence between college and high school graduates of the younger generation is greater and potentially more hazardous for society than is the gap between the generations. As the workplace is now organized, individuals without college degrees will have difficulty finding fulfillment; yet they live in a world where they are inclined to take "less crap" on the jobs (Yankelovich, 1974b, p. 85).

Men versus women. Even today vocation has different implications for young men and young women. For one thing, women expect to work more often than men expect their wives to work (Scanzoni, 1976). Yet the woman who tries to combine marriage with career, observes Sheehy

(1976), can hardly give as much to her career as a man can. She can hardly establish a firm commitment to a job, given the problem of coping with "competing priorities." Hence the career that bolsters her husband's confidence and stability may simply create havoc in her life. For another thing, most men are hardly prepared to cope with the situation when their wives make more money or achieve higher status than they. Blue-collar men, especially, who have little status outside the home, are jealous of their prerogative as breadwinner within the home. Women encounter additional obstacles if they delay by some years returning to the work-place. New developments with which they are unfamiliar have occurred in their field of specialty, and they must often settle for work below their potential. Meantime they must somehow reconcile the demands of their jobs and those of their young children.

LIFE STYLE

The achievement of all the foregoing tasks must somehow be integrated into a way of living which reflects an individual's skills, habits, goals, values, and philosophy of life. It is in early adulthood that a relatively permanent life style is established (Newman & Newman, 1975). During this period an individual experiments and evolves a style of life. Those who marry—the vast majority of young adults—must "develop a pace that reflects the activity levels of both [partners]. Within that framework, most couples find that the presence of children requires somewhat more planning and less freedom for spontaneous activities. Finally, the work setting largely determines the structure of time, including when one goes to work and returns, how tired one feels after work, how much time is allotted for vocations, and what kinds of preparation must be made during nonwork hours for one's daily occupation" (Newman & Newman, 1975, pp. 267–268). The way one lives is also influenced by the community and climate in which one lives. In places where winter is severe, it is likely that activities will be carried out within the home, although in summer there may be considerable social and community activity.

One aspect of developing a life style is determining how to apportion one's time effectively, for example between work and leisure, (Newman & Newman, 1975). For some individuals time spent with the family has higher priority than that spent in occupational advancement. The life styles of wife and husband may develop somewhat separately, depending partly on the degree to which they split or share their roles. If both wife and husband work, there may be little time except on weekends for any activities other than those involving care of the household and family. This makes it all the more important that they devote weekends and vacations to personal growth.

Several young adults describe below certain aspects of their preferred life style.

> I expect to travel as much as possible, see Europe, and the U.S.A. I like to spend a lot of time camping and fishing as I love the out-of-doors. I'd love to remain fairly active sports-wise, pursuing my bowling. I like a life style in which I'm not afraid to spend some money. I really don't want to be high on the hog but to live comfortably. I want to own a boat and a really nice sports car. Most of all, I want good health so that I can pursue the above life. (*Male*)

> I enjoy the life style which allows me to do the things I enjoy, such as fishing, and camping, as opposed to working 24 hours a day to reach high social status. (*Male*)

> I'm pretty much of a home body. I like to spend evenings by the fire, reading, baking breads, etc. On the other hand, I want to take advantage of cultural activities—plays, movies, etc. I'm very adaptable, so any environment suits me fine. (*Female*)

> I want to live in a community where there is a lot of land, and I would like to have neighbors but not too close. I come from a family-oriented home and therefore would like to spend a lot of time with my family—camping, traveling, cultural activities—and any kind of activity that would include the whole family. (*Female*)

Life styles, as will become obvious in the next chapter, vary according to many factors including sex, age, and social class; and they reflect the extent to which developmental tasks have been mastered. These life styles may be either relatively ineffective or rewarding; and in any case, are important harbingers of all the years that follow.

PERSPECTIVE ON YOUNG ADULT TASKS

Overall, young adulthood is a busy period, critical for the stages to follow. The early 20s are so chock-full of such major tasks as getting established as an adult, starting a family, and embarking on a career that there is little time for reflection. Following this relatively stable period comes a more uncertain time when doubts regarding one's success to now arise. Such doubts, though tension-producing, are healthy because only through reassessment and change can growth occur. The danger is in getting bogged down with the many details of life that progress toward more basic goals suffer. Indeed it is the nagging suspicion that one is stagnating—that one's life isn't headed in any particular direction—that often provokes unrest in people in their 30s. How well they resolve this dilemma depends on their accumulated personal resources. There has been little recognition of this problem by society, and for the most part no preparation or education for it. Consequently, young adults generally must work this out on their own.

SUGGESTED READINGS

Bernard, J., *The future of motherhood.* New York: Penguin Books, 1974. In this both scholarly and readable volume Bernard considers society's institutionalized modes of childrearing, and the forces that shape their operation. She considers in detail such topics as pressures on women to become mothers, the status of mothers, the divergent roles of mother and worker, and the status and tasks of the mother.

Crites, J. O., "A comprehensive model of career development in early adulthood." *Journal of Vocational Behavior,* 1976, *9* (1), 105–118. Some of the theoretical and research issues regarding how and why beginning workers establish themselves in the workaday world, are explored. A comprehensive model of career development is proposed, and ways are suggested for translating it into operational terms.

Edwards, J. N. & Booth, A. The cessation of marital intercourse. *American Journal of Psychiatry,* 1976, *133* (11), 1333–1336. Among the more than one-third of a sample of 365 young adults married an average of 11 years, who had not had marital coitus for a definable period (median, 8 weeks), the cessation of such behavior proved markedly different for both sexes, and more predictable for the men.

Elder, G. H., Jr., & Rockwell, R. C. Marital timing in women's life patterns. *Journal of Family History,* 1976, *1* (1), 34–53. This study of women born shortly before the Great Depression indicates that the age of marriage has critical effects on future life patterns, and underscores the importance of having a life-course perspective.

Falk, G. Mate selection in America. *International Behavioral Scientist,* 1975, *7* (1), 68–80. Forms of mate selection and factors that enter into the process are analyzed and discussed.

Goudy, W. J., Powers, E. A., & Keith, P. The work-satisfaction, retirement-attitude typology: Profile examination. *Experimental Aging Research,* 1975, *1* (2), 267–279. The initial phase of a longitudinal study of 68 males, from the time they enter college until their early 30s, suggests that personality traits are significantly related to the vocational adaptation of professional and managerial men.

Houseknecht, S. K. Reference group support for voluntary childlessness: Evidence for conformity. *Journal of Marriage and the Family, 1977, 39* (2), 285–292. Certain hypotheses were tested regarding the parents' reference group as a factor in deciding not to have children. The evidence disclosed the nature of pressures placed on young couples to have or not to have children, and the couples' reactions to those pressures.

Kerckhoff, A. C. Patterns of marriage and family formation and dissolution. *Journal of Consumer Research, 1976, 2* (4), 261–275. Those factors associated with mate selection and the dissolution of marriage are identified; they include such variables as race, religion, age, and socioeconomic status.

Marcia, J. E. Identity six years after: A follow-up study. *Journal of Youth and Adolescence, 1976, 5* (2), 145–160. In a longitudinal study of identity status in which 30 young men were originally tested as undergraduates, and retested six years later, factors were identified that related to persistence or change in type of identity.

Richardson, M. S., & Alpert, J. L. Role perceptions of educated adult women: An exploratory study. *Educational Gerontology, 1976, 1* (2), 171–185. This study of 93 adult women graduate students in a large urban university, concerned the women's perceptions of their marriage, work, and motherhood roles; and the interaction between them and age-role status variables.

Russo, N. F. The motherhood mandate. *Journal of Social Issues, 1976, 32* (3), 143–153. The adult female's core task is characterized as having two children and rearing them well. An attack on this mandate is judged essential to eliminating sexism. An analysis of the purposes of childbearing and rearing are basic to understanding sex-typed behaviors.

Sherman, R. G., & Jones, J. H. Career choices for women: The new determinants. *Journal of College Student Personnel, 1976, 17* (4), 289–294. Comparisons of young women in 1959 and in 1974 indicated significant changes in matters of career choice.

Titus, S. L. Family photographs and the transition to adulthood. *Journal of Marriage and the Family, 1976, 38* (3), 525–530. An examination of family photographs was made in order to study the transition to parenthood. There were more pictures of first babies than of later ones, and more of the parents holding the babies than of the babies alone.

4
CHAPTER

Life Styles
of
Young
Adults

THE CONCEPT OF LIFE STYLE

The concept of life style—the ways in which individuals bring together all aspects of their lives—is considered increasingly important today. Life style is the self in action, the pattern of one's life. It represents all the things that an individual characteristically and most typically does. It includes such matters as how people structure their days, the relative amount of time they devote to specific activities, and what those activities are. It involves whether people live in a hectic, stressful fashion or a leisurely, composed one; in a closed or open family style; a good deal outdoors or almost wholly indoors, and so on.

Throughout childhood and adolescence life styles are strongly influenced by schooling, but when youth moves into adulthood, life styles must be restructured. Although it is true that the new life styles bear a relationship to the earlier ones because basic personality characteristics remain the same, still the way of living must be completely restructured to accommodate the special tasks of this age. And while young adult life styles may have certain overall similarities, they differ according to subgroups, as we will discuss in this chapter.

THE YOUNG MARRIEDS

4b The Prechildren Stage

The most common young adult life style involves marriage, whose life cycle in turn involves three levels of commitment: minimum, limited, and maximal. The matter of couple involvement is most significant at the initial (childless) stage and again at the "empty nest" stage, when husband and wife associate constantly with each other. Involvement is either minimal or limited during the period in between, depending on how many children there are, whether both wife and husband work, compatibility, and other factors. Once the children arrive some people, the mothers in particular, concentrate on the children. They do not realize the problems that such a focus may produce after the children grow up and leave home (Lowenthal et al., 1975).

4c **Young adults at the preparent stage.** In one study the happiest of (any group) studied—including both singles and marrieds, young and middle-aged—were married couples in their 20s who had not yet had children.

To a certain degree this prechild period is a time in which both partners share the delusion that they are more alike than they actually are, "a happy, but fragile stage" (Stern, 1976, p. 18). Later on reality destroys this delusion; but at least while it lasts, couples are transcendently happy. Each spouse becomes lost in the other and robbed of his or her own individuality. The young wives, particularly, are "positively euphoric," apparently enjoy housework, and are relieved to have arrived at what may still be judged "a woman's greatest achievement..." (Campbell, 1975a, p. 38). The young men are also happier after they marry, although they feel more stress about money. In the above-mentioned study three out of four of the young women worked, and only 20% of them worried about household bills, compared to 38% of their husbands. Only 18% of the young wives portrayed their lives as hard, while 34% of the husbands did. However this difference disappeared after the first child arrived. From then on the original euphoria became tainted by brushes with reality; and the young couples' submerged egos reasserted themselves, so that they no longer believed in the fantasy that their identities were the same.

The couples' life style before the children arrive is often distinguished by considerable joint activity to the exclusion of others, at least on an intimate level. Sheehy (1976) concludes it is unhealthy, this "closed dyad [pair]: the in-turned husband-wife, mommy-daddy pair of the idealized American family". While the closed dyad functions well

1978 © Sybil Shelton

As young adults at the preparent stage, time together is usually spent in exclusion of others.

enough to insure speedy success in vocation and economics and a rapid climb to social status, it can also mean shutting out the support of others. Anthropologist Ray Birdwhistell believes that the closed dyad constitutes a "diseased social form" (Sheehy, 1976, p. 147). The woman especially, after getting married and beginning a family, often lets friendships with other women deteriorate. She also gives up her nonsexual friendships with men because she feels her husband wouldn't like them.

The prechild couple obviously has more time for activities than do older couples with children at home; they also have access to a greater variety of activities than do retired couples. In one study (Lowenthal et al., 1975), high-school seniors and newlyweds engaged in more activities, more frequently, than did older persons. To the degree that time and money allowed, the newlyweds were constantly "on the go." But since many of them were both working and continuing to attend school, they had little money and chose inexpensive activities.

Social relationships vary considerably according to social class. Except for the closed dyad variety, young middle-class couples associate individually with persons of their own sex and jointly with other couples, often because of the husbands' jobs or interests. While they may visit and go out most often with these other couples, these couples may not be the most intimate friends of either husband or wife (Hess, 1972). Blue-collar couples have fewer mutual friends than do middle-class ones, and interact chiefly with neighbors or relatives.

Marital Problems of Young Adults

4d **Problems relating to personal development.** In time, says Sheehy, the male, having attained a certain competence on his job, and feeling increasingly sure of himself, may become bored with his wife's role as his substitute mother. He now expects his wife to extend herself as he has, and be more of a companion to him rather than remain in a dependent position. He perceives that his wife has not grown much and is discontent with her less worthy status. If he could admit it, he would say that he cannot bear his wife's relatively dull and nonproductive way of life. Perhaps he is willing to tolerate, even encourage, his wife to do something on her own, as long as it is not at any cost to himself. That is, he could not bear to think of her becoming as tied to a job as he is because she would pay less attention to him. Yet he has no guilt feelings on this score because he has learned from early childhood that it is women's nature to nurture their men and tend their children. Given that, what might be boring to him just comes naturally to her.

For her part the wife may feel that her husband has gotten ahead of her in the world—that he has become more sophisticated and has developed more as a person. At other times a wife may also feel somewhat impatient, though she may not yet be prepared to do anything about it. Her readiness to undertake something new will depend upon what she has accomplished in the past, for most people are afraid to take changes. Or she may realize that if she does break out of her domestic bind, her husband may not be able to tolerate her new freedom, or like doing without all the domestic comforts to which she has accustomed him. Hence she may retreat, and try to keep him from making progress along with her. If he sees through what she is doing, he can change from feeling secure to feeling trapped.

Aside from matters of personal development, couples disagree mostly at first about in-laws. Later on, especially if the wife gives up her job to have a baby, they argue over money and not having time for joint recreation. They do not fight over specific modes of child care until the children are old enough to get into trouble (Troll, 1975).

4e **Infidelity and divorce.** For such reasons the age period 28 to 32 involves increasing strains in marriage (people feel their mates don't accept them as they are); and couples feel less strongly that marriage was a good idea (Sheehy, 1976). It is generally during their 30s that husbands are unfaithful for the first time, usually with someone they meet on the job. This new woman is often young and interesting, although her job is subordinate to his, and she poses no real challenge to his own status. Sometimes the man who becomes bored with his wife and seeks a divorce finds out later on, after the divorce, that his ex-wife has broken out of her shell and become more interesting. In fact, for many young women, divorce becomes a rite of passage. While the man may have divorced his wife because she was dependent and uninteresting, after the shock wears off she may become a far more dynamic person than before. Parenthetically, whether or not a dissatisfied couple will actually obtain a divorce relates to their values, socioeconomic status, personality, and religion (Troll, 1975).

4f **The gradual diminution of problems.** During their 30s most young marrieds are somewhat less involved in activities and social relationships, and focus instead on their families. This age period involves many psychological changes, including preparation for the 40s. Life begins to appear harder and more complex (Gould, 1975). Couples still have their dreams, but these are now closer to reality. Such people are now fully part of the mainstream of adult society. Most of them have either found their niche or made some compromises.

Young Marrieds and their Children

49 **Rewards and problems.** Some young couples observe Jurich and Jurich (1975), over-idealize "the single carefree life," especially if they married early or had limited dating experience. As adolescents, some individuals may have had inadequate opportunities to experiment with different roles, or to choose those that were most suitable for them. That is, their adolescence was "short circuited" before they could firmly establish a satisfactory identity. This produces a "lost adolescence syndrome" once the responsibilities of parenthood begin to mount up. After the children are born, either one or both spouses may simply feel trapped, burdened by their responsibilities, and bored by marriage routines. They envy the lives of their single friends and yearn for the same freedom themselves. Often their solution is simply to give up on their marriage in order to live a single life. Meantime they must somehow cope with their children, which some of them do by giving up the child to the other parent.

At least some young women are beginning to question the institutionalization of motherhood in our society. Some books suggest that mother's day is over, and point out the negative features of having babies (Radl, 1973). It is not that mothers do not love their children, but that many of them do not care for motherhood as it has been institutionalized. Formerly when mothers felt like protesting about their roles, they did so in secret, often with feelings of guilt; now they often do so openly and unashamedly.

However, most couples welcome the arrival of the first child, especially if the child has been planned. They feel a certain wonder at this small creation of their own flesh and blood who simultaneously establishes a link between themselves and future generations. Even young fathers almost immediately feel a bond with the child. After a time the bubble bursts. For both sexes satisfaction of life in general drops to average, and does not rise much again until the children have grown up and are about to leave home (Campbell, 1975b).

Indeed couples with young children feel more stress and pressure than any other group. Young mothers between the ages of 25 and 34 are more likely than their husbands to portray themselves as tied down, feeling doubts about their marriages, and sometimes wanting to be free of parental responsibilities. In addition, working women still perform the major role in the home, and three out of four wives are also working. This makes the case for women's discontent quite clear (Campbell, 1975b).

The husbands may also experience problems after the children arrive (Campbell, 1975b). Inevitably the wife now has less time for the husband, he may resent her preoccupation with the child. He may also become strapped financially, especially if his wife stops working until the children are older. In a replication of a 1965 study Hobbs and Cole (1976) found that nowadays significantly fewer men (46%) than women (31%) rate their marriage as more satisfying after the birth of their baby. Apparently present-day couples consider their babies less essential to marital happiness than did young marrieds in the mid-1960s. Both in the 1960s and 1970s beginning parenthood was characterized by problems, but not crisis. In any case the strength of the parent-child bond may be greater than even the parents realize. While a growing body of research concerns the attachment of infants to their mothers, the parents probably become as attached to the infants as the infants do to the parents (Hartup & Lempers, 1973).

In order to test these views, Russell (1974) questioned a random sampling of couples in Minneapolis whose first babies ranged in age from 6 to 56 weeks. The results indicated that the third family member did not disrupt affection and intimacy between the parents. Although both parents did report certain problems, the women most often checked the following items as bothersome: worrying about their personal appearance, becoming physically tired, interruption of rest and sleep by the baby, worrying about their loss of figure, feeling somewhat edgy and upset. The husbands were most often bothered by interruptions in sleep and rest, suggestions from in-laws about the baby, increased money problems, interruption of plans, and the housework required by the baby.

The degree of satisfaction with the infant involved a number of factors. Parents with higher education felt less gratification, perhaps because they had other satisfying elements in their lives. Those with more occupational prestige were not as gratified as those with less prestigious jobs. Those women who were not pregnant before they married and had time to adjust to marriage and motherhood after marriage were happier at becoming parents than were younger women or those already pregnant at marriage, possibly because the former were more mature and the child was planned. Those children who were consciously planned definitely received a heartier welcome.

In general the respondents in the survey felt there was more gratification than crisis in their lives. Over all, 42% said their marriage relationship improved after the birth of the baby, 43.5% said it remained about the same, and only 7.5% of the women and 5.5% of the men felt that it had worsened (Russell, 1974). In general the parents found the first year of parenthood only "moderately stressful" and quite rewarding.

Still, parents (especially fathers) welcomed calm babies more than they did noisy babies.

4h **The optimum age for having children.** A question of growing importance today is: When is the best age to have children? Formerly so much pressure was placed on young couples to have children, and birth control methods were so ineffective, that the question was almost irrelevant. Nowadays, with the pill widely prevalent and effective male contraceptives on the way, the question becomes relevant indeed. Besides, working women must work out an appropriate calendar for combining childrearing with their careers.

Most couples prefer to wait a time at least until they establish themselves. Just how long a couple can wait is perhaps more of a psychological than biological matter. Although the chances are greater that older mothers may have children with Down's Syndrome (mongolism), the condition can be detected prenatally and the fetus aborted.

The psychological impact of delayed childbearing is another matter. It has to do with the childbearing pace of one's peers, one's own ideal life cycle, and the expectations of others who matter ("The social limits of fertility," 1976). If a couple waits for very long to begin or add to their family they become out of phase with their peers who are further along in the childrearing cycle. Thus the later childbearers may lose a significant source of support. That is, they must rear their children when their friends have already completed that part of their lives.

The research with regard to the spacing of children is not clearcut. In general, Thompson (1974) reports that single children tend to be ambitious, independent, intelligent (especially verbally), and achievement oriented. One could, on this basis, make a case for having just one child, or else widely spacing children so that they in all have the positive attributes of only children. However, adds Thompson, there is still no irrefutable evidence that single children or widely spaced children all possess these positive qualities, nor that those traits they possess would be desired by all parents (p. 117).

4i Sex Roles among Young Marrieds

For the average young woman who marries at about age 20, the "traditional roles include housewife and mother, companion, and partner. In the beginning of marriage, the companion role is usually at its peak, partly as a carry-over from the courtship relationship. Young wives turn to their husbands both for sympathy and in anger. But as time passes—and particularly if children intervene—intimacy wanes, and wives turn to God, other people and housework" (Troll, 1975, p. 80). Of course the situation is somewhat different for those women who work outside the home.

Mothers of young children, in particular, lead a sharply restricted life, and since most of them stop working at least until their children become enrolled in school, their situation now stands in stark contrast to their former more sophisticated, broader, adult oriented lives. Now the young wife relies chiefly on her husband and the TV set for a "pipeline" to the outside world. When the children grow older her world broadens more, perhaps through returning to work or participating in community activities. Nevertheless, since childbearing is still considered to be more the mother's obligation than the father's, her own development as a distinctive personality slows down. Instead her satisfactions come from her contributions to the happiness and success of her husband and children.

Thus getting married changes the woman's role more than the man's. Until this time she has typically held a job outside the home; and while she may continue to do so, homemaking tends subtly to become her main occupation while she becomes correspondingly less committed to her vocational role. The young woman changes from Miss to Mrs., which in her own eyes and the eyes of others constitutes a sharp change in social role. While some young women use the designation Ms., they ordinarily assume the husband's name, in effect becoming a less distinctive individual.

Problems relating to differential sex roles. The better-educated achievement oriented woman, in particular, may grow tired simply of nurturing her husband unless he nurtures her dreams as well. Levinson (1973) portrays "the dream" as a critical aspect in the development of both sexes, and of two key relationships for the young man, the mentor and the loved woman. The mentor serves as something of a model or guide for the young man, and maybe a woman in a high position on the job who takes an interest in him. The loved woman may have functions resembling those of the mentor, for she may help her husband both to realize what identity the dream has and help make it come true. However, Levinson cautions that this relationship will last and aid his development only if it also helps hers.

Gail Sheehy (1976) comments on the significance of Levinson's advice. Tongue in cheek, she hazards a guess that if women had people to keep house for them and take over all their chores—including child-rearing, shopping, cooking, and caring for their husbands–then doubtless women would be equally as productive and even as politically powerful as men. She notes that many high-achieving women must maintain expensive housekeepers in order to perform these services for their husbands.

4K **Problems relating to personal development.** Initially both wife and husband may work. However the wife ordinarily interrupts her career after the first child arrives. Now her main focus shifts from husband to children while he concentrates more on his job, partly because of greater financial strain. In time the wife may return to work, which relieves him of financial strain. But it may also damage his sense of self worth.

A Study of Young Marrieds

4I **Young adult men.** After interviews with many young adult couples Sheehy (1976) concluded that both sexes are still slave to the traditional "shoulds," at least among those with a college education. For a time young American men would not involve themselves in what society thought they should. They shunned big business and power. At the same time young women entered the job market and took the young men's places. While they were interested in running for Congress, many young men were looking for "meaningful relationships." These men and women believe that people should live together rather than marry, and should not have children. The picture today has changed somewhat, and it is uncertain what will happen in the future.

Certainly young adult men are not the corporation-defying, emancipated-from-money-making freelancers that the alienated youth of the late 1960s and early 1970s might have become. Instead they, like their fathers before them, are preoccupied with making it in the world and establishing a career. In Sheehy's interviews young male adults talked chiefly about actions that they had undertaken—that is, what progress they had made in their careers; and they measured their lives in terms of how close they were to achieving their career dreams. Their wives were really secondary in importance to what they wanted—success through work. When they spoke of their wives and children it was chiefly in terms of how they had contributed to their own progress in fulfilling their dream.

Not all young men follow the same pattern. Some of these young men settle down quickly; others, the seekers, experiment and explore and make tentative, reversible decisions. Such individuals simply breeze through one job after another during their 20s. Other men may try out combinations of these two patterns.

Nevertheless young men are changing. While career is still most important, their lives have taken on a subtly different orientation. They are more expressive than men of earlier generations and they take more interest in their children. They are on a more equal plane with their wives; and the middle-class males, at least, help more around the home. They spend more time pursuing interests unrelated to their careers and feel unembarrassed about having aesthetic concerns. To some degree, at least, they are throwing off the baggage of having continuously to prove their masculinity.

4mm **Young adult women.** The middle-class young adult women interviewed by Sheehy (1976) fall into several categories. One group of women, the transients, keep their options open, at least during their 20s. They simply avoid permanent commitments to either work or a man. Single healthy young women, especially, may pile up a wealth of life experience by postponing firm commitments. However, ultimately many of these women do settle down or perhaps marry, thus assuming a more traditional way of life. Some of them are forced to the realization that as they grow older it becomes increasingly more difficult to acquire new jobs.

Another group, the either/or women, feel called upon in their 20s to decide between husband and children or vocation and achievement. The either/ors involve two types. First is the nurturer who

The role of young adult males is changing in our society. They take more interest in their children and homelife now.

delays her career until she has married and started a family. However she does expect from the start to go to work at a later date. At the opposite pole is the achiever who defers nurturing, and who may spend a half dozen or so years completing professional preparation and postponing motherhood and marriage. The nurturer who puts off achievement may have a difficult time realizing her dream. Sheehy feels it was terrible that many women were led to expect that they would find work they cared about once they had put in their 15 or so years as a homemaker. By the time a woman has had her children and is ready to move back into her field, many advances have been made in it, and she may be no longer qualified. Such women are becoming increasingly common, for today's mother ordinarily bears her last child by the age of 30, and that child will have entered school by the time she is 35 (Norton, 1974).

The most traditional category of women includes the caretakers, those who marry early and have nothing else in mind but to pursue the domestic role. Even in their early years they do not look ahead to anything else. In the past this option has been the most popular; women have simply lived for others and taken vicarious satisfaction in the achievement of their husbands and children. Society has placed its stamp of approval on this pattern which has been the one most favored around the world and through the centuries. Many women may hold part-time jobs, or work occasionally, simply to supplement their husband's salary or to provide some extra money for things around the house, but it has nothing to do with their own self-realization.

In a study of Radcliffe graduates (1974), the majority of caregivers discovered that even when their marriages were good, they simply were not enough. Almost two-thirds returned to school or sought jobs. Among the job seekers two-thirds are still looking. While many of these women were highly talented, the overwhelming majority found it necessary to return to school and to training in areas which related to their caretaking skills (e.g., teaching, library and social work)—areas already saturated with workers. The 36% of women who remained full-time caretakers faced two hazards: what to do if left without a husband as a result of divorce, death, or whatever; and their own fear of not growing in any way. Such conflicts and situations do not ordinarily arrive until the late 30s or even early 40s.

Having become entrenched within the caretaker role, and without the desire, courage, or means to escape it, such women tend to rationalize their position by defending nonequal rights for women. They act as though the women's movement had never occurred. Recently there has been a certain popularity among some of these women of books like *The Total Woman* (Morgan, 1974). Books of this type recommend that the woman simply surrender her house to her lord and master, that she cater to his every whim, and do whatever she can to remain alluring and seductive. They insist that God preordained such arrangements. The result, such self-appointed authorities claim, is that their husbands become completely rejuvenated and treat them as they did in the early days of love. Sheehy dismisses such nonsense as "total personal dishonesty" and this writer strongly agrees. Women are not encouraged to be honest and express their feelings; instead they are encouraged to be manipulative and to indulge in play-acting. Such advice encourages neither the wife nor the husband to become a true adult.

4m **The weaknesses of traditional roles.** Neither sex gains much satisfaction sticking to traditional sex roles. This was clearly shown in a longitudinal study by the Institute of Human Development of the University of California at Berkeley. The 171 randomly selected individuals had grown up in the San Francisco Bay area and were perhaps more than ordinarily upward mobile for their time. To date the study has followed their lives from birth over a period of 30 to 40 or more years (Haan, 1972). In their 30s the women had become even less certain of themselves than they had been as young adolescents, when they were considerably ahead of the boys. By now they were "submissive, fearful, guilty, over controlled, and hostile." Their only gains in personal development were in their roles as wife and mother. They were introspective, protective, and sympathetic, but they had also experienced losses. Their feelings of sexual pleasure and their confidence in their youthfulness had both declined. They no longer felt secure in their role as attractive women. They only felt safe in the one role, that of mothers.

By contrast, from junior high school age into their 30s, the males' self confidence had steadily increased. They had made progress toward increased social control and assurance. In terms of the characteristics studied, they proved to be productive and assertive, dependable, increasingly proud of their independence, and as capable of giving advice to their colleagues. The men were also self-confident with regard both to their sexual and social powers. Nevertheless their increasing self control was accompanied by some loss in self-expressiveness and tenderness.

4o **Symptoms of failure.** The failure to find healthy ways of expressing sex roles in young adult marriage is reflected in the divorce rate and the incidence of runaway wives. The most common age of divorce for women is 28 and for men, 30. Thirty-four is the average age of remarriage for divorced women. On the average, 13 years have passed since she married the first time (Norton, 1974). Thirty-five is the age when most wives run away. Their numbers are rapidly increasing. In fact in the past dozen years the ratio of runaway wives to runaway husbands has increased from 1:3 to 1:2. Typically the runaway wife is 35 years old, was married at 19, and bore her first child within 11 months of the marriage. After that she dedicated her life to home-making. In her mid-thirties she concluded that her current life was not rewarding, often because her husband no longer thought of her as a person. Ordinarily these wives had enough money but they had no value for their families, and that their lives lacked any real meaning. Perhaps they feel it is their last chance and that the only way to start a new life is to break out completely.

Very recently a new pattern has developed which some couples, especially better educated ones are attempting to follow (Sheehy, 1976). Educated young women try to break out of their shells with more or less success. Some of them simply make halfhearted stabs at it. They may take a few courses, sometimes in the area of their husband's profession. Yet even these young women develop psychological doubts, having been brought up to believe that their role is simply to take care of their husbands and not become too independent. Few women are committed as yet to a fully competitive position in the larger society, though many of them have become committed to personal freedom and independence.

Meantime young men are inevitably affected by whatever new roles young women assume. They have, to some extent, launched their own liberation project. They have forced the draft to be voluntary; and increasingly they resist paying alimony. They want wives who can be companions, and not just sex objects. While career remains their primary concern, the balance is slowly tilting toward a more human and expressive existence.

4p **Looking ahead.** In this new scheme of things young adults must set the pace, for the only ones who need not first unburden themselves of many old-fashioned ideas from the previous generation are those in their 20s or younger. It is still too early to know what the final outcome will be—whether a considerable number of them will develop new life styles that will prove lasting, or whether, after several years of career commitment and delayed childbearing, today's young women may beat a retreat, stay home, and have babies (Sheehy, 1976).

LIFE STYLE VARIATIONS BY SOCIAL CLASS

Most of what is written about the life styles of young adults, or of any age for that matter, derives from research about the middle class. The picture of the upper and working classes is fuzzy, for so little research on them has been conducted. The following thumbnail sketches of young adults in these neglected classes are based on two of the rare articles that deal with them specifically.

4q The Upper-upper Class

In the first of these articles, Blumberg and Paul (1975) observe that many have foretold the end of the upper class. Factors accounting for this forecast include the continuing thrust for equality within society; efforts to include students from all classes in private schools and Ivy League colleges; the increasing affluence of the general population; and "the challenge to the aristocracy of birth by the aristocracy of talent ... " (p. 63). However a study of upper-class young adults today reveals the upper-class way of life to be alive and well. In this study, which was based on the society pages of the Sunday *New York Times,* young people listed in the social register were classified as upper-class, while the merely rich were classified as upper-middle class. The survey shows that upper-class education distinguishes the social-register rich from the merely rich and those below. In fact private school attendance at the secondary, if not the primary, stage is practically a must for upper-class youth—and that means not just at any private school but at a particular set of highly select nonchurch-related schools in the northeast. Indeed 90% of the social-register men, compared to 57% of the merely rich, attend private schools; and nearly 47% of the social-register men attend one of 12 private schools, compared to 19% of the merely rich. From among the over 2000 accredited institutions of higher education in the United States, over half the upper-class men choose the eight Ivy League schools.

These select private schools, in turn, serve as "an antichamber to the upper-class marriage market"; Their students are invited to fashionable dances and debutante parties. The trend toward coeducation in such schools has actually strengthened their matchmaking function. This factor, in turn, has increased the already strong tendency of the upper class to marry within that class.

For upper-class youth of both sexes higher education is taken for granted, and 19 in 20 attend college. Most of the females go to the elite eastern private schools. Three in 10 attend the female counterpart to the Ivy League, the Seven Sisters Schools (Smith, Wellesley, Radcliffe, Vassar, Barnard, Bryn Mawr, and Mount Holyoke). Most of those who do not attend the Seven Sisters attend quality private schools elsewhere. Overall 95% of the social-register women compared to 74% of lower-upper class or merely rich attend private schools. Nor do most of the young women stop there. Over the past decade the number of upper-class women in graduate or professional schools had doubled from 7% to 14% even now. Yet only 12% of the young women, compared to 49% of the young men, had a postgraduate education.

Despite their excellent education vocation is not part of upper-class women's tradition. Certainly the working wife has been more characteristic of lower- and middle-income families. Only 18% of husbands making over $25,000 a year have working wives, compared with 45% of husbands earning between $4,000 to $10,000 a year. In this study only 20% of the women mentioned an occupation, and among those who did, a number said they would quit working after they got married. However the picture is rapidly changing. The percentage of upper-class women reporting jobs has tripled since the early 1960s from 8 to 23%, and often in high-level professions. These include professors, doctors, lawyers, clinical psychologists, biologists, and editors. Even in this group the majority pursue vocations traditionally associated with females, including teaching and social work.

The young women, like the young men, are maintaining upper-class traditions. True, the great debutante affairs of past generations have become less frequent, and coming out is becoming less popular. Upper-class girls have come to look on elaborate debutante balls as simply "wasteful and pretentious status-seeking," and many of the remaining debutantes now prefer tea parties or small dances at home. Nevertheless, 69% of the upper-upper social register young women and 45% of the lower-upper, merely rich, young women still announce their debuts. Whether the gradual diminution of the debut is a temporary or a more lasting phenomenon is as yet uncertain.

Some of the literature about this group gives the impression that upper-class young people are now tending to "drop out of the system en masse, refuse to enter the corporate world of their fathers, and instead join communes or become craftsmen and peddle home-made belts, jewelry or sandals off campus" (Blumberg & Paul, 1975, p. 71). While some of this picture is true, and young people question traditional upper-class patterns more than they used to, the extent has been grossly exaggerated. Instead only the rare upper-class male youth fails to choose upper-class businesses or professions. About 47% plan to be business men and 43% professionals, so that the career picture today is much like that for earlier generations. It is true that more of them are now entering professions (compared to 12% a few years ago) than business occupations. However this figure is misleading because many of the young professionals enter business later on, often because they are given preferred status in their fathers' business. In any case there is no indication that upper-class male youths today are rejecting the traditional occupations of the upper class.

There is some indication that growing numbers, though still a minority, of upper-upper class youth are turning away from elite schools to more mixed-class institutions. Also a small minority are attending colleges across the country and not simply those in the northeast. For one thing, certain other colleges in the country have become more attractive. For another, some of the more competent upwardly mobile public high-school graduates are choosing the Ivy League colleges, which dilutes their upper-class make-up. In other cases, upper-class youth may attend certain other schools because of their outstanding curricula in particular fields. Thus the upper class may become less isolated, which may lead to more interaction with other classes.

Despite this and other leveling forces that have erupted in American society in the last generation, the "upper class has maintained itself remarkably intact, and having done so, is perhaps the most untouched group in American life. Moreover, it is the upper-class territory of school, neighborhood, club, and bluebook that remains the most racially segregated turf in America" (p. 75).

4r The Working Class

Youth and young adults of the blue-collar class differ sharply from those of the upper and middle classes (Simon, Gagnon, & Buff, 1972). Working-class youths move into the work force early, sometimes before finishing high school. Such boys may hold several part-time jobs, and then a fulltime dead-end one. Their major motive for beginning to work at such a young age is to gain economic independence. Their parents are often hard-up, so that their own spending money has been severely limited. They buy a car immediately and make the first of never-ending car payments. While their jobs are appropriate enough for ages 22 or 23, they represent an uncertain future in years ahead. Other boys, perhaps through some family connection, may obtain an unskilled or semi-skilled factory job. By contrast the boy who finishes high school may obtain a job in a post office, on the police force, or in the fire department. Especially after they marry and have a child, the main aim of all these young men is job security.

The working-class girl who does not go to college is committed mainly to becoming a wife and mother. Before then she obtains some low-paying job, perhaps as a salesgirl. Only if marriage fails or becomes indefinitely delayed does she become more committed to her job. Even then, because of their sex and educational limitations such women find it hard to get ahead. Hence they are committed to maintaining a job rather than working toward a career.

Aside from work the initial task of these young people is to get married and establish their own household. Their ideas are somewhat vague about what this life should be, partly because they often fail to find in their own parents adequate role models. Both sexes are relieved once they have decided to marry—after all, others of their own age and social class are settling down. Besides they want to be adult, and being married and having a job is considered the proper route to adulthood.

Sex roles are more strictly traditional than among middle-class couples. In the home, sex roles are strictly divided: the woman does the traditionally feminine chores and the man the masculine ones. If the wife works, as blue-collar women are increasingly doing, she nevertheless continues to do most of the domestic chores. The man may help out a bit, but far less than his middle-class counterpart. After marriage couples, but particularly the young men, return to the same-sex friendships they had before marriage. Unlike middle-class couples they do not ordinarily indulge in recreational pursuits together. The young wives associate mostly with other married women, from whom they learn much about homemaking and childrearing, while the young husband hangs out with "the boys" during nonwork hours, often at the bar. He finds married life less supportive than does his wife because it eats up his extra money and to a degree limits his freedom.

The values of the working class have remained pretty stable: "patriotism, personal responsibility, self-help, hard work, and resignation all still coexist with values of political cynicism, distrust of strangers, male dominance, demands for obedience from children, and relative moral and personal inflexibility" (pp. 32–33). Their unchanging values widen the gap between them and the dominant urban middle-class society. The very "success" of this segment of society in maintaining itself intact has reduced its youths' and young adults' opportunities for flexible life styles and made it difficult for them to adapt to a rapidly changing technological world.

SPECIAL CATEGORIES OF YOUNG ADULTS

4s The Young Servicemen

For a considerable fraction of young adults, a stint in the service produces a distinctive life style, yet little research has been done on this score. This writer's own informal research on the topic has been limited to males, so the following discussion will apply only to them.

Almost all young ex-servicemen report that their period in the service left an indelible and significant imprint on their lives. They also report many rewarding outcomes of the experience such as the following.

> Traveling around Europe, meeting people my own age who were nationals of that particular country and learning about them first-hand. I still write back and forth with a few. Confidence in myself that I could do "the impossible" at times. Learning to operate heavy equipment. I drove a tractor-trailer for 2 years after being discharged and made $250 a week.

The young men also felt that being in the service had altered their habits and life styles. Here several men tell how it affected their habits, including drinking, smoking, and drug use.

> I did not drink before I was in. By the time I got out I was almost an alcoholic and still do drink to excess occasionally. I smoked before I was in but by the time I got out I smoked four packs a day. I am now down to one pack a day. It has been said that anyone who was in the service who says they did not experiment with drugs is a liar. I'm not a liar.

> I really started to smoke cigarettes in the service—nerves I guess. Not too much drinking. Started smoking grass in Nam though.

> Became a heavy drinker in an effort to socialize with the boys.

Most of the young men had problems such as these in adapting to life in the service.

> While in boot camp, I realized that I resented taking orders from fellow recruits who were in a higher position yet they were younger than I was.

> It was my first time away from home. Taking orders from persons I had no respect for and had no respect for me.

> Lack of personal freedom and having to take orders from people who you didn't feel were fit for their rank.

Almost all the men, with a few exceptions, said that the experience affected them as people, usually for the better.

> I felt that being in the service made me a better person. I was encountering many problems with my family at the time of my entry into the service. By being in a neutral environment, and away from my problems, I was able to develop and mature. I was better able to accept responsibility and perform under pressure.

> Made me lose any values I had and corrupted me totally.

For the most part it changed me for the better. I became stronger (mentally). The military madness caused me to become stronger.

Confident in myself and I now question many of the values the government has tried to socialize me to. The worst part is that I am much more racist.

The change from service life back to civilian life was not always easy. Here several men tell what they found most difficult about readjustment.

Finances were the biggest problem I encountered when I got out of the service, as there were no jobs available to me.

I had to learn to hide what I really felt, you had to be "insane" to keep your sanity and do what you were told even if it was against your better nature. This presented many problems when I first got out because after being in for so long it was difficult for me to realize I was no longer in. I also found myself resenting people who had not gone in and experienced what I had. I had been trained to be violent and "on my toes" at all times. I scare myself sometimes (even now) when somebody comes up behind me or wakes me unexpectedly because at times I will still lash out before I can stop myself. Hopefully I will break myself of this some day.

Relating to persons not familiar with problems of vets. Resocialization process.

There is no question but that life in the service is a maturing experience. It causes young people to assess their own values, their former life style, and their goals for the future. It is strange indeed that researchers have almost totally ignored the effect of this period on young peoples' personality development.

4t Young Adult Students

Young adults in college from their early to their late 20s include those whose earlier education was delayed or those who are pursuing graduate study. They may have taken time out for travel, to make enough money for further study, to begin a family, or for other reasons. They include both marrieds and singles, undergraduates and graduate students. Often such students have worked enough to save up money to return to school. Their funds may be supplemented by some form of scholarship. Young men may also receive help from their wives, especially if they remain in school a long time.

Until 1940 married undergraduates were unwelcome on college campuses and somewhat rare in number. Today, however, such students comprise approximately a fifth of the American undergraduate college population. While such students have characteristic problems, they seem somewhat better adjusted overall than do the single ones (Busselen & Busselen, 1975). They get higher grades, are better satisfied with their living quarters, have better places to study, and are better off economically. The married students' good adjustment may derive from several factors. For one thing, those who marry in college may simply be more mature than other students. Besides, since they have already chosen their mates, they need not concern themselves with dating. On the other hand, these students have their special problems, one being that domestic activities leave them little time for cultural experience. Also, since they are more vocationally oriented than single students, they lead a narrower life. Much of the foregoing also applies to adult, single undergraduates. The latter usually combine work with schooling, and otherwise associate with persons their own age. They, like the married undergraduates, take little part in campus life.

By means of a series of interviews Taylor (1976) concluded that graduate students are alike in many ways. For one thing, they are observers, which causes them to separate themselves from objects and people. They have few outside involvements because they must spend long hours in libraries and laboratories. So to a certain extent they are in exile. They often have less money than is required for truly adequate living. They rarely share the dominant values of our culture. They come to value intellectual distance both in their work and in their personal lives. On the other hand, they develop a strong emotional attachment to their field of inquiry, which they believe is truly significant for

As a special category of young adults graduate students have few outside involvements and must spend many hours studying.

life itself even though their studies may be very esoteric. They seem to have faith in authority and to desire a pretty clear authority structure; and they often assume a "holier-than-thou attitude" (p. 34).

Graduate work does have its positive features. Graduate students insist on intellectual freedom; and they believe that they can be different so long as they are decent human beings. They do not seek the same kind of power and wealth as people in nonacademic surroundings. They take a tremendous satisfaction exploring the depths of their culture. Ideally they will transcend the bounds of scholarly authority and attain a sense of their own scholarly worth.

Young-adult Singles

4u **Characteristics.** Young-adult singles—older ones will be discussed later —include those who never intend to marry and those who for one reason or another are putting off marriage. In defining singles Stern (1976) excludes cohabiting singles and those involved in an exclusive homosexual relationship.

The number of singles is increasing for a variety of reasons, one of which is there are now three times as many young women enrolled in college as there were in 1960. Other reasons include expanding economic opportunities for women, the woman's movement, the availability of birth control methods—which limits the number of marriages precipitated by pregnancy—and the increasing numbers of young people who declare that they will never marry.

Single women include a disproportionate number of superior individuals, perhaps partly because men feel threatened by them and avoid marrying them. (Glick, 1975b). Or such women may deliberately postpone marriage until they are well established in their careers or find husbands of their own caliber. Tidbal (1975) studied 1500 achievers randomly selected from several editions of *Who's Who of American Women*. Slightly over half of these women had married, but once they had received their bachelor's degrees they had devoted an average of seven years exclusively to their careers before getting married. Since no such factors operate among men, male singles are more representative of the general population. In consequence women who remain single are superior to young men in terms of occupation, income, and education (Bernard, 1972).

For women, age 30 is an important marker. The majority of women under 30 are married while those over 30 are far less likely to do so. Older single women are more positive about life and feel less stress than do younger ones, perhaps because they are better adjusted to being single and also may possess a better paying, more satisfying job. Still another reason is that most women who had much concern about getting married eventually did so. Therefore the older ones represent a higher percent of those who had wanted to remain single all along.

Single men experience both advantages and disadvantages because of their unwed status. They are often viewed as swingers who are somewhat carefree, frolicking merrily through life. Hence they invoke a less responsible image than married men. Perhaps for this reason they are discriminated against in terms of salary and promotion, especially after they reach the age when most of their contemporaries are married. On the other hand, they have had many experiences with women that they could not have had if they were married. Perhaps for this reason they are more liberal and sympathetic with movements for social change than married men. They also have more money to spend exclusively on themselves, which permits them to exploit their greater freedom.

Life styles. Young-adult singles have their own life styles. Many often want to spend some years traveling or just having a broad range of experiences before settling down. Society's reduced pressures on the young to marry constitutes a subtle but real factor in prolonging singlehood.

Young singles can and do live a more varied, less rooted, life than young marrieds. They socialize chiefly with other young singles, especially those with similar interests and outlook. For this reason those who do or do not plan to marry eventually will tend to associate with each other. The singles who definitely intend to marry one day will spend more time dating and looking ahead to marriage. They may have the feeling that they must crowd into the here-and-now whatever extensive traveling and fooling around they want to do. They will deliberately cultivate the sort of social life that will permit them to meet eligible members of the other sex and to test their relationships with different kinds of personalities. Growing numbers live, at least for a time, or even for several years, with the person they eventually marry. The women who anticipate marriage spend relatively more money on clothes and their social life than do those who expect to remain single.

Those who believe they will remain single early on establish a commitment to career. They too travel, and have varied experiences, but with less of a sense of urgency. They are fully aware that their chosen life style is sufficiently flexible to accommodate such experiences at any stage in life. Some of them associate mainly with their own sex, others with both sexes. They may have both casual and more serious sexual encounters, but they avoid legally binding commitments. While they may lack the security and satisfactions that young couples achieve in establishing a family, they can lead an equally full and satisfying, though quite different, life style.

Single people may be involved in some serious and/or casual homosexual or heterosexual affairs. However, many women, even sexually liberated ones, find sex acceptable only within the framework of warm relationships (Hunt, 1973). These relationships may, or may not, signify future intent to marry. In one study 30% of the college men and women questioned felt that traditional types of marriage are growing obsolete, and 25% agreed that the traditional nuclear family (father, mother, and children living together) no longer works (Stein, 1976). Some young people move from campus to city and form friendships with persons quite different from their families and former friends. While they may find the city somewhat threatening they do have a chance to meet varied people, to gain valuable life experience, and to have fun.

4w **Cohabiting singles.** Growing numbers of young adults are electing to live together for weeks, months, or even years, without getting married (Edwards & Stinnett, 1974). Whether or not this trend will last or increase is uncertain.

Most young adults (80% in Macklin's study) report cohabitation to be pleasant, maturing, and helpful in understanding themselves and the other sex. They approve cohabitation as a practice and believe its effect to be healthy. Even those individuals who experience problems in the relationship report that personal growth has occurred (Macklin, 1972). Such individuals differ in some ways from young adults generally. In a comparison of unmarried couples who simply "went together" with those who lived together, the going-together couples held more traditional views of each other and were more committed to marriage. Among the living-together couples more of the young women than men wanted ultimately to marry their cohabiting partners. When young women pressured them to marry, the young men often broke off the relationship and eventually chose new living mates (Lyness, Lipetz, & Davis, 1972).

While families of cohabiting couples for the most part are not radical in life style or ideology, they are generally liberal politically, sexually, and religiously (Croake, Keller, & Catlin, 1974). Nevertheless in terms of the division of household labor young couples, whether cohabiting or married, still divide work along somewhat traditional lines. Young wives bear the brunt of domestic tasks, but less so if they work or go to school. On the other hand husbands help with the laundry and dishes more than their fathers did, while the young women share home repairs and lawn mowing more than their mothers did. Still there are no significant differences in proportion of time spent on traditional tasks when parents are compared to their adult children. For the most part the women perform household duties whether or not they are employed outside the home.

Despite the persistence of the traditional division of labor, there is no significant power struggle between spouses regarding the performance of household tasks, either among married or cohabiting couples. Those young people who are most strongly committed to traditional sex roles tend to come from families in which there is a traditional division of labor, to be of lower rather than higher social class, and to be Catholic rather than Protestant. A minority of couples simply structure household tasks along traditional lines while attempting to some degree to implement a conscious ideology for more equalitarian relationships. It appears that cohabitation and the erosion, to a certain extent, of traditional male authority, will not automatically end traditional sex roles. It seems that young women are still too conservative, and perhaps concerned about their femininity, to alter the current situation.

4x INDIVIDUAL TESTIMONY

The foregoing discussion has dealt with subgroupings of young adults. Within each subgroup, however, there are individual differences. For a better perspective on life styles from the individual point of view, here are several young adults' replies to several questions about their lives.

What do you find most satisfying about your present life?

Good family, challenging job, and recreational opportunities. (*Male, age 23*)

That my past education and experience, coupled with my capabilities, make it possible for me to do just about anything I want. (*Male, age 33*)

My family and career—also that I am able to choose to stay at home for a year or two and not feel guilty about it. (*Female, age 33*)

The free open feelings I have about my life style. (*Female, age 35*)

I'm assertive, love myself for the first time, and feel completely turned on and in tune with God and the rest of the world. My work with

Spanish-speaking migrants makes me feel very needed and worthwhile. (*Female, age 29*)

Is there anything unusual or different about your life style?

I am so traditional in my work, marriage, etc., that I am "unusual." I have a happy home and marriage—that's unusual. (*Female, age 27*)

I guess being gay is different in that we're a minority, but I feel better about myself, having found my true self. I don't feel that I am different. (*Female, age 33*)

I've lived on several socioeconomic levels, sunk to the lowest levels of life (drugs, prostitution, alcohol) have risen above my past and now live a respectable satisfying Christian life. (*Female, age 29*)

I'm socially reclusive. (*Male, age 33*)

Ninety-five percent of my time is regulated by me. I eat when I'm hungry, sleep when I'm tired; work when I want to. (*Male, age 29*)

What are your chief and most pleasant forms of recreation and interests?

I obtain a great deal of joy from travelling and several hobbies, such as woodburning and making things from wood. (*Male, age 33*)

Fishing; reading. (*Male, age 33*)

Chess; listening to interesting people; making money. (*Male, age 29*)

Sewing; my children. (*Female, age 35*)

I enjoy creating things. I watch TV, sometimes for diversion, sometimes for escape. Crocheting; sewing; reading. (*Female, age 33*)

4y PERSPECTIVE ON YOUNG-ADULT LIFE STYLES

Changes in the life styles of young adults in the United States have been less dramatic than is commonly believed; yet they are significant in certain ways. Most young adults focus their main energies and commitments on family and vocation, but in ways that differ from their parents. Since most young women work, sex roles are changing, but the changes have not yet been worked through well enough to satisfy adequately the needs of husbands or working wives. Ordinarily parents find real satisfaction in their children, the more so because childbearing has become a matter of choice rather than an obligation or the price of sex.

No homogeneous picture of young-adult life styles can suffice because life in the United States is increasingly complex and there are so many subgroupings within society. True, certain generalizations apply to most young adults—that they are searching for a style of life that suits their needs, and that they experience an increasing desire for a more satisfying life rather than a largely life-sustaining existence. Beyond such broad goals considerable differences exist according to such variables as sex, social class, marital status, and vocation. No longer is membership in the nuclear family viewed as the only valid life style, although it is still by far the most popular. It is increasingly accepted and understood that nontraditional ways of life are most satisfying for some people for part or all of their lives.

There is nothing in the picture to suggest that today's young adults are any less emotionally healthy than their counterparts of earlier generations. In fact the reverse is true. As birth control methods have improved, as the great majority are becoming better educated, and as economic and technological gains reduce the need for drudgery, young adults are expecting more and gaining more from their lives. Even such transactions as obtaining a divorce, joining a commune, or participating in consciousness-raising groups of various kinds may be less symptoms of failure or acute discontent with their present life than a positive reaching-out for greater personal fulfillment.

SUGGESTED READINGS

Askham, J. Identity and stability within the marriage relationship. *Journal of Marriage and the Family*, 1976, *38* (3), 535–547. Interviews with young adults involved in a variety of living arrangements (single, married, cohabiting, living in communes) yielded certain hypotheses concerning intimate relationships. For one thing, people seek to develop and maintain a sense of identity in such relationships; however, the conditions required for attaining this goal tends to produce conflict.

Clayton, R. R., & Voss, H. L. Shacking up: Cohabitation in the 1970s. *Journal of Marriage and the Family*, 1977, *39* (2), 273–283. On the basis of data obtained from 2,510 young men, the practice of cohabitation is analyzed in terms of prevalence, correlates, and significance. Differences in cohabitation are also examined with regard to age, social class, ethnic background, and size of city.

Cotton, W. L. Social and sexual relationships of lesbians. *The Journal of Sex Research*, 1975, *11* (2), 139–148. A study of lesbian relationships of 30 middle-class women, ages 20 to 47, living in New York City, provides a picture of their personal characteristics, life styles, and social activities.

Craig, G. J. *Human development*. Englewood Cliffs, N.J.: Prentice-Hall, Inc., 1976. See chapter 19, "Early Adulthood: Roles and Issues," for a discussion of life styles—married or single and at work—during this period of life.

Crummette, B. D. Transitions in motherhood. *Maternal-Child Nursing Journal*, 1975, *4* (2), 65–73. The transition in motherhood from feelings of inefficiency and disorganization to those adaptation and confidence are analyzed in relation to various factors, including the development of the child, the assumption of new roles, the values the mother holds for herself and the child, and matters of personal deprivation associated with the mothering role.

Friedrich, W. N. & Boriskin, J. A. The role of the child in abuse: A review of the literature. *American Journal of Orthopsychiatry*, 1976, *46* (4), 580–590. The role of the parent is ordinarily stressed in matters of child abuse, while other factors, especially the role of the child, are ignored. Young parents may find it extremely difficult to accept children with such disabilities as a physical handicap or mental retardation, who can never fulfill their dreams and expectations.

Rich, A. *Of women born: Motherhood as experience and institution.* New York: W. W. Norton & Co., Inc., 1976. A feminist describes the ambivalent feelings of mothers, whose satisfactions are diluted by never-ending responsibilities and feelings of frustration. Of special interest are her comments on such topics as abortion, and relations between mothers and daughters.

Sheehy, G. *Passages: The predictable crises of adult life.* New York: E. P. Dutton & Co., Inc., 1976. In Sheehy's book about adult life stages, see the chapters "The Trying Twenties" and "Passage to the Thirties" for a discussion of how the young adults she interviewed, coped with this period.

Shuptrine, F. K. & Samuelson, G. Dimensions of marital roles in consumer decision making: Revisited. *Journal of Marketing Research*, 1976, *13* (1), 87–91. Despite recent trends toward equality between marital partners, questionnaire data from 350 families indicate that each spouse still has a clearly defined role regarding areas in which he or she will have greater influence in purchasing decisions.

Stafford, R., Backman, E., & Dibona, P. The division of labor among cohabiting and married couples. *Journal of Marriage and the Family*, 1977, *39* (1), 43–57. Matched samplings of married and cohabiting couples at a university were compared with regard to the division of labor in household tasks. Among both samplings the traditional division of labor persisted, probably because of a "nonconscious ideology" acquired through modeling after their own parents.

Westenmeyer, J. & Rosenberg, P. Role, ritual and grynnflnk. *American Journal of Orthopsychiatry*, April 1977, *47* (2), 341–347. An examination is made of the relationship between unmarried cohabiting couples and their families. Since cohabitation is becoming a firmly established alternative to courtship, their situation becomes involved in the dynamics of their respective families and kin.

Youth '74. New York: Research Services Institute of Life Insurance (277 Park Avenue), 1974. This report of a national sampling of young people aged 14 to 24, describes their life styles and attitudes toward such fundamental matters as marriage and childbearing. Single copies may be obtained free of charge.

III PART

The Middle-Aged Adult

5
CHAPTER

The Characteristics of Middle Age

THE SIGNIFICANCE OF MIDDLE AGE

What is Middle Age?

Definition. When does middle age begin? Middle age has no generally accepted boundaries: some United States census reports define it as covering ages 45 to 64, while other studies date it from 30 to 70 (Kerckhoff, 1976). In terms of human biology, the climacteric—the end of one's reproductive potential—might be considered the end of the middle years and the beginning of old age (Troll, 1975). Socially, however, the climacteric is considered as occurring in middle age. Definitions of middle age may also involve life developments. For example middle age may be defined as the period when the children leave home and the parental breadwinners retire from their jobs (Kerckhoff, 1976). Middle age may also be defined in terms of the way people perceive themselves.

It is apparent from these middle-aged peoples' reactions to the question, "How old do you feel?" that there is usually a gap—though it varies in size—between the way people see themselves and their actual chronological age.

> Forty mostly, although there are days!!!! I feel younger because I think young always and so does my husband. (*Female, age 58, married*)

> I think I feel my age. If I don't, and I get too overactive, I know soon enough. (*Female, age 54, widowed*)

> I don't feel any particular age, but rather I feel 41 is a label and I will get another at 42 because aging is slow. I don't feel any different than I did at 31. Physically I can see some change. That and other people's attitude about 41 make me aware of my age. I never feel older, probably because I feel healthy and active. (*Female, age 41, married*)

> On my good days I feel 18. When I have a bad day, which is more often than I like to say, I feel much older. (*Female, age 53, married*)

> Some days pretty old, but usually young at heart. Don't have the stamina I used to. (*Female, age 64, married*)

> I've always felt extremely young—I have no feeling of growing older,

physically or otherwise. I have never felt "middle-aged," regardless of how others may view me. (*Female, age 62, single*)

Self-perceptions of middle age. The process of seeing oneself growing older is gradual and often begins in the 30s. Sheehy (1976) refers to the years 35 to 45 as the "deadline decade," in which the majority experience a complete authenticity crisis. In the earlier adult years an individual may simply have steered from one channel to another when the going became difficult. In the late 20s and early 30s, Sheehy asserts, peoples' lives seem to be at their peak—their health is good, their sex lives satisfying, their incomes rising. But they often begin to feel old. They notice that their peers look older, and realize that they do too. At the same time they joke about growing older and discuss its compensations.

Self-perceptions of age vary greatly according to health, social class, how well life crises have been resolved, and personal outlook in general. People who have led a hard life, experienced much sickness and prematurely aged physically may feel old. Working men may feel themselves to be middle-aged at 40 and old by 60, while professionals and business executives may not perceive themselves as middle-aged until 50, or old until after 70 (Neugarten, 1972). In a study of middle-class men, about half those over 80 considered themselves old, while the other half saw themselves as middle-aged (Eisdorfer & Lawton, 1973).

Still another factor in how people feel about middle age is how successful they have been at resolving middle-age crises. Neugarten (1968) describes middle-aged persons as those who determine the norm and make decisions; and though society is "oriented toward youth," it is "controlled by the middle aged" (p. 93). Until people have resolved the crises of entering middle age they find no satisfaction in promises of middle-aged power. Yet, most people come ultimately to accept middle age, to enjoy its many advantages.

A final factor in determining how one sees middle age is personality. Some people wrap up their lives at a relatively early age. They tend to dwell in the past and the present, not the future. Others always look eagerly ahead and live too full a life to be aware of the passing years. In other words, middle age may be meaningful for one individual but not for another. For example the empty nest stage—after the children leave home—would have meaning for a mother but not for a childless woman. Thus it might be appropriate to think of middle age and other ages in the functional sense rather than as arbitrary age designations (Nydegger, 1976). There is a vast gap in the self-perceptions of these two types in terms of psychological and functional age.

Symptoms of middle age. According to Butler (1976) there are several signs of middle age, one being that people begin counting "backward from death instead of forward from birth" (p. 30). That is, an individual begins thinking of the amount of time left to live. Another symptom is that people begin sizing themselves up and evaluating what they have done, deciding whether they have achieved what they had hoped. This is often very painful. A third sign is a growing preoccupation with the body, or "body monitoring". This period is sometimes characterized by drug addiction, excessive drinking, or obesity. Conclusions about the significance of middle age—or any age—depend upon its frame of reference. Does the assessment involve the way this age relates to an anticipated future, or does it concern the impact of experience on oneself during middle age, or is it about the effect on individuals who play certain roles during a specific age range? It might be more appropriate to speak of middle ages, which would include all the social roles and functions under discussion here (Nydegger, 1976).

The Tasks of the Middle Years

The tasks defined. Various authorities have attempted to define the most significant tasks of the middle years—and while these authorities differ

1978 © Sybil Shelton

As people enter middle age they often begin evaluating what they have done and whether they have achieved what they had hoped.

considerably, collectively they provide a general picture of what the middle aged are expected to accomplish in modern western society. Kerckhoff (1976) believes that people at middle age must redefine their identity just as they did at adolescence. He compares middle age with adolescence because both ages involve answering the important questions, "Who am I? Where am I going? What is life all about?" (p. 9). That is the middle aged, like adolescents, face an identity crisis. McMorrow (1974) spells middlescence with an "o" (midolescence) in order to stress its likeness to adolescence. He perceives middle age as "characterized by a reverting to the bizarre, irrational, sexually confused status of adolescence" (p. 9).

LeShan (1973) believes that middlescence provides a real opportunity, another chance to find out what it means to "do your own thing," to become truly oneself, to discover one's own truths, especially one's own identity. She compares the process that the middle aged experience in examining their identities with the lobster's periodic shedding of its shell. It makes the lobster vulnerable, but it also permits it to grow.

Rhona and Robert Rapoport (1975) define life tasks or preoccupations in terms of four major life stages: youth, young adult, establishment, and retirement, each with its own focal preoccupations, interests, and activities. The establishment (middle-aged) phase paves the way for the retirement phase, which is a time of personal and social integration. Young adults identify with social institutions; in the next, the establishment phase, people are concerned with life investment, performance, productivity and evaluation.

Levinson's (1977) concept of middle age is similar. He refers to it as a settling down phase which involves greater control over one's life, and stronger feelings of security and stability. It means "building a nest" and also "making it: planning, striving, moving onward and upward, ambition" (p. 104). Settling down means getting married and having a family, although building and making the nest can be separated. Both the Rapoports and Levinson perceive middle age as a time when things get done, since goals have already been defined.

The tasks of middle age depend somewhat on the relationship of people at this age to older or younger generations. As members of the older generation die, their adult children become the oldest generation and assume certain of the characteristics peculiar to it, while the older generation's grandchildren then become the second generation (Duvall, 1971). Members of the oldest generation feel to a certain extent that they have fulfilled their destiny and that the main task of activating society now belongs to the second generation. While they are no longer actively involved, they nevertheless constitute a conserving force through their now adult children and grandchildren. To a degree they are watchdogs over the society, evaluating current trends against earlier ones. And while they have too little power and are too out of date with the times to block change, they can nevertheless have an effect on what occurs. The in-between middle-aged generation to some extent serves as a moderator between the older and the younger generations. The younger generation is often impatient and wants to make radical changes in society, while the older generation remains somewhat cautious, unwilling to turn its back on solutions to societal problems that have proven themselves over the years. In addition the middle generation must take care of the dependent older and younger generations.

A critique of Erikson's theory. As we discussed in Chapter 1, Erik Erikson (1968) perceives middle age as the phase of generativity, which means the ability to look out for oneself and to be concerned for others. Those who do not achieve it because they have not resolved earlier conflicts become self-centered instead of happy and productive. Generativity helps to resolve the crises which occur when people realize that what they have dreamed of achieving is not what they have actually achieved. If to some extent they have failed to arrive at more selfish goals, they compensate, finding satisfaction in the accomplishment of other goals. Generativity, in short, refers to caring for others in the broader sense, though being productive and creative, thereby making a contribution to others. For example, many men in their 40s move away from dedicating all their energies to their own personal career advancement and undertake community service.

On the other hand for every individual who becomes philanthropic or assumes the role of guide to younger individuals, there are several who hang on to their career fantasies as zealously as ever (Sheehy, 1976). Some men at this period, realizing they will never attain their goals or finding that those goals no longer mean anything to them, will drink too much or over eat in order to cope with feelings of disillusion or failure. Other men, by contrast, take a more enlightened approach to similar problems. They may lighten their work loads or engage in off-the-job activities that provide self-fulfillment.

Sheehy calls attention to a major limitation in Erikson's theory, which is that he, like most life-cycle theorists, is concerned only with the male life cycle. After all, women have always been concerned with generativity or serving others. It is not simply through more generativity that women manage to recreate themselves during the second half of their lives. True, they may indulge in such generative activities as working for local, social, or political reforms. However if the crisis for men at midlife is a matter of overcoming stagnation through generativity, the midlife task for women demands that they overcome their dependency and realize their wholeness.

Sheehy clearly differentiates between men's and women's tasks in middle age. Like Kerckhoff she perceives the early middle years as a time for redefining the self and for assessing the worth of what one is doing. Like Erikson she perceives people at the "deadline decade," from the mid-30s to the mid-40s, as undergoing a crisis and feeling their lives approaching an end. Several factors, including fading youth, a decrease in physical power, and the obsolescence of former life roles— may lead to a crisis of authenticity. As a result, middle-aged people ask themselves what they really believe in and why they are doing what they are doing. Women approach this crisis earlier than men, often by age 35. They feel that it is their last chance to indulge in a bit of extramarital sex or to have a final fling before settling down and aging. They feel exhilaration and a sense of release. Meantime their husbands are also feeling that it is their last chance, and they find themselves working harder too. Yet a husband is less exhilarated than his wife, for no matter how much he has achieved, a man of 40 generally feels worn out, overworked, and unappreciated. Sometimes men of this age seek a second career, or they may break out of their marriage. Some even attempt suicide.

Sheehy, like other theorists, feels that people who resolve their crises in a satisfactory way become rather mellow and stable. Those who rethink the way their life is structured may find that the best years of their lives lie ahead. They become more tolerant and understanding. Friends become of greater value than ever before, but so does having a fair share of privacy. Men become more sensitive to and concerned for others.

Indeed, concludes Sheehy, it is only during the late 30s and early 40s, when entering the second half of their lives, that most people begin to attain genuine adulthood. At that time they either stagnate and become resigned to it, or they change and improve their lives. The stagnaters become alienated from their own children, and their mates grow away from them. Their work does not become more than just a job, and the crisis, instead of being buried, rises again at about age 50.

Crisis as a spur to growth. This survey of theories about the tasks of middle age suggests that middle-age crisis is normal, and if properly resolved it can produce growth. The new stage may be on a higher, not lower, level than that of young adulthood. It is important for researchers to identify the factors that distinguish people who experience renewal after middle-aged crisis from those who get stuck in the same old rut.

MENTAL AND PERSONALITY CHARACTERISTICS

Mental Characteristics

The pattern of mental development. Various authorities, Piaget among them, believe that mental development proceeds through relatively discrete stages. After going through the first three stages in childhood, normal individuals presumably reach the highest, formal operations, stage in adolescence and become capable of systematic deductive reasoning. That is, they can now use abstract rules or generalizations to attack a whole class of problems, and think abstractly without the use of concrete proofs. According to this theory, abilities stabilize at this point and remain reasonably constant until later adulthood when they begin to decline.

This theory has been subject to several important criticisms and changes. In the first place the pattern of adult intelligence may sometimes emerge prior to early adolescence (Fitzgerald, Nesselroade, & Baltes, 1973). Second, only half the adult population ever reaches the stage of formal operational thinking, or the problem-solving stage. In the third place, formal operational thinking is not necessarily the final stage. Instead, thought structures, or patterns of intellectual function, may continue to change progressively beyond this level throughout adulthood (Gruber, 1973). The implication of this theory is that formal structures, or the intellectual underpinnings of problem solving once developed, are stable and remain accessible (or constitute a potential resource) throughout life. They may also constitute "building blocks for new structures that go beyond those traditionally defined as formal" (Arlin, 1975, p. 602).

As a case in point Gruber (1973) analyzed the development of creative thought in adults, especially those who had accomplished exceptional things. He noted that important changes in adult thinking parallel the developments in children's thought. Among both children and adults these changes are characterized by processes of grouping, experimenting, discarding, and restructuring ideas. This concept of continuously learning and perceiving new things in adulthood represents a significant challenge to the traditionally held idea that adult thinking establishes an ultimate equilibrium beyond which new structures do not appear. This concept is substantiated to some degree by a 38-year follow-up of intelligence from preschool to middle age (Kangas & Bradway, 1971). In these cases there was no limit to mental growth, and increases in adult mental function related to preadult intelligence.

We should add that when the peak of one's powers is attained depends upon the activity involved. In some sports decline begins at about age 30, but in such fields as painting and philosophy, high achievement may continue until very old age. After all, Verdi composed his Othello at 73, Cervantes wrote *Don Quixote* at 55, and Benjamin Franklin invented bifocal lenses when he was in his seventies (Butler, 1976).

Differences according to age and sex. It is true that younger people react more speedily behaviorally, and by inference, mentally, than older ones, but to what degree is uncertain. Older people are often more deliberate, having grown accustomed to weighing alternatives before accepting answers as conclusive. Troll (1975) suggests that it may be functional that young people process new information more quickly than older ones. In earlier years when intelligence is somewhat fluid and information-processing common, younger people assimilate quickly at a time when rapid learning is most useful to them—that is, when they have had little experience. Later on speed is displaced by a certain rounding-out or filling-in process.

Sex differences in adult intelligence may also exist. Women perform well in verbal meaning, reasoning, and word fluency, which reflects their more verbal type of life, while males are superior in numbers, space, and general intellectual ability (Schaie, Labouvie, & Buesch, 1973). Nevertheless such differences vary greatly within each sex and can easily be explained in terms of differential social sex roles.

It is relatively easy to explain most of these differences. For adults of all ages, sex differences vary according to the respective roles that men and women play. For example men's superiority in space and numbers is due at least partly to the nature of the games they played and the toys they had in childhood (Schaie, Labouvie, & Buesch, 1973). For individuals of both sexes mental performance in childhood and all subsequent years is strongly modified by their own experiences. Retests over a period of 38 years on the Stanford Binet Intelligence Test indicated that males with higher IQs at age 12 increased more in IQ by their mid-twenties than those who began with lower IQs; while females with higher IQs at age 12 gained less than did those with lower

IQs. Troll (1975) suggests that "it is as if women use their intelligence to grow dumber, at least in the early years of adulthood." Perhaps the real reason is that bright men are engaged more often than bright women in tasks that help them to do well with the kind of problems included in IQ tests. Besides, in the competitive male world, brighter men find greater challenge while less intelligent ones will be consigned to less mentally demanding tasks. On the other hand since both brighter and duller women tend during early adulthood to perform approximately the same tasks, the gap between their IQs becomes less.

Personality Characteristics

The process of personality development. The bulk of evidence suggests that once established, basic personality characteristics, as distinct from more peripheral ones, are relatively persistent across the years. Although personality development throughout life is an often obscure, and always a complex process, its basic design persists. Overall personality "development is a cyclic process with competencies developing and then disappearing to reappear anew at a later age; development is not a continuous process but rather a series of waves, with whole segments of development reoccurring repetitively" (Bower, 1974, p. 322).

Tendencies toward stability or change are not necessarily built in, but relate to peoples' social environment. On the one hand personality development is at least partially a response to changing internal and external demands. On the other, personality cannot simply be changed on demand (Nydegger, 1976).

A relevant study. In one study Woodruff and Birren (1972) made both longitudinal and cross-sectional comparisons in order to distinguish between age differences and age changes in personality. Adolescents tested in 1944 on the California Test of Personality were retested 25 years later when they had become middle aged. The subjects were asked to answer the inventory the second time as they believed they had answered it in 1944. Meantime contemporary high school and college students also answered the test. Longitudinal comparisons suggested that actual age changes in personality were small although subjective age changes were large. In other words, changes in personality had been much less than the subjects believed. The large differences in personality scores between the two groups represented a difference in cohorts, or a generation gap. That is, differences between the groups were not so much a matter of difference in age as of "unique socio-historical forces" which affect the "members of each generation when they are in different stages of development" (p. 256). The researchers concluded that the differences in personality of individuals over the years—from adolescence to middle age—are small.

General characteristics: miscellaneous findings. Certain studies have concerned the personality characteristics of adults in general. As indicated earlier, some authorities suggest it is important to redefine oneself and one's goals in middle age. However a survey which included adults and university students in Los Angeles, Australia, and Britain indicated that few adults, even the youngest and/or most highly educated, (with the exception of the university students) had thought at all about the question, "Who am I really?" (Turner, 1975a).

We have also suggested that adults undergo a certain mellowing in middle years. They acquire greater tolerance regarding both self and others, as well as greater insight into the complexities of their world. Nevertheless various factors can slow down this process or even get it off the track altogether (Gould, 1975). Certainly aging gracefully cannot be taken for granted. It requires foresight and preparation. The great majority settle down and look upon themselves as relatively stable; for whatever is done, "the die is cast" (Gould, 1975). Such understanding in healthy persons does not represent resignation, but the resolution of conflicting alternatives and the definition of a life style based on their experiences.

Results of Selected Studies of Adult Personality

Common middle-class personality patterns. Sheehy (1976) categorized the middle-class middle-aged couples whom she interviewed in terms of characteristics that limit or encourage personal growth. "Transient individuals", for instance, are given to exploration. They make tentative, easily reversible decisions and are unwilling to make more than limited commitments. They might drift from one occupation to another, tackling each with enthusiasm, some constructively and some destructively. On the surface such individuals may appear to have mature commitments, but they are not deeply involved in them. The question arises: when does postponing making adult commitments become destructive? George Bernard Shaw gave himself until age 30. At 20 he left his homeland, became involved in the socialist movement, and finally developed his unusual talents by writing about whatever interested him.

At the other extreme, young people who invest very little of themselves in their early choices may have little on which to grow. Such individuals may become locked out of many future possibilities. In general young people who are transient through their 20s, feel a compelling need at around 30 to establish goals and attachments, which may or may not include marriage (Norton & Grymes, 1973). Those in the locked-in group are "safe but stifled." They make commitments in their 20s, without undergoing any crisis and without any in-depth self-examination. Their goal is to have a goal and to follow it; and they do not normally engage in much questioning about the values that underlie those goals. As they enter their 30s they may, however, regret not having spent more time in exploration. At that point some of them may try to break out of their early commitment if it does not suit them. Such an effort to change will be difficult, but not nearly as much as for those who wait until they are 40 and realize they have charted the wrong course. The locked-in type includes people who get into safe jobs and never dare leave them. They are reluctant to take risks.

The well-adjusted Harvard students at middle age. Certain studies—for example, one that Sheehy cites by Vaillant and McArthur—suggest how early personality characteristics and life styles relate to later adjustment. A group of Harvard students, initially selected for study because of their psychological health and their high level of independence, had been studied from their freshman year to age 48. The results indicate how people with relatively similar backgrounds and apparently similar personality characteristics eventually follow different paths, and either grow or stagnate. Between the ages of 25 and 35 these young men worked hard at their careers and dedicated themselves to their nuclear family. They were poor at self-reflection and resembled latency children. They followed the rules, were good at performing tasks, anxious to become promoted, and dedicated to the system. By age 30 they had simply given over to conformity. In the meantime most of these young men were masterful at deceiving themselves. Their early 30s were especially empty and there had been little personality expansion during the previous years. By the time they were 35 they couldn't wait to take charge. However, at 40, most of the young men found themselves in a state of turmoil greater than anything they had been through in adolescence. The years 40 to 50 proved a difficult decade for all aspects of their lives. Yet they proceeded with self-appraisal in midlife and came out with their lives restructured. They looked back on the years 35 to 49 as the happiest of their lives. But some of them, who had been adventuresome in their 20s (especially the lawyers) seemed to settle down in a very mundane fashion in their 40s. In midlife they simply failed to grow, and compared with their classmates, they appeared to be prematurely aging.

Those individuals who came out best became less concerned in midlife about their personal advancement, and shifted away from an emphasis on making money and winning career awards, to caring for others. This reorientation included concern for children, consulting, teaching, and serving as models and guides to younger men. These men were a perfect example of Erikson's generativity-as-opposed-to-stagnation thesis.

The Oakland Growth Study. Let us have a look at one more study, one that shows how characteristics that may interfere with adjustment at one age may prove functional at another ("Freeing up after forty," 1976). The Oakland Growth Study began in 1932 and involved 200 11-year-old boys and girls. They were observed in depth in their junior and senior years in high school and were interviewed again at ages 40 and 50. At 40 the more traditional subjects had moved smoothly into middle age with little change in life style; they appeared emotionally healthy. Those individuals who had been "sex-role rebels" in adolescence experienced some conflict and depression at age 40, perhaps because they had "suppressed their freer instincts and emotionality." The male sex-role rebels were more expressive than most males and the females' interests lay outside the home (p. 50). However, apparently something had happened between the ages of 40 and 50 because by 50, these individuals had come to appreciate and respect their inner natures. These nonconformist men were outgoing, giving, sensual, and freely expressed their feelings. They also needed much less power. The women sex-role rebels became more perceptive, nonconformist and strongly intellectual. Researcher Livson concluded that both sexes had become more androgynous by age 50, perhaps because the women no longer devoted themselves to mothering, and the men no longer needed to prove their prowess. Or it may simply be that sex norms are more flexible by this age. In any case, the study suggests that age 50 rather than age 40 is the real beginning of life for some people.

Limited generalizations. Such studies suggest the complexity of personality research and the difficulty in drawing conclusions. Rough patterns of personality development can be defined within various segments of the population according to social class, ethnic group, and other such factors. Considering the large number of cultures around the world and the many kinds of life styles within a single culture, such patterns could be endlessly noted. To what extent they can be categorized according to overall patterns of human personality development, and pinned down to the forces that produce them and define the processes involved, is uncertain. The task is to integrate findings from the various longitudinal studies on a continuing basis, and to derive sound principles from them.

MORALS AND RELIGION

Adult Morals and Values

Stages of moral development. Moral, like mental, development is often portrayed as developing by stages. Kohlberg's well-known theory (1975) depicts the development of moral reasoning in three stages. The first, or preconventional, stage involves somewhat egocentric, self-centered concepts of right and wrong. In the second, or conventional, stage of morality of late childhood, the individual simply accepts and follows social standards of law and order. At this stage people may not behave according to their own beliefs about what is right and wrong, but neither do they challenge the idea that morality is unchanging and supreme, sanctioned by social standard and divine law. In the third and highest, or postconventional, stage, an individual follows personal principle and abstract reasons. Originally Kohlberg believed that the final stage of conscience, or principled orientation, was reached by the end of adolescence. He later found support for the idea that moral development continues in adulthood (Bielby & Papalia, 1975).

This theory, like cognitive stage theory, has undergone some revision. For one thing, it has been assumed that once people reach the advanced stages of moral development, they stay there forever. However, there is reason to believe that there can be a certain amount of regression to earlier ways of cognitive and moral functioning. For another thing, the majority of adults operate chiefly at the conventional level, and perhaps it is good that they do. Society may depend for its stability on a population willing to support its fundamental laws and morality. Basic changes in those principles can be made by new generations and by the minority of thoughtful persons who operate on the postconventional level.

The stability of values. In general, concludes Troll (1975), most adults remain rather stable in their interests, values, attitudes, and feelings about themselves and others. True, "there are fluctuations in values, goals, attitudes, and interests over the adult years, [but] they seem more like waves on the surface of a slow-moving tide of historical shifts than like impressive individual changes" (p. 48). And while the principles governing our behavior differ somewhat for people in their 20s, 30s, 40s, and 50s, they are "just as likely to be cohort differences as age changes" (p. 48).

On the other hand, some values and interests are more variable among certain individuals and in certain areas of behavior than others. In a longitudinal study (Kelly, 1955) in which several hundred engaged couples were tested in their mid-20s and again 20 years later, the most stable measures were values, but even in this area about half the subjects indicated some change. The least stable measures regarded such matters as church, marriage, childrearing, entertaining, house-keeping, and gardening. Few individuals felt the same way about these matters as they had two decades before; and the men had changed more than the women.

Values in middle age. As people move through their 40s they become less concerned with career and more with human factors. A comparison of junior and senior psychoanalysts at the William Allenson White Institute of Psychiatry (Lionells & Mann, 1974) yielded this conclusion. For the junior analysts, career and status were related to competing with younger people. They felt it necessary to remain as physically attractive as possible in order to compete with those younger than themselves. The senior analysts, whose average age was 53, perceived the midlife crisis as an individual experience, and defined themselves as distinctive from parents, spouse, or children. They were evaluating their own lives, had relaxed in their competitiveness with others, and found the middle years a welcome release from a number of involve-ments. They felt freer to be independent within their relationships. The researchers translated these changes as a transition from *us*-ness to *me*-ness.

Individual testimony. In the process of life evaluation, people arrive at conclusions that together make up their philosophy of life. In the following, several middle-aged adults talk about the most important conclusions that they have reached about life.

> Not to be afraid to take a chance, to explore every avenue. Like a book, there's always something we learn now. Nothing is impossible if you really want it. (*Female, age 58, married*)
>
> I always thought the phrase "life begins at forty" meant things would be much better and always considered the author of the phrase a little shortsighted. However, now I think he meant what he said, but in the sense that most problems—health, financial problems, etc.—begin to be a major part of your older years. I think from age forty and on one's life is put through a wringer of emotions, problems, etc. (*Female, age 51, separated*)
>
> Life is a constant struggle. (*Female, age 54, widowed*)
>
> One of the definite conclusions is to educate my three children. (*Female, age 43, married*)
>
> Don't cry—pray. Don't worry. Leave it up to God. All things are possible with Him. Accept people the way they are and don't be shocked

if you are deserted by husband, children, or friends. We see it happen to others. (*Female, age 61, widowed*)

One's attitude toward life reflects an individual's state of mind. We have the capacity to control our minds and in turn, our lives. People need an honest identity. They must feel life has worth, or mental destruction is inevitable. (*Female, age 41, married*)

Your energy slows down after middle age. Make the most of every day. Thank God always for the blessings we do possess. (*Female, age 53, married*)

Life, especially in these times, is rather rough. Money doesn't go as far as needed. (*Female, age 64, married*)

If you make mistakes, don't constantly wish you hadn't made them. Have a healthy self-respect, and also respect others to the extent that they deserve to be respected. Life has a lot to offer if you know how to avail yourself of opportunities. (*Female, age 62, single*)

Factors that modify values. Various factors are involved in causing certain values to be accepted by most people. One of these factors is historical. A recent trend in the middle years has been toward seeking greater self-realization, especially among more affluent people, who can afford the leisure time required for it. Earlier in life, and among people who are not well off financially, one's energies are consumed by the struggle to make a living. Later, as peoples' obligations decrease, they become more preoccupied with their inner selves, and concern themselves with two special characteristics of these years: philosophical concern and insight (Lionells & Mann, 1974). In fact the eccentricity sometimes observed among the middle aged who are beginning to enjoy doing what they please, may actually be a healthy freedom from trying to please everyone else. Gail Sheehy (1976) quotes Dr. Estelle Ramey, a physiologist almost 60 years old, as saying that she had become more truthful as she got older; that is, she had not intentionally lied, but she had wanted to be liked. She has now lost the need to be liked by everyone, and is content to be liked only by some.

Values are also modified by the so-called generations effect. This means that cohorts of people who experience radically different circumstances will have correspondingly different values. In other words, differences in values within a generation are not the result of aging, but of the circumstances they experienced during unusually impressionable periods of their lives, especially adolescence and youth. For example the teenagers and their young middle-aged parents of the 1970s both grew up in somewhat affluent times. When you add this factor to the significant impact of home life on values, it is hardly surprising that these two generations are generally more alike in personality and values than people of the same generation.

The growing consciousness among the middle aged that they must keep up with the times or become hopelessly out of date also narrows the gap between current generations. They realize that otherwise they may be surpassed by their children in acquiring the skills and attitudes needed to adapt to a technological society. They may resort to continuing education, or travel, or discussion groups on topics of current importance. In some cases parents may take on counterculture ethics and life styles, at least in fantasy. In the past parents served as mentors and interpreters of emerging life styles and values; and they were able to bring "perspective and experience to the generational dialogue" (Dragastin & Elder, 1975, p. 138). Nowadays the generations learn together and share views and values.

An especially significant factor in shaping values is social class. About five years after ideas regarding sex, family, and life style are put forth by the middle class, working-class people take them over (Yankelovich, 1973). The working class, or blue collars, differ in turn from the lower-lower class. The blue collars accept the dominant value system, and have a great respect for such qualities as self-direction, obedience to parents, and the worth of work. Since they do essential work, they are genuinely integrated into the industrial society. On the other hand, they experience more marital stress and have a higher rate of divorce than white-collars probably because of economic strain and their relatively lower rank in the social hierarchy. Among the lower-lowers, or "disreputable poor," the situation is quite different. They have no real

College professors serve as significant mentors and role models for young adults.

status in society and are alienated from it. They are often unemployed or on welfare, which is quite different from the respectable blue collars, who hold regular jobs. One spouse may simply desert the other rather than go through a socially approved divorce (Segre, 1975).

Values always reflect a country's overall culture. Today's technological society is often portrayed as unfriendly to the establishment and maintenance of stable values; and May (1974), among others, believes that the values long associated with America are rapidly dissolving. Consider, for example, the frontier myth. According to this notion, "each isolated person or family was part of the manifest destiny of the American dream" (p. 271). Self-reliance and objectivity were valued because they were needed for survival. But these values have become distorted. For instance, "the gun that was a tool for self-reliance has now become a tool for excessive violence. . . . " (p. 271). Moreover, "courageous loneliness has become neurotic alienation" (p. 271). And that strength (or power) which formerly helped individuals develop character has become power for power's sake.

Others are more optimistic about the times. According to Dubos (1976) "history shows that crises usually [result in] . . . new phases of creativeness . . . " (p. 172). The change in values is often wrongly identified with a dissolution of values. Crises pave the way for new values which will be more effective for guiding current behavior.

Religion in Middle Age

Relevant research. Comparatively little research exists regarding present-day adults and religion in terms of the way it functions in their lives. We do know that people of various religions tend to give different weight to different kinds of behavior. We also know that family experience, age, and sex importantly modify religious behavior. Very religious parents are likely to have religious children, and if the parents are not religious their children are not either. Both sons and daughters are more likely to follow the mother's religious values than the father's, and daughters are more likely than sons to share parental attitudes (Braun & Bengtson, 1972).

We also know that age and sex relate to differences in religious behaviors. In a study which involved four life stages—high school, newlywed, middle age, and pre-retirement—the majority of the respondents had some religious affiliation. Among the men church membership was 76% for those in high school, 24% as newlyweds, 59% for the middle-aged and 50% for the pre-retired. For the women it was over half at all stages except pre-retirement, when it increased to 60%

(Lowenthal, Thurnher, & Chiriboga, 1975). It is uncertain, however, to what extent these differences can be attributed to aging, or whether they result from the times in which particular cohorts lived.

It is also uncertain just what part religion plays in adults' lives today, or even how people define religion. The vast majority say that religion is meaningful for them, but different people interpret both religious concepts and meaning in highly varied ways. It is obvious that religion does not play as great a role in life today as it did formerly. On the basis of data obtained from Gallup Polls in 1957 and 1968, some scholars of religion believe that the United States is moving rapidly into a post-Christian era. Data suggest that the churches no longer provide the meaning and psychic comfort they used to. While the vast majority express belief in life after death and in the devil, there is a marked increase in the number of those who no longer hold such beliefs (Hertel, Bradley, & Nelson, 1974).

Individual testimony. Here several middle-aged people indicate what religion means to them.

> A great deal. It always has been and always will be of most importance in my life.

> Religion is a major part of my life. It means more today than when I was younger. Your problems are fewer and your outlook is entirely different when you are younger.

> A small part—less than the past. I feel at present that I am on trial. I feel better at times when I look around me and see some of my friends enjoying life with their husbands.

> Religion is a big part. To live content and to find happiness, one must have faith; more now than ever before.

> It has never meant anything at all, except negatively. I was compelled to go to Sunday School as a child and I hated it. I gave up any idea of God at about the time I found out there was no Santa Claus—they were both just fantasies of early childhood. However, I am certain that religion contributes a great deal to many people—and I fully respect other people's religious beliefs.

SUMMARY

Middle age is a somewhat fluid concept. Over time it changes as society revises its image of what people in these years are like. What are now the middle years in the United States were once the later years for most of the population. This is still true in certain countries. The middle agers' self-image reflects both society's notion of what people at this stage are like, and personal experiences with aging.

The middle years have their own special significance. Life's goals are often redefined after the strains of childrearing and vocational competition are nearing an end and preparation for retirement is being made. They are years of accomplishment, and change between the earlier and later phases. The younger middle-ager is a doer who controls society and serves as advocate for children, youth, and the very old.

In later middle age, adults re-evaluate their goals and life styles. They may not have achieved all their vocational objectives, but they are resigned, even relieved, that the struggle is over, and these years are often their best. They often settle back and enjoy a less hectic, fuller life.

In terms of both mental and personality characteristics, middle agers fare well. They are no longer considered to be victims of the inevitable but slow decline in mental powers. While they may not learn or respond as speedily as younger people, their experience often more than compensates for whatever decline may occur. To what degree their mental prowess declines or improves depends largely on the quality of their experience over the years.

Middle agers' personalities depend on the interaction of their genetic makeup with all their experience to date. Hence personality is more an individual matter than a reflection of how long someone has lived. Nevertheless since people at any stage in life do share the rewards and strains of that stage, they may display certain similar behaviors. For example, the so-called mellowing of the middle years may result from no longer having to be concerned with childrearing and status seeking. Since life experiences vary according to subcultures of sex, race, and social class, personalities at middle age will likewise vary.

Middle-aged peoples' morals and values, too, are based on foundations built up over the years. Since they have by now tested themselves in many situations, their values have stabilized somewhat. Nevertheless regressions or progressions can still occur, depending upon the stability of one's life and an individual's continued capacity to grow.

Whatever religious views people have when they emerge into adulthood, they usually retain, in broad outline, into middle age. While the middle aged today are not as overtly religious as were their forebears, most of them profess that religion is important in their lives. While research on this topic is inadequate, it is clear that people vary greatly in their religious views and practices.

SUGGESTED READINGS

Alpaugh, P. K. & Birren, J. E. Are there sex differences in creativity across the adult life span? *Human Development*, 1975, *18*, 461–465. This study was designed to examine sex differences of young, middle-aged, and older adults, in creative problem solving, and to determine the significance of sex-role identification in order to account for such differences. The degree of sex-role identification was found not to relate significantly to creativity.

Arlin, P. K. Cognitive development in adulthood: A fifth stage? *Developmental Psychology*, 1975, *11* (5), 602–606. Recent investigations of the Piagetian stage of formal operations are cited to suggest that progressive, consistent changes may extend beyond this level. Two formal stages are operationally defined: the problem-solving stage of formal operations as proposed by Piaget, and a problem-finding stage.

Baltes, P. B. & Schaie, K. W. On the plasticity of intelligence in adulthood and old age. *American Psychologist*, 1976, *31*, 720–725. While these writers do not entirely reject the idea of intellectual decline in adulthood, they stress plasticity, or flexibility, as it is manifested in individual differences, multidimensionality, and directionality of intellect, and the significance of cohort-related effects.

Brim, O. G. Theories of the male mid-life crisis. *Counseling Psychologist*, 1976, *6* (1), 2–9. After reviewing the literature, Brim takes issue with the prevailing view that little of consequence transpires in the male personality during middle age. Certain middle-life transitions over a 10- to 20-year period, involving goals, endocrine changes, stagnation-versus-growth, confrontation with death, family relationships, and role and social changes, are examined. The available data failed to support the notion of age-specific crises. Instead transitions may involve crisis when they are accompanied by numerous simultaneous demands for personality change.

Craig, G. J. *Human development*. Englewood Cliffs, N.J.: Prentice-Hall, Inc., 1976. See chapter 20, "The Middle Years of Adulthood: Continuity and Change," for a discussion of this period as a developmental stage of midlife crises, biological continuity and change, and theories of adult development.

Davitz, J. & Davitz, L. *Making it from 40 to 50*. New York: Random House, Inc., 1976. A husband-wife team reports the results of their research and interviews with over 200 middle-class women and men, often providing first-person anecdotal material regarding their everyday feelings and behavior.

Hertel, B. R., & Hart, M. N. Are we entering a post Christian era? Religious belief and attendance in America. 1957–1968. *Journal for the Scientific Study of Religion*, 1974, *13* (4), 409–419. One may wonder what may take the place of religion to support the morale of adults in distress in the post-Christian era. According to Gallup Polls taken in 1957 and 1968, there was a marked increase in the proportion of Americans who disbelieved in life after death and the devil, although the vast majority still believed. Church attendance has declined among believers as well as disbelievers, which suggests that churches no longer provide the psychic comfort they did in the past.

Horn, J. L., & Donaldson, G. On the myth of intellectual decline in adulthood. *American Psychologist*, 1976, *31* (10), 701–719. After exploring the popular hypothesis that intellectual decrements relating to age are a myth, the writers conclude that such a view may stem from faulty research and wishful thinking.

Levinson, D. J., et al. Periods in the adult development of men: Ages 18 to 45. *Counseling Psychologist*, 1976, *6* (1), 21–25. Through comparisons of biographical data obtained from 40 35- to 45-year-old men during interviews and a follow-up session two years later, six developmental periods were identified despite the high diversity of the individual biographies.

Majeres, R. L. Semantic connotations of the words adolescent, teenager, and youth. *Journal of Genetic Psychology*, 1976, *129* (1), 57–62. A study of attitudes of 38 9th and 10th graders, 53 college students, and 30 28- to 56-year-old adults toward the words "youth," "adolescent," "teenager," and "adult," indicated relative attitudes toward youth and adults and the degree to which such attitudes resemble common stereotypes of youth.

Ryff, C. D., & Baltes, P. B. Value transition and adult development in women: The instrumentality-terminally sequence hypothesis. *Developmental Psychology*, 1976, *12* (6), 567–568. A study of 57 middle-aged, and 62 older women (mean ages 43.1 and 70.4 years respectively), based on data from the Rokeach Value Survey, indicate certain differences in values according to age group. The findings also revealed the existence of self-acknowledged transitional reorganizational phases in adult years.

Simmons, H. C. Theory and practice in religion and education: II. The quiet journey: Psychological development and religious growth from ages thirty to sixty. *Religious Education*, 1976, *71* (2), 132–142. Data are presented regarding the adult years as a transition from major concern with external events to developing an inner life, including faith, feelings of self-worth, and typical crises from the ages of 30 to 60. Religious faith is perceived as part of the meaning system of the adult years.

6
CHAPTER

Physical
and
Mental
Health

PHYSICAL CONDITION AT MIDDLE AGE

Aspects of Physical Aging

Physical aging is basic to all aspects of the aging process (Palmore, 1974). It involves a progressive "decline in physiologic competence that inevitably increases and intensifies the effects of accidents, disease, and other forms of environmental stress" (Timiras, 1972, p. 465). Such changes are most commonly associated with old age, but are already apparent in middle years. The changes described below are typical; however, the physical condition of middle-aged adults, like that of people of all ages, varies greatly.

Height and strength. These kinds of changes are easily recognized. Most people arrive at their full height by adulthood, although some reach it in their early teens and others in their 20s. Maximum strength is usually attained sometime between the ages of 25 and 30, after which there is a slow but steady decline, perhaps 10% between the ages of 30 and 60. Much of the loss of strength is in the leg and back muscles, and less in the arm muscles. Exercise can help to retain, even to restore, strength to muscles that have not been used for a while; and individuals can keep up their strength in later years by exercising regularly. For some people muscle tone declines greatly in their 20s, and for others not until their 70s (Timiras, 1972).

The senses. All body systems, including the senses, become less efficient over the years. There are lens changes in the eye that occur over the years. Increasing numbers of people require corrective lenses, and by age 50 almost everyone has at least a pair of reading glasses (Timiras, 1972). With regard to taste there is little change up to age 60. The number of taste buds decreases from about 250 for young adults to fewer than 100 in 70-year-olds. For men the decrease begins between ages 50 to 60 and for women, from 40 to 55. A study of subjects aged 15 to 89, indicated a sharp decrease after 60 in terms of experiencing particular taste sensations. The ability to taste sweet substances was the first to be affected. Nevertheless food complaints of older persons, especially those in institutions, do not relate to taste receptors so much as to particular food preferences and emotional attitudes (Bischof, 1976).

Both speech and hearing change somewhat with age. As the voice-producing apparatus ages, the vocal chords lose their elasticity, and the ability to speak clearly diminishes (Botwinick, 1973). Plentiful evidence indicates that hearing declines with age. In general the ability to discriminate between high and low sounds begins to decrease at about age 25, continues to decrease gradually until about 55, and after that, drops more sharply. All adults hear more poorly as they age, and high frequency tones are heard more poorly than lower ones (Marsh & Thompson, 1973).

Physical Disorders

Heart ailments. Heart conditions are especially common in middle age. In fact, high blood pressure or hypertension affects approximately 22 million Americans and plays a direct role in the deaths of at least 60,000 women and men each year, most of them in their 50s. Glass (1976) differentiates between persons who are or are not candidates for heart attacks. Type A persons, who are likely to have heart attacks, are competitive, feel time pressure, and react to frustrations with hostility. They set deadlines for themselves, which Type B people do much less often. Type A people bring work home, while Type B's do not. Type A's push themselves a lot, while Type B's take it easy. The Type A's earn greater rewards, but at a larger cost to the body.

Middle-aged men are far more susceptible to heart attacks than women. For that reason much of the research about heart disease involves men. In one study of men aged 39 to 59, those who were aggressive, competitive, ambitious, and restless were especially prone to coronary collapse. Those who were relaxed, patient, and unconcerned with high achievement were apparently immune from coronary disease, despite such high-risk factors as family problems, smoking, and lack of exercise (McQuade, 1972).

Illness. Respiratory illnesses are the most acute ones for people of all ages. After about age 45 heart disease, high blood pressure, and arthritis begin to increase. Other conditions such as diabetes, chronic bronchitis, asthma, and hay fever do not increase consistently after 45 or 50 (Kimmel, 1974). The leading chronic conditions, and the sex most prone to them, are as follows: "diseases of heart, male; arthritis and rheumatism, female; lower extremity impairments, male; back spine impairments, male; mental and nervous conditions, female; hypertension without heart involvement, female; visual impairments, male; asthma, male" (Verbrugge, 1975, p. 401).

Of course the status of illness in adulthood will change as medical and biochemical breakthroughs occur. Between 35 and 55, males have a higher incidence of internal clotting. Testosterone, a male hormone, increases the chance of high blood pressure, while the female hormone estrogen suppresses it. Estelle Ramey believes that ways may be found of protecting men from the effects of testosterone without simultaneously interfering with their sexual function (Kolbenschlag, 1976).

Overall Physical Status

General vigor and functioning. Many middle agers enjoy excellent health, chiefly because they have maintained sound health habits over the years. Indeed, overall physical condition declines so gradually that one may hardly be aware of it until many years have passed. After ages 50 to 55, for example, the eyes and teeth may deteriorate more rapidly than muscular strength. Unfortunately these differential aging processes have neither been adequately measured nor researched.

The declining death rate. Generally the health of both young and middle-aged adults has been steadily improving over the years, as we can see from the steadily declining death rates. In the years 1900 to 1975 the death rate declined for ages 25 to 34 from 8.1 to 1.7 per thousand, for

1978 © Sybil Shelton

Maintaining good physical health is a concern during the middle years and exercising regularly helps keep one's strength and muscle tone.

ages 35 to 44 from 10.6 to 3, for ages 45 to 54 from 15.5 to 7.8, for ages 55 to 64 from 28.5 to 20, and for ages 65 to 75 from 59.1 to 45.7. The reduction for the elderly has been even more dramatic: for ages 75 to 84 it has gone from 128.2 to 101.8, and for ages 85 and over, from 269.2 to 184.2. Since deaths from accidents, especially automobile accidents, have sharply increased during this same period, the decline in nonaccidental deaths is even more dramatic (Golenpaul, 1977).

Sex differences in longevity, illness, and disease. Females have higher illness rates, but die later, than males, and the greater female longevity (life span) is increasing (Verbrugge, 1975). The reason for this discrepancy in womens' illnesses and longevity may lie partly in the distinction between clinical (illness as diagnosed) and social (illness as experienced) definitions of illness. While there is some overlapping of the two, it may not be high. Verbal statements about illness reflect both an individual's attitudes and other such factors as social status and education. For one thing, females are apparently more willing to report ailments and are more sensitive to body discomfort, while males are taught to ignore their symptoms and simply continue as usual when they are ill. There are fewer women than men in the labor force, so they may be more prone to recognize and take care of lesser illnesses. Indeed, employed females report less illness and disability than do unemployed ones, perhaps because they have less time to be ill. On the other hand, they may simply be psychologically healthier, and hence less prone to illnesses of psychosomatic origin.

On the other hand, not all differences in illness between the sexes are a matter of social definition. Undoubtedly, males have a greater chance of getting sick or being injured because of their jobs. They also tend to drink, smoke, and drive more than females. That is, their life style is associated with more occupational hazards and causes of chronic diseases. In addition, females may have greater resistance to degenerative diseases because they are protected by estrogen (Moriyamo, 1968). Certainly the higher rate of prenatal deaths and birth defects among men suggests that they are inherently less resistant to disease than females. In short, it may be that males "are physically sicker from both acute and chronic conditions, but . . . social and psychological factors enhance females' reports to such an extent that" they appear to be sick more often than men (Verbrugge, 1975, p. 399).

Another important factor also inflates the statistics for adult females. Whenever crises, major or minor, arise within the home, whether it be the husband's or child's illness or any other emergency, it is usually the employed woman rather than the employed man who remains at home. In such circumstances the simplest way to get time off the job is to take sick days. Verbrugge did not take this factor into account.

It is uncertain to what extent the female's tendency to take it easy and seek medical help when feeling ill may increase longevity. This kind of behavior may not only help women to recuperate from a sickness; it may also slow the progression of more acute and chronic conditions. By utilizing available health services women have a better chance of early diagnosis and treatment of serious conditions. Even if females do have a higher incidence than males of certain conditions, their tendency to take time off for illness may transform a short-run disadvantage (losing time on the job) into a long-run benefit (a longer life), but this hypothesis would be hard to test.

Still, womens' tendency to give in more often to illness may have certain negative outcomes. For one thing, as we mentioned, women are less productive on the job, whether at home or at the work place. Female medical costs are higher than those for males, even excluding conditions relating to childbirth. Also, the way people feel about their health relates to the way they feel about the quality of their lives. Among middle-aged persons, in fact, the way they rate their health correlates more highly than any other variable with life satisfaction (Palmore & Luikart, 1972). It would appear, therefore, that females experience a less satisfying life with regard to health. This suggests to us that it is important to determine the ways in which female roles and socialization influence perceptions of their own illnesses.

Individual Reaction to Own Health

In middle age most adults feel that their health is reasonably good, and they have their own informal and varied ways of maintaining it. Here several individuals answer the question, "How good is your health, and what do you do to preserve it?"

I'd say my health was pretty good except for the usual aches and pains that come with old age (*Female, age 51*)

Yes, [it's good], except for arthritis. [I] watch my diet, keep active. (*Female, age 54*)

Fairly good. [I] visit the doctor, [get] plenty of exercise, rest, [have] good eating habits. (*Female, age 43*)

Yes [,it is good. I do] all the wrong things. Smoke too much. Eat too much. I am grateful for good health. (*Female, age 61*)

I am in good health. I take vitamins daily and am fairly active. My health currently is not of major concern. (*Female, age 41*)

[My health is] fair. [I care for myself by] rest and doctoring. Yes, I am concerned as I have always been real active and ambitious. Now arthritis in my feet has slowed me considerably, as well as other minor ailments. Its hard to slow down as I have always hurried. I never want to be a burden to anyone. (*Female, age 53*)

I have good health. I take exercise. (*Male, age 55*)

Yes [,I am healthy]. I try to eat right—that is, a lot of roughage with bran. I take setting up exercises every morning. I drink only an occasional glass of wine and do not smoke. Consequently I feel good most of the time. My careful diet and daily exercise probably take me out of the average life style category. (*Male, age 53*)

Awareness of aging. Perhaps one of the first ways that people become aware of their own physical aging is that those who suffer from heart disease and cancer are not simply old people but also their own contemporaries. As a result, death and illness become less impersonal. Another reminder of passing years is gradual physical deterioration. More often than their wives, men develop ulcers, poor hearing, bad eyes, and even diseased gums (Berland, 1970). Middle-aged individuals also experience a jolt when they recognize the gap between themselves and youth, often as a result of quite casual episodes, sometimes merely from gazing at themselves in the bathroom mirror (McMorrow, 1974).

TOPICS OF SPECIAL CURRENT INTEREST

The Climacteric

The female climacteric. In recent years much attention has been focused on certain physical phenomena of middle age, among them the climacteric. While the climacteric is a normal physical process, it can be a cause of stress. Since most people associate the climacteric with menopause, they believe it applies only to women. But many professionals feel it also happens to men. While menopause refers to the permanent cessation of menstruation due to aging, climacteric is a broader term which includes a complex of physical and emotional changes. Technically speaking, the term climacteric, but not menopause, is applicable to men, although the two terms are often used synonymously (Katchadourian, 1976).

Females follow the same general pattern of sexual maturing and decline. They are born with several hundred thousand ova, which begin maturing at puberty. About 300 to 400 cycles later, ovulation becomes quite erratic and finally stops. The period of menopause, which marks the end of ovulation, generally occurs around the age of 47, although it can occur before 45 and after 50. The cessation of ovulation results in infertility and decreased levels of estrogen. As the levels of estrogen go down, they no longer counter or offset the masculinizing effects of androgen, which continues to be produced by the adrenal cortex. In consequence a woman's voice becomes lower and her face hairier. The reproductive system atrophies. Other symptoms which may accompany the climacteric include headaches, dizziness, joint pains, palpitations, and hot flashes. While practically all women experience such symptoms in menopause, only about one in ten is significantly disturbed by them. Nevertheless menopause need not produce either sexual dysfunction or apathy. In fact some women become more erotically responsive, perhaps because of the effects of androgen as well as because they are no longer concerned about the possibility of pregnancy.

In terms of overall psychological effects, women are highly variable. Some of them report practically no disturbance, while others experience a good deal. Probably some women's discomfort is a result of their own expectations that stress at this time is inevitable. Other women may feel somehow less feminine after the menopause. Still others lead such busy active lives that disturbance is minimal, and has almost no effect on their lives.

It is easy to exaggerate the effects of the menopausal period. After comparing the behavior of middle-class women with that of their husbands through two menstrual cycles, Alice J. Dan found no more overall variability in women's than in men's behavior. That is, the men too had their peaks and depressions. While the women's ups and downs related somewhat to the time between the end of one period and ovulation for the next, neither sex proved any more erratic or unpredictable than the other. Nor did Dan find any support for the common belief that there are behavioral deficiencies in women at any special time of the month ("Menstrual myths," 1977).

The male climacteric. The male climacteric is a somewhat vague concept, for the male reproductive function does not ordinarily diminish as abruptly as it does for females. Only in rare cases does the male climacteric involve symptoms such as hot flashes. More often there is a gradual decline in testicular function along with diminished fertility and potency, beginning in middle age. On the other hand males can remain sexually active, and sometimes even fertile, into old age. For both sexes, more direct tactile stimulation in sex is required; and putting the penis into the vagina is physiologically more difficult because the penis is less rigid, the vaginal opening smaller, and there is less vaginal lubrication. Achieving orgasm also takes longer, and it may be less intense than before. Thus sexual activity changes but does not cease.

Therapy. Problems associated with the climacteric have been approached both psychologically and physically. In years past estrogen was often administered to women in order to ease the biological changes and stresses of the climacteric. However, hormonal replacements are coming under increasing criticism because of the potentially dangerous side effects. It is also of "dubious value for males" (Katchadourian, 1976, p. 44). Both sexes may sometimes profit from psychological counseling at this time.

Mastectomies

An operation which has gained considerable publicity in recent years, especially because it was openly discussed by Happy Rockefeller and Betty Ford, is mastectomy, or the removal of a cancerous breast. Three researchers at the University of California questioned 41 women who had had mastectomies during the previous two years. Almost all the women had experienced the greatest emotional difference immediately after discovering the lump. The majority had talked little with their husbands about their problems. A quarter of the women admitted that they thought about suicide after the mastectomy, a third used more tranquilizers, a sixth drank more, and another sixth consulted psychiatrists. On the other hand, two-thirds of the women rated their adjustment to the operation as excellent or very good, and another quarter of them as good. For their part, nearly half of the husbands reported trouble sleeping, a quarter of them experienced a loss of appetite, and almost half had problems with work, because of their wives' operations. About a quarter of the women found sexual adjustment harder than before, but the others reported no difference. Almost two years after the operation, 20% of the men had not seen their wives unclothed, often at the women's request. The women themselves told the researchers that the men's responses varied greatly, from complete reassurance to repulsion. In general a couple's relationship before the operation was the best index to their subsequent adjustment ("The emotional pain of mastectomy," 1977).

Alcohol, Drugs, and Cigarettes

Alcohol. Too little attention has been paid to the problems of drinking, smoking, and pill-taking in adults, except for the most extreme cases. Alcohol can be especially troublesome, marijuana is the drug of the young, and alcohol, that of adulthood. While most people aged 50 to 70 drink less than younger people, it is unclear whether this difference relates to age. It could simply be a generational effect. That is, today's youth may drink more heavily in later years than older people do now, because of youth's changed drinking patterns.

In order to dilate the arterial-venous system, some physicians prescribe a certain amount of alcohol (often wine) for their older patients. Others caution against this, believing that it is addictive (Zimberg, 1974). In any case, as many as nine million Americans may be alcoholics, and alcoholism is certainly among the nation's most serious health problems (Butler, 1975b).

Drugs. Addictive drugs are dangerous because they require increasing dosages if they are to have any real effect, and withdrawal from them produces physiological and psychological stress. Such effects do not ordinarily accompany the use of such nonaddictive drugs as aspirin. Drug addiction is more prevalent among young adults, especially those in large urban and suburban centers, because drugs are more available in the big cities. There is some decrease in drug use after young adults marry, especially after they have children (Henley & Adams, 1973). In general such usage was a phenomenon of the Viet Nam War period. There have been significant decreases since then, partly as a result of better treatment programs (Harris, 1973). Consider, too, that the long-term use of addictive drugs reduces longevity, whether because of general bodily deterioration, overdoses, or suicide. Hence there are few heavy drug users in the older age group (Capel et al., 1972).

The worst form of drug addiction among adults is excessive or unwise pill-taking, and this trend is increasing. Among the most popular pills are tranquilizers, which are widely prescribed. Since little is known about their long-term effects, these habits might prove hazardous.

Smoking. The effect of cigarette smoking on health is, to some extent, controversial. Most authorities stress its relationship to poor health and longevity, especially when combined with such factors as overweight and inactivity. A minority say that this is not proof, and observe that genetic factors provide the disposition toward cancer. They believe that smoking simply constitutes a precipitating factor. Certainly lung cancer is more common in some families than others. Moreover since smoking satisfies certain needs, people who stop may instead become victims of hypertension or overweight (Botwinick, 1973). Attempts to reduce or eliminate overeating, smoking, and drinking have at best a 50% chance of success, regardless of the program used, be it group therapy, hypnosis, or whatever (Bischof, 1976).

A Brief Comment

In concluding this discussion of adults' physical health a few general observations are in order. (1) To focus on reducing adult illness and disease is not sufficient. It is essential not only to maintain one's health, but to assure that it is good enough to support a rewarding life style. (2) Because of constant medical and biochemical advances, the public should be more effectively educated so that it can make better use of the newly emerging knowledge. (3) Peoples' knowledge about health should become better integrated with other kinds of information so that they can adjust their lives accordingly. For example, what are the hazards to family nutrition when both partners work? In many cases childless couples develop haphazard eating habits. Or one might ask, what is the relationship of stress to drug use? Are present-day tensions so great that popping tranquilizers is becoming a serious form of drug abuse? (4) Exercise is an especially important factor because it improves strength and the circulation to cardiac muscles. Exercising the leg muscles facilitates the flow of blood to the heart, which indirectly improves body function in all areas, including the brain (Timiras, 1972). Yet what may be good for one individual or group in terms of climate, exercise, and diet may be poor for others. (5) There should be health education even for children, so that they are aware of how to take care of themselves throughout their lives. This is a real challenge, since younger people characteristically focus on the here and now. As longitudinal data clarify the long-term effects of various health habits and remedies, such information should become a part of health instruction at all levels.

EMOTIONAL HEALTH

Emotionally Healthy Behavior

Criteria. There is no generally agreed-upon formula for what constitutes emotionally healthy behavior. Smithson (1974) gives these criteria: being independent, and having the ability to accept reality, adapt to change, respond sensitively to others, and handle feelings of hostility. Emotionally healthy persons are distinguished by other characteristics as well.

> They accept their right to be human and enjoy life. They express normal anger or fear without feeling guilty about it. They control their emotions, rather than being controlled by them. They experience inner

freedom derived from confidence in their ability to utilize emotions properly. Emotionally healthy individuals can express feeling in whatever gradation is appropriate. If doors are stuck, they do not smash them down. Such individuals keep things in perspective and do not constantly seek molehills to make into mountains (Rogers, 1977, p. 108).

The optimum state of tension. Emotional health does not imply a state of zero tension or stress. Individuals can feel under considerable pressure and yet be relatively satisfied with the quality of their lives. Conversely the individual who feels little stress may sometimes not feel satisfied with life. In one study of stress (Campbell, 1975b), widows and widowers whose lives were generally unsatisfying, nevertheless reported feeling the least pressure. Married couples with small children reported more happiness than singles, but also felt the largest amount of stress of any of the groups questioned.

Hans Selye (1974) distinguishes between stress and distress. Stress is "the nonspecific response of the body to any demand made on it . . . any kind of normal activity—a game of chess or even a passionate embrace—can produce considerable stress without causing harmful effects. Damaging or unpleasant stress is distress" (p. 43). In order to prevent the transformation of stress into distress, people should not be engaged for too long in stressful activities. It is the stress of frustration rather than that of hard muscular work which produces disease, including migraine headaches, high blood pressure, peptic ulcers, and even back pains. Finally, all individuals have an optimum stress level, and they must find out what it is for themselves.

Common Middle-aged Problems

Unusual responsibilities. Certain stresses are especially characteristic of middle age. Adults make and carry out the major decisions of the world, so middle age may be full of strains and competing pressures. If responsibility is too great, the temptation may be to overcompensate in the other direction until the pressure dissolves.

Adults are also in control at home, and sandwiched between the demands of youth and the needs of the aged, the middle-aged person often reports feeling "caught, pressed, squeezed" (Kerckhoff, 1976, p. 6). In fact, contrary to the common assumption that the adult in early middle age is happier than the one in later middle age, parents whose children have left home are happier than those whose children are still with them.

Impending old age and changing physical image. Certain other problems relate directly or indirectly to the coming of old age. There are increasing physical disabilities in addition to such concerns as making certain that enough money has been saved for the years ahead. There is also the problem of adjusting both to one's own aging physical image, and others' perceptions of that image. Some individuals almost panic; others who have long since learned to accept rather than deny the inevitable, accept it, often with a sense of humor. One 62-year-old man, upon being shown a picture that his son had made of him on vacation, jokingly asked, "Who is that old man?"

In general those individuals who derive feelings of self-worth from their bodies—among them athletes and beautiful women—are more devastated by their changing appearance than those who base their feelings of self-worth on other criteria. People who take special pride in their strength or looks will begin aging psychologically as soon as they perceive their bodies aging; while those whose self-concept depends on nonphysical characteristics such as intelligence or vocational competence, may feel young until relatively late in life. In some cases, the former try desperately to remain young-looking (Troll, 1975).

Whatever our own image of ourselves, we must also cope with the image that we create in the eyes of others. In one study of physical image (Adams & Huston, 1975), a sample of young adults whose mean age was 24.7 years, and older females whose mean age was 66.3, were shown six pictures of males and females aged 48 to 52, six pictures of very attractive men and women (three of each sex), and six of unattractive people (also three of each sex). The subjects were then asked to rate the persons in the pictures according to what appeared to be their honesty, level of self-esteem, amount of social ability, and other factors. In general, physical attractiveness appeared to be of considerable significance in many ways. The physically attractive, as compared to the physically unattractive, middle-aged persons were judged to be more socially desirable, to have attained a higher occupational status, to possess higher self-esteem, to be more socially outgoing, and to provide more pleasant companionship. The physically unattractive females were ascribed a lower vocational rank than their more attractive female peers, or than the physically unattractive males; and the physically unattractive females were perceived as having lower self-esteem than the physically unattractive males. On the other hand, the attractive females were perceived as possessing self-esteem equal to the attractive males. The older women stereotyped the middle-aged persons in terms of pleasantness, honesty, and being socially outgoing, in a more favorable fashion than did the young adults. The young adults, as compared with the elderly, did not have a greater tendency to look favorably on middle-aged females as compared with their middle-aged male peers (Adams & Huston, 1975).

Issues relating to vocation. The middle aged also experience vocational problems, which will be discussed in greater detail in a later chapter. Another major source of stress is making a living in a competitive society. To a large degree because it is approved and encouraged by the society, most adults endlessly struggle to improve their financial position, even after they are well off. Often vocational stress is a factor in physical problems, depression, and excessive drinking (Kiev, 1974). People at middle age may also go through a period of indecision as to whether they should retire. They may feel the impatience of younger workers to push them out. For instance, when the State University of New York ran short of funds in 1976, older faculty members were individually called to determine whether they were planning to retire—thereby receiving an unsubtle hint.

Sex-related problems. Other problems in middle age relate to sex, pregnancy, and menopause (Kisker, 1974). Extramarital sex may cause stress, though less than it did formerly because of changing attitudes and the pill. Pregnancy and childbirth may also produce stress, and the incidence of mental illness following this period is relatively high (Cohler et al, 1975). In some cases psychological instability occurs during pregnancy, and in other cases, after childbirth.

Stress may also be connected with abortion, particularly among women with ambivalent feelings about it. Problems also are relatively greater when there is a prior history of illness or suicidal behavior (Marmer, Pasnau, & Cushner, 1974). If the pregnancy was unwanted the consequences are less damaging (Adler, 1975). If social attitudes are negative, or the woman's desire to keep the child is strong, the experience can be very upsetting. Spontaneous abortion, too, can be very stressful, and accompanied by feelings of inferiority, inadequacy, and guilt ("What did I do to bring it on?", 1977).

Health-related problems. Another threat to happiness is ill health, especially from late middle age on. In early adult years one may have an acute illness or an occasional need for surgery. The potential for more chronic disorders increases with age. In case of surgery the part of the body affected is especially important. Anxiety is unusually great when it involves the eyes or vital organs, especially the heart. Reactions to open-heart surgery include hallucinations, delirium, and mood disorders (Braceland, 1974). Gynecological operations may also prove traumatic. For example, removal of the uterus is associated with a loss of femininity. Those women who deliberately choose hysterectomy as a means to avoid pregnancy show few, if any, negative symptoms; but women who have experienced therapeutic abortions may show signs of depression and an impaired concept of their femininity.

Extent of Dissatisfaction

Relevant research. Even when middle-aged subjects report satisfaction with their lives, a closer analysis may reveal a somewhat different picture. In research by Lowenthal and Chiriboga (1972), middle-aged men reported considerable satisfaction with sex and marriage in middle years, although their wives reported less frequency and satisfaction in sex activity. The men seemed to be either reluctant to report negative circumstances, or were repressing them.

Similarly Cuber and Harroff (1965), in a study of upper-middle-class Americans from 35 to 50, reported widespread cynicism and disillusion. During long in-depth interviews they often rationalized away unpleasant aspects of their lives, both with regard to their self-concepts and maintaining a front before others. Often they were involved in marriages which they described as lacking in vitality and conflict-ridden. Nevertheless husbands insisted that their marital situations are reasonably satisfying, although their wives were more inclined to describe them as disappointing. A survey of other studies suggests that the male's apparent calm may be a cover for more serious interpersonal difficulties.

Individual testimony. Individually middle agers report quite varied problems, as indicated by these answers to the question: "What are the most serious problems that you face at the current stage of your life?"

> Trying to save enough so that when I retire I won't have to depend on my children. (*Female, age 54*)

> I don't feel I have any serious problems. Or maybe at this age I have learned things work out. (*Female, age 61*)

> Old age. (*Female, age 46*)

> Health problems; it seems that since I reached 50 years of age, I have many ailments. (*Female, age 53*)

> Trying to sort out from my many life goals those most worth doing; I've roughly a couple of thousand years' of projects in mind and somewhat less time than that for doing them. (*Female, age 62*)

Lack of energy. I do not experience financial problems. We live within our means. No foolish spending. (*Male, age 55*)

The struggle to make both ends meet. (*Male, age 63*)

The Midlife Crisis

Conflicting evidence. Life is often portrayed as involving a series of crises which, because there are aspects of human development and the environment common to most people, are presumably shared by those people at similar periods in life. Most observers agree that a certain midlife change, sometimes called a crisis, occurs, although they differ about when it occurs. Levinson (1978) speaks of a crisis in the late 30s or early 40s, Neugarten (1964), in the 50s, and Lowenthal and Chiriboga (1972), in the 60s. Some observers portray the crisis as involving a reevaluation of one's life pattern, while others describe it as a decrease in life-satisfaction and the ability to cope. Some of them believe this period to be temporary, others see it as a time of irreversible decision.

Rosenberg and Farrell (1976) feel that the middle-aged male undergoes crises that are intensified by demands made on him by the outside world. At the same time he has to be a role model for his maturing children, who are having identity conflicts like his. While his own physical strength is declining he is reaching the height of his personal and social power. On the job, in the community, and in his family he is expected to demonstrate a commitment and strength appropriate to his status. He cannot give expression to his conflicting feelings about arriving at middle age, because that would threaten his own stability. At the same time his own father is getting older, losing his status, and giving up his dominant roles in family and society. The middle-aged son now assumes the status of a patriarch. He is the family head in the eyes of the larger culture, and "the rock" which supports the family network. This new role symbolizes the standard against which his adequacy is measured by both himself and others. At one time he may have desired to outdo his father; but now that he is actually on top, his "victory" holds no meaning for him. By now his father arouses his sympathy, so that any enjoyment the son might feel at his own success is tinged with guilt. Now that he is in a position of control he feels weak if he admits feeling vulnerable, or if he leans on others. Thus like an adolescent, a middle-aged man is "confronted by biological, status, and role changes" that makes him try to redefine who he is. Unlike the adolescents, he is not allowed to take time off to explore these questions. "Instead, he is more constrained than ever by expectations of others, his obligations to them and his concern for his already established identity, which is . . . known, if not entirely satisfactory . . . " (Rosenberg & Farrell, 1976, p. 165). Meantime, "by reaffirming those values by which he has lived, the middle-aged male can both justify himself and support normative integration." This permits him to "retain symbolic potency" to compensate for his "declining physical and emotional vigor." (p. 168).

By contrast, in their study of middle-aged San Francisco couples Lowenthal and Chiriboga (1972) found no evidence of midlife crisis. While many of them indeed had critical problems, they appeared to be a continuation of past ones rather than new developments. For the most part these couples felt considerable relief after the youngest child left home, and when asked to name the most significant turning points of their lives, most often mentioned such life events as completing their education, obtaining their first job or a better job, getting married, and having children. None of the men, but some of the women, also named beginning to date, meeting their future mate, or perhaps having an affair. Few of either sex mentioned economic depression or war. Some of the women, but none of the men, named separation from others because of illness or death, moving, or getting divorced as important turning points, and a few women named the children's leaving home. More of the women than the men perceived these turning points negatively, but women report more stress than men anyhow. This sex difference may exist partly because it is less acceptable for men to admit that there is anything wrong with their mental health. Or it may be that women's life roles are less healthy (Bernard, 1973).

With regard to his San Francisco subjects Lowenthal (1972) decided that adults' reactions to stress can be predicted from their earlier life styles. Those who have been strongly directed toward a goal, may experience a temporary period of lowered morale while they are reestablishing new goals. Those who are somewhat defensive and self-protective may remain somewhat detached from others so that they can continue to protect themselves.

The meaning of midlife crisis. In addition to conflicting evidence regarding the prevalence of midlife crisis, it is also unclear what the significance of such a crisis is. At best, it can be liberating, for it allows a person "to take a fresh look at himself and his environment and emerge with a kind of wisdom, maturity and insight which are beyond the grasp of youthful capacity. At worst, the crisis is kept from becoming fully conscious and results in destructiveness toward both the self and others." Attitudes may become more rigid and people may feel a "dominating need for others to confirm the very mode of being that is experienced as painful" (Rosenberg & Farrell, 1976, p. 157).

Factors that Relate to Mental Health

Sex and marital status. Different kinds of adults vary both in terms of life satisfaction and mental health. There is usually, but not always, a positive relationship between the two. Some individuals who report satisfaction, nevertheless lead very dull, unself-fulfilling lives. They may have developed defense mechanisms that make them blind to their own deficiencies or the emptiness of their lives. For example, married women express greater satisfaction than single women, but single women are emotionally healthier. Women also describe their lives as no less satisfying than men do, yet mental-health surveys indicate that women are unhealthier mentally than men. They have a greater incidence of mental illness of all kinds, from depression to suicidal tendencies. In terms of reported life satisfaction, at least, married people of both sexes, with or without children, fare better than the unmarried, widowed, or divorced (Campbell, 1975).

The emotional health of housewives depends chiefly on the women's own personalities, goals, and individual situations. In a study of working-class women near Boston, almost twice as many housewives as working wives were dissatisfied with their lives, and thought their husbands' work was more interesting than theirs. The dissatisfied housewives felt that they hadn't had a fair chance in life and wanted their

The middle years for many married women are satisfying both mentally and physically.

daughters to lead a different life (Ferree, 1976). On the other hand, not all American housewives are unhappy. An important determinant is whether or not the woman wants to work. In a study by Fidell and Prather, many housewives proved healthy, comfortable, and happy in their roles because they did not want to work. They had happy marriages, felt in control of their lives, and had better physical and mental health than working wives. The working wives were less happily married than the fulltime housewives, but felt more competent, and had greater self esteem (Tavris, 1976).

Campbell, Converse, and Rodgers (Campbell, 1975) studied a national sampling of American adults in order to appraise the quality of their lives. Both sexes seemed generally contented. Fewer than one in ten described their lives as miserable, boring, useless, lonely, or empty. One-half believed their lives to be interesting, hopeful, worthwhile, and full. They confessed to experiencing some stress (a fourth felt it almost all the time), frequently about money. Nevertheless in general they were reasonably happy.

Social class. Another factor in mental health is social class. Sheehy (1976) concluded that members of the well-educated middle class have the greatest number of options and the fewest obstacles to choosing their own life styles. They do not have the traditions of the upper class which tend to predetermine their life styles, and which result in a certain inertia. Nor are middle-class persons frustrated by a lack of education and economic disadvantages like lower- or working-class people. On the other hand, all these life options produce greater confusion, and sometimes stress. Thus as they move from one life period to another, there is a greater feeling of flux and a greater chance for human development variation.

It is easy to underestimate the mental health of the lower socioeconomic classes. Among the more affluent strata of society there is comparatively little of the alienation and apathy that working-class people experience (Sheehy, 1976). However, white-collar professionals usually lack the family network that poorer people often rely on for companionship and assistance. Besides, poverty is a relative concept. People who have always lived frugally may not feel as poor as they are perceived to be.

Even within the same social class, mental health will vary according to the type of personality involved. A study of 300 managers ("Coping with stress," 1976) revealed both high- and low-stress types. Among the high-stress groups many had a specific behavior pattern: "excessively competitive, aggressive, hostile and often neglectful of all but job-related aspects of their lives—that is, significantly related to heart disease" (p. 38). The high-stress people dealt with their tensions by working harder. The low-stress men typically used five coping mechanisms: "building resistance by regular sleep and good health habits; keeping work and nonwork life separate; getting exercise; talking things through with on-the-job peers; and withdrawing physically from a situation when necessary" (p. 38). The researchers concluded that the difference between the two groups was "the difference between working smarter and working harder—of changing gears or keeping the foot on the accelerator" (p. 38). The same distinction, of course, could be made in other occupations as well.

Personality characteristics. In another study, Chiriboga and Lowenthal (Horn, 1975) defined the positive and negative personality characteristics which interact to produce a feeling of well or ill being. Positive factors, which they call resources, include such characteristics as self-satisfaction, hope, insight, and competence; while the negative elements, called deficits, include self-criticism, anxiety, hostility, and emotional problems. They tested four groups, including high school seniors, newlyweds, middle-aged parents whose first child was about ready to leave home, and persons within two or three years of retiring. The percentage of those who reported high or low deficits remained pretty constant across the years. The high school seniors were high with regard to both deficits and resources—a "psychologically complex" combination (p. 34). The happiest newlyweds were characterized by many resources and few deficits. The happiest middle-aged persons had few deficits but only moderate resources, while the happiest retirees were low in both deficits and resources. Perhaps, concluded the researchers, when various avenues of self-expression are closed to older people, having a complex personality may become maladaptive, at least from the individual's own perspective. It is possible that complex persons can grow old gracefully in this society, only if they belong to privileged classes, where a variety of options remain open for them.

Age as a factor. Longitudinal studies suggest the limitations involved in attempting to assess mental health on a one-time basis at a particular point in the life cycle. In 1932 researchers from the University of California's Institute of Human Development interviewed 200 11-year-old boys and girls in the San Francisco area (Casady, 1976). They followed them through their junior- and senior-high-school years and studied them again at ages 40 and 50. Of these 200, Livson concentrated on the 45 individuals who appeared psychologically healthiest at 50. Of these well-adjusted people, 14 had been especially stable at both 40 and 50. During adolescence they had followed conventional sex roles and moved smoothly through early and middle adulthood. Most of the women as teenagers had valued warmth and closeness; and as adults they had been family-oriented, warm, gregarious, and charming. The men had been self-controlled adolescents, as males are supposed to be, valued thinking more than feeling, and focused on career achievement. As adults they had valued self-discipline and rationality, qualities that helped them achieve professional success.

The remaining two-thirds, 31 of the 45 under study, had followed a different route. They were somewhat nontraditional, and as teenagers were not in step with society's usual sex roles. Both as teenagers and as young adults they had a more difficult time. The men were sensitive and expressive but had suppressed these presumably feminine traits in order to become self-controlled and ambitious. By age 40 they were more anxious and hostile than more traditional men. They had also overcompensated for their gentleness by becoming power-oriented. However, by age 50 these men had given up acting like the people they were not and had relaxed into being warm and emotional. Meantime the nontraditional females who had sacrificed their intellectual and career interests in order to assume family roles, had also undergone a period of stress. At age 40 they were more psychologically constricted, depressed, and anxious than the well-adjusted traditional women. But by age 50 their intellectuality had revived and they were seeking outlets for expressing their needs for personal realization and accomplishment. The nontraditionals of both sexes were able to be their true selves at 50 because by then the women had dispensed with their mothering duties and the men had arrived at their achievement goals. Or it may be that by then, society's sex norms had relaxed sufficiently that both sexes could be comfortable with themselves.

In any case this study poses two interesting questions. Since a larger number of those following the nontraditional sex pattern attained superior adjustment by age 50 despite social problems in the meantime, might not most individuals profit by following such a pattern? Wouldn't their adjustment have been even better, given a social environment more supportive of flexible sex roles? Many present-day psychologists answer yes to these questions, asserting that freeing people from rigid sex roles and permitting them to be androgynous (*andro* from the Greek for male, and *gyne* from the Greek for female) would produce more flexibility and fewer limitations on what people can do. In other words, observes Beur (1975) "We need a new standard of psychological health for the sexes, one that removes the burden of stereotype and allows people to feel free to express the traits [of both] men and women" (p. 59). The ideal, according to Lee and Gropper (1974), is not to produce masculinized females or feminized males but to let all persons be individuals.

The Status of Mental Health at Middle Age

Overall assessment. Despite the problems and crises we have discussed here, most middle-aged people are reasonably content. For one thing, the large majority have begun to withdraw from activities which they never really cared for anyhow. They modify their style of life in order to be able to do what they consider truly important. Meantime they profit from their past experience, take stock, and develop a healthy perspective (Kerckhoff, 1976).

The years of the 50s are also characterized by stability, despite a certain concern that over half of life is already gone. In their early 40s people feel that their personalities are pretty well stabilized, and between 44 and 50, "with a slight sigh, there is an acceptance of the new ordering of things. Life is even. Not even better, not even worse, but simply even up" (Gould, 1975, p. 78). People now increasingly say, "I try to be satisfied with what I have, and not to think so much about the things I probably won't be able to get" (p. 78). There is a growing concern about health and an acceptance that "I can't do things as well as I used to do" (p. 78). The picture of stabilization is again underscored. People feel less confusion than they did in their young-adult years.

Indeed adults at all ages regard middle-age as the healthiest adult period, except those in the upper class. Cameron (1974) questioned 317 white adults in Detroit regarding generational differences in happiness and then asked them to rate their own degree of life satisfaction. The respondents, regardless of sex or age, believed middle-aged persons aged 40 to 55, to be the happiest; followed by young adults aged 18 to 25; and finally by older people, 65 to 79. Only the wealthier, better-educated subjects disagreed, declaring older persons to be the happiest, perhaps because later years can be satisfying if there is sufficient money. Perhaps most considered the middle years as the happiest because by then "you have life pretty well in hand, while the young are still struggling and the aged have lost most of their reason to live" (p. 64). With regard to feelings about their own happiness there were no important differences between the generations. All age groups believed themselves above average in happiness compared to all other adults. Significantly the better-educated, more affluent subjects reported greater happiness and recognized the true value of their advantages. They realistically viewed money and education as establishing roots to happiness (Cameron, 1975).

It is difficult to reconcile the crises and problems of middle age with evidence of general satisfaction at that age. Often such crises occur on the brink of middle age, and once resolved, a period of calm follows. Besides, the resolution of crisis is growth-producing and personally satisfying. In the developmental sense, crisis is not equivalent to stress, but is rather a critical or significant point in life.

Individual testimony. On the individual level, too, middle-aged adults, with some exceptions, feel reasonably well satisfied with their lives to date. The majority do have certain regrets.

> It's been a very exciting life, socially, and materially better than average. (*Female, age 58*)

> I'm not particularly satisfied with it. I'm sorry I married. (*Female, age 51*)

> I am happy. I'm married and had four beautiful children and eight lovely grandchildren. But I wish I had stopped to smell the roses more often. I also wish I were a more outgoing person. (*Female, age 54*)

> I'm well satisfied; no regrets. (*Male, age 55*)

> I feel that I could have accomplished a lot more in my early adulthood. Young people have far more opportunities today. I spent my first few adult years teaching public school—and that work is so taxing that there's little time or energy left for a really stimulating life. Nor did I feel any real satisfaction with such teaching. I felt I was marking time. (*Female, age 62*)

Here are some responses to the question: Is your feeling about the future one of hope, fear, dread, resignation—or what?

> At times I feel all of these—fear, hope, dread, and resignation. One hopes for the best, fears the worse, dreads the present, but then resigns himself to all. (*Female, age 51*)

> Sometimes fear; but most the time I have hope. (*Female, age 54*)

> The older we get we certainly can't expect things in any area to get better; not health, wealth, or love of life. I don't feel dread or fear and I hope to accept whatever comes with a smile. (*Female, age 61*)

> I think very little about the distant future; when I do, it is vague but optimistic. (*Female, age 41*)

> I fear suffering in sickness. (*Female, age 53*)

> I hope to enjoy my retirement years. (*Male*)

In summary, life satisfaction at middle age is relatively good, although it varies by category and individual. However, such a situation should not obscure the challenge to make life more fulfilling. Becoming satisfied without being mentally healthy can be counterproductive and make one pull away from potentially enriching activities.

PREVENTION AND THERAPY

Commonly Used Techniques

Everyday self-help devices. Certain informal approaches, as distinct from more formally organized ones directly guided by professionals, may serve to upgrade the level of mental health and the quality of life. One of these is facing up to, rather than running away from, reality. Regular exercise is also recommended, especially for the relaxation of tension. In one study a group of women ages 50 to 79, participated in a three-month exercise program which involved jogging, stretching, calesthenics, and other activities. The results indicated that their capacity for training wasn't much different from that of younger individuals (Adams & deVries, 1973). Regular exercise improves body chemistry and muscle tone, which in turn facilitates blood circulation and elimination (DeCarlo, 1974). However, periodic exercise is neither safe nor helpful.

Another important ingredient for good mental health is change, and even crisis, if an individual is to grow (Sheehy, 1976). The alternative is simply to settle back in a rut and dredge up rationalizations that justify having done so. After an individual has weathered life's cycles up to this point, and developed a life style that is truly satisfying, that individual has achieved what Erikson calls integrity. However, getting there may require breaking out of life patterns which have kept a hammerlock on the development of one's best self. Such a step requires awareness that this kind of counterproductive behavior exists, and the courage and persistence to break out of it.

Ways of coping with the inevitable, but continuing, daily tensions may be healthy, unhealthy, or somewhat neutral in effect. For example couples may avoid strife in their daily interaction by such apparently trivial activities as shopping, going to a bar, escaping to home workshops, watching television, reading newspapers, or simply sleeping. Parents may also take out on their children the tensions they feel toward each other (Rosenblatt, 1974).

While they may not specifically call it such, people are increasingly engaging in environmental engineering. This means that they seek to create, or locate, and settle in, environments that are supportive of personal growth. A favorable environment suggests not only factors conducive to preserving sound physical health, but also to promoting aesthetic and emotional satisfaction (Dubos, 1976). Of course environments must always be evaluated in terms of the age, personalities, and life styles of persons concerned.

Education. Another potentially important aid to effective living is education. Bailey (1976) observes that we have done little to help people to
prepare for the predictable stresses and strains of middle age. True,
certain education programs have offered classes and workshops to teach
adults how to spend their leisure time more profitably and pleasantly;
but little attempt has been made to help them deal philosophically with
the crises of middle life. And only just recently have researchers begun
to compile systematic data concerning the characteristics and stresses
of middle age which may serve as reliable bases for personal development and therapy. Ideally training for adulthood should begin in high
school and college in the form of courses and modules so that adolescents and young adults will understand their parents' behavior.

This lack of adequate preparation thus far, has several reasons.
For one thing, we think of formal education as confined to the first
quarter of life. For another, systematic information regarding middle
age is only just beginning to emerge in a form which constitutes a
sound basis for preventive education and therapy. In addition, most
of the stresses of middle age have been accepted as inevitable, a conclusion on which emerging research is casting growing doubt (Bailey,
1976).

Special New Kinds of Approaches

A random sampling. In addition to the well-known techniques discussed
above, people nowadays may become involved in certain lesser-known,
special therapies. The potential range is wide: a single publication entitled *Personal Growth,* deals with such approaches as encounter groups,
gestalt therapy, meditation, hypnotherapy, relaxation techniques, peak
experiences, creativity, primal therapy, biofeedback training, psychosynthesis, self-actualization techniques, and self-analysis (Jordan, 1976).

Let us briefly define a few of these therapies. Suinn recommends a
combination of relaxation and environmental control (Jordan, 1976).
More specifically, he suggests learning to relax, perhaps through deep
muscle relaxation, meditation, using imagery to breakup emotional reactions that are aroused by pressures, managing the environment properly by such means as scheduling appointments realistically, and
walking, talking, and eating more slowly.

In primal therapy the origin of problems is said to be psychic pain
arising from early childhood experiences. The pain becomes locked in
corners of the brain and can only be relieved by experiencing it again
in its entirety under the guidance of a therapist. Often the experience
is punctuated by "piercing screams, writhing, vomiting, and general

discomfiture, during which the person makes the proper mental connections between the pain and its origin" (Torrey, 1976, p. 62).

Certain therapies are clearly designed to meet newly emerging needs. For example, "encounter groups and therapeutic communities and growth centers serve people's social needs by offering instant intimacy in a culture in which" people move around a great deal, and the nuclear family is very unstable, so that people cannot always rely on one another (London, 1974, p. 68). As a result people are seeking deep relationships wherever they can find them. They even attempt to transform brief encounters into intimate ones.

Meditation. For many people have rejected traditional therapies in favor of "biogenics, sex therapy, food, dance, art, music therapies . . . massage [and] breathing-relaxation therapies. These techniques serve people's sensory needs in a culture where" there is so much leisure time available that it must be given some deeper meaning in order for people to truly enjoy it. Still other therapeutic forms, including yoga and nude therapy, combine social and spiritual activities (London, 1974, p. 68).

Many researchers, as well as laymen, are turning to nonchemical ways to cope with stress. Coleman (1976) speaks of his sojourn in India while on a Harvard fellowship, where he met Indian yogis, Tibetan lamas, and Buddhist monks, who impressed him with their general warmth, openness, and intellectual alertness. All were from highly different backgrounds, possessed highly varied beliefs, and shared just one thing in common—meditation.

Meditation itself involves a relatively simple process. If you want to try it, simply choose a quiet place, and sit in a straight-back chair in a comfortable position, with your eyes closed. Focus on your breath as it enters and leaves your body, observing the full passage of in-and-out breathing. Whenever your mind tends to wander, simply draw your attention back to the rhythm of your breathing. Don't try to control your breath; just be aware of it. Whether it is fast and shallow, or slow and deep, doesn't matter. If you have difficulty concentrating on your breathing, count inhalations and exhalations up to 10, and then begin again. Another version is to say some simple word such as "one," in rhythm with your breathing. You should meditate for 20 minutes, and do it regularly, twice a day at the same time and place.

Medical research shows that meditation does indeed prove helpful. After being shown stress films in laboratories, the meditators feel more relaxed the entire time than do nonmeditators. The long-term meditators show a lower degree of anxiety and psychosomatic disorders than do nonmeditators. They perceive what is threatening in life more accurately, and become aroused only when necessary. Once aroused, they recover more quickly than anxious persons. All the meditation techniques seem to be about equally effective in reducing anxiety and helping to handle stress.

A warning. Unfortunately it is difficult for people to decide among therapies because there are so many of them. Moreover there is nothing to prevent licensed practitioners from devising new therapeutic techniques about which they may make claims of great success and use them as they like on their patients. In addition large numbers of unlicensed individuals under no professional control, practice their own particular brands of psychological counseling and psychotherapy, and may call themselves marital therapists, counselors, and psychotherapists (Bergin, 1975).

Another weakness which exists in all psychotherapy, is the lack of any firm criteria for what constitutes a healthy life. Since humans are infinitely variable, so may optimum life styles and characteristics also vary endlessly. For example it is commonly assumed that change is important for continued growth, and hence is a basic ingredient in the good life. But what constitutes the good life is inevitably debatable, even among the so-called experts.

Assistance for Serious Problems

It is beyond the scope of this book to deal with major mental problems which would require consultation with professionals. However, people should have some idea of the effectiveness of such treatment for themselves or others for whom they are responsible. In general about 55% of untreated persons show no change for the worse or better, 40% improve, and about 5% get worse. Improvement among untreated patients is often called spontaneous remission, but this term overlooks disturbed persons' efforts to help themselves, or help that they may receive from others. A survey of studies designed to measure the effects of therapy on wide-ranging types of disturbances, indicates that 65% of those who enter therapy improve, compared with the 40% who never see a therapist who also improve. This suggests that 25% more people improve when they receive therapy. Nevertheless, changes are not always positive. In 10% of the therapy cases the patient's condition deteriorated significantly—which is twice as many as in the untreated groups. That is, one in ten therapy patients becomes worse off while in treatment. In at least half of these cases this worsening condition can clearly be attributed to the therapy itself. The key factor in such cases is apparently the type of therapist. Those who have poor therapists end up in worse condition than those with no therapy at all. The better therapists tend to be those who are more empathic, warm, and genuinely concerned about the patients (Bergin, 1975). Yet it is impossible to define precisely what the ideal therapist is, because no single type of therapist definitely relates to patient deterioration; and the type of therapist who may be successful with one individual may not be with another.

Current Trends

In general there are signs that people are assuming a more active and positive approach toward their physical and mental health. For one thing, they are taking a long, hard, and realistic look at themselves. In fact, self-ratings are better at predicting future physical health than physicians' predictions (Palmore, 1974).

People are concerned not simply about unhealthy, perhaps imagined, aches, pains, and anxieties, but also about the sort of physical and mental health that increases their potential for living a full life. Lionells and Mann (1974) observe that those who seek clinical counseling today have changed dramatically from patients of a few years ago. Formerly the middle-aged expressed their psychosomatic complaints in vague terms—they felt tired or lacked energy—but now they are concerned about fulfillment and self-realization. In order that such efforts have a positive pay-off, people in general need help in gauging the effectiveness of the many possible approaches to maintaining sound mental health. Because there are inadequate legal regulations over therapy, many gullible people pay a lot of money for inept, inappropriate, or even harmful "assistance."

SUMMARY

Aging inevitably changes all the parts and systems of the body. People first become consciously aware of aging in middle adulthood. Certain disorders, such as heart disease, high blood pressure, and arthritis, become more common. Also people become aware that their physical image is changing, as grey hair and a paunch begin to appear.

For better perspective on the foregoing, certain other factors should be taken into account. First, many middle-aged persons are in excellent health and their appearance shows few effects of the passing years. The extent of crisis and change varies widely according to social class, sex, and individual health habits and emotional status over the years. Furthermore the physical health of those in middle age and older is progressively improving because of the widespread and growing interest in nutrition and exercise.

While there are no clear-cut criteria for determining what constitutes emotional health it is certain that middle agers have their characteristic problems. These include concern over their changing physical condition and body image, responsibilities for both the old and young, and midlife crises relating to vocation, sex, and personal goals. Such crises have a positive effect when they result in a realistic assessment and rearranging of goals and life styles. Most individuals somehow muddle through their problems alone, although growing numbers make use of such preventive and therapeutic measures as transcendental meditation, participation in encounter groups, and sometimes psychiatry.

Overall the outlook appears promising. People today are not merely concerned with resolving problems that cause difficulties in their lives, but are striving for genuinely rewarding lives. While they may find this goal somewhat elusive, and always in need of redefinition, a large majority achieve relative contentment after they emerge from their midlife crises.

SUGGESTED READINGS

Campbell, A., Converse, P. E., & Rodgers, W. L. *The quality of American life: Perceptions, evaluations, and satisfactions.* New York: Russell Sage Foundation, 1976. Variations in life satisfaction are determined for a national sampling of the population over age 18, on the basis of class, age, education, and income; and implications for social policy are discussed. Specific subjects considered, include work experience, marriage and family life, personal resources and competence, and woman's status.

Clemente, F., & Sauer, W. J. Life satisfaction in the United States, *Social Forces*, 1976, *54* (3), 621–631. A study of 1,347 adults indicates the relative impact on life satisfaction of race, age, socioeconomic status, social participation, and perceived health.

DeMarchi, W. G. Psychophysiological aspects of the menstrual cycle. *Journal of Psychosomatic Research*, 1976, *20* (4), 279–287. A review of studies of the effects of hormonal variation during the menstrual cycle indicates that certain physiological changes during this period may relate to the degree of stress experienced at this time.

Goleman, D. Meditation helps break the stress spiral. *Psychology Today,* Feb. 1976, *9* (9), 82–86, 93. One of the more popular of the current modes of self-psychotherapy is described as helpful in maintaining a serene outlook on life.

Golub, S. The magnitude of premenstrual anxiety and depression. *Psychosomatic Medicine*, Jan.-Feb., 1976, *38* (1), 4–12. The magnitude of premenstrual mood changes in fifty 30- to 45-year-old women was assessed by using an anxiety inventory and a depression adjective checklist. Premenstrual depression scores proved higher than those at midcycle, but lower than those at any time of persons with psychiatric disorders.

Harry, J. Evolving sources of happiness for men over the life cycle: A structural analysis. *Journal of Marriage and the Family,* May 1976, *38* (2), 289–296. Among a national sampling of men, the principal correlates of happiness varied according to the men's progression through stages of the life cycle. Because of the rigidity of men's work commitments, they change their definitions of happiness rather than their behavior, in order to adapt to varying circumstances at successive life stages.

Illich, I., with Keen, S. Medicine is a major threat to health. *Psychology Today,* 1976, *9* (12), 66–77. In his conversation with Sam Keen, Ivan Illich considers the various ways that medicine is hurting rather than helping the American people—through unnecessary surgery, unnecessary medication, excessive costs and so on. He deplores the power of doctors, the dehumanization of treatment, and the growth of a patient mentality.

Ineichen, B. Neurotic wives in a modern residential suburb: A sociological profile. *Social Science & Medicine,* 1975, *9* (8–9), 481–497. A comparison of 42 neurotic women of childbearing age and 42 without psychiatric problems indicated no significant differences in number of children, length of marriage, or education. However, more of the neurotic women were married to manual workers, and had less satisfying environments.

Meyer, E. E., & Saintsbury, P. (Eds.) *Promoting health in the human environment.* Geneva, Switzerland: World Health Organization, 1975. This discussion of public health administration, based on documents from the 1974 World Health Assembly, has sections that cover a broad range of environmental factors that affect health, the negative consequence of such conditions, and the promotion of health through constructive exploitation of the environment.

Montagu, A., with Goleman, D. Don't be adultish! *Psychology Today,* Aug. 1977, *11* (3), 46–50, 55. In this brief but stimulating article, a well-known authority on people talks with an associate editor of *Psychology Today* about how to retain the desirable characteristics of childhood and discard inhibiting traits of adulthood.

Mostow, E. & Newberry, P. Work role and depression in women: A comparison of workers and housewives in treatment. *American Journal of Orthopsychiatry,* July 1975, *45* (4), 538–548. A comparison of depressed housewives with a matched group of depressed working women indicated important differences in social functioning in relation to work roles. For women of lower socioeconomic status, as for those of higher status, work apparently has a positive psychological effect.

Palmore, E. & Likert, C. Health and social factors related to life satisfaction pp. 185–201, in E. Palmore (Ed.) *Normal Aging II.* Durham: Duke University Press, 1974. (Originally published in *Journal of Health and Social Behavior,* 1972, (13), 68–80.) In the Duke Adaptation Study, which involved 502 persons aged 45 to 69, correlates were determined for life satisfaction, including health, social-psychological and socio-economic variables.

Rogers, K. Crisis at the midpoint of life. *New Society*, August 1974, *29* (619), 413–415. Five interrelated studies, two in London, two in Nassau County, N.Y., and one in New York City, and involving 2,500 respondents, concerned crises during the critical years of middle life. These crises produced feelings of frustration, inadequacy, depression, alienation, which were caused at least in part by the onset of aging, and individual reaction to it.

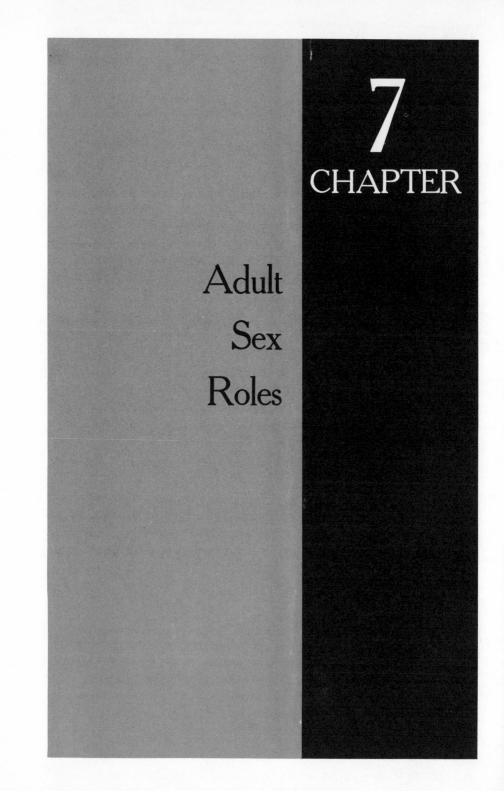

7

CHAPTER

Adult
Sex
Roles

The first part of this chapter concerns adult's psychobiological sex roles, or the psychobiological consequences of the sex drive, sex awareness, and sex interest. In the second part of the chapter, the discussion will turn to social-sex roles, or the broader roles of men and women in society.

PSYCHOBIOLOGICAL SEX ROLES AND BEHAVIORS

Female Sexuality

Psychoanalytic theory questioned. A survey of major research regarding female sexuality indicates that much of the past psychoanalytic and related theory about it, must be seriously questioned (Chilman, 1974). For example, Fisher (1973) failed to find any support in his research for certain Freudian theories. For one thing, women who have physical problems with infertility, pregnancy, menstruation, and childbirth are not, as the Freudians assert, more likely than other women to be mentally ill or neurotic, or to deny their sexual role and functioning. Nor do problems in one area of sexual functioning relate to difficulties in others. For example, women who have problems with menstruation are no more likely than others to have difficult pregnancies; nor does a difficult pregnancy mean there will be a difficult childbirth. Fisher also found that women are more accepting of their bodies and less anxious about "their body safety" than most males are. He found no support for the penis-envy concept so often mentioned by the Freudians.

On the other hand middle-class women, at least, may indeed be more dependent than males on their mate relationships, partly because they equate sex with love. In one study sexually active women college students who were dependent on their male partners, and found their sense of identity was wrapped up in them, perceived their sexual relationship as a way of approaching intimacy and "holding their man" (Bardwick, 1973). By contrast males can enjoy sexual relationships for their own sake, without becoming emotionally involved with their sex partners. It is even uncertain how many "liberated" women can engage in random sex without developing psychological problems. Studies of women in certain communes indicate that women cannot take several simultaneous sexual relationships for long because they tend to fall in love with, and become dependent upon, one man (Bernard, 1972).

On the other hand, the old notion that women passively submit to their husbands without enjoying sex themselves, is no longer valid. Robert and Amy Levin reported that among women who voluntarily answered a sex survey, sex frequency varied little at different ages: 12 times a month for those under 25; 9 to 10 times for women 25 to 34; 8 to 9 times between the ages of 35 and 39; and 6 to 7 times a month from age 40 on. Almost 3 out of 4 of the strongly religious wives between the ages of 35 to 39 attained orgasm almost all the time, compared to 68% of the moderately religious and 61% of the nonreligious. Over 7 in 10 of the respondents reported the sexual aspects of their marriage as good or very good, and 2 in 10 rated it fair. Those under the age of 20 rated sex most highly, 80% declaring it very good or good. Even 60% of the women over 40 rated their sex lives as good or very good. Almost 80% of all the wives said that they were usually or always active partners in sex. Almost all the rest were active half the time or sometimes. While these respondents were better educated and had relatively higher incomes than average Americans, other more representative samplings show similar trends. In a study at Princeton over a 5-year period the typical wife in the early 1970s was making love 14% more than she did a half a decade before (Horn, 1975).

The Redbook study. According to a *Redbook* magazine poll, which is the largest survey of female sexuality ever undertaken, mostly white middle-class married women have changed significantly since their "sexual pulse" was taken by Kinsey just over two decades ago. In the *Redbook* survey 4 out of 5 had had premarital intercourse, the first time at the average age of 17, and 9 in 10 of those were under 25. By comparison Kinsey had reported that just one-third of women under 25 had had premarital sex. Almost a third of the *Redbook* women had had extramarital relations, and another third confessed that they would like to. Over 90% have orgasms, the majority within ten minutes, and practically all have both practiced and enjoyed oral sex. Over three-fourths are active sexual partners, and nearly 65% masturbate occasionally or frequently. Over two-thirds sometimes have sex under the influence of alcohol, and 63% under age 25 sometimes smoke marijuana prior to having sex. Almost 40% of the respondents felt that they were not having enough sex.

The Hite Report. The Hite Report gives the results of responses by over 3,000 women to a questionnaire that was distributed to them. Its findings have been considered controversial by many. One of the major conclusions is that women can and do masturbate to orgasm easily and regularly. It has been wrongly believed that women slow in arousal are frigid, rather than understood that men are simply unskilled and more quickly aroused. Moreover, intercourse is not the only way for women to reach orgasm, since orgasm is typically clitoral rather than vaginal. Even the sexual revolution hasn't freed women; instead it has put more pressures on them. Hence many women are having homosexual experiences. But how valid are these conclusions, at least for women generally? Since the subjects surveyed did not represent a random sampling, and since persons who voluntarily answer such surveys are hardly typical, the results may only be applicable to a small fraction of the female population (Hite, 1976).

Other research. There have been other reports regarding female sexuality. Chilman (1974) found that physiologically the female's sexual response was much like the male's, and that women probably have as strong a sex drive as men. Within a specific time period females are more capable of multiple orgasms than males. According to Fisher (1973), females have more difficulty than males in attaining orgasm, at least in heterosexual relationships. About one-third of them fail to achieve orgasm at least some of the time, and at least 8% all of the time. Nevertheless all females are readily orgasmic if and when they engage in masturbation or lesbian relationships. The female clitoris is analogous to the male penis and it, rather than the vagina, is the female's chief erogenous zone. In many cases females achieve more satisfaction through clitoral than vaginal stimulation.

Male Sexuality

Relevant data. Traditionally, males have been relatively more physical and less psychological than women, in their approach to sex. For example males place a high value on their "reproductive equipment" and are quite concerned about their potency (Chilman, 1974, p. 126). This attitude probably relates "to the actual physical vulnerability of the penis and testicles, the need for males to have an erection, to have intercourse and impregnate, their inability to hide erectile or orgasmic failure from their mates, and the fact that, unlike females, they can never be sure that they are actually biological parents" (p. 126). A man's penis is so important to him that he believes it should also be important to the woman, and that she must feel deprived in lacking similar equipment.

Healthy well-adjusted males can have a satisfactory sex life throughout middle age, and even until extreme old age. The common decline in mens' sexual activity during middle age is often due to alcohol, drugs—especially tranquilizers—and poor medical advice. In general, doctors are relatively uninformed regarding sexuality (Butler, 1976).

Many middle-aged men, perhaps because they are bored with their spouses, seek sexual stimulation on the side. Usually they have no intention of breaking away from their wives, although they may tell their mistresses otherwise in order to keep them from feeling exploited. In any case they have more trouble establishing these kinds of relationships than they did formerly. Traditionally the successful businessman who needed to prove that he was still a sexual sensation, would seek out a rather young woman. However young women are now far more sophisticated, and in the process of taking, the man may find himself taken. Besides, such men may find themselves in greater competition than before with younger men, because young women today hold their own jobs and are less impressed by older men with money.

Vasectomy. In recent years some men have been undergoing vasectomies, which permit intercourse without conception. In general, postoperative attitudes of persons who have had a vasectomy have been positive, although there are exceptions. It is extremely important that individuals be counseled in advance about this operation. At present, estimates of the success rate in reversing a vasectomy by rejoining the cut ends of severed vas deferens, range from zero to 100% (Cole & Bryon, 1973). Research into a new kind of birth control has recently begun. It involves the male production of antibodies, which sometimes cause infertility. In any case, "re-joining the vas is an expensive, tedious procedure that requires full hospitalization and offers absolutely no guarantee of success, even if the vas deferens are reunited" (p. 216). The chances at present are probably no more than 50/50.

Research Regarding Both Sexes: The Playboy Foundation Study

There has been little comprehensive research about current sexual attitudes and practices of the entire American adult population. Most people are familiar with the landmark studies by Dr. Alfred C. Kinsey and his associates, *Sexual Behavior in the Human Male* (1948) and *Sexual Behavior in the Human Female* (1953). The most comprehensive studies in the 1970s have been of female sexuality by Redbook magazine, and of the general population by the Playboy Foundation. Otherwise studies have involved only limited populations or have been concerned with specific aspects of sexuality, such as unwed motherhood, rather than general sexuality.

While the study commissioned by the Playboy Foundation did not involve a strictly random selection, it nevertheless represented a reasonably good sampling of the American adult society. It involved over 2,000 questionnaires, which were filled out by people 18 and older, in 24 cities. Data gathered by a professional public-opinion survey team were supplemented by in-depth tape-recorded interviews in order to determine the meaning of trends that showed up in the questionnaires.

This report provided considerable evidence that sexual liberation has indeed taken place. When the Kinsey studies appeared, most of the public, and even many academics, looked upon Kinsey and his researchers as "unwholesome and somewhat unclean" (Hunt, 1974, p. 5). By the late 1960s, however, such research had become respectable, and grants were being awarded for projects having to do with such phenomena as prostitution and homosexuality. In the 1940s, sex in the presence of third parties would have been considered obscene, but just a decade later Masters and Johnson watched couples having intercourse in the laboratory and recorded the condition of their body organs at each stage of the process. Marriage and sex manuals have become more open, freely advocating and illustrating a variety of coital positions and approaches. Thousands of couples are receiving direct sexual instruction at various sex therapy clinics and in nude encounter groups. In groups, married couples and single people feel each others' bodies in order to acquire effective sexual techniques. Premarital sex has become widely accepted, especially among the younger generation. At the same time the search for sexual partners has become more noticeable and widespread. Most cities have public places where sexual pickups are the norm. Growing numbers of underground newspapers and magazines carry advertisements by people seeking sexual partners. Many people have openly admitted their sexual attitudes and preferences. For example feminist author Germaine Greer has confessed having one-night stands, and women's liberationist Kate Millett has freely admitted her homosexuality. Homosexuals have organized into over 600 gay organizations, they have their own meeting rooms on campuses, and their publications are circulated nationwide. Some of them are attempting to make homosexual marriage legal. Most dramatically, by 1974 about 1500 transsexuals had switched from one sex to another through radical surgery. Perhaps of more fundamental significance is the increasing numbers who have begun to advocate and even practice alternatives to monogamous marriage, including open marriage, swinging, and homosexual unions. Finally, the courts in certain states have made fundamental revisions in sex laws. For instance, all private sex acts between consenting adults have been decriminalized. While traditional laws against cohabitation, adultery, and sodomy still exist in most states, these laws are not generally enforced.

The Playboy study also reported far more permissive attitudes and practices than those of a generation earlier. For example, (1) three-fourths of all males and over three-quarters of all females believe that schools should teach sex education. (2) Over four-fifths of the males and all the females said that the man should not always be the one to initiate sexual intercourse. Only 1 in every 40 females and 1 in every 20 males took a strong stand against the female assuming the initiative. (3) There was little change in permissiveness regarding premarital intercourse in the two decades between 1937 and 1959. However in the following 15 years there was a strong shift toward greater permissiveness. In earlier years fewer than a quarter questioned believed that premarital intercourse was all right for both sexes; 8% said that it was all right for men only; and over half that it was all right for neither. In the Playboy study, depending on the extent of emotional involvement or affection between sexual partners, from 60 to 80% of the men believed that premarital sex was all right for men, and from 44 to 81% for women. Among the females, 37 to 73% believed it was all right for men, and from 20 to 68%, that it was acceptable for women. Over half of the males and nearly half of the females agreed with the statement: "People who have sex before marriage are more likely to have happy and stable marriages later on "(p. 21). Only half the men in the sample believed that "most men want to marry a virgin," and over two-thirds of the women disagreed that the woman who goes to bed with a man prior to marriage forfeits his respect. (4) Over half the women and almost half the men did not feel that "homosexuality is wrong," and almost half of both sexes believed that it should be legalized. A slightly smaller number felt it should not, and the rest expressed no opinion. (5) Only 1 in 5 adults viewed masturbation as very wrong, and over two-thirds stated that it was not wrong. Thus the general population has come around to a view of masturbation held only by "the enlightened and psychologically sophisticated" a few years ago (p. 22). (6) A majority favored legalizing prostitution and abortion, and adopting divorce laws that do not require people to present reasons for divorce to the court. (7) Only a third of all American adults believe that they should have access to any sexual materials they might desire, but over half would feel this way if it were proven that such materials are not harmful.

Overall it appears that "the average American now holds many opinions about sex that a generation ago were rarely held by any but highly educated, big-city sophisticates and Bohemians." (Hunt, 1974 p. 24). Nevertheless these attitudes were not the same for the entire population. Permissive sexual attitudes are more common among males and the young in general; and they are associated with such factors as higher education, higher occupational status, political liberalism, and lack of strong religious feeling. By contrast more conservative attitudes are more common among females, older people, blue-collar workers, the less educated, the politically conservative, and the devout. Of all these factors, the most significant is age. Only on issues that are not personally threatening and represent no danger to social stability are the age groups in complete agreement. In every age group, nine-tenths or more of both sexes agree that sex is one of the most beautiful parts of life and that women have as great a right as men to initiate intercourse. Otherwise conservatism increases with age: for example, women under 25 are over three times as likely as those over 55 to endorse premarital intercourse. Nevertheless the more permissive attitudes held by the young do not stem from rebelliousness or youthful irresponsibility. Instead they are simply part of the contemporary culture and are learned by their age group.

The question arises as to whether these differences are a result of the shift from permissiveness to conservatism that always occurs with age. Or, we might ask, are these findings specific to the generations concerned, reflecting the times in which they grew up? People do grow somewhat more conservative as their own children arrive at puberty, perhaps because they feel responsible for what their children might do. Although the changing sexual attitudes reported by the Playboy study have affected almost all age groups to a certain degree, the greatest difference is found in those whose sex attitudes were learned in their late teens and early 20s. Still, sexual attitudes also depend on the era in which a particular generation grows up. Most individuals arriving at adulthood in the late 1920s and 1930s were three or four times more likely to consider anal intercourse wrong than those now entering adulthood. Another interesting finding is that there is a narrowing gap, at least among younger people, "between the devout and the nondevout, blue-collar people and white-collar people, the college- and the non-college educated, the political liberals and the political conservatives" (Hunt, 1974, p. 29).

With regard to sex practice, certain acts have become more common, and others less so, and the gap between male and female practices has narrowed. Young women are more likely than in the past to have a sexual life before marriage, but only if there is some emotional involvement. In effect, the double sex standard has weakened. Extramarital sex has become more common only among women, who have simply reached the male level of activity. For most Americans sexual liberation simply means enjoying all parts of the body, the right to employ "caresses previously forbidden" by law or tradition, and to be sensuous and enjoy sex, rather than be too serious about it. For these people, sex must be "within the framework of meaningful relationships. Sex, for the great majority of Americans—including the liberated—continues to express loving feelings, or to [produce] them, or both. It has not been successfully [removed] from love and remade into a simple appetite, except for a tiny majority of swingers" (p. 38).

A summary view. In sum, adults' sexual attitudes have shifted toward permissiveness. This trend cannot be regarded "as an obligation to do anything and everything, but as a freedom within which they have the right to remain highly selective, choosing only those sexual acts that meet their emotional needs" (p. 31). Many people who are advocates of sexual liberation would not do many of the things that they defend the right of others to do. Moreover certain practices are still as unacceptable and uncommon as ever. In general adults have added to their sexual activity only what is biologically and psychologically free from disease (p. 32). Emotional gratification continues to be very important. Even masturbation is not practiced purely for sensual purposes, but is often combined with fantasies about love. Married couples masturbate more than they used to; it is simply a way of relieving sexual frustrations that arise in marriage, or occur when sex is forbidden because of illness, pregnancy, or other factors.

It cannot be assumed that such trends are irreversible, for in history there have always been swings from conservatism to liberalism and back again. Already the tendency to sexual liberalism that occurred in the late 1960s is showing signs of slowing down and even reversing. In the second half of the 1970s, such free-swinging behavior as engaging in group sex has been increasingly criticized. Publishers of pornographic books and magazines are being fined and even jailed. The movement for the passage of the Equal Rights Amendment appears to be crumbling. Authorities on the family, ordinary citizens, and the President of the U.S., are rallying to the defense of the family and declaring it the only legitimate outlet for adult sex.

Issues Relating to Both Sexes

The double standard. A long-standing subject of controversy is the sexual double standard. This means that the sexes are judged differently by society for engaging in the same behavior. The double standard is based on certain mistaken assumptions, especially that males have stronger sex drives than females and therefore cannot be expected to control their sexual behavior (Chilman, 1974). "Good" women are perceived as being relatively asexual; they have intercourse primarily to satisfy their husbands' sexual needs. Their "sexual purity" supposedly makes them superior mothers and guardians of the family morals.

Perhaps in earlier times the double standard had a certain value. Before contraceptives were available the woman was vulnerable to pregnancy and needed the husband to support her if she had a baby. Since property was the chief form of wealth and was passed down from father to son, the man wanted to be sure that the children born to his mate were really his own. Besides, in the days when masculine physical strength was vital both for occupation and security, the female wanted a male to protect and support her. In order to insure that her husband stay with her and fulfill these needs she gave him special sexual consideration. The situation has dramatically changed today, for women are able to support themselves and control their own reproduction. Anyhow, like their husbands, they can easily have sex outside of marriage (Chilman, 1974).

Masturbation. Although masturbation among both sexes is common, it is associated with deviance, and discussion of it is still taboo. Research, however, indicates that such behavior is completely normal, unless it is compulsively excessive. In fact, contrary to the common theory that married women who masturbate are likely to have neurotic problems, these women apparently masturbate because they are open to their sexuality and derive pleasure from both intercourse and self-stimulation (Fisher, 1973).

The freeing of sex morals. There is a general feeling, supported by considerable research, that people are becoming either more open or promiscuous sexually, depending upon one's values. Far more unmarried couples are living together for varying lengths of time, before deciding whether or not to marry (Silverman, 1974). In addition, three times as many wives have extramarital affairs today as they did a brief generation ago.

An assessment. Are sexual morals declining, or are they simply adapting to new conditions? Some persons see changing sexual behavior as symptomatic of decay, both within the family and the larger society. By contrast many authorities believe that today's freer, more egalitarian sex practices healthier than the traditional, often distorted, views and practices of former years (Cowing, 1975). According to O'Neill and O'Neill (1972), having affairs can have a therapeutic effect, for men and women can see for themselves that the grass "is not greener on the other side of the fence." Or affairs may help people to work out some sexual inhibitions. Some professionals believe that more liberal sexual practices are simply the result of more effective contraceptives (Gallagher, 1974).

Sex Therapy

Even if sex relationships are growing healthier, 4 couples in 10 still report problems of sex adjustment; and treatment centers, many of them phony, are increasing in number. Quackery in sex therapy is almost impossible to prosecute, considering the current status of the law. William Masters and Virginia Johnson estimate that only 50 to 100 out of the approximately 5000 new clinics devoted to sex problems are legitimate (Koch & Koch, 1976). During New York State hearings on abuses by unregulated therapists many horror stories were told. For example, some therapists punched women in the breast or pulled out their pubic hairs. When the victims protested, the therapists asked, "Do you believe in healthy play?" While the American Psychiatric Association specifically states that therapists are not to have sex with patients, the American Psychological Association has been unable to pass a resolution condemning such activity (Rogers, 1973, p. 37).

Both psychologists and psychiatrists get away with this kind of behavior because their patients, or victims, are too embarrassed to press charges.

> In one case a young homosexual woman, who was having difficulty accepting herself, went to a psychiatrist for help. He recommended that she "get herself screwed" by a man and volunteered to do the job. She declined and never returned to his office. In another case a psychiatrist pretended to fall in love with his gullible woman clients, until the irate husband of one of them broke his jaw. Despite the policy of the American Psychiatric Association and the jaw-breaking, which took place in the clinic, the psychiatrist returned to work as usual as soon as his jaw healed.

Responsible and effective marriage counseling involves certain basic ground rules. One is that both husband and wife should be involved. They are helped to gain an objective view of their relationship and to talk through their problems under guidance. Aspects of the relationship that cause difficulties for the couple are treated as symptoms of larger problems rather than as problems in themselves. Responsible therapists would hardly encourage extramarital sex relations, because they realize that few sexually open marriages last. Nor do therapists try to change people's moral beliefs (Koch & Koch, 1976). Needless to say, proper counseling also depends on the integrity and the professional training of the counselor involved. Since marriage problems often stem from fundamental personality conflicts, and always relate to the total personalities of the individuals concerned, the therapist needs an in-depth knowledge of psychological processes and human behavior.

SOCIAL-SEX ROLES

Introduction

Earlier we briefly discussed social-sex roles in terms of young adults. Here we are concerned about sex roles for adults in general, especially those in their middle years. Social-sex role is a way of describing the various behavior patterns that are considered proper for each sex. It "distinguishes the behavior patterns of male and female from birth to death. This role carries with it a whole array of attitudes, feelings and activities. In short, it may involve anything and everything associated with being a male or a female within a particular culture" (Rogers, 1977, p. 335).

Certain other terms place the concept in sharper perspective. The term sex-role identity suggests an awareness and acceptance of one's biological identity, and a consciousness of what attitudes are associated with being male or female (Dreyer, 1975). Most American children develop this sex-role identity by the time they are 6 or 7, and they maintain it for the rest of their lives. The term "sex-role preference", on the other hand, suggests an individual's conscious preference for particular sex-typed attitudes and behaviors. While sex-role identity is stable, sex-role preference may change over time. Because of societal pressures, the way most individuals perform their sex roles represents a compromise between their own sex-role preference and social stereotypes of what each sex role should be.

Factors Affecting Sex Roles

Historical origins. The traditional sex roles of man, the doer, and woman, the nurturer, have deep roots. Western religion and philosophy themselves are based upon patriarchal principles. In the Bible it is stated that "man . . . is the image and glory of God; but the woman is the glory of the man. . . . Neither was the man created for the woman, but the woman for the man" (First Corinthians, 11:14). In another place it says, "Let the woman learn silence with all subjection. But I suffer not a woman to teach, nor to usurp authority over the man" (1st Timothy 2, 11:15). As a result of this tradition, which has been reinforced through the years, the vast majority of adults today were socialized as children by family, school, and the mass media, to accept traditional sex role stereotypes.

The question of the extent to which sex roles are rooted in biology or simply shaped by environment, has caused considerable controversy.

Although it is probably true that those sex-roles that function best, harmonize with biological potential, further research is needed to define that potential. According to Erikson (1963), a fundamental difference between the sexes, which is inherent in the capacity to be either an impregnator or a childbearer, is suggested by the way young boys and girls utilize space. When they play with bricks, boys build outward and upward while girls construct enclosed spaces. Thus one sex manifests its presumably fundamental psychological and biological makeup in erecting, constructing, and elaborating; and the other is concerned with enclosing and holding safely.

On the other hand there is considerable evidence to support the belief that sex differences are cultural. On neuroses inventories, clear-cut differences in emotional stability between individuals of different cultures do not appear until the adolescent years, at which time they become increasingly apparent. Such findings may be accounted for concludes Anastasi, (1958) by increasing sexual differentiation in terms of social pressures, privileges, and expectations in certain cultures, with the male sex-role increasingly favored (Rogers, 1977, p. 352).

Early socialization. The most important environmental influence on sex role is family experience. Even by the age of two and a half, children are pretty familiar with sex roles. From birth children are exposed to all sorts of sex-related symbols including hair styles, posture when going to the toilet, and different kinds of behavior by the mother and father. That is, children unconsciously acquire concepts of sex role in innumerable, subtle, and constantly recurring ways.

Other influences on sex-role socialization include school, church, society in general, and the mass media. According to Stanford University psychologist Sharon Nash, for instance, the sexes are shown in quite traditional roles in advertising. Women's professional status is all but ignored and there is no indication in advertisements that women comprise 40% of the working force. When women are shown working, it is in the lower-status "women's" occupations. On most television commercials, the woman's world is portrayed as purely domestic. Products aimed at women fall into two main categories. The first includes beauty aids and underwear, which suggests that women are "obsessed with the need for masculine approval" ("The television image of women," 1975, p. 424). The second involves products for maintaining the home and caring for the family. Overall the commercials portray "women as homemakers with cleanliness compulsions, forever sniffing the kitchen floor or the family wash. All those commercials about ring around the collar and perfect rice are designed to make the female feel guilty if she's not preoccupied with becoming a launderer, an immaculate house cleaner, and a cordon bleu chef" (p. 425). By contrast, "men are portrayed as rational, independent, advice-giving professionals" (p. 425).

In addition, the afternoon soap operas foster the notion of "female passivity, ineptness, and subservience. Even professional women somehow "manage to get themselves in the damnedest messes from which only strong, brave, intelligent males can extricate them" (p. 425).

Recent influences. In recent years several factors have had an unsettling effect on sex roles. Since machines now perform most of the work that once required masculine brawn, the vast majority of jobs can now be performed equally well by both sexes. Women's entry into the workaday world has also freed many men from the exhausting burden of being the sole family provider. Meantime higher education for both sexes has increased interest in humanistic values and developed peoples' desire for self-realization. This naturally transcends traditional sex roles. The woman's liberation movement is simply an outgrowth of such factors. It has actually had a large impact on liberating men from their traditional and perhaps even more confining roles.

The Female Sex Role

Disadvantages. Certain aspects of women's roles are damaging to their personalities. Even some of the presumed advantages of those roles, when they are carefully examined, are of questionable worth. Women often feel protected by men, but is it healthy to the need for protection? Many women feel it is a divine blessing that they can become mothers, but don't males become parents with far less pain and trouble? Besides, isn't it extremely difficult for women who spend most of their time in the home, often tending young children, to remain intellectually active and involved? Even the married woman who goes to work finds that her status depends on how important her husband is. She is treated as though she is hardly a person in her own right (Felson & Knoke, 1974). Ordinarily her own education and job do not significantly affect the status of the family. Working wives and their husbands feel the family has less importance than homemakers do.

While the majority of wives are working today, those who do not work—either because of their children or their husbands' attitude—may have a difficult time adjusting to staying home. In a study of working and middle-class London housewives aged 20 to 30, the majority were dissatisfied with housework, finding it endlessly demanding, fragmented, and monotonous. They liked neither the long hours nor the isolation from others with their young and demanding children. Nevertheless oddly enough, the majority of housewives defend their roles. Even though housework has low social status, it is the primary work of the housewife, a role long associated with femininity. Besides, gender identity is rooted in the idea of sexual division of labor. Hence women are often defensive about the housewife's status, probably to sustain the rationality of their own position (Oakley, 1975).

In addition women in general are taken less seriously and respected less than men. Consider the difference in status accorded women's and women's sports, or a woman's airplane competition frivolously labeled the Petticoat Derby. Moreover female household heads have less prestige in the community and less status than men with the same education and economic level; and they may have less status than married women who take their status from their husbands. Reduced prestige, in turn, lessens the status for the family as a whole and gives the family less power in the community (Brandwein, Brown, & Fox, 1974).

The woman's role also subtly interferes with her potential for professional success. For one thing, women fail to take themselves seriously enough, for they have not been brought up to have confidence in their abilities (Movius, 1976). In addition, by being responsible for child care, working women don't have enough time to spend reading in their field, to do overtime work, and to have the sort of personal involvement on the job which helps win promotions. If the children are ill it is simply assumed that the mother, not the father, will take time off from work to care for them.

Advantages. Nevertheless the woman's role has its good points, too. For one thing, the female role is more flexible than the male's, and women are penalized less for stepping out of it. Many people believe women are warmer than men, since traditionally they have been freer to express emotion. It could also be argued that many of the presumed disadvantages of traditional women's roles result from using masculine criteria of satisfaction to evaluate women's status.

> Even the presumed disadvantages of woman's role may have diminished . . . (Rogers, 1977). [Douvan] attributes the change in women's status chiefly to those factors having greatest impact on female socialization, such as improved education, vastly improved birth control technology, and the contemporary women's movement. The higher level of woman's education today permits an intellectual companionship with the opposite sex, both before and after marriage. Education has also increased the expectations of intrinsic satisfactions and intellectual stimulation in a woman's life. Meanwhile, birth control technology has separated sex and maternity from the core of feminine identity, permitting "a new integration in which the woman conceives of herself as fully developed, adult, sexual, and nonmaternal" (Douvan, 1975, p. 33).

The impact of the women's movement. The effect of the women's movement on women's sex roles is as yet unclear for a variety of reasons.

First, the movement is not a single entity. There are radical feminists who desire drastic change, there are moderates, and there are those who are primarily concerned with obtaining better salaries and day care for children, both of which are supportive of their family roles. The problem in defining proper goals for women, asserts Laudicina (1973), is the difficulty of harmonizing such contrasting role demands—that is, the occupational, marital, and familial. She suggests broadening the scope and meaning of the women's movement in order to make it more congruent with the needs of more women and men. Through reassigning tasks and conventional work roles, and making occupational time demands more flexible, women could assume an equal position in the work force and still find satisfaction in family and home life. Meantime men would be freed of the excessive occupational demands which have hitherto prevented them from fulfilling a satisfactory paternal role within the family.

A major obstacle to sex-role change is woman's internalized feelings, which are rooted in her past. Although women are gaining more

One of the areas that has been effected by the women's movement is the area of conventional work roles for women.

freedom, the individual woman will profit little from them if she is not psychologically prepared to do so. Women must take responsibility for creating environments most appropriate to their own needs. Too many women have unquestioningly taken on the traditional sex roles, and simply assumed a passive, colorless way of life because of their limited horizons (Neugarten, 1972).

The Male Sex Role

Disadvantages. The male is typically thought of as a rather efficient doer, an achiever. According to Fasteau (1975), men are brought up with the attitude that they must work, take on difficult jobs, and overcome obstacles. They are competitive and like to win. However, they do not have much insight into themselves or others, they cannot achieve closeness with other men, and their emotional needs are met by women.

This thumbnail sketch fits no male exactly, but it is important because people believe it. Males may be no more competitive than females (Maccoby & Jacklin, 1974). Many of them are warmly loving and place human values ahead of material achievement. Nevertheless each male must somehow cope with the stereotype of men as hard-as-nails. Indeed the male's greatest handicap is the cultural concept of masculinity itself. For one thing, males are taught to be self-sufficient. This is often interpreted by men to mean that they should not be intimate with others; so they are often awkward in relationships. For example, in unstructured groups males are competitive and less comfortable about expressing warmth and support than females (Ariès, 1975). For another, the excessive stress placed on masculine achievement prevents males from relaxing.

According to Fasteau (1975), the masculine stereotype converts sports into compulsion rather than pleasure. In addition, since violence is viewed as masculine, males resort to it more than females do, both in personal and impersonal relationships. Finally, the idea that men must be in control (like Don Juan) in sexual relationships, forces both men and women into certain roles, and discourages spontaneity (Fasteau, 1975).

Many persons question whether the traditional cultural concept of masculinity is mentally healthy. The ideal is too aggressive, too competitive. Furthermore the concept of masculinity is overidealized. The "complete male" is the embodiment of courage, independence, effectiveness, success, and a host of other traits. The individual male's reach is almost sure to exceed his grasp. He applies the cultural measuring rod to himself and often feels like a failure. In fact, reports Long (1970), statistics show male suicides and mental breakdowns exceed those of females (Rogers, 1977).

Advantages. The male's role has its advantages. For one thing, men ordinarily are assumed to be the heads of households. It is legally impossible for a woman to head a household if the husband is present, regardless of her own relative income, power, and status. Brandwein, Brown, and Fox (1974) recall that one couple was threatened with federal arrest for giving false information because they listed the wife as head of household in their census form.

[In addition] it is ego-strengthening for males to live in a world of work, and a world of big affairs in general, that is ordered by males. Men usually are trained for the higher positions that carry the most power and prestige.

Also ego-strengthening is the male's sex advantage. . . . From adolescence onward, females outnumber males. In social situations, an extra male is an asset, an extra female is a liability. Besides, the unmarried male has a freedom of movement and action denied the unmarried woman (Rogers, 1977, p. 348).

Why men's sex role is changing. The male's sex role is subtly changing for several basic reasons. For one thing, advances in technology have weakened the firm division of sex roles. In our earlier agrarian and pioneer economies men were called upon to perform tasks requiring physical strength, while women's roles required interpersonal skills and dexterity, including childrearing and homemaking. With the coming of the industrial and postindustrial economies, the family lost most of its economic function and became more of a social, emotional, and recreational unit; and the sex roles became even more inflexible. The men performed their tasks away from the home, while the women typically remained at home. Nowadays, however, in our affluent society, such factors as shorter working hours, increased leisure time, more service occupations which involve interpersonal skills, and the increased availability of mechanical devices to take care of household chores, have weakened the need for earlier sex-typed roles (Dreyer, 1975).

These changes are also rooted in history. In the early years of this country the most respected activities were instrumental. That is, work was a means to an end rather than an end in itself. However as productivity increased, and along with it the average person's free time, instrumental activities lost some of their status in favor of expressive activities—that is, those which are valued for themselves rather than for a product resulting from the activity. Thus an individual who farms in order to make a living is engaging in instrumental activity, while one who grows exotic plants just for fun is engaged in an expressive activity.

The transition from the instrumental to expressive way of life sneaked up on the American people so that few are aware of it.

Nevertheless it is now apparent that the emphasis in the U.S. is shifting away from quantity to quality. This is partly because Americans now have enough free time to be concerned with how to use it. No longer does their life style consist chiefly of work, with barely enough time for rest and a little relaxation (Havighurst, 1975).

The effect of women's liberation. Men's sex roles are also responding to changes in women's roles. Prejudice and discrimination, which have prevented women from becoming complete individuals, have also kept men from achieving their full potential. Certainly neither sex can have a full life unless both sexes share a common humanity. That is to say, men, like women, have been the victims of sexism. Anyhow, women cannot change the patterns of society alone. Men must come to understand that they too need women's liberation.

Future prospects. For at least two reasons, changes in male sex roles may require more radical adjustment than those currently taking place in women's roles. For one thing, men have had higher status, and what dominant group wants to concede its superior position? For another, men may be called upon to express and develop values which they were encouraged to suppress throughout their early years. Consider, for example, the man who is called upon to take care of the baby while his wife is at work. He must diaper the baby, tend it when it cries, feed it, and perform various tasks that he learned as a boy to associate with femininity (Douvan, 1975). The concept of being a sissy has been so strongly associated in the male mind with being repulsive, weak, or even mentally sick, that it is extremely difficult for men to rid themselves of these feelings.

Sex-role Relationships in Marriage

Changing relationships. In several ways the relationships between husbands and wives are changing. Because the average family now has fewer children, married couples frequently have no children at home for most of their lives. Hence for a significant portion of their lives, sex is leisurely and private (Long, 1976). In addition, sex-role responsibilities are shifting in the home. Sixty percent of married women with jobs outside the home are sharing responsibility for family support, while married men are assuming greater domestic responsibilities. In many cases men are assuming a larger role in shopping, cleaning, and cooking, while women are spending more time working in the garden and fixing things around the house (Weitzman, 1975).

Meantime the whole concept of marital roles is changing, partly because far greater numbers are now college educated. Traditionally marriage was viewed as providing for sex, procreation, and the rearing of children, while the marital partners filled rigidly defined complementary roles. One reason for the change in this concept is that greatly increased geographic mobility has removed married couples from their kin and thrown them increasingly on their own resources. The result is that wife and husband look more to each other for friendship and support. At the same time increasingly better-educated wives have become more satisfactory companions and social assets for their husbands. However, increased demands on the marital relationship have also contributed to the rate of its failure.

Women who have received a good education have heightened expectations of intellectual stimulation and intrinsic satisfaction. The young college graduate who has grown accustomed to being curious, sensitive, analytical, and achieving, discovers all too often that she has no chance to express these characteristics, either in the currently defined world of work or in the home. In fact, observes Douvan, "her dreams of being a literary editor [conflict] badly with the actual secretarial jobs proffered. And during the years of active mothering she [is] likely to discover little satisfaction for her intellectual needs isolated in a home in the suburbs with preverbal children" (1975, p. 32). By the middle years her nagging feelings of discontent may have hardened into a sense of failure as a person.

Another factor that has fundamentally altered marital relationships is birth control. Until recently there was no way for a woman positively to avoid pregnancy unless she gave up sex with men (Douvan, 1975). In consequence girls were taught both to expect and look forward to maternity, and they thought it essential to their fulfillment as women and as an expression of complete femininity. If for some reason, a woman did not have children, her maternal feelings might be directed into nurturant activities such as nursing or teaching. These were considered legitimate alternative expressions of her femininity. However, birth control has divorced maternity from the core of feminine identity. It permits the development of a personality in which the woman may conceive of herself as fully developed without being a mother. Perhaps the most dramatic indication of the separation of the maternal from the sexual role is the rapidly increasing number of young women who expect to have no children at all. In earlier studies almost no women expressed these wishes; however, in the early 1970s a full 10% said that ideally they would have no children (Hoffman, 1974). These young women intended to marry—they simply thought of themselves as women, and as sexual, but not as mothers.

Many of them still define themselves in terms of their relationships to their family, while others form identities around their vocation. The latter, "who anchors her identity in work, asserts the legitimacy of an internal anchor based on her individual talent and integration" (Douvan, 1975, p. 34). The change to this new ethic is not yet complete. Those women who have rejected the old ethic without achieving a clear new one, may be somewhat confused and anxious about their intimate relationships, as well as about their life roles.

The effect of the women's movement on marriage. Perhaps to some degree the women's movement is altering marital sex roles. The more radical branch of this movement has tried to do away with patriarchy. They often question the organization of the family itself and the traditional sex-role dichotomies. These women have forced the public to re-examine basic assumptions regarding family forms, sex roles, abortion, and childbearing.

While the woman's movement has effected certain improvements, it has been distorted by some people who raise absurd fears in women's minds concerning being conscripted for the armed forces or fundamentally harming the family. Such objections are actually a ruse which diverts women from the more significant aspects of the movement. As a result women are sabotaging themselves by not fully supporting the very movement that has done more for them than anything else in recorded history except, perhaps, suffrage. As a result of such distortions many women will support few of the ideas promulgated by feminists except equal pay for women. Less radical groups, such as the National Organization of Women (NOW), have sought changes in law and education which would expand women's opportunities and provide them with greater power. Groups such as NOW have succeeded in effecting changes regarding women's employment, opening up colleges and clubs to more women, and making textbooks in public schools nonsexist.

Studies indicate how little most women really know about the women's movement. Halas (1974) studied 63 mature women, all married or previously married, who were enrolled in community colleges, as well as their acquaintances who were not enrolled in school, with regard to sex stereotypes and the women's movement. Most had been stereotypically socialized as children with regard to career and marriage, but they had become more liberal as adults. In a projective portion of the study the subjects indicated a strong tendency to subordinate their own needs to those of their husbands and children, to take care of their own needs only after making extraordinary efforts to see that their families' needs were met, and to seek excuses for their behavior in the few cases where they put their own welfare first.

For the vast majority, their life styles had been determined by their sex-role socialization. They had been encouraged to marry, for marriage was seen as the only fulfilling and appropriate role for women. At the same time they had been discouraged from having a college education or career goals. The results suggest that those who experience pressure during early development to limit their goals, take on those stereotypes and become docile, passive, and obedient.

A large majority (82%) of the mature students and 56% of their women acquaintances in the study approved of the women's movement. However their interest in it was narrow; they viewed receiving equal pay for equal work as the chief objective of feminism. The small minority whose earlier socialization experiences had been less stereotyped, had gone to college, had liberal attitudes, and identified more closely with the feminist movement. But even those who expressed strong feelings about the women's movement had only limited information about it.

Currently husband-wife sex roles are in too great a state of flux to predict what they will be in the years ahead. There are those who feel that the emancipation of women will make men feel increasingly emasculated and cause women to lose that elusive essence of subservience and nurturance traditionally identified as femininity. On the other hand, most psychologists and college-educated persons believe that recent changes in sex roles, if they persist, will make marital relationships far healthier than before. Perhaps it is most realistic to view sex roles as continuously evolving and reflecting changes in the total society.

New Types of Sex Roles

The modern role. New concepts in sex roles have two main features. One is the idea of sex-role equality. This primarily means putting females in the work force on an equal basis with males. There has been little consideration of how male roles would or should be changed to effect this equality (Osmond & Martin, 1975). The second new concept in sex roles is more fundamental, and involves a complete reorientation of sex-role concepts. Traditional sex roles clearly differentiate the roles of men and women. Modern sex roles, by contrast, are characterized by "flexible and dynamic transcendence of sex-role constraints. That is, modern definitions of social roles are not specified by sex" (p. 745). Instead they focus on "individual human potentiality" (Naffziger & Naffziger, 1974, p. 257). The ideal is that both sexes learn to "define themselves solely in terms of humanness and not what men do that women should not do" (p. 257).

This new type of orientation has several advantages. First, it acknowledges repressed needs in both sexes. For example, males, who are presumed to be unemotional, need some emotional outlet; and since love is portrayed as all powerful the male can feel control without feeling a loss of masculinity. It also permits women to experience a hitherto repressed need to escape domination. A mutual need for love equalizes the sex power in the relationship. The new roles also "facilitate individual growth so that females and males are primarily human beings, sure in ego strength, and capable of making actualized, caring relationships" (Hirsch, 1974, p. 170).

The androgynous and bicultural concepts. There are several alternative interpretations of these new sex roles, although they are basically much alike in rejecting the rigid dichotomy of traditional ones (O'Leary & Depner, 1976). One conception, the androgynous gender role, suggests that individuals of either sex should freely incorporate characteristics traditionally associated with either males or females. That is, both sexes may develop attributes characterized as extremely masculine or extremely feminine without violating their own gender identity. Thus the woman who has confined her development to the so-called feminine characteristics is only partially a person and functions inadequately unless she gets married. She requires a husband to do many things that her feminine role denies her. O'Leary and Depner (1976) warn that the androgynous role may produce a superwoman syndrome, in which a woman enacts both male and female gender roles. That is, she may strive to compete professionally while at the same time performing all the traditionally female domestic duties. This dual role may prove extremely exhausting both physically and psychologically. It is better to encourage either sex to function without any limitations imposed by biological gender; but neither sex should feel compelled to enact all the roles traditionally associated with both sexes. That is, it becomes essential to establish priorities instead of trying to take on all the responsibilities of both sexes.

For his part the androgynous male would simply be concerned about developing his own unique potential, without regard to proving his masculinity or having a fear of appearing feminine. The male artist or teacher might devote considerably more of his time and thought to expressive activities than the forester or construction worker, yet neither would feel less masculine than the other. According to the androgynous concept, the most effectively masculine male is the one who comes to appreciate and develop those characteristics which are uniquely his own.

Lee and Gropper's (1974) concept of biculturalism is similar. Each sex has been confined to its own way of life or culture, and thus deprived of a whole cluster of abilities, feelings, and interests reserved, on altogether arbitrary grounds, for the other. The ideal is not to produce masculinized females or feminized males but to let all persons become complete individuals, with free access to the total environment.

The concept of equity. The Rapoports' (1975) concept of equity between the sexes agrees, in the main, with the foregoing views, but it has a different twist. Various aspects of heterosexual relations become involved in attempts to establish equity, including friendship between a couple, sexual activities, and concepts of the meaning of masculinity and femininity. Traditionally, the male-female stereotypes have involved assigning different values, ideals, and behaviors to each sex. A woman could strive to achieve, so long as it was in the area of woman's activities. The man could be nurturant, so long as it was appropriate to his vocation. Indeed sex roles inevitably overlap and operate in a complex, interrelating fashion, despite the tendency to dichotomize them. Moreover peoples' bisexual nature has long been recognized, although incorporating this notion into concepts of self and everyday life styles is difficult. It "threatens learned responses in relation to one's own maleness or femaleness, and therefore oneself as a person" (p. 426).

The concept of equity does not necessarily mean an equal division of tasks, or performing the same tasks. Instead it means providing for equal and fair opportunity when conditions are not strictly equal. This suggests possibilities for variation instead of a rigid adherence to a new stereotype, that of equality. It embraces the principle of equality of choice, and of fair distribution of both responsibilities and privileges. It may involve inequality in the sense of not being exactly the same, provided that this situation is freely entered into and approved by the individuals concerned.

Implicit in the equity concept is the danger that traditional arrangements will simply be accepted as equitable because the parties concerned lack any real awareness of the inequities actually involved. Nevertheless, argue the Rapoports (1975), it is better to devote our energies to raising consciousness than deliberately to impose a new form that may be uncomfortable for both parties concerned. That is, equity means balancing the rewards as well as the more unpleasant duties in ways that are fair, if not exactly the same. Over the life cycle the balance will change and shift, and at various times partners to the arrangement will be doing and receiving more or less.

Current Status and Prospects of Change

Current status. The data concerning the current status and future prospects of sex roles are confusing. Considerable research suggests that most of the changes resulting from women's liberation have been peripheral rather than fundamental. In a nationwide survey of young people aged 14 to 25, regarding their choice of adult life style, 36% of the women judged the life of the "average housewife, raising children, with time for own interests, the most appealing" ("Youth attitudes," 1975, p. 64). In another study, this one of middle- and lower-middle-class adults, Lowenthal, Thurnher and Chiriboga (1975) perceived few signs of sex-role change, even in adolescents and young adult groups, and even less in the older groups. Instead the life styles anticipated by both sexes were "family centered and male dominant" (p. 244). Only the college and university students were making substantial changes in traditional sex roles. Even younger persons were somewhat conservative.

A survey of juniors and seniors at a Florida University also revealed surprisingly traditional sex-role attitudes (Osmond & Martin, 1975). Both sexes approved a relatively sharp sexual division of labor within the family; and females were given chief responsibility for home and child care. Only a slight majority (55%) of both sexes favored passage of the Equal Rights Amendment. Since these results were from a sampling of well-educated young adults, it might be anticipated that a lower middle-class sampling would assume an even more traditional position. Furthermore, if the views of upper-class college students can be taken as the weather vane of social change, this study suggests that little fundamental difference in the distribution of family sex roles can be anticipated within the near future.

Yet other evidence suggests that fundamental changes in sex-role attitudes have occurred. Among a sampling of college freshmen, a "dramatic shift" occurred in favor of the women's movement between 1967 and 1972. In 1967 38% of the females and 61% of the males agreed that "the activities of married women are best confined to the home and the family." By 1972 these figures had become 18% and 39% respectively (Yankelovich, 1972). Meantime college women are becoming more aggressive in lovemaking and men more tender, thus improving chances for mutual understanding and satisfaction (Walsh, 1972).

Often middle-aged women are even more strongly feminist than younger ones. As Bernard (1975) points out, the life style of middle-aged women (ages 35 to 55) has changed. Often they do not have elaborate hairdos. They use less make-up, and some use none. Their clothes are more casual, and they often wear slacks instead of skirts. Entertaining has also become less formal. Instead of encouraging their daughters to be coquettish, many mothers are often disappointed if their daughters do not take initiative in asking boys to dance with them at high-school parties.

Gardner (1974) believes that women's lib has had its most dramatic effect on the blue-collar woman. Traditionally "her life was captive to the triangle of husband, children and home. Her role in life was to be the wife, mother and homemaker—and . . . her primary goal and duty was to fulfill that role as best she could" (p. 17). As the result of her restricted role the blue-collar woman was isolated from the outer world. She felt ill at ease and that she had little worth in the world outside her home. She accepted without question that women must serve their husbands, and that women workers must receive lower pay than men and have fewer opportunities for advancement. Moreover they reared their sons and daughters to look on the woman's role the same way. They did not feel their daughters needed much education because it was not necessary for homemaking.

However, many working-class women today are demanding a better deal. They expect to be able to combine homemaking and career if they choose, and to receive the same pay, choice of jobs, and opportunity as men. They still want to keep up with the Joneses next door, not with people in an elegant neighborhood across town. Apparently they don't care as much about social mobility as they used to, although their desire for material possessions is growing. Increasingly, such women are doing volunteer work, taking part in protest groups, working at full- or part-time jobs, and developing interests outside the neighborhood. After the children grow up they don't think they will feel useless, but rather will continue to be involved in many activities. They expect to do things with their husbands, such as taking winter vacations together. They have more egalitarian relationships with their husbands than working-class women had in the past. The majority want no more than three children, and the trend among the younger ones is toward two.

The truth is that the traditional divisions in sex roles remain basically the same but that numerous more peripheral changes are occurring. To what degree these changes will work their way through to the core is uncertain. It cannot be assumed that a trend will continue in the same direction. Already a subtle change has occurred in the women's liberation movement itself.

The new feminism is not

> an organized movement; nor does it hold meetings or press conferences. It is an all-pervasive rise in female awareness that has permeated virtually every level of womanhood in America, at all ages. Today women believe they have more options, that they can do things that will change their lives, that they have the wherewithal to improve their economic status (Adler, 1975, p. 114).

Reasons for modifying sex roles. People have questioned whether sex roles should or even can be modified. To what extent are they biologically decreed? Is the liberated woman or the happy housewife the ideal?

Those who urge conformity with the old standard say that individuals who find it easy to go along with the prescribed roles are happier. In the area of sex role, as in any other, those who can accept the status quo are naturally more comfortable (although not necessarily happier) than those who attempt reform (Rogers, 1977, p. 352).

There are reasons for altering sex roles other than those given in the foregoing discussion. For one thing, strict adherence to traditional sex roles is emotionally unhealthy. Sandra Bem reports that women who have strong traditionally feminine traits also consistently have "high anxiety, low self-esteem, and low self-acceptance. And although high masculinity in males has been related to better psychological adjustment during adolescence, it is often accompanied during adulthood by high anxiety, high neuroticism, and low self-acceptance" (Bem, 1975, p. 59). Freeing people from rigid sex roles would also make them more flexible and would place fewer restrictions on what they can do. According to Montagu (1968), "males have long stood in need of such feminine qualities as tenderness, sensitivity, compassion, and gentleness," and women would benefit from "the adoption of traits hitherto considered purely masculine, such as courage, adventuresomeness, enterprise, and intrepidity." That is, "men need to be humanized; women to be energized. Men need to become more secure, compassionate, and less violent, women to achieve their full status as human beings . . ." (p. 481). (Rogers, 1977, pp. 351–353).

A CONCLUDING STATEMENT

While research reports regarding middle-age sexuality do not agree in detail—primarily because different categories of sampling were employed—it seems clear that practices have become more liberal and attitudes healthier. While sexual problems still exist, there is a more open attitude toward acknowledging and dealing with them.

The same can be said of sex roles: that they have evolved in a healthier direction. Each sex role still has its disadvantages, but these are being more widely recognized and are diminishing. It is unclear at present whether sex roles will become increasingly depolarized or whether they will regress in the years to come. The author believes that a rigid dichotomization of sex roles limits the development of personal potential, and that artificial restrictions on behavior, in the name of sex-appropriateness, should not be tolerated. In a free environment, differences in sex roles would reflect natural predispositions and individual preferences. The result would be widely assorted interpretations of sex roles by both sexes, in ways most comfortable and self-enhancing for each individual.

SUGGESTED READINGS

Bell, R. R. Religious involvement and marital sex in Australia and the United States. *Journal of Comparative Family Studies*, 1974, 5 (2), 109–116. This study of Australian and American working women, whose mean age was 35, concerns their attitudes toward sex roles, and the relationship between their religion and their sexual patterns. In general those women who were more religious also displayed more conservative sexual behavior. Sex roles were more polarized in Australia, and the Australian women were more confused about their sexual roles.

Biegel, H. C. Changing sexual problems in adults. *American Journal of Psychotherapy*, July 1976, 30 (3), 422–432. On the basis of emotional reactions in professional reports, Biegel concluded that researchers are often more interested in promoting their own values than in honestly reporting their findings. The effect is to jeopardize progress in the search for knowledge, and to act against the best interests of society.

Bloom, L. J. & Houston, K. The psychological effects of vasectomy for American men. *Journal of Genetic Psychology*, June 1976, 128, 173–182. Evidence concerning the psychological effects of vasectomy on American men is conflicting. While surveys indicate effects to be generally positive, clinical interviews provide a somewhat different picture.

Dixon, R. B. Measuring equality between the sexes. *Journal of Social Issues*, 1976, 32 (3), 19–31. Women's status in the spheres of sexual relationships, reproduction, homemaking and child care, economic production, and political decision-making are traced in terms of relevant statistical data from 1900 to 1970.

Easton, B. Industrialization and femininity: A case study of nineteenth-century New England. *Social Problems*, April 1976, 23 (4), 389–401. This analysis of the concept of femininity and how it emerged in an industrial economy suggests that ideas regarding women in the 19th century were shaped, to some degree, by the development of capitalism. As women lost their role in the family economy, their dependence on men became greater, and their power diminished. Books of the day declared that woman's role was subordinate to the husband's, and should be devoted to homemaking and childrearing.

Hunt, M. *Sexual behavior in the 1970's*. Chicago: Playboy Press, 1974. On the basis of a nonrandom but well-selected sampling of American adults, this book describes a wide range of sexual attitudes and practices, and compares these findings with data from other research.

Johnson, P. Women and power: Toward a theory of effectiveness. *Journal of Social Issues*, 1976, 32 (3), 99–110. Access to and use of power are examined in terms of sex-role stereotypes; and the hypothesis that women and men are expected to use different bases of power, is supported.

Kaplan, A. G. & Bean, J. P. (Eds.) *Beyond sex-role stereotypes: Readings toward a psychology of androgyny.* Boston: Little, Brown and Company, 1976. Sex roles are discussed in terms of their traditional and alternative conceptions, and their sexual and biological aspects, as are the consequences of sex-role socialization, and influences on sex-role development.

Maccoby, E. E. & Jacklin, C. N. *The psychology of sex differences.* Stanford, California: Stanford University Press, 1974. The writers review and analyze research regarding sex differences, and conclude that the sexes are remarkably similar in many respects and that such differences as exist are largely the result of socialization, not biology. They also evaluate various theories that have been proposed to explain the nature of sex-role socialization.

Pleck, J. H. The male sex role: Definitions, problems, and sources of change. *Journal of Social Issues,* 1976, *32* (3), 155–164. Traditional and modern male roles are discussed from several perspectives including sex-role identity, role strain, and distinctions between the male role in relation to women and that in other areas of life experience.

Seiden, A. M. Overview: Research on the psychology of women. I: Gender differences and sexual and reproductive life. *American Journal of Psychiatry,* 1976, *133* (9), 995–1007. In this first part of a two-part article the author discusses research regarding gender, differences in behavior, and women's sexual and reproductive lives. It is concluded that much that has been reported about the psychology of women should be re-examined, and that research by women would yield different data from that conducted by men.

Socarides, C. W. Beyond sexual freedom: Clinical fallout. *American Journal of Psychotherapy,* July 1976, *30* (3), 385–397. In his evaluation of the nature and meaning of "radical" changes in sexual customs, the writer portrays them as threats to psychological well-being, family structure, and social cohesion. He deplores especially the erosion of gender role and sexual identity, the downgrading of mothering and of the exclusive heterosexual pair model of sex relations, and the acceptance of "severe sexual disorders" as merely alternative modes of normal sexual functioning.

Van Dusen, R. A. & Sheldon, E. B. The changing status of American women: A life cycle perspective. *American Psychologist,* February 1976, *31* (2), 106–116. As a result of changes in recent decades, the family life cycle is coming to assume declining importance in the woman's life cycle. Moreover the social distinction is diminishing between the married and unmarried (no longer married, never married, or not yet married). It is predicted that such trends will have a profound effect on the family, the economy, and social values.

Middle Age in the Nuclear Family

The nuclear family is composed of the father, mother, and children, as distinguished from the extended family, which also includes one or more relatives. The former plays a highly signicant role in our society. Except for a tiny minority, all young people expect to marry, have children, and live only with them and their spouse. Despite attacks on it, there is plenty of evidence that marriage within the framework of the traditional nuclear family is still popular in this country (U.S. Bureau of the Census, 1976). Fewer than 1% of couples live together, in a "quasi-familial" relationship, without marriage (Glick, 1975). Despite the rising divorce rate, two in three couples maintain intact marriages as long as they both live. Society itself has become so rootless, observes Kirkpatrick (1974), that only the nuclear family remains to fulfill the role of persons of unusual significance in an individual's life.

MIDDLE-AGED PARENTS

Parental Roles

Within the nuclear family parents still play a large parenting role, but the emphasis has changed. Even motherhood is not static; it contains at least three stages: (1) early motherhood, when the children are preschoolers and the mother is about 25 to 34; (2) middle motherhood, when the children are school aged and the mother is in the 35-to-54 age range; and (3) late motherhood, when the children are 18 or over and the mother is past 55. When women live to old age the mother-child roles sometimes become reversed (Bernard, 1975). In middle age, therefore, the mother—and of course, the father—have children of high school age or older. The mother often becomes an important confidant of her daughter, and sometimes of her son.

The father's role changes somewhat too. The very young father takes an interest in his children for a while and then, because of work pressures, becomes much less involved. Later on, in middle age, middle-class men, at least, often seek to establish a closer bond with their children (Sheehy, 1976). To some extent they may succeed—adolescents typically admire their fathers—but at this age teenagers are seeking autonomy and spend little time with either parent.

The father's role depends partly on his social class, for lower-class fathers are generally less involved and more authoritarian than middle-class ones. Fathers with a poorer education may feel somewhat inadequate as their children's education equals or surpasses their own. In general the more children there are in the family, the more authoritarian and controlling the father becomes. Both middle-class parents reason with their children more, while lower-class parents use physical punishment (Troll, 1975).

As children move into and through adolescence, the parents' roles subtly change. In the family, middle age is associated with children growing up and leaving home. The man may be threatened by the increasing power of his almost-grown sons at a time when his feelings of "physical potency" are declining (Fried, 1967). There may also be a shift in "locus of power" within the nuclear family in middle age (Neugarten & Guttman, 1964). The man may become guilty about his aggressiveness up to now, and the woman may become the central figure in the family constellation. During earlier middle age her nurturance and aggression were important to the family's emotional life. However as time goes on she becomes increasingly important, to the point that "she pushes the father from the stage and seems to draw strength from his decline" (Rosenberg & Farrell, 1976, p. 163).

The Pluses and Minuses of Middle-aged Parenthood

Problems. There are certain problems involved in being a middle-aged parent. Young people often try out various activities their parents would not approve of, including cohabitation, smoking pot, and having premarital sex. Parents also worry about their almost-grown children's choices of dates, driving habits, and vocational choices. Nevertheless they must tread softly and avoid appearing to dictate to their children for fear of alienating them and severing the lines of communication.

Parents must also help them to establish their autonomy, or independence; and must resist the need to bind them to themselves. While considerable attention has been paid to parents' attachment to their children, observes Bardwick (1974), far less has been paid to their separation from them. Nevertheless the bonds must be loosened if children are to mature. In other words the concept of parenting, and especially maternity, as "forever nurturing," is simply not consistent with the best needs of the child. Healthy children are created not only through attachment but also through separation.

As middle-aged parents, the emphasis of parenting shifts to a role of helping the teenager establish his or her own identity and independence.

Sometimes parents may feel overwhelmed, especially if they both work, and have aging parents besides. In such cases they may be torn between feelings of obligation to their children, spouse, and work, and those to their parents. For the most part, in such dilemmas they give priority to their own children (Kalish, 1975).

Rewards. There are compensations, too, in childrearing, which are somewhat different from what they used to be. In the past many parents relied on their children to perform chores in the home or supplement the family income by working. Parents also used to expect their children to support them when they grew old. Nowadays, in some cases, the children help to strengthen or extend the family's economic control. For example, consider the family control of major corporations. Children's own occupational achievements may provide prestige and esteem to their parents, particularly at a time when they are leaving the working world themselves.

There is less child-parent conflict today, too, perhaps because the gap between the generations in basic values has narrowed. In a study in which the members of 73 three-generation families were questioned regarding their views on eight major social issues, the liberal parents had a higher percentage of liberal children than the conservative ones (Fengler & Wood, 1973). While generational differences do exist, they are mostly superficial (Troll, 1972).

As a result of the reduced parent-child conflict, as well as the growing equalitarianism in spouse relationships, the formerly hierarchical power relations in the family have diminished. The matter of power within the family, predicts Yorburg (1973), will ultimately disappear, for parents will "defer to and learn from children, if the occasion suggests, as they will defer to and learn from each other" (p. 258). Indeed there has been a reversal in the traditional socialization patterns. Considering the current rate of social change, youth's more flexible adaptation to change, and the parents' desire to comprehend their children, parents often imitate their children's behavior rather than the reverse. Thus parents may seek to keep up with and link themselves to the changing world through their almost-grown-up children. Examples might be "language accumulation, even four-letter words, music patterns, and the new dance steps, and in some cases, hair styles and drug experimentation" (Gunter & Moore, 1975, pp. 203–204). On the other hand some authorities believe that the erosion of adult authority can go too far (Baumrind, 1974). They believe that "the roles of guide and guided are essentially hierarchical. . . . and that youth will hardly seek advice from those whose status is exactly on a par with their own" (Rogers, 1977, p. 430).

Individual testimony. Here several middle-aged men and women indicate to what degree and in what way they have found their children satisfying.

> My greatest satisfaction has been having a family and watching them grow through their changes. (*Female, age 43*)

> My children have enriched my life enormously. I'd probably be a rigid old female without them. (*Female, age 59, housewife*)

> I loved bringing my children up. They have their own interests and families and don't enjoy my company much, but that happens, too. I am sure if I was sick or less independent they would be concerned, if it weren't too time-consuming. (*Female, age 61, activity director*)

> I am enjoying them more now as a parent-friend since they are older and we can mutually share in our enjoyment of the things we do together. (*Female, age 41, teacher*)

> I have always been so busy with my work that I haven't had much to do with my children. However, I do love them and am proud of them. (*Male, age 50, stockbroker*)

> I've always enjoyed my children and, as they have grown older, have felt increasingly close to them. (*Male, age 55, physician*)

The Middle-aged as First-time Parents

So far our discussion has concerned children who are almost or completely grown, but sometimes couples have their first child when they are middle-aged. The do so despite certain risks. The chance of having a mongoloid child after age 40 is much greater, about one in a hundred. However, as we mentioned earlier the process of amniocentesis, by which a small amount of amniotic fluid is drawn by a needle from the uterus, has become 100% accurate in detecting Down's Syndrome (mongolism) and various other chromosomal abnormalities. If it is discovered that a woman is bearing a seriously handicapped child the fetus may be aborted. Besides, a growing body of data suggests that the physical dangers of having a baby after age 35 have been vastly exaggerated.

The wisdom of having children at this age depends partly on the parents' motive. In some cases a woman may become pregnant in order to avoid making certain decisions, perhaps that of re-entering the work world. Sometimes the wife becomes pregnant because she finally decides that she does not want to miss the experience of childbearing and rearing. When older couples genuinely desire the child, they are usually very successful and level-headed parents, and better prepared financially than younger couples to provide superior care.

The "Empty-nest" Stage

The increasingly long empty-nest stage, the time after the children have grown up and left home, may be "the most dramatic change" in the typical family life cycle. This time has increased from 2 to 13 years, chiefly because of improved survival rates. It has many implications, the most significant being that not only does the empty-nest period occupy a notably longer fraction of the parents' total life span, but also husband-wife relations subtly alter—for better or for worse—after the children leave home. In fact, since the birth rate is declining and people are living longer, in the very near future married couples will spend more post-parental years alone together than they did as parents (Cleveland, 1976). In addition, many wives seek employment to fill the gap created by the children's leaving home. Meantime a substantial number of such couples find it practical to live in smaller yet more modern living quarters (Glick, 1977).

In the empty-nest period, parents are often portrayed as feeling desolate and alone. With certain exceptions, especially among women, the opposite is more often true. In fact many middle-aged couples feel considerable relief when their children no longer consume so much of their money and time (Kalish, 1975). In a sampling of 54 middle- and lower-middle-class men and women whose youngest child was about to leave home, Lowenthal and Chiriboga (1972) concluded that they anticipate a somewhat simpler life style and look forward to relaxing. Thus, "raising a family seems to be one of those tasks, like losing weight or waxing the car, that is less fun to be doing than to have done" (Campbell, 1975, p. 39).

Certain women may indeed have problems, partly because this period often coincides with menopause. Women who have centered their lives around motherhood may experience an identity crisis similar to that their husbands may experience upon retirement (Troll, 1971). Even well-adjusted professional women may find it hard to learn to let loved ones go. Eleanor Luckey (1974) recalls that "I was not ready to let go of my parents when they died; I hadn't finished working through my own dependency" (p. 312). Then she recalls that after her children grew up she had to let them go and "if there is a way of loving and letting go without pain, I have not found it!" (p. 312).

A great deal depends on the mother's total situation. Data from six national surveys give strong evidence that children's leaving home does not typically have negative or lasting effects on the mother's psychological well being. Instead these studies indicate that middle-aged women whose children have left home are somewhat happier and enjoy life more than women of the same age with children living at home. On the other hand these data concern only women who are currently living with a husband or other adult, and they probably conceal many less fortunate cases (Glenn, 1975). Only if other aspects of their lives are good—in terms of finances, health, and emotional support from their husbands—do women make a satisfactory adjustment. While they may not especially care about romance, at least companionship is important to them, and their level of marital satisfaction may be similar to that of newlyweds (Troll, 1971).

In general the children's departure from home doesn't affect the fathers as much as the mothers because children have typically played a lesser role in their lives. The father of adult children may assume an even lesser role than he did when the children were small (Troll, 1975). Later on, after the children establish their own families, the fathers experience less conflict with them but also gain less pleasure from them. Again the foregoing is a generalization. Because of special situations— perhaps the father is unusually attached to a particular child—a few fathers may find the adjustment hard.

MARITAL RELATIONSHIPS

The Family Career

The matter of husband-wife relationships is many-faceted, involving multiple roles and several "subcareers." The lifetime family career involves several of these subcareers: the sexual experience career, the marital career, the parental career, and the adult-parent career (Bernard, 1972). There is also a distinction between "her marriage" and "his marriage." Most family studies involve primarily those who simultaneously embark upon the marital and sexual experience careers and then, after an interval, move into the parental and adult careers. However, among couples studied by Trost (1973), only 38% followed the usual plan for the family career. These exceptions included 26% who began marriage with the bride pregnant, and 16% who had a child who was preschool age or older. Other couples omitted the more common stages of rearing a child from birth and adopted a teen-age child shortly after they married. Thus for many individuals, sex experience and parenting exist either before or outside a particular marital career. Meantime individual life career changes affect both the adults and children involved. These critical points include "entry into work by the wife, the onset of a critical illness, or [problems with] a delinquent child . . . " (Hutchinson, 1975, p. 282).

Marital Roles

The wife-mother role. At all stages of these family careers the marital partners play their respective roles. Traditionally the woman has been nurturant and self-sacrificing—a role sometimes portrayed as demeaning. It also has its advocates: Chilman (1974), for one, believes that many people have gone too far in criticizing "self-sacrificing mothers" and observes that there are gains as well as losses in serving others, including one's children. Gains may include developing such personality traits as "compassion, generosity, self-respect, and endurance" (Chilman, 1974, p. 129). The sacrifice becomes undesirable if at the same time, it excludes filling one's own needs, and/or when it unconsciously breeds feelings of resentment toward those being served, or makes them overdependent.

Certainly many women find their greatest fulfillment in the role of wife and mother. As Eleanor Luckey, a highly respected professor of child development and family relations, observed:

My own richest experiences—my most growth-provoking—my most joyful and most painful have been because I have been a daughter, wife, and mother. I believe that I have learned to value myself and what I have to offer others because I was cared for and valued as a child by my parents, and especially because I have been loved and accepted by a man who knew me as I was and loved me anyway . . . . Overall, the most prevailing thing I have learned about family life is that it is worth the effort! (Luckey, 1974, p. 312).

Nevertheless, inherent in this often-glorified role are certain major problems which have their roots deep in the past. One such difficulty is that the very origin of this role is surrounded with some unhealthy associations, one being that women were considered too weak and emotional to do anything else. In 1873 the Supreme Court held that "the natural and proper timidity and delicacy which belongs to the female sex evidently unfits it from many of the occupations of civil life. . . . The paramount destiny and mission of women are to fulfill the noble and benign offices of wife and mother. This is the law of the creator" (Bradwell vs. Illinois, 1873, pp. 130, 147; cited in Weitzman, 1975). The same Supreme Court upheld an Illinois State Court decision depriving a married woman of the right to practice law (Kay, 1974). The court's opinion states that "Man is, or should be, woman's protector and defender" (Bradwell vs. Illinois, 1873, pp. 130, 147). In those days it was also the married woman's task to cater to her husband's emotional needs, and in so doing, to derive vicarious satisfaction, which would amply satisfy her (Pleck, 1974).

Such attitudes are by no means obsolete today. One provision that the state-designed marriage contract imposes on women is almost total responsibility for child care, both during marriage and after divorce. This social assignment is perhaps the "most stubborn and intractable bastion of discrimination" (Brief for Appellees in Geduldig versus Aiello, 1974, p. 41; cited in Weitzman, 1975). In other words, the courts are not in tune with changing sex roles (Weitzman, 1975).

The wife-mother role presently is a somewhat fluid one, and represents a wide spectrum, from the quite traditional to the very modern. The general trend is in the modern direction. Mousseau (1975) declares that in recent times the woman is taking on increasing importance in the family, not only as her husband's companion and "economic associate," but also in educational and emotional functions. At the same time family duties are becoming less rigidly divided. It simply is not fair, observes Weitzman (1975), to burden men with the total burden of financial support. It is also unfair "to impose on women exclusive responsibility to perform household chores and to take care of young children. Such prescriptions derive from sexual stereotypes and produce both an unnecessary rigidity and specificity" (p. 540).

The husband-father role. The husband-father role is evolving, too, in a healthy direction. In a sense the changes in the wife's role are forcing men into a different, more constructive one. For one thing, as women begin to acknowledge their own needs, they have less time to cater to men's. Men may also be expected to express themselves emotionally, rather than having women do it for them (Pleck, 1974). The liberation of males from their emotional bonds is gaining additional impetus from young adults. Part of the result of youth's alienation in the late 1960s was a rejection of the strait-jacketing of males into narrow, unemotional roles.

Men are also being liberated from role of sole provider. This obligation has caused many males to have a sense of failure in the past. Even today, in two-thirds of the states a woman is not responsible for the support of her husband no matter what the circumstances. In the other states, she is responsible only if he has become a public charge or incapacitated (Kay, 1974). The husband, however, may be required to pay alimony in case of divorce. This is based on the assumption that women, like children, are incapable of supporting themselves. Today alimony is awarded in fewer than 15% of all divorce cases, and non-compliance with alimony awards is common (Kay, 1974). Nevertheless the threat of being placed in this position still hangs over men's heads.

On the other hand, support for more rational policies regarding alimony is growing, with a concern for equity for both spouses. Even more promising in terms of the man's financial burden, is the massive influx of women into the work world, so that the family's well-being does not rest on his shoulders alone. When only a minority of women worked, some men felt emasculated because they depended on their wives to help them fulfill what was traditionally only their role.

A study of marital roles. A study of 210 couples aged 28 to 50, in Yakima County, Washington, suggested that while certain marital roles persist, others are changing. The traditional family roles of child care, child socialization, and provider are still widely accepted and enforced. Either one or both parents is assigned the role of child socialization, and the same is true for the child care role. The provider role is unanimously considered to be the father's responsibility. Two other roles, the housekeeping and kinship roles, are weakening. A majority of the respondents felt an obligation to keep in touch with relatives and to help them in financial emergencies; yet fewer than 40% expressed any great disapproval of those who failed to discharge such obligations. Practically all of the respondents still perceived housekeeping as either the duty of the wife or of wife and husband jointly; nevertheless only a minority of both sexes would strongly disapprove of a woman who felt no strong commitment to the housekeeper role. Three other roles are attaining increasing importance, one being the therapeutic role. Approximately 70% of the husbands and 60% of the wives believed that each spouse should help the other solve problems. Also of increasing importance is the recreational role. The respondents believed that both parents have obligations to provide recreation for the family, and strongly disapprove of parents who fail to do so. Traditionally only the wife's sexual duties have been recognized. However, in this study, 90% of both sexes believed it was each spouse's duty to be available to meet the other's sexual needs, and the spouse who rarely or never consents to have sexual intercourse was strongly disapproved. Nevertheless a few men and a sizable minority of women fail to respond to the sexual needs of their spouses (Nye, 1974).

The interaction of husband-wife roles. It should be apparent that whatever changes occur in the roles of one spouse automatically have repercussions for the other. As women enter the work world, men become pressured into sharing duties of housekeeping and childrearing. While the majority of women who hold full-time jobs still do more of the household chores, the trend is toward equality. As younger women emerge into adulthood they will take with them the values of equity and of self-actualization they now take for granted.

Often husband and wife roles interact in complex, subtle ways. Take the case of some couples in their early 40s, who fall into a 20-year marriage slump, perhaps because in our youth-worshipping culture they still carry around fantasies that may have fitted the first half of life, but not the second (Sheehy, 1976). The second half of life has its own special styles and significance. Sometimes the husband who has failed to realize his life ambition simply projects the blame onto his wife. At other times the wife is tired of living vicariously through her husband's successes rather than achieving her own status. Or the husband may be tired of working toward a goal, and somewhat bored from living such a narrow, vocationally-oriented life. By contrast the wife, perhaps freed of young children, may begin to blossom. She begins to see the husband for what he is. When husbands become uncertain of themselves, wives have traditionally built-up their egos. If they do it conspicuously, however, their husbands may feel resentful. Instead of feeling nourished a husband simply begins to feel trapped. He may be made more conscious of the failings he was trying to hide from himself. For her part the wife may feel almost compelled to get her husband's permission before taking steps on her own. However, she must get over perceiving him as something of a surrogate parent, with the authority to give or withhold permission, if she is to grow. In short the marital contract must be renegotiated, not in one dramatic step, but through a series of steps across the years.

The Equable Relationship

The concept of equity. Rhona and Robert Rapoport (1975) believe that people should not aim to make husband and wife roles equal, but equitable. As people shift and change at various stages in the life cycle the domestic load will be redistributed, and each party will assume an active responsibility for many household duties (Rapoport & Rapoport, 1975).

Couples with children must also consider the matter of children's equity, especially in terms of family decision-making and the family division of labor. The allocation of tasks and activities such as cleaning, bed-making, and shopping, must be made regardless of sex. Ideally parents and children resolve these matters together; and the children may actually participate in reeducating the parents. With regard to decision-making, there is the question of whether children should be protected from more critical conflicts within the family. It is still uncertain, in terms of both research data and clinical experience, to what degree and when children should become involved in, or be shielded from, parental crises (Rapoport & Rapoport, 1975).

Obstacles to change. It is no simple matter to modify roles deeply rooted in tradition. One significant obstacle is the internal feelings against change experienced by both sexes; these derive from their early socialization into traditional sex roles. That is, it is difficult to

> disentangle one's sex-stereotypes from an assessment of what one's actual capacities are. Is the man who dislikes cooking and makes a mess of it doing so because he is really "bad" at this kind of thing, or because he has powerful internal resistance, conscious or unconscious, to being typed as "feminine"? Is the man who does not like to sew on buttons expressing a free inclination to have his dislike respected as an individual taste, just as many of his wife's individual tastes should be expressed, or is he responding to sex typing? Conversely, is the woman who cannot change a fuse, or who cannot handle financial accounts, only expressing personal inclinations, or is she tied to sex-role binds? (Rapoport & Rapoport, 1975, p. 430).

Such introjected resistance—incorporating external events (in this case, role changes) and reacting to them (by resisting) as if they were internal—to real equity in parenting is great, and there is no single way to achieve equitable marital arrangements. The parents may arrive at various solutions, perhaps alternating part-time and full-time work conditions in order to be more home-based. Some couples may attempt to develop forms of child care within the community.

Another obstacle to achieving equity has been the traditionally lopsided division of the parenting function. Child care has been associated with mothers, and all sorts of rationales have been used for stressing the importance of their physical presence during the children's early years. The removal of the workplace from the family setting after the industrial revolution had the effect of removing parental functions from the man. This separation of sex roles in the family has existed for so long that it is difficult to change. Even today businesses operate on the assumption that families must adapt to the needs of the worker-husband and father. And until the workplace adapts in terms of schedules and other matters, readjustments of familial sex roles will encounter resistance.

Ways to achieve equity. Despite such roadblocks, progress toward equity can be developed in several ways. Dialogue and discussion groups about sex-role change would permit people to arrive at conclusions in more relaxed ways than would be possible if only the couple was involved. It is also important that males perceive that they will gain more than they will lose by such readjustments, chiefly through living a fuller life instead of a unidimensional one (Rapoport & Rapoport, 1975).

Help may also come from consciousness-raising groups that participate in developing and disseminating new ideas. Important, too, are friendships and supportive networks through which persons with common problems can talk together about critical issues and take advantage of each other's skills and resources. Implicit in such resources is the need to decrease the degree of privacy involved in most family life. While many couples may not care to join communal groups, they may at least establish ties through participation groups, voluntary activities, and other links with the community (Rapoport & Rapoport, 1975).

Other Marital Problems

Shortcomings of the spouse. Not all problems relate directly to the sex-role dichotomy. Sometimes the marriage relationship is strained because one partner has outgrown the other (Tsoi-Hoshmand, 1976). A lag by one partner may develop for a variety of reasons; for example, a working wife may have supported her husband through college. In other cases mothers may spend all their time looking after their husbands and children while neglecting the development of their own potential. Such a situation can have quite unpleasant effects. For one thing, the marriage partner who has dedicated all her time to the children may resent the other's participation in activities outside the home. This situation also invites unfavorable comparisons by each spouse of the other.

A second and related problem is the new focus on escaping traditional sex-role stereotypes, among them that many men simply do not know how to behave in the tender, warm, and sharing fashion that women are coming to demand (Koch & Koch, 1976). For their part, women often have ambivalent or guilty feelings about placing their own needs on the same plane with those of their husbands and children; yet they are no longer willing to settle for the selfless, passive role bequeathed them by earlier generations (Koch & Koch, 1976).

Traditional problems. In addition marital partners still experience traditional problems—a lack of communication, unfulfilled emotional needs, problems with the kids, sexual problems, infidelity, money, in-laws, alcoholism, and physical abuse (Koch & Koch, 1976). The very fact that such problems are common may tend to perpetuate them. We may come to look on them as inevitable instead of developing new and creative ways to solve them. Yet their very persistence alerts us to the fact that they are extremely difficult to solve.

Here several men and women evaluate their married life and its chief problems.

> My wife has not grown over the years. She's a bore and I've only endured it by having affairs over the years. (*Male, age 45, teacher*)

> My marriage is very satisfactory. The hardest problem has been trying to understand my wife and having her understand me. It's not a serious problem but one of constant concern. (*Male, age 41*)

> My chief problem in married life has been the struggle to make ends meet. Finances were strained during the 1940s and 1950s. (*Male, age 63, real estate broker*)

> My chief satisfaction in marriage has been good companionship and mutual love. We have adjusted our own individual goals to mutual goals. I enjoy my husband's company. (*Female, age 59, housewife*)

> Marriage is a great institution; it can be beautiful. (*Female, age 61, activity director*)

> I found my married life unsatisfactory due to mother-in-law problems plus a husband who wouldn't face reality and grow up. (*Female, age 51, office clerk*)

Wife abuse. Sometimes marital problems end in wife abuse, a topic which is finally receiving the attention it deserves. In-depth interviews with members of 49 families in which women had been beaten, disclosed that there are certain important factors which influence the actions taken by abused wives (Gelles, 1976). First of all, the less frequent and severe the abuse the more likely the woman will not seek outside support. The second determinant is how much violence the woman experienced as a child. The more she was hit by her parents, the more likely she is to stay with an abusing husband. Wives are also more likely to seek help who have completed high school and are employed. In general the fewer resources the wife has, and the less power, the more abuse she will take from her husband before seeking outside help. Another deterrent to seeking help is the lack of support on the part of police, the courts, and social agencies, which often treat marital violence as a private matter. One woman who called both an agency and the police without receiving any real help, was eventually strangled by her estranged husband. In Gelles's study over three-fourths of the women had sought outside help, but it did not prove entirely satisfactory. For women who have few resources and no job the situation is particularly stressful.

Looking Ahead

Despite marital problems most authorities have an optimistic view of husband-wife relationships in the future. They feel that there will not be turn-arounds, but rather a gradual upgrading of marriage. For example Yorburg (1973) predicts that people will not become more sexually promiscuous. Instead the current trend in male-female relationships in industrial societies has been toward increased mutual respect, recognition of individual differences and needs, stronger affectional ties, and less exploitation. Mace and Mace (1975) believe that the traditional marriage "with its legal rigidity and hierarchical structure, has no future ... " (p. 133). They believe that the "companionship marriage, based on intimacy, equity, and flexible interpersonal interaction, offers a promising new life style, a type of relationship that is being chosen by many couples in American society today" (p. 133). Other new life styles they believe to be of minor significance, and for the most part see them simply as pioneering social experiments which do not represent a viable substitute for more traditional marriages.

Saving and Improving Marriages

Marriage contracts. Efforts to improve marriage may be in the nature of advance planning to insure a happy marriage; or they may be of the maintenance variety, intended to preserve or improve upon what is already good; or of the curative kind, when problems exist. Among the more innovative ideas designed to improve chances for a happy marriage is the personal contract, or premarriage contract, as it is sometimes called (Kelly, 1975). Such a contract is negotiated between the pair before they marry and is signed by both. Its contents vary a great deal from one couple to another, since they reflect the topics which are of greatest concern to each. In general they relate to such matters as division of labor in performing household tasks, division of responsibility for personal finance, number of children to have and when, relationships with in-laws, and where to live. Some couples go further in attempting to anticipate any possible crises that may arise later in the marriage, such as divorce, alimony, or child custody.

These contracts have certain drawbacks, one being their questionable legality. One state, Massachusetts, has provided legislation for upholding the validity of such contracts, but the vast majority have no laws pertaining to them. If the contract violates any existing laws, or if its provisions are clearly contrary to tradition, judges would probably not uphold it. There are other very real problems, too, one being that young people who have never been married before do not know what the marriage relationship involves. Persons capable of devising the most effective contract would be those who have been married before. Another problem is that marriage relationships change over the years, and so do the marital partners themselves. For another thing, such contracts may be so tightly drawn that they are not sufficiently flexible to allow for alternatives within the marriage relationship. Moreover the effort to deal with such contingencies as divorce may involve a self-fulfilling prophecy.

On the other hand, such contracts may serve useful purposes. In drawing up a contract a couple will make a serious effort to anticipate their married life realistically. Negotiating a contract may even persuade them that they should not marry at all. In addition the contract may be a flexible one, with a built-in provision for periodic renegotiation on the basis of what the situation is at a given point in time. The contract may also help to clarify and facilitate communication between the couple, and to determine whether, in fact, they can arrive at harmonious outcomes. There has been little empirical evidence to determine how such contracts fare in the long run.

Marriage counseling. Of late, much attention has been paid to marriages in trouble, and couples are increasingly resorting to therapy. In the process they seek to learn how to communicate with each other and to gain new insight into their problems. Whether they do or not depends upon a number of factors—the type of therapy employed, the therapist, the couple themselves—and the special "chemistry" of all of these combined. Marital therapy often involves two stages. In the first, couples simply arrive at making their lives tolerable. In the second stage they seek not simply to make their relationship tolerable, but actually good.

The types of therapy are numerous. Some of the best-known are network family therapy, in which the entire network of persons significant to a particular family—including neighbors, employers, and friends—may be involved; conjoint family therapy, which involves the entire family and stresses communication, interaction, and generational information; systems theory, an objective analysis of the family system focusing on the roles and needs of each family member as an individual; and multiple impact therapy, which requires two days of intensive work involving not only the whole family but a clinical team of professionals. In this last one, there are meetings with various combinations of family members, in which the division of authority, the marriage itself, and children's views of the family, are analyzed. Six months later the team visits the family to assess its progress. In addition, there is multiple family therapy, in which several families or couples come together with a therapist, and family members share similar experiences. All these approaches stress individual family members' interactions with each other and with the therapist (Keebler, 1976).

Therapists vary widely in personality, competency, and approach. Some of them simply seek to help the couple make the marriage functional again. They assume that if the partners are happy about it, the marriage is indeed working. Others seek actively to improve the relationship, often according to their own concepts of what constitutes a healthy marriage and their special role in helping a couple achieve it. Psychologist Israel Goldiamond of the University of Chicago views himself as a teacher. He feels that he can teach a couple how to get what they want out of life. It may be impossible to get those things if one's choice of mate is bad. In that case, a couple may divorce. Goldiamond does not consider his therapy a failure if divorce occurs, for he believes the most important thing is for people to learn how to get what they are after (Koch & Koch, 1976).

Even the most skilled therapists are ineffective if the couple does not have a strong emotional investment. They must cease blaming each other, children, in-laws, or even the women's liberation movement, and interact as individuals who have plenty of self-esteem. Each will have to give up something, particularly habitual and destructive behavior patterns (Koch & Koch, 1976).

Changing emphasis in marriage counseling. If counseling is to be effective it must also take into account changing concepts of marriage. One of these is that the family must be altered so that those within it can develop alternatives as they come to appreciate each other's limitations and potential. This change would involve more flexible concepts of motherhood, sex roles, and the privacy of the family. Neither parent now lives exclusively for the children, but more openly weighs the anticipated benefits of rearing them. In other times parents received some compensation for their sacrifice through various material and symbolic benefits. But nowadays young people are more likely to go their own way, without inviting their aging parents to reside with them. Unless marriage and family counselors remain abreast of such developments they cannot help marital partners to deal effectively with current problems.

Another change in counseling involves the current emphasis on equalitarian relationships. Couples must now be understood on the level of both being friends and lovers, rather than one being a breadwinner and the other a housewife. It is especially important, observes LeShan (1973), that middle-aged marriage partners become each other's friends who know and respect each other, in spite of knowing each other's weaknesses.

Another change regards divorce. Formerly—and in some quarters even now—divorce has been considered a symptom of failure of the persons involved. Now many people are coming around to the view that it may simply represent the best solution for people who do not help each other grow—not because they are failures as people but because of the effect they have on each other. Tsoi-Hoshmand (1976) observes that a marriage which is destructive to either partner and fails to produce personal growth for both may not be worth maintaining. O'Neill and O'Neill (1972) agree, pointing out that divorce is sometimes essential, for if maintaining a marriage means giving up your own identity, it is better to give up the marriage.

Finally the concept of marital adjustment suggests a dynamic process, not a static condition (Medley, 1977). The marriage itself is a dynamic relationship involving continuous change; hence, studies of marital adjustment must take into account the evolving nature of marital relationships. Marital adjustment is a creative process and "not a fixed mechanical sequence. Therefore, no mere list of suggestions for enhancing marital adjustment will do justice to the complexity of the process" (p. 10).

Defining the Good Marriage

The characteristics of a good marriage as defined by Tsoi-Hoshmand (1976), reflect the underlying philosophy of many marriage counselors. In the first place a good marriage has an unusual degree of mutuality (Levinger & Snoeck, 1972). Mutuality suggests the sharing of values and personal feelings as well as the rewards and strains involved in living. A good marriage will survive even demanding changes within the relationship. Over a period of time the partners will change in the process of seeking increased psychological maturity; and the relationship should have the capacity to stretch and adapt to the stresses of change. Marital partners should also develop problem-solving skills which help them to make the necessary adjustments during all phases of their relationship. In the process they should neither compromise their own personhood or mental health, and in this respect humanistic values are especially relevant. Such values connote each partner's capacity to respect the other's direction of self-fulfillment, and to see marriage as the context of personal growth rather than an obstacle (Tsoi-Hoshmand, 1976). In addition, mutuality involves learning how one's partner is affected by one's own self-satisfying behavior (Levinger & Snoeck, 1972). Middle-aged men, especially, have often been characterized in literature as "feeling drowned in the dullness of life." Sometimes marriages at middle age are described as good, simply because they "are to a great extent unpainful and unexamined, rather than . . . stimulating and challenging. They may be comfortable, and they are easy to endure *and* easy to ignore." Often problems arise between middle-aged couples, having to do more with boredom than with real stress. The middle-aged marriage, therefore, can often be described as "suffering from success"; and this very security may contain within it "the seeds of destruction" (Tsoi-Hoshmand, 1976, p. 9). In time, however, the so-called middle-age crisis may become a stimulus to growth which challenges a couple to take stock of themselves and live a good life (LeShan, 1973).

Appraisals of Marital Success

Marriage as good. Most authorities on the family give it high marks. Eleanor Luckey (1974) believes that the "great quest of life is seeking how to be a loving person. And . . . living in a family provides most of us our greatest opportunity for loving one another" (p. 312). A large majority of families perceive themselves as healthy, too. In the General Mills American Family Report, which was designed to determine the mood of American families, 83% of adults polled believed that their family was in good shape; 78% were pleased with the way their family works together; and 69% expressed a high level of satisfaction with "the amount of fun and enjoyment" in their lives (p. 141). Although over half felt somewhat insecure about their financial future, because of inflation, especially positive feelings predominated ("American family . . . ," 1975).

Comparisons by life stages. Comparisons of marriage satisfaction at different life stages reveal no great variation, despite the common belief that satisfaction decreases after the early glow wears off (Rollins & Cannon, 1974). It is true that marriage satisfaction dips slightly in middle years and rises again in later years; nevertheless the dip is slight. There are unavoidable marriage crises, observes Stern (1976), usually about middle life, but after this, they settle down in their marriage or develop a "new, more stable equilibrium. . . . " (p. 18). Nor is there much difference in marital satisfaction between men and women. Hence both the idea of sex differences in marital satisfaction and the negative effect of the family life cycle itself have been overplayed.

Medley (1977) describes three ideal types of conjugal relationships, which may or may not last throughout the marriage. All three may provide each partner with feelings of self-fulfillment and well-being. The husband-wife type emphasizes the couple's shared, more intimate relationships. While the focus is on husband and wife roles, other roles are not excluded. In the parent-child type, one partner assumes the role of parent, and the other, the child. The parent-spouse acts in a dominant, nurturant, protective manner, while the other behaves dependently and submissively. Such a relationship may develop when one party becomes incapacitated or assumes a sick role. In the associate relationship, couples are more or less friends who appreciate each other's company and find their most rewarding moments outside the more intimate marital relationships. They are effective in managing the business of marital and family life. All three types are found at each stage in the life cycle, in different proportions and varying with passage of time.

The negative view. Although evaluations of family life today are sometimes negative, most are positive. One detractor, France's great historian of the family, Philippe Ariès, contends that the family which has evolved over the past few centuries has become "both an all-purpose refuge and a prison" (Mousseau, 1975, p. 52). Beginning in the 17th century the family's function was not only economic, it also served to socialize and educate the young. Meantime families became not just practical arrangements, but places of more intimate love, so that divorce became an absolutely necessary "safety valve" (p. 52).

Feldberg and Kohen (1976) perceive married life, present and future, as stressful because it is continually subject to external pressures. Such stresses are personal (in the sense that they affect the person involved), and they may derive from problems that that person has. In consequence the relationship often breaks up. Personal differences between marital partners may exist, yet what are presumably personal problems may actually derive from powerful institutions "structured for profit, broadly and narrowly defined, which force family members to compromise their personal commitments in order to maintain their families" (p. 158).

Marriage as boring. LeShan (1973) perceives marriage as having both strong and weak points, but considers it generally somewhat dull. The pressures exerted by jobs and grown children may decrease, which permits a couple to apply more energy and thought to their marriage. However the question may arise as to whether the marriage can endure without the excuse of maintaining it for the sake of the children (LeShan, 1973). Similarly, Kerckhoff (1976) warns that unless both spouses consciously strive to enrich their marriage, middle age may "lead not to marital bliss but to the marital blahs" (p. 9).

New Directions

Suggestions for improving marriage. Despite its apparent success, most authorities believe that marriage could be improved. Mace and Mace (1975) are of the opinion that society should provide married couples the support, training, and guidance that they need. According to Philippe Ariès, it is essential to re-open the family structure, an idea promoted by the women's movement. The important thing, says Ariès, is not so much the insistence of women who stay home that they be granted equality with women in the work world, as the need to get away from the home "where the nineteenth century had imprisoned her, and where the baby boom had chained her even more tightly" (Mousseau, 1975, p. 57).

Future prospects. Others predict that specific changes will take place in the future. Yorburg (1973) believes that the family's responsibility for socializing children will become further restricted. The parental role will be supplemented by experts trained in effective techniques for childrearing. Ariès's (1975) predictions are even more radical. If the life span is extended, an individual would hardly expect to stay with the same spouse for the duration. For instance, a woman might choose to remain attached only during her childbearing years.

Most authorities believe that the family will persist for the foreseeable future, but with some changes. Mace (1974) perceives the family "as a very tough institution" that is nevertheless undergoing a significant transition from institution to companionship (p. 291). This new form is based on "depth relationships combined with individual autonomy" in which marriage partners enjoy

> warm, loving, highly creative relationships; and children develop in a setting which gives them all the emotional security they need, into mature and responsible adults ... [Such families] reach out in every direction and join hands with a wide circle of friends and neighbors with whom they share their lives richly and deeply. In these families no one's personal development is thwarted; they know that those who love them wish only to help them realize all their powers and capabilities. The members of these families suffer no identity crisis; they know who they are, and are proud and glad to belong to each other. Their lives are filled with creative, meaningful activities that enrich them and all who know them (p. 192).

Unfortunately, observes Mace, there is a "curious cult at present which seeks to villify the nuclear family" (p. 191). Many persons have become "fascinated and intoxicated by the contemplation of the extreme, the pathological, the bizarre, and the far out. And all the time, not far from our doorsteps, nuclear families are functioning magnificently and blazing the trail to health and happiness" (p. 192).

In his own wide experience, Mace has observed no satisfactory alternative to the nuclear family. Even extended families have typically been based on hierarchical systems with rigorous and often ruthless discipline. When such families are democratized they ordinarily splinter. With regard to communal groupings, unless they focus on some special purpose such as religion or patriotic goals, they commonly prove unstable (Mace, 1974). In short, Mace perceives in the nuclear family the model of the ideal human society, for "it is a microcosm of the larger world in containing both sexes and a variety of ages. In a manageable setting it enables its members to give and to get in just proportions. It trains them to be sensitive to the needs of others, to work together for common goals, to succor each other in times of crisis, and to find joy and gladness in shared delights" (p. 193).

Bernard (1973) agrees with Mace, predicting that the future of marriage is "as assured as any human social form can be," although it may change in form or name (p. 301). People may even refer to themselves as pair-bonded instead of married. The chief characteristic of the marriage of the future will be "the array of options available to different people who want different things from their relationships with one another ... there will, in brief, be marriages in the future as different from conventional marriages of today, as those of the present are from those of our forebears in the nineteenth century ... " (p. 303).

SUMMARY

Most middle-aged persons are parents within a nuclear family. During their earlier middle age their children are often teenagers, and by later middle age, have left the "nest." Parents find both rewards and frustrations in dealing with their nearly grown children, but the rewards have become greater as families have grown more democratic and the generation gap has narrowed. Despite pride and satisfaction in their children, they often lead a more relaxed, satisfying life after the children leave home.

The family roles of men and women are distinctively different. Most women—even those who work outside the home—still find their greatest satisfaction in the wife-mother role; nevertheless they have their problems. Their dual role in family and on the job is exhausting, for husbands do not assume an equal work role at home. However men are gradually assuming more responsibilities in the home; and middle-class men, at least, are taking their father role seriously.

So far it is unclear what is the healthiest form of relationship between a couple, or how best to achieve it. A complementary relationship, where the ideal is equity, not simply equality, has been proposed as one solution. In order to prevent problems or cope with them when they arise, such techniques as marriage contracts and marriage counseling are employed.

Overall it seems that most middle-agers find family life reasonably satisfying, with the inevitable problems found in all close human relationships. While family roles and married life are changing as the result of changing times, the family remains the cornerstone of society.

SUGGESTED READINGS

Allen, R. C. Men and women together. *Mental Hygiene,* Fall/Winter 1975, *59* (4), 21–25. This analysis of progress toward the elimination of sex discrimination since 1800 focuses on marital relationships and their potential for permitting maximum growth and freedom for both partners.

Bernard, J. *The future of motherhood.* New York: Penguin Books, 1975. In this book, as well as in her earlier one, *The Future of Marriage* (New York: Bantam Books, Inc., 1973), Bernard presents a critique of current marriages and a blueprint for future ones in which equalitarian spouse relationships will prevail.

Booth, A. & Edwards, J. N. Crowding and family relations. *American Sociological Review,* 1976, *41* (2), 308–321. Interviews with 560 families in Toronto whose living places range from open to highly compressed, revealed little or no effect on family relationships between the spouses, between parents and children, or between the children.

Broderick, C. B. Fathers. *The Family Coordinator,* July 1977, *26* (3), 269–275. An analysis is made of the roles of fathers and the range of life styles, based on available research.

Bush, S. A family-help program that really works. *Psychology Today,* May 1977, *10* (12) 48–50, 84–86, 88. A unique program, Family Power, has successfully served as an intermediary between families and service agencies on New York's Lower East Side. In too many cases a maze of programs affords overlapping services so that people often misuse or fail to use them at all.

Chadwick, B. A., Albrecht, S. L., & Kunz, P. R. Marital and family role satisfaction. *Journal of Marriage and the Family,* 1976, *38* (3), 431–440. On the basis of data collected from a random sampling of adults in Utah, factors were identified that contribute to marital and family role satisfaction. Adequacy of role performance by the marital partners, and the spouse's fulfillment of expectations, proved the strongest predictors of satisfaction.

Gelles, R. J. Violence and pregnancy: A note on the extent of the problem and needed services. *Family Coordinator,* 1975, *24* (1), 81–86. A period of pregnancy is represented as the time of crisis when many wives state that they are physically attacked. The pregnancy period as a crisis deserves greater attention, and so does the violence which often accompanies it.

Mace, D. R. & Mace, V. G. Marriage enrichment—Wave of the future? *Family Coordinator,* 1975, *24* (2), 131–135. The concept of marriage enrichment is analyzed, and marriage is portrayed as evolving from an institutional to a companionship relationship in the contemporary world. Marriages are portrayed as requiring interpersonal competencies for which couples need special training, guidance, and support if they are to succeed.

Nichols, B. R. The abused wife problem. *Social Casework,* January 1976, *57* (1), 27–32. Cases of wife abuse are portrayed as having been grossly mishandled, and suggestions are made for improving the situation. Sometimes assistance may take such forms as providing caseworker advocacy for the abused wife, referral of the wife to consciousness-raising groups, and group treatment of couples.

Nilson, L. B. The social standing of a married woman. *Social Problems,* 1976, *23* (5), 581–592. A study of 479 adults was undertaken to identify factors that determine the social status of married women. Variations in assignment of women's status are also analyzed according to sex of respondent.

Nobody home: The erosion of the American family. A conversation with Urie Bronfenbrenner, *Psychology Today,* 1977, *10* (12), 41–43, 45–46, 47. A child development authority deplores the state of the family and feels that it is currently providing an inadequate support system for its members. Society, including employers, should create conditions that will help the family hang together.

Oakley, A. *Woman's work: The housewife, past and present.* New York:

Pantheon Books, Inc., 1975. After reviewing historical attitudes toward woman's work, the author briefly reports an interview sampling of housewives regarding their activities and their attitudes toward them. She then discusses the division of labor by sex and offers certain highly untraditional solutions (abolish the family as well as gender and housewife roles).

Roby, P. A. Shared parenting: Perspectives from other nations. *School Review*, May 1975, *83* (3), 415–431. Roby examines the impact of several nations' public child care services on womens' status and family structures, and then recommends policies that will encourage fathers to share domestic and childrearing responsibilities. Only thus will it be possible for women to share equally in the social, economic, and political life of the nation.

9
CHAPTER

Alternative
Life
Styles

ALTERNATIVES TO THE NUCLEAR FAMILY

Family Groupings

The extended family. The most common type of family in America is the nuclear one. It is composed of the mother, father, and children. Yet there are other forms; they will be reviewed in this chapter. One current alternative, the extended family, was once the norm, and there are still many such families in the world. Even in this country there are some extended families in which the grandparents or other relatives are included in the home.

Extended families fulfill certain important needs, both instrumental and psychological. Relationships within such families provide the members with feelings of esteem and well-being. Parents are not the only source of care and affection for the children, or the only adult objects of identification and social learning. The presence of grandparents helps children develop the capacity for being helpful to older persons, including their own parents, as they grow older; and since such families include several generations they permit "anticipatory socialization"—that is, they prepare children for the age roles they will occupy in the future (Kempler, 1976). The presence of several generations also gives children a feeling of historical continuity, and familiarizes them with various stages of the life cycle. Finally, extended kinship groups make it easier to pass on stable value systems, especially in times when youth appears to be searching almost desperately for a meaningful ideology. In particular, such families provide their members with such important values as security and tradition.

On the other hand, the extended family may provide individuals who have less independence, initiative, creativity, and sensitivity to the need for change. The achievement of adulthood involves detaching and differentiating oneself from the parental models, and attaining a distinct sense of self. Hence the extended family functions best when at least some of its members are capable of responding to environmental and historical change (Rudolph & Rudolph, 1976).

The commune. In the commune, a number of families join together in a sort of miniature socialistic society. Communes vary greatly in purpose, composition, and durability. Hall and Poteete (1972) observe that hippie communes, which are based simply on the principle of doing your own thing, are "merely passing phenomena. They are shanty towns held together temporarily by a love-everybody philosophy spouted by people who are frightened by the dynamic interresponsibility of love" (p. 326).

Occasionally communes do last. Leach describes one which has lasted for over 20 years. It is made up of middle-class professionals who have continued in their jobs. The children are all in a play group and those wives who want to care for the children do so, while the others work (Hall, 1974). In other communes babysitting cooperatives are used. In many others children are excluded altogether (Kinkada, 1973).

It is debatable to what degree communes constitute a viable alternative to the family. Anthropologist Edmund Leach describes kibbutzim, communes, and group marriages as "artificial," and doubts that such groups can hold together, for he feels that people do not experience the same sense of obligation to those who are not kin as they do to their own families (Hall, 1974). Yet such arrangements do sometimes work out. The growing need for communes—for example, among single parents, never-marrieds, and the elderly—may result in sounder, more creative approaches to communal living. Sufficient testimony already exists, from those in more successful communes, to prove their potential worth.

The family network. Other useful variations—the family network, affiliate family, and family cluster—constitute possible substitutes for the extended family (Stoller, 1970). The family network may consist of three or four nuclear families who decide to live together in the same neighborhood, and meet together regularly to exchange services, and share problems and leisure pursuits. Such an arrangement permits families to provide feedback to each other about themselves and their problems. Also it reduces the isolation often experienced in nuclear families today.

On the other hand, some of the same criticisms made of communes apply to the family network. The mobility of its members may make such networks temporary. Moreover the families involved may not succeed in developing a style that will mutually meet all their needs.

The affiliative family. Still another alternative is the affiliative family. It consists of any combination of husband-father and/or wife-mother and their children, along with one or more older persons (Clavan & Vatter, 1972). This alternative may be especially appropriate for older women such as widows and single women with children, who desire to continue in an occupation while caring for their families. In one example, a 41-year-old divorced woman with five children lived with an elderly female divorced college professor whose children had grown up (Clavan & Vatter, 1972).

The affiliative family has several values, one being that, like the extended family, it establishes a three-generation network. It facilitates modeling by older generations for the younger; and it permits supportive emotional experiences and socialization opportunities similar to those in extended families. On the other hand, the affiliative family presents potential problems. In the first place, as all the parties get to know each other the arrangement may not always work out. Besides, in this, as in other alternative family forms, social and legal sanctions are missing which would provide such family structures with the support they need.

The family cluster. The deficiencies of these living arrangements are, to a considerable extent, compensated for in the family cluster, in which persons of different age and marital status and their children meet regularly together. They participate in leisure-time activities together, and afford mutual help and personal growth in solving problems—all without living together, pooling incomes, or swapping mates. For several reasons this living arrangement may become a means of reducing isolation in a complex, impersonal urban society. For one thing, household units rarely embrace more than two parents and two children, and sometimes include only one of each. Also there is an increasing number of adults who are single, divorced, or widowed (Pringle, 1974). Nor do many people have the advantage of living in three- to four-generation households.

Cluster members need not necessarily live in the same neighborhood: the composition of the group is the important factor. One study was made after several family clusters had been in operation for over four months (Wolfarth, 1973). About three-quarters of the participants mentioned having gained interesting companions; and over half said that they now spent more time doing things for fun, profiting from others' experiences, and having friends with whom to share their ideas and feelings. In terms of overall satisfaction with the experience, 15 of the 46 respondents rated it as very positive and 19 as positive, while 4 said it had been negative, 1 very negative, and 7 that it was equally positive and negative.

Several factors may contribute to a cluster falling apart, including lack of effective leadership, the departure of key members, disagreement as to activities and procedures, and personality clashes. Nevertheless some of them have operated successfully for a considerable period of time (Pringle, 1974).

Cooperative enterprises. Progress toward forming support systems between individuals and families also takes the form of various cooperative arrangements; "for example, car pooling, the common ownership
of machines like snowblowers and tractors and co-ops, especially in
urban communities" (Kempler, 1976, p. 148).

The Childless Couple

Another alternative to the nuclear family—in composition if not
living arrangement—is the childless couple. This falls into two categories; those who would like to have children and cannot, and those
who prefer to remain childless. A study was made of 555 women aged
30 to 49, living with their husbands. Forty-four (8%) were childless,
and of these 44, 22 could not have children. Those who chose to be
childless numbered about 4%, while another 4% would have preferred
to have children but could not (Rao, 1974). Those who prefer to remain
childless are few, but their numbers are steadily increasing.

Reasons for voluntary childlessness. There are several reasons for this
phenomenon. Among them are adults' increasing concern for their own
self-realization, and for the demands that children place on their time,
energies, money, and psychological resources. Those who are concerned
with these factors, increasingly consider parenthood undesirable. Another reason for voluntary childlessness is the population explosion,
which is making unlimited reproduction dangerous to the human race.
In addition, couples are feeling that the decision to have children is more
critical than the decision to get married (Veevers, 1975). Individuals
considering marriage have a chance to get to know their potential mates;
but one cannot know in advance the characteristics of the unborn child.
A marriage can be terminated by divorce, but the decision to have
children is irrevocable. People can give married life a try in the form
of a trial marriage or premarital cohabitation, but with two exceptions,
there is no way to try out parenting in advance. One exception is in
the case of foster parents, for whom there is a trial period before the
adoption is final. Another possible, but inadequate, rehearsal for parenthood, may consist of taking care of someone else's children for a while;
but this is quite different from having children of one's own.

The pluses of childlessness. Childless couples are better satisfied than
those with children. In fact, childless husbands feel unusually satisfied
with their lives and experience less pressure than other men their age.
The quality of their lives is higher than of any other grouping of males,
except possibly those whose children are past the age of 17. Part of
the reason is that childless couples are freer of financial worries. Child-

less wives past 30 are just as satisfied as women with children. They usually describe their lives quite positively, though less than their husbands do. These womens' status is relatively good, for childless marriages are typically far more equalitarian than those with children (Veevers, 1974). Indeed, Movius (1976) refers to the child-free marriage as woman's ultimate liberation. It permits women to have a life of their own. Women who seek to combine marriage and career, trying to get the best of both worlds, they deny themselves the opportunity of having the best of either. Of course only longitudinal studies will determine whether these couples may feel differently regarding having children after they grow older or after the spouse dies. However, grown children do not always pay as much attention to aging parents as they once did (Campbell, 1975b). Besides, the decision to remain childless is reinforced by the satisfactions couples derive from their flexible life style. The following testimony indicates the advantages that several couples have found in being childless.

> The chief advantages my husband and I have found are these: (1) We have enough money to do things we like, beyond just paying for necessities. (2) We don't really enjoy children, so why have them when they might somehow detect that we would prefer not having them? (3) We don't have to worry about how they will turn out. (4) As a female, I haven't been encumbered with the sort of domestic responsibilities that children impose on a mother. (*Female, age 40*)

> We haven't felt tied down. We can travel when we please and move when we please without feeling that we are disrupting children's school and social lives. Since we both work, and find considerable fulfillment in our vocations, we are not diverted by distractions imposed by children who would probably be about teen aged at this stage in our lives. (*Male, age 42*)

> My wife and I put off having children until a time when children would have proved an intrusion upon the life style we had developed. We simply felt complete as a marriage and family unit and had no feeling of anything missing. Originally we had intended having children simply because it was expected of us. Now the population explosion makes us feel we've done our bit toward helping society cope with the problem. (*Male, age 44*)

Reasons for having children later. Of course some long-time childless couples ultimately have children. As women progress through their 30s they may panic at the realization that they must have a child now, or never. In other cases children become a couple's compensation for the future because of failures or deficiencies in other areas of life. Voluntarily childless wives most often reconsider their decision when they suffer some setback in career (Veevers, 1974). In other cases a wife may unintentionally become pregnant, and for religious or other reasons, the couple may decide against abortion. Parenthetically, since the voluntarily childless are also among the better educated, such late-in-life parents usually do a good job of parenting.

> Bill and Susan Hobby were both well educated, reasonably well off financially, and committed to having no children. Bill taught in a university and Susan did part-time teaching. Otherwise, they mostly stayed at home, engaged in many joint interests, including raising flowers, boating, and reading. To their chagrin Susan became pregnant at age 40; however, after the baby, a son, arrived, Bill and Susan transformed into very proud parents. The son, who was attractive and precocious, simply became programmed into their erstwhile way of life.

Essentials for happiness. Veevers (1975) concludes that remaining childless may be a valid family life form conducive both to personal and marital adjustment for some couples. In order that voluntary childlessness prove a viable family form it should meet certain criteria. First, both wife and husband should be fully in agreement that they do not want children. The one condition necessary for the satisfaction of the voluntarily childless wife is that she participate in meaningful activities outside the home, and even outside the bounds of man-woman relationships. Such activities might involve holding a job; and almost all childless women do so. In addition they may gain satisfaction from avocational pursuits such as dancing, painting, writing, or other expressive activities. It is important that both husband and wife take advantage of the free choices made possible by the child-free life style. Another essential criterion is that such couples be able to cope with the social sanctions against them. Through the centuries, having children has been viewed as natural and normal. It has been considered a reflection of sexual competence, as well as a religious, civic, and moral responsibility. Having children is still perceived by most people as making marriage complete and giving it a deeper significance. It is often portrayed as necessary for attaining true social and personal maturity, and for maintaining a healthy personality in adulthood (Veevers, 1975). Therefore those who voluntarily decide to have no children are viewed, especially by older generations, as somehow deviant—ethically, socially, and psychologically (Veevers, 1975).

In general childless couples themselves are undisturbed by criticisms relating to "the dominant fertility norms" (Veevers, 1975, p. 485). In effect they succeed in "discrediting [their] discreditors" (p. 485). They are typically unconventional in other ways as well. For one thing, ordinarily they are somewhat nonreligious. They also associate mostly with those who are childless or who would prefer to be, which reinforces their own commitment to childlessness. In addition they realize—either from first-hand observation or experience—that following conventional norms is no guarantee of good adjustment. In general they are quite committed to their careers and they seek varied experiences. They highly idealize the husband-wife relationship; and they also view themselves as advantaged compared to couples with children. They may perceive most mothers as having had little choice about, and having been dragged reluctantly into, parenthood.

Childless couples conclude that many people who display toward them various blends "of scorn, hostility, or of pity, are in fact secretly jealous of the freedom and other advantages which the childless enjoy" (Veevers, 1975, p. 482). Relevant data support the view that many parents do indeed envy childless couples, or would enjoy participating in a child-free life style. Regardless of how real such views are, the fact that childless couples believe in them renders their own status more palatable to themselves.

The outlook. What is the future of childless marriages? Will the present trend continue, and perhaps accelerate? Among young adults the childless marriage, once "pitied or disparaged," is already widely accepted as a "fulfilling life style"; and many young couples say quite frankly that they prefer not to have children (Campbell, 1975b). They are supported by at least two important developments. First is the scientific debunking of the myth that women have a maternal instinct. This theory holds that because of their biology women want to have children, and that once the children are born, they will instinctively love and know how to care for them. Such a myth is blind to certain exceptions: (1) the many women who seek to terminate their pregnancies through legal or, if necessary, illegal abortions; (2) the cases of flagrant child abuse and infanticide; and (3) the large number of women who remain voluntarily childless without any apparent distress (Silverman & Silverman, 1971). The second major factor that puts right on the side of the childless, is the concern with overpopulation. Veevers (1975) believes that people are increasingly questioning their right to procreate.

Obviously, voluntary childlessness will never become a consideration for everyone; yet, concludes Veevers (1975), it may be for about 5% of all couples. Therefore if a diversity of life styles is to be encouraged in order that people may find that which is uniquely congenial to them, voluntary childlessness must be considered a viable option.

Three Unconventional Family Life Styles

Swinging. Other less socially acceptable alternatives to marriage include swinging, or the agreed-upon exchange of married couples, at least on occasion. To gain some insight into such arrangements, Gilmartin (1975) compared a sampling of 100 middle-class married suburban swinging couples with 100 socioeconomically matched nonswinging couples. The swinging couples attended swinging parties about once every two weeks. In other words, swinging was no more important than other leisure activities. At swinging parties wives typically engage in erotic activities with perhaps three or four different persons, while husbands may average two or three for each party. Ordinarily they indulge in petting, massaging, mutual masturbation, and oral-genital sex; and the majority have intercourse at least once at each party. Over half the women sometimes engage in sex with other women, often with the husbands watching, but none of the husbands reported any homosexual activity.

By comparison with the nonswingers, the swingers had looser ties to family, community, and church. As might be expected, the swingers were considerably freer in their attitudes on such matters as sex education for children, abortion, premarital sex, nudity, and contraceptives for teenagers. Nevertheless swinging does not seem to have an adverse effect on their marriages. In fact, 85% of them felt that it constituted no threat to their marriages or to their marital love. Not a single one of them believed that their marriages had become worse as a result of swinging; instead the great majority felt that their marriages had improved. Nor had swinging negatively affected their sex lives, for they normally had sexual intercourse with each other more frequently than the control couples. Among the controls, 31 of the husbands and 8 of the wives had engaged in adultery. By comparison the swinging husbands were much happier than the adulterous control husbands, and the same was true for the wives, though less so. The swingers were even slightly happier than were the nonadulterous controls.

The swinging couples insisted that they did indeed value fidelity in marriage, but to them fidelity signified an open, trusting relationship. Certain of them spoke of "faithful adultery," in which everyone concerned understood the emotional limitations of adultery (Gilmartin, 1975). In today's pluralistic society, concludes Gilmartin, there are various ways that human sexuality can be properly and effectively organized, and monogamy appears to be merely one of them. As the study shows, psychological or emotional monogamy can exist and even grow stronger without a coexisting sexual monogamy. In fact the swinging couples characterized themselves as monogamists. Except for their sexuality, "the most remarkable thing about the swingers is how unremarkable they are" (p. 58). For certain people, concludes Gilmartin, traditional ideas about the relationship of sex to marriage may actually be less conducive to marital happiness and stability than swinging, because they are less congruent with individual needs.

Group marriage. In the group marriage, two or three couples live together and share sex partners. Such marriages can work, even on a relatively short-term basis, only when they begin with relatively happy monogamous unions. Certainly group marriage does not solve pre-existing neurotic problems. In such marriages, observe Hall & Poteete (1972), sexual sharing isn't the chief problem. Instead these arrangements dissolve on the same basis as conventional unions do; for example, in both monogamous and group marriages, one person may dominate. In addition, group marriage partners may indulge in too much mutual soul-searching, when they might better come to know each other by doing things together and interacting in everyday matters. Neither swinging nor group marriage is a genuine alternative to conventional marriage. Such arrangements are too few, fragile, and hazardous to attract the more traditional majority.

The homosexual union. In the United States there is a minority of uncertain size, that is composed of homosexual or gay couples who live together in quasi-marital unions. The vast majority never proclaim their status, and are therefore generally indistinguishable from any other roommates or housemates of the same sex. They experience the disadvantages of belonging to two minority groups—the singles, whom we discussed in an earlier chapter, and the gays. The general public still looks upon gays as deviant, socially undesirable, and psychoneurotic, and considers their unions as illegitimate, sick, and undeserving of legalization. For example, a male homosexual couple was denied a marriage license in Minneapolis (Weitzman, 1975). Such couples lack the economic advantages of heterosexual couples in filing joint income tax returns, as well as in obtaining certain disability, unemployment, social security, and pension benefits. They also lack certain prerogatives of heterosexual couples in obtaining mortgages, apartments, homes, and insurance.

Admitted homosexuals are also generally not permitted to adopt children; they are usually not even granted custody of their own children (Basile, 1974). In some cases the judge will award custody to a lesbian, provided that she separates from her homosexual partner. In other cases the father may obtain custody because he claims the mother is providing the child with a potentially destructive environment. The assumption is that the homosexual is promiscuous, abnormal, and unfit to be a parent. However, in a few isolated cases, appellate courts have overturned orders that lesbian mothers must live apart, indicating that homosexual relationships do not necessarily render a home unfit for children. Homosexual fathers' rights both to visitation and custody have also been upheld (Weitzman, 1975).

Researchers do not fully agree about whether gay couples assume polarized sex roles. In studying 34 female homosexuals who had been "married" to another homosexual for two or more years, Jensen (1974) concluded that they organize themselves into subgroups according to age, education, income, and life style, and these married homosexuals follow the same principles of group behavior that heterosexuals do. In many instances one of the pair assumes a masculine (butch) role and initiates the action: lights the other's cigarette, holds her coat, and opens doors for her. Typically butches may be friends and roommates, but do not dance together or make love to each other. Fifteen of the seventeen females who took the butch role repaired things around the house, while only two did not. Only one of the females who played the traditionally feminine (fem) role did household repairs. In general the butches were a little older than the fems, had a higher income, and were more often interested in typically masculine occupations than their partners. The butches were much less likely to desire children, and far less likely to have had sex relations with the other sex. By contrast the fems had had more sexual experience with males and often wanted to be mothers. Ordinarily the butch within the homosexual "quasi-marital" union perceives herself as "100% homosexual, a woman lover, and identifies with males in terms of cultural expectations" (Jensen, 1974, p. 366).

On the other hand, Freedman (1975) reports that homosexuals do not adhere to standard sex roles in their living relationship or otherwise, an observation that most gays themselves would endorse. When two men or two women live together, they quickly perceive the limitations of stereotyped sex roles. The dichotomies of breadwinner-versus-homemaker or dominant-versus-submissive simply are not important to most of them. The women homosexuals appear better adjusted sexually and play more active sexual roles than do heterosexual women. They focus especially on sex as an expression of tenderness and warmth. While some of them "come out," or make their homosexuality known, the majority live quite inconspicuously. They have both gay and straight (heterosexual) friends and possess a remarkable adaptability. For example:

Kim was a college teacher, a pilot, and a very personable, athletic young woman. When she was visiting her parents at their cottage on a lake she met Gladys, an attractive divorcee with a small son. Before long Kim and Gladys established a homosexual relationship and lived together, along with the son. Formerly the boy had been a young terror but Kim, the butch in the combination, took firm but kindly control of him. Kim's parents sharply disapproved of the arrangement; therefore Kim broke off with them. These things happened 20 years ago. Kim and Gladys, with the boy in tow, went to the West Coast, and prospered.

They were both creative, active, and congenial. Ultimately the boy grew into a fine young man and left home. Kim and Gladys are a happy middle-aged couple with many friends, fond memories of the past, and optimism for the future.

The commonly held belief that gays are more psychoneurotic than straights has been disproved, and homosexuality is no longer classified as an illness by the American Psychiatric Association. In fact, when homosexuals and heterosexuals not in therapy are compared on personality tests, researchers cannot tell one group from another (Freedman, 1975). In some ways gay people seem better adjusted. They often show a wider range of emotional expression because they are not limited by standard sex roles. They even report that their minority status has caused them to develop such important capacities as social criticism and creativity, and has made them more sensitive to others.

Gay couples experience two major categories of problems. One is that they must either keep a tight lid of secrecy on the real nature of their union, or they must cope with the social rejection that coming out, or proclaiming their status, would entail. The other problem is that, being legally single although psychologically married, they fall prey to all of society's very considerable discriminations against the single person, to be described in the next section. Many gay couples manage to cope by maintaining supportive relationships with other couples like themselves with whom they can be fully open.

THE SINGLES

General Information

Identification. Single adults in the United States include the never-married, the widowed, and the divorced. They include people before marriage and between marriages. Among single adults in this country, 58% have never married, 27% are widowed and 15% are divorced ("The economics," 1976). About 35% of all Americans over 18 are single; and adult singles now head one household in five. By 1990 it may be one in four mainly is because people are divorcing more often, getting married later, and waiting longer to remarry. Older singles consist mostly of the widowed, separated, or divorced because by this time, many of the formerly single have married. If a person is single or entering middle age, that individual is likely to remain so, for only 1% of all first marriages involve the middle-aged (U.S. Public Health Service, 1973).

Reasons for remaining single. The reasons that people remain permanently single are somewhat different for males and females. Women who remain single are more likely to be better educated than their married peers. In fact, Davis (1973) found that female scientists and engineers are six times as likely to be single as their male counterparts, perhaps because such women choose not to marry (Havens, 1973). Single females are also more likely to have grown up in democratic families, perhaps because such women are more likely to achieve, and the achievers are less likely to marry. By contrast, males with high occupational achievement, who have been brought up in democratic families, are least likely to remain single (Spreitzer & Riley, 1974). It should be kept in mind that the factors that predispose people to marry may change over the years.

Males may remain single for somewhat different reasons. They may dislike feeling tied down; and they have easy access to sex, anyhow. Among the very young, at least, couples may simply choose to cohabit without marriage, in which case, in a sense, they are not single. Nevertheless cohabiting couples are subject to certain of the limitations of the single person, including much higher tax rates than married couples.

The Divorced

One group of singles who share many of the advantages and problems of singles in general, are the divorced. This category of adult is rapidly increasing. Between the year 1970 and 1975 the proportion of divorced persons increased 37% for women and 50% for men (Stein, 1976). Moreover about 29% of today's teenage marriages will end in divorce (Glick & Norton, 1972). As yet there seems to be no leveling off or decline in the divorce rate (Bernard, 1973).

Causes of divorce. There are several reasons that the divorce rate is growing. Today couples feel less restricted by societal sanctions against divorce than in the past. They are also more assured that a wife can make a living on her own ("What future," 1976). In other cases couples simply grow apart.

Feldberg and Kohen (1976) believe that divorce is most often the result of problematic situations rather than deficiencies or incompatibility of the marital partners. For example the couple experiences pressures from external organizations. The sex-based division of labor within the family can also cause problems. Since the man works outside the home and brings in the pay check, his family life participation is perceived as strictly voluntary instead of essential to the family's success. Meantime women still take the major responsibility for housework and child care, even though the majority now also work outside the home. Families must also cope with demands on their time by neighborhood organizations, the church, and other institutions and agencies. As a result couples often have little time to share together.

Still another reason for divorce, suggests Ariès, is that couples may simply become fed up with each other after so many years. In earlier times couples were often separated by death, but because of increased longevity, today's couples spend over a half century or more together. Hence adults simply have replaced death with divorce. Current acceptance of divorce assures a couple who cannot tolerate each other for too long that they can separate (Mousseau, 1975).

The adjustments involved. The problems involved in divorce are both immediate and long-term. For one thing the decision to seek divorce is usually made only after a considerable period of time and much emotional strain. Nevertheless the actual separation is often the most painful event (Fisher, 1973). William Nichols, a psychologist and marriage counselor, says that people go through the same process of emotional loss in divorce as in death; but in divorce there is always the possibility of renewing the relationship. Even if the couple intensely dislike each other, Dr. Nichols believes that they still experience grief because of the feelings they once had. He says that stages in the adjustment process differ in degree of intensity. The worst part is when one partner moves out, or when the divorce papers are served. After that there is a numbness, a sort of anesthesia, and a struggle with reality in which it is hard to believe what is happening. Finally there is the emotional breakthrough in which one accepts what has happened ("Rising divorce rates," 1975). This is followed by plans for the future, although one must still cope with memories.

The next task is to readjust one's role, one for which society lacks adequate guidelines. Perhaps women have the most difficult time, for a large majority (71%) have to work and 84% must care for children, ordinarily without any real psychological or economic support from the ex-husband. They earn less than single women of the same age, and only 4% can afford to hire someone to help with housework. Moreover they have less opportunity than divorced men to date and remarry. For such reasons they feel great stresses and describe their lives in somewhat gloomy terms. A quarter of these women fear that they might have a nervous breakdown, compared with only 8% of divorced men ("Rising divorce rates," 1975).

The divorced woman also suffers socially, and dwells in "social limbo" (Brandwein, Brown, & Fox, 1974, p. 506). No longer does she enjoy the pair-relationships that she and her husband shared with other couples. In addition she suffers a certain "stigma" because of her presumed failure to keep her man. For example, "the societal myth of the gay divorcee, out to seduce other women's husbands, leads to social ostracism of the divorced woman and her family" (Brandwein, Brown, & Fox, 1974, p. 499).

In the following a 38-year-old woman who has been separated for three years and is now finishing the divorce procedure answers several questions.

I imagine that you did a good many things as a couple when you were with your husband. Since you have not been with your husband have you found much difference in your social life? I am a person who likes to be alone a lot and I'm not lonely. I think I experienced loneliness for the first time going through the process of divorce. I really didn't know what was happening to me.

Why would you feel more lonely during this process? I really never dwelled on what it meant to be lonely for the first 30 years of my life. For the first 12 years there was a certain intimacy in being married; a feeling I had that someone was always there and that I could talk to, and during some periods after he left I was depressed. What am I feeling? I guess that is what people call loneliness. But I have to say that the kind of socializing that we did as a married couple I don't miss at all. I found it phony and superficial. You tend to go to functions because it's expected rather than out of genuine friendship. My real friends, people I have shared the most with, have not changed. They are my same friends, whether I am married or not. I have not been to any occasion where there have been couples for the last three years.

That particular feature hasn't bothered you? No, I feel relieved at missing these couples' affairs—you never ever get a match. I mean that either the husband part of the team was okay and the wife was a dog; or the husband was a dog and the wife was wonderful. But I never found both interesting at the same time.

I would gather that your feelings have changed from the time that you first separated until now. In other words, there has been a process of adjustment. How long has that been? It has been about three years. At first I had been aware for maybe five years prior to the separation that I had to find myself in terms of my husband. A lot of people said I was really lucky to get this person, and unfortunately a part of me still reacts to this. It's become much diminished but I do feel a tinge of failure. That I failed something, especially because of the terms on which he wanted to end the marriage—that I have physically failed him. That I was physically repulsive to him. After all, I'd married at 19, and married with all of those norms that were prevalent in the 50s and early 60s—that you stay married to one man, that you had children, and settled in the suburbs, while he got a good job and became successful. Then came living through those years of finding out that that was really so much crap, and that I didn't want to live in someone else's shadow, that I really did want to have a career, that I didn't want to just be a mother.

Do you think now that you might ultimately get married again? No. Right now I can't envision myself ever again living with someone in a possessive relationship. I'm sure that a psychiatrist would say it's because I fear rejection, but I'm not going to get close to anyone. I would like to meet someone at a convention and say, "Hey, I'll meet you again next year" or "I'll meet you next month. Let's fly here for a vacation but no strings attached, strictly a relationship that has some caring and involvement but in which there are no demands on either party to perform to the expectations of the other."

Divorced men have certain advantages, but their handicaps are greater than is commonly believed. On the one hand they feel less pressure than married men, and only 42% worry about paying bills. Only one in eight divorced men always feel rushed, while one in three divorced women do. Forty-two percent of divorced women, but only 25% of the men, describe their lives as difficult. Nevertheless divorced men have their problems. Sometimes they have to make alimony payments that keep them financially strapped. Also, it is they who lose

With divorce becoming a way of life in today's society, parents often find it hard to remain in close contact with their children.

their homes and their children, and that hurts them. In many cases they simply are not used to cooking and housekeeping for themselves and lead somewhat haphazard, dreary lives. Certainly the image of the "free-swinging ex-husband" is a distortion ("Rising divorce rates," 1975).

Nevertheless divorced people do adjust, and some of their lives become better than before. The vast majority eventually remarry; mean-time they carry on, often quite well, after the shock of the divorce wears off. Many of them literally learn to live alone and like it, especially when they have been overshadowed by their former mate's personality. After the bereavement of the divorce is over, some of these persons develop real feelings of satisfaction in looking out for themselves. They also enjoy their new freedom and develop a new self-reliance. Consider the case of Catherine Graham, who was shy and dependent as long as her forceful husband was living and directing the Washington Post. After he committed suicide, she assumed control; and after her own managerial talents blossomed, she became one of the most powerful women in the country.

Single women who are widowed or divorced and have subsequently gained status socially and economically via their own careers, report increasing feelings of self-worth. At the same time they feel a stronger personal identity and a greater interest in their own careers. And while they still make only 60% of what males do for the same type of job, in recent years they have become more hopeful about improving their economic status (Ehrlich, 1975).

Divorced men feel they gain less, partly because their roles are different. What they experience as their chief benefit, and one shared by women, is escaping a relationship which had somehow failed to foster personal growth and a compatible, shared way of life. They are also able to look for new wives who may be more congenial to the personalities they have become since they married before. By contrast with women, it isn't hard for them to find and choose from a variety of women, partly because there are more unmarried women than unmarried men.

John and Mary Taylor had been married for fifteen years and had three daughters. John was handsome, personable, and very successful in business. Originally he had found his rather childlike wife appealing, but in time he grew bored with her lack of sophistication. Meantime she had become increasingly prone to nagging and fault-finding. One of his out-of-town business contacts was a highly personable woman, whose tastes and maturity matched John's own. Finally he sued for and won a divorce. He remarried, at the cost of an almost exorbitant alimony. Fortunately his ex-wife remarried too, and only his child support payments remained. Although he misses his children he sees them from time to time; and he is, in general, far happier than before.

The Single Parent

Problems and adaptations. Single parents may be either widowed, divorced, or unmarried. More children than ever before are being reared by one parent today. In 1960 8% of all children in the U.S. lived with one parent; in 1975, about 18% ("What future," 1976). Over 85% of these parents are women, most of them legally separated or divorced. Unfortunately society portrays the one-adult family as a deviant rather than a workable, increasingly common, alternative family form. In addition such women are tainted with the stigma of being divorced, separated, or single, and the notion that they have been unable to win or to keep their husbands. It is also assumed by many that these women should either marry or remarry, and the situation would then be all right. Single parents have some special needs including children's day care and part-time jobs which carry full benefits. These parents also need health care clinics and leisure activity centers (LeMasters, 1973).

Single parents may resort to various devices for easing their jobs. Sometimes they simply remarry. Others hire housekeepers to care for their children, while they are working. A minority join communes and find a certain economic and emotional stability there, along with freer relationships for themselves and their children (Brandwein, Brown, & Fox, 1974). In some cases divorced parents work out a situation which is to the advantage of both—that is, they alternate parenting tasks. In so doing, the father gets to know his child—perhaps better than he did before; and the mother has a chance to pursue a serious career because of the help she has from the father (Sheehy, 1976). Fathers who obtain full custody manage to do a good parenting job while maintaining their careers. They generally hire someone to help, and themselves help during evenings and weekends.

The single father. For at least three reasons the number of single-parent families headed by fathers can be expected to increase. Society is placing greater stress on the importance of fathering than ever before. In consequence boys will, in time, begin to receive family-life training along with girls—in fact, some already do. Second, men are coming to enjoy and insist upon their rights as parents. And finally, the equal-rights-for-the-sexes movement suggests that fathers' claims to children are equally as valid as mothers', and women who care little for mothering should not have the children foisted on them. When Jack and Susan obtained a divorce the judge wisely awarded custody of the three children to Jack, on the grounds that the mother was somewhat unstable. With the help of his own mother Jack's children thrived. He took a real interest in the children and had a far better disposition than the mother, who was a perpetual nagger and fault-finder.

The man who is a single parent has his own special problems. Society tends to question his ability to be a parent at all, an attitude reflected in part by the prevailing practice of awarding custody of children in divorce cases to mothers. The father may in fact be somewhat inept because he has not been socialized to be a good parent.

On the other hand, no research exists to prove that single fathers do a poorer job than single mothers. Indeed they are usually quite conscientious and resourceful about their tasks (Sheehy, 1976). In one study of single fathers (Mendes, 1976), a large majority (28 out of 32) did the cleaning, cooking, and home management, and none of them felt they lacked masculinity for performing these functions. While most of them knew something about cooking already, those who did not proceeded to learn from cookbooks or girlfriends. Over half experienced some difficulty in attempting to coordinate work and the various tasks of taking care of home and children.

All the fathers loved their children and all but two believed that the children loved them. The fathers typically showed preadolescent children considerable physical affection, but gave much less of it to adolescents. Instead they reassured the older children by the way they took care of them. Only 5 of the 32 fathers expressed any special problems about the emotional needs of their preadolescent children, and after

1978 © Sybil Shelton

In recent studies single fathers were most adept at handling domestic chores and giving love to their children.

receiving psychotherapeutic help three of these achieved significantly better relationships.

Among the 32 fathers, 20 were rearing daughters aged 2½ to 15. They felt no special concern about taking care of their daughters except with regard to the girls' sexuality. Indeed the fathers were more aware of the daughters' sexuality than of the sons'. In particular they expressed concern about how the daughters would accept their sexuality as adolescents. They also expressed some anxiety that their daughters lacked appropriate female role models for learning to be feminine. The older fathers, especially, were reluctant to discuss sexuality with their daughters, believing that such information should be provided by women. Sometimes the daughter still had a good relationship with the mother; in other cases the fathers had girlfriends with whom the daughter interacted.

In general the fathers did a pretty good job, though their role was not always clear. Nevertheless certain recommendations can be made. For one thing, males should be taught the art of homemaking. They also need to learn more about what constitutes normal child development and should have a grasp of sound general principles of childrearing.

Society and the Singles

Social attitudes. Traditionally singles have been considered somewhat deviant, even a bit pathetic. In the 19th century the superintendent of the Western Lunatic Asylum declared that single and widowed persons were more likely to become insane than married people. As he expressed it:

> We remember that the unmarried so often give unbridled indulgence to the feelings, propensities, and passions of depraved human nature, and that uninfluenced by the wholesome and purifying restraints of matrimony, they plunge recklessly into dissipation and vice, reaping as their reward, a broken constitution, ruined fortune and blasted reputation. We must cease to feel surprised, that in so many instances, they present the pitiable spectacle of a "mind in ruins" and become the tenants of our asylums for this afflicted class of citizens (Stribling, 1842, pp. 15–16).

American society still tends to stigmatize single people, and to impose social sanctions, often subtle ones, on them. It also stereotypes singles instead of noting their great diversity. It frequently portrays them, especially single males, as making nightly rounds of the bars and having endless sexual adventures (Jacoby, 1974). Singles of both sexes, but particularly women, are viewed as threats to married people.

As a result many single people simply avoid married couples. While they obtain support from associating with others whose life style is similar, they nevertheless must face the negative reactions of society.

Reactions of single people to social stigmatism. Single peoples' reactions to societal criticism are highly variable. They depend on the personalities of the individuals involved and the reasons they are single. Because of their socialization, single persons often feel ambivalent, torn between the traditional values of marriage and parenthood, and just recently acknowledged values of remaining single, changes in traditional sex roles, equality between the sexes, and self-actualization. The result is that some singles have problems with their personal and social identity. Part of the problem derives from pressures from parents, relatives, colleagues, and friends. One young man, a writer, reported "a nonspecific pressure, a sort of wonderment that at 35 I can be alone. I sometimes feel pressure from my own confusion, of how come I don't conform to the patterns of people who are in the same situation as I am in terms of career and age" (Stein, 1976, p. 96).

Those who are single by choice often feel no defensiveness at all about their status. They may feel that their way of life is superior, at least for them. Their only real concern is that they are the subject of various kinds of discrimination that casts them into the role of a minority group.

Stein (1976, p. 65) identifies the major factors that tend to make people remain single.

Pushes	*Pulls*
Restrictions within relationship:	Career opportunities
Suffocating one-to-one relationship, feeling trapped	Variety of experiences and plurality of roles
Obstacles to self-development	Self-sufficiency
Boredom, unhappiness, and anger	Sexual availability
Role playing and conformity to expectations	Exciting life style
Poor communication with mate	Freedom to change and mobility
Sexual frustration	Sustaining friendships
Lack of friends, isolation, loneliness	Psychological and social autonomy
Limited mobility and availability of new experiences	

Discrimination against the single person. Society discriminates against the single in many ways. In some countries women alone cannot be served at certain bars. Even in this country there are public places where women cannot go without an escort. While hardier women have always defied tradition, less defiant ones have succumbed to such discrimination. In fact, until just recently some women have reported difficulties in maintaining an active social life without mates; and in some segments of society this state of affairs persists. Stereotypes of loners relate more to unmarried women than to bachelors, since women have traditionally defined their identity in terms of marriage and motherhood.

Singles are also victims of legal discrimination. For example, they pay up to 20% more in taxes than a married couple filing a joint return ("The economics of being single," 1976). Joint-return taxpayers normally don't pay 50% of their income in federal taxes until their gross income reaches about $53,000, while single persons are in that bracket when they earn $40,000 a year.

Singles must also cope with job discrimination. A man's marital status makes little difference in his job until he reaches his early 30s; but after that age the single man may be suspected of homosexuality or of not being socially well adjusted ("The economics of being single," 1976). Married, or even divorced, adults often receive job preference over singles who have the same qualifications. In a survey of major corporations only 2% of the executives, including junior ones, were single. Over 60% of corporations responding said that single executives tend to "make snap judgments"; and 25% portrayed singlehood as "less stable than marriage" (Jacoby, 1974). In the case of women it is hard to distinguish discrimination based on sex from that due to being single (Stein, 1976). In any case young single women have to convince employers that they are indeed serious about their careers. In addition there are various fringe benefits the married have that the single do not. For instance, companies often provide married employees with free group life insurance. Employees can often take their spouses on company trips, but single employees cannot bring along the people they live with. Childless singles who have neither a husband nor children to depend on when they are old, have a special need to plan carefully for retirement. Yet even in social security, single people suffer some discrimination. Currently the single man who retires at the age of 65 receives $387.37 a month, while the married man whose wife has never worked at all receives $580.70 a month. Nevertheless both men have contributed exactly the same amount in social security taxes ("The economics of being single," 1976).

Singles are also exploited commercially. They may be lured to participate in a singles weekend or a singles cruise, or to go to single bars. Allon and Fischel (1973) reported that patrons of single bars chiefly look for excitement, affection, companionship, and social acceptance. Other commercial arrangements specifically for singles, include special tours, resort areas, dances, and singles-only housing units.

The Advantages of Being Single

Being single carries a variety of potential satisfactions. One is having the time and opportunities to make friends. The singles' most important support is from like-minded individuals. One young man, once married for 10 years, found support from "the three guys I share an apartment with, and with whom I share similar attitudes about life." Singles also can lead more varied lives in terms of "taking classes, dating widely, learning music or a sport, travelling, trying new roles they have been afraid to try before" (Stein, 1976, p. 98). For many singles, living with others provides a strong source of emotional support as well as certain economic advantages. Singles also have a degree of choice about work that the married do not because they do not have to look out for the well-being of their families. They can make vocational choices on the basis of motivation, and they can afford to take chances. Both sexes feel a certain satisfaction in not having to spend their money on the basis of a joint decision (Stein, 1976).

In in-depth interviews Stein (1976) determined why 20 people, ages 22 to 45, planned to remain single, and what satisfactions they found in being single. While some of them kept marriage as an option, at the time of the interview they felt that having an exclusive partner would limit both their own personal development and their freedom. In fact the most negative feeling toward marriage was its restriction on human growth. One man said, "When I was in an unofficial marriage with a woman, I would see only her and would be totally focused on her as the deciding factor of how my mood would be. It was a way of keeping myself out of having anything for myself and depriving myself of friends" (Stein, 1976, p. 93). Another young man, divorced after a 10-year marriage, observed that "it's simplistic to think that one person is always going to fill all my needs, and that I'm not going to change and she's not going to change" (p. 93). A second reason for rejecting marriage was that it produced feelings of isolation, sometimes because of failure to establish satisfactory communication with one's mate. In addition several respondents noted the tendency of marriage partners to associate only with mutual friends.

Marriage was also perceived as restricting opportunities, and as a trap requiring constant adaptation to one's mate. As one young man said: "There aren't any conditions under which I would consider getting married . . . I want freedom of choice, freedom to do what I want instead of being tied to living with just one person and doing the same, mutually satisfying things over and over" (p. 94). The majority of them agreed that marriage, though secure, decreases exploration, freedom, and learning. They disliked what they perceived as "a stalemated, boring situation" (p. 94). As one young woman said: "There are so many things I want to do. Now that I have completed school and am making a good living, there is fun to be had. I've started a dance class, learned pottery, and joined a women's group" (p. 94). Other factors pulled these people toward remaining single. One was the greater psychological autonomy they have. While theoretically, women can combine marriage, career, and stimulating experiences, it is hard to do so. The majority of single women had felt themselves secondary to males when involved in exclusive relationships with them, and had a tendency to put their boyfriends' needs first. One young woman who had lived with a man for a year, while concentrating more on his interests than hers, broke off the relationship and felt far more satisfied with her life. She became involved in various professional interests, helped organize a regional conference on health care, and reported extreme satisfaction with her new freedom. When she tried to be "friend, lover, mother [and] shrink," she had ended up by feeling a "victim." Today her life style stresses growth through sexual freedom and varied friendships; and instead of centering her life on a mate, she is "moving outward, enjoying a diversity of human contacts that she is convinced have helped her attain a stronger and clearer sense of selfhood" (p. 95).

The males, in particular, mentioned the pull toward a less rigid, more loosely structured life style. Instead of being confined to the family roles of father, husband, and provider, as singles they could freely experiment with a variety of roles through which they could seek out and integrate their own identity. One young man, a writer, describes his options as "clown, promoter, radical, friend, playboy, priest ... you name it, the possibilities are there. I'm in a situation to discover my potentials and act on them. It's an exciting process, sometimes frightening, but I like having alternatives to choose from" (p. 95). After being married for six years, he is now enjoying making his own, often spontaneous, decisions, while a flexible schedule and increased mobility have "helped him create a free flowing, integrated life, as opposed to the disjunctive pattern of his marriage. He writes, studies, travels, and relaxes, without the guilt and constraint associated with his former life" (p. 95).

Being single can also produce conditions conducive to increased confidence and self-respect. Since they felt fewer pressures, the singles we have discussed often believed that they had a better chance to realize their capacities. As one man who had been married twice, but had now been single for five years, observed:

"I am having an experience I never had before, since I was always answerable to someone—my family or wife. I never had the experience of being completely self-motivated, having to consider someone else's reaction to what I do—approval or disapproval—does the job pay enough. It makes me feel potent . . . and very responsible for what I do. Productive, capable of dealing with life's exigencies, and capable even of seeking friendly help when I need it. Whether you are self-realized or not cannot be blamed or credited to someone else" (p. 95).

Another attraction of remaining single was sexual freedom, opportunities for open-dating patterns, and cross-sex relationships, especially in terms of friendship.

Selected Aspects of Life Style

Housing. Singles have a variety of living situations. Some live alone, others live with roommates, and still others live in urban communal groups and share large apartments in buildings where they find support and friendship (Stein, 1976). In one urban project almost 700 adults, most of them single, live in various communes including "religious, political, craft, music, art, and therapeutically oriented communes" (p. 94). In certain of these communes people have a particular ideology, and in others they gather together simply for economic advantages.

Singles find this kind of living quite supportive because they meet new people there, and they have help with emotional problems. They can be the kind of people they want, can relate to others freely and actively, and are cared for when they need it (Zablocki, 1975). Most of the singles who live in communes are quite "normal," and not at all "freaks" or "way out people" (p. 96).

Social relations. The greatest need of single people is to develop networks of human relationships that provide the basic satisfactions of "intimacy, sharing, and continuity" (Stein, 1976, p. 109). Single people place a lot of emphasis on friendships. Such relationships differ from family support in that they are more fluid and open, and are established by free choice. While single people value varied and changing relationships, they nevertheless place a high value on enduring, close friendships. As one young woman said, "The intensity with which we talk is not a function of any category of time . . . it varies, but the intensity is pretty much a result of how much we communicate . . . feeling really connected and excited about what I'm talking about with the other person" (Stein, 1976, p. 83).

Group activities. Singles are also finding considerable support from various groups and group activities. One of these is an organization called Zero Population Growth, which is for those who wish to have few or no children. Another, the National Organization of Nonparents, includes both married and unmarried people, and is concerned with developing workable options outside of marriage. Perhaps more important are the networks of human relationships outside the traditional family structures, which provide for sharing and intimacy, such as rap sessions and consciousness-raising groups.

Still other areas of involvement for singles are therapy and encounter groups, as well as associations that focus on specialized interests. While often not restricted to singles, they are usually adapted to the needs of singles and are more frequently patronized by them. Carolyn Bird (1972) observes that the degree of caring, interpersonal involvement, and personal support permitted by such groups is often stronger than in traditional marriages. And, she adds, "not the least of these is the frankly experimental and informal character of the group which encourages exploration of psyche of the other and dispenses with sanctions that shrivel mutuality" (p. 348).

The Status of Singles' Mental Health

Since singles are quite heterogeneous, their mental status must be discussed in terms of subtypes. Older single men are more likely than married men to have mental problems, including neurosis, passivity, and depression; and they are more likely to commit suicide. Never-married men are also twice as likely as never-married women to have mental health problems (Srole et al., 1962). Apparently, observes Campbell (1975b), "women can get along better without men than men can get along without women, [for] single women of all ages are happier and more satisfied with their lives than single men. So much for the stereotype of the carefree bachelor and the anxious spinster . . . " (p. 38). Single women are also more active and work through their problems more realistically than men, partly because single men are less likely to become parts of warm supportive networks. Nevertheless single men are now participating more in friendship organizations and networks.

Given such a situation, it is strange that society persists in depicting single women as lonely, maladjusted spinsters. Many of the outstanding women in history have been single. Their male biographers have assumed that such women shunned marriage because they shunned involvement in the outside world (Sheehy, 1976). After reconstructing the lives of women poets over a period of four centuries, Louise Bernikow observed that "women who do not love men, and women who do not have sex with men, in the eyes of men, have loveless and sexless lives . . . [but] most of these women poets have loved women, sometimes along with loving men. Women have found in other women exactly that companionship, encouragement, and understanding that they did not find in men" (Bernikov, cited in Sheehy, 1976).

Another factor in singles' mental health is age. Older singles are more concerned about their careers, and less about how to get along in the world. They have money for leisure-time activities and for advanced educational experiences (Glick, 1975b). Yet despite their more stimulating lives, they may feel more discouraged than younger singles. They may feel anxious about the prospects of future loneliness; and if they have not established warm supportive relationships, they may find the middle years depressing (Stein, 1976).

While older single women are at least as healthy as married ones, the reverse is true of men. In a study of single men, Gilder (1974) reported that they were more subject to suicide, crime, emotional and physical problems, and low incomes. However Stein questions the methodology of Gilder's study. Even if the data are valid, such factors may result not from failure to marry, but rather from society's rigid attitudes toward single persons.

The Future of Singlehood

We might ask: What is the future of singlehood? Certainly as greater numbers of people choose to remain single, singlehood will assume a more attractive status. At present there is growing social support for the decision to remain single. If still more support becomes available, there may be even fewer people who model their life styles around marriage and the nuclear family (Stein, 1976).

The statistics tend to support these projections. In one study (Stein, 1973), only 2.7% of the women college freshmen questioned did not expect to marry, but as seniors 7.7% of them did not expect to marry. Still later, in 1973, a full 40% of the women seniors did not know whether they would marry.

Singlehood is emerging as a viable alternative life style, but whether it will attain the status of a movement is debatable. Certainly the growth of such a movement, and the development of singles' political power, holds the only real hope for reducing discrimination against the unwed. Yet major obstacles stand in the way. One such is that singles are so heterogeneous that agreement upon objectives for single programs would be difficult. Another is that most singles eventually marry, so that the enduring, hard-core support for singles programs would be relatively small.

The greatest help may come, in future years, from the population threat. In order to encourage more people not to have children, society may decide to reward singles rather than risk worldwide starvation and poverty because of excess numbers.

The Future of the Family

In view of all the foregoing alternatives, the question naturally arises as to whether traditional marriage is doomed. On this score authorities seem to differ. Although the phrase "do your own thing," has become widely adopted, observes Sheehy (1976), society continues to provide little real support for those who depart from the mainstream. On the other hand, Bernard (1975) suggests that within the lifetime of today's youth, the stable lifelong marriage may become "deviant"; and the views of youth today lend some support to that theory. In one survey (Stein, 1976), the number of college students who believe that traditional marriage is becoming obsolete increased from 24% to 34% within just two years. But if family forms do change, observes Ariès, it is unclear at this time what forms they will take, and whether we may be moving in the direction of ways of pairing off that are quite different from those ever known before. Ariès perceives attacks against the family as simply one part of the current revolt against technological society, for people are rebelling against a more and more confined, restricted world (Mousseau, 1975).

Kempler (1976) recommends that society experiment with alternative marriage arrangements, and provide them with support and encouragement. In the process different families and individuals may find the mode of life most suitable for their own and their dependents' welfare. Ultimately society itself must provide the environment and technological support, including human service systems, which will help all kinds of families and group living arrangements to function successfully.

AN OVERVIEW

While the nuclear model remains the most common, and popular, family form in America, alternatives do exist, although their levels of popular acceptability vary widely. The childless couple, the single-parent family, and communal living are increasingly, though not universally, approved. Other life styles such as homosexual marriages, swinging, and group marriage, are still widely condemned. The divorced and the single no longer provoke the pity and criticism they used to.

Meantime researchers have disclosed that single-parent families ordinarily fare far better than has been assumed, especially if there are no financial problems. In short, while the nuclear family shows no sign of being displaced as the chosen life style of the vast majority of adults, certain alternative family forms appear to work quite well.

SUGGESTED READINGS

Adams, M., *Single blessedness*. New York: Basic Books, Inc., 1976. Basing her discussion on interviews with single women as well as on relevant research, the author provides insight into the feelings of these women about themselves, their singlehood, and their personal and social roles in a patriarchal society.

Curtis, J. *Working mothers*. New York: Doubleday and Company, Inc., 1976. This quasi-empirical book, based on interviews with 200 mothers and involving also their husbands and children, focuses mainly on the impact of the mother's employment on all parties concerned, and discusses controversial issues relating to this non-traditional female role.

Davitz, J., & Davitz, L. *Making it from 40 to 50*. New York: Random House, Inc., 1976. This report, based on interviews with over 200 middle-class adults, provides insight into the way people of this age think, feel, and behave in the U.S. today.

Denfeld, D. Dropouts from swinging. *Family Coordinator*, 1974, 23 (1), 45–49. A questionnaire submitted to 965 marriage counsellors regarding problems experienced by swinging dropouts, discloses the problems associated with the consensual exchange of marriage partners. These problems include guilt, jealousy, threat to the marriage, boredom, loss of interest, disappointment, divorce or separation, and fear of discovery by parents or professional colleagues.

Duberman, L. *The reconstituted family*. Chicago: Nelson-Hall Publishers, 1975. Drawing her data from a study of 88 reconstituted families (where one of the spouses has remarried) the writer deals with the effect on these families of such variables as religion, age, social class, and education. She also discusses husband-wife relationships and critical problems of family functioning.

Feldberg, R., & Kohen, J. Family life in an anti-family setting: A critique of marriage and divorce. *Family Coordinator*, April 1976, 25 (2), 151–159. Despite the high rate of divorce, the vast majority of people continue to try to meet their emotional needs through marriage. While failures in family life are ordinarily portrayed as reflecting inadequacies of the parties involved, the authors state that they often derive from outside factors in our capitalistic society. The writers stress the woman's heavy responsibilities for the emotional lives of her spouse and children.

Glazer-Malbin, N. (Ed.) *Old family/new family*, New York: Van Nostrand Reinhold Company, 1975. Although a few of these selections are somewhat difficult to read because of the complexity of their content, the majority are easy to comprehend. The collection deals with both traditional and new family forms. The new types include such alternatives as swinging, cohabitation, and same-sex relationships. The chapters by Seiden and by Bart afford useful interpretations of issues in the male and female socialization processes.

Glenn, N. D. & Weaver, C. N. The marital happiness of remarried divorced persons. *Journal of Marriage and the Family*, May 1977, *39* (2), 331–337. A study of the happiness of persons who remarry after divorce supports the view that remarriages are, on the whole, almost as successful as first marriages, and that American marriage still effectively serves the needs of individuals.

Heckman, N. A., Bryson, R., & Bryson, J. B. Problems of professional couples: A content analysis. *Journal of Marriage and the Family*, May 1977, *39* (2), 323–330. A survey of 200 psychologist couples indicated that their differential scientific productivity stemmed partly from sexual discrimination, but mostly from the women's giving priority to their families' needs and their husbands' careers. The problems posed here have become increasingly common as the numbers of dual-career marriages have grown.

Kempler, H. L. Extended kinship ties and some modern alternatives. *Family Coordinator*, April 1976, *25* (2), 143–149. With the waning of kinship ties among certain modern middle-class families, various alternatives have arisen. Three of these—the commune, the family network, and the affiliated family—are evaluated as being far from ideal in fulfilling the needs traditionally supplied by kinship ties.

Kobrin, F. E. The primary individual and the family: Changes in living arrangements in the United States since 1940. *Journal of Marriage and the Family*, May 1976, *38* (2), 233–239. Census data are presented to show that increasing numbers of adults are living alone or apart from relatives. Marriage in adulthood is portrayed as involving three stages of family membership: premarital independence, marriage, and post-family independence. The development of such clearcut stages suggests that segregation by age is increasing and that the family is decreasing as a place for primary relationships.

Movius, M. Voluntary childlessness—the ultimate liberation. *Family Coordinator*, January 1976, *25* (1), 57–63. Since working mothers experience excessive demands on their time and energies, career-oriented wives may come increasingly to view childlessness as an attractive alternative. The career woman who is childless has many advantages which may prove almost essential for competing successfully in today's vocational world.

Rogers, C. *Becoming partners: Marriage and its alternatives.* New York: Dell Publishing Co., Inc., 1972. This book provides rich insights into marriage alternatives in modern America. Through taped interviews, anonymous individuals involved in such varied relationships as premarital cohabitation, interracial marriage, remarriage, and married life in a commune, discuss their relationships freely.

10
CHAPTER

Work
and
Leisure

WORK

The Significance of Work

The meaning of work. Being a worker has different meanings for different people. For some, work is marginal or even unpalatable; for others it is the core of their identity (Troll, 1975). Work becomes the "scaffolding that holds up the adult life." In some cases one's preoccupation with work can become too "compulsive and neurotic," because it is the only thing that glues life together (Stegner, 1976, p. 42).

The burden of work is heaviest for the middle-aged because it is during this time that they normally reach the peak of their influence in all areas of business and government. Although Americans in the 40-to-65 age category comprise only a quarter of the population, they earn over half the nation's income; and the average age of top business executives is 54 ("Generation in the middle," 1970).

The new work ethic. Nevertheless, observes Yankelovich (1974b), certain trends are transforming the American work ethic and reducing the work burden. One of these is a new way of defining success. From World War II until recently most Americans defined achievement in terms of material things. Today, however, new concepts of success involve quality rather than quantity; self-fulfillment rather than high earnings. The stress is on the self and its unactualized potential, a self that demands full consideration. Parallelling this change has been a shift in feelings about obligations to others, including family, society, and vocational associates. In the past, the "key motif . . . was 'keeping up with the Joneses'; today it is 'I have my own life to live, let Jones shift for himself' " (p. 81). While concern for material things still exists, these things are now considered no more important, and perhaps less, than such self-fulfilling activities as "being closer to nature, finding ways to be creative, spending more time with friends, and more time on self-understanding" (p. 81). As a result employee-employer relationships have changed, and employers can no longer count on the complete support of their employees. Today people are not willing to submit passively to whatever is good for the company. They will be loyal to the company if the company will provide fulfillment for them.

A third development, equally important for the work ethic, is decreased anxiety over economic matters. While those persons who lived through the Great Depression of the 1930s, still feel the effects of having lived through it, most young people assume that, once employed, they won't have to worry about jobs. They have grown up during a period of affluence and it is deeply bred into them that it is not hard to earn a living. People still attach considerable importance to economic security but for the young, at least, any notion that they may not be able to earn a satisfactory livelihood appears "curiously unreal" to them (Yankelovich, 1974b, p. 82). While three out of five adults still name economic security as their number one goal, 40% would take economic risks in order to improve the quality of their lives. This new value orientation is significant and has wide implications both for them personally and for the world of work.

A fourth development has been a "spreading psychology of entitlement." That is, people are moving away from feeling that they would like something, to a feeling that they have a right to have something (Yankelovich, 1974b). Rather than saying that they would like to have a job that might provide satisfaction, they believe they are entitled to such a job. These "rights of entitlement" were reflected in the various social movements of the late 1960s, including the student movement, the consumer movement, and the women's movement.

A fifth development is "disillusionment with the cult of efficiency" (p. 82). Although most people do not attack it as harshly as some "counterculture radicals," nevertheless, many of the younger generation question whether the present-day passion for efficiency isn't making them pay too high a price in terms of missing out on "life's excitement, mystery, romance, and pleasure" (p. 82).

These new trends have not affected all segments of the working population in the same way. Older workers, whose chief motive is to earn enough money, are perhaps least affected. However, middle-aged males, aged 30 to 50, in the middle-income range, are becoming concerned about self-fulfillment and the quality of their occupational life. Lower-class workers are demanding a better deal on the job than before, but they lack the sophistication to focus their attention on the quality of life. Anyhow, their low incomes make family necessities their first priority. Lower-order, biologically rooted survival needs must be met before higher-order, psychological ones can be considered.

Middle-aged Women at Work

Statistics. For women, work outside the home has become the norm for several significant reasons. Over half the women aged 16 to 64 are in the labor force, as well as half the mothers who have children 6 to 17 years of age; and these figures are growing. In 1960 about 31% of married women were working, compared with 45% in 1975 ("What future," 1976).

Reasons for working. The great majority of women work because they need the money, but many of them want to work outside the home anyway. In the home women often work without getting much expression of appreciation from their families, and they have little or no financial compensation or feelings of accomplishment (Mainardi, 1972). By contrast on the job they receive pay, have chances to interact with their peers, and have a stronger feeling of individual identity. In one study 51% of the mothers of preschoolers questioned, and 56% of the mothers of older children, said that they would continue to work even if the husband's earnings alone permitted the family to live comfortably (Popenoe, 1976).

Professional women, especially, find self-fulfillment in their work. Eleanore Luckey has "professional fun" in doing research. She has taken it seriously, she says, but "I think I have found the same sense of pleasure in it that some people do in reading whodunits, or in working crossword puzzles, or perhaps in playing poker. Starting with a problem or an idea that I want to check out, finding a way to design a study that will get the answer, and then seeing how it comes out is great fun" (Luckey, 1974, p. 311).

The situations of single and married women workers are different. For many married women success on the job is not critical. Most of them look upon the family as their primary responsibility, and their pay as supplementary to their husbands'. By contrast single women must support themselves while earning less for their work than men do. In addition the single woman's job is more likely to be critical for her own feeling of self-realization.

Special problems. While other minorities have more power on their jobs than ever before, women have less. Women have moved into the work world in great numbers, but the pay differential between the sexes has not narrowed. In fact it is widening; 15 years ago fulltime women workers earned 61% of what men did, and now they earn only 57% as much. In a study of 2000 industrial concerns, only 40 women who had had two years of experience were earning at least $20,000 a year ("Executive Woman," January 1975). The fraction of women in professional and technical positions has also declined. In Massachusetts, where 56% of the teachers are women, only 25% of school principals are women, and none are school superintendents. Women workers are still disproportionately represented in traditionally female jobs (O'Leary & Depner, 1976).

In addition career women often encounter the attitude that they will inevitably put family welfare ahead of their jobs. A survey of 1500 male executives indicated that they had more confidence in men's than in women's abilities to meet the needs of both family and employer (Gaylin, 1976). The man who is devoted to his family is judged to be a well-rounded, emotionally healthy individual; while the woman with exactly the same feelings is seen as lacking commitment to the firm. Employers look with favor on family men, but do not expect the family to intrude much on their work. If the husband of a career woman lets it be known that he is helping out much in the home, the boss is not pleased. Meantime his wife has to cope with bosses who believe that she both should and would give precedence to the family over her job.

The truth is that married women often do put their families first, because they have been taught from early childhood to do so. They are also brought up to hold certain false notions about a career. They assume they can take time out for childbearing and then without penalty, continue their career. However only in very exceptional cases can such women compete on an equal basis with men. It is also a fallacy to assume that women possess the time and energy to maintain two full-time jobs—that is, their careers in the work world and at home—without cost to themselves or their families. While many women attempt this, they simply cannot dedicate enough time, nor invest as much of themselves in their career, as men do. Those women who spend a good deal of time with their children simply lack the time necessary to make an outstanding success of their career.

Despite such problems, employed women express more satisfaction than housewives with regard to their daily work, their relationships with their children and the community (Popenoe, 1976). Working-class wives are the exception to this rule: their marital situation is better when they are not employed. For one thing, the working wife who makes a good salary may be a real threat to the husband who did not graduate from college. Such men may work hard, and have a rough time on the job; yet they manage to eke out a living. They find their chief fulfillment in their families. They are also willing to make sacrifices in order to provide their families with the best living that they can. However if their work and sacrifices are no longer necessary for the family's well-being, their low-status jobs become increasingly abhorrent to them. Moreover when their wives rival them as providers, they may feel "emasculated." Thus the women's movement may indirectly "endanger the fragile psychosocial balance which has supported less educated men in their jobs for many years" (Yankelovich, 1974b, p. 87).

The remedy in such cases ought to be to re-educate people about these attitudes rather than to discourage women from working. This is a challenge to the schools, the writers of children's books, and the producers of children's television programs. As both spouses come to recognize the need for a well-balanced life that includes vocation, avocation, and family activities, new life styles can be worked out that will prevent marital discord over such matters.

A comparison of housewives and working wives. In interviews that included both women who did and did not work outside the home, Ferree (1976) found that 67% of the working wives believed themselves to be relatively good homemakers, and their jobs provided an additional source of self-esteem and fulfillment. Nor did they work merely to supplement the family income, as has been commonly believed. Rather, they share men's motives in working both for money and personal satisfaction.

True, a minority of the housewives were not dissatisfied. A quarter of them were quite happy with their lives. These were the women who believed their work at home was appreciated, and who participated in "social support groups." For example, neighbors, relatives, and friends might come to the house daily.

The working wives had their share of problems, chiefly the triple responsibility for job, housework, and child care. Those who worked part-time had an easier time discharging these roles and were better satisfied than the fulltime workers. Nevertheless part-time workers also had difficulties. They did not feel entitled to demand much help from their husbands with household chores; nor did they have much chance for raises and promotions.

Among those housewives who were dissatisfied, it was not merely their role, but certain features of it, that caused their discontent. Not many years ago housewives shared a mutually supportive network of kinfolk and friends. Working-class women in particular usually lived near their relatives and long-time friends. As people have moved more often, and as large numbers of women have gone to work, these "housewife networks" have become less common, and the role of housewife has become a lonely, "solo pastime." If the husband is at work all day and the children at school, the wives feel isolated; they spend their days doing housework and watching television, and often feel they are "going crazy staying home," seeing only their four walls (Ferree, 1976). Almost half these relatively isolated housewives reported feeling discontented, compared to fewer than one-fourth of those who had frequent social contact.

A woman's work provides contact with varied kinds of adults, and offers her pay which signifies the worth of her work. By contrast the housewife's work is never completed and provides neither "tangible rewards" nor social contacts. Despite housewives' never-ending work, these women are taken for granted, and their husbands often feel that they simply sit at home and do nothing all day. At the same time their husbands remind them that their duty is to stay at home and take care of the house. Sometimes wives wanted to work outside the home, but didn't do so because their husbands objected. A third of the fulltime housewives said that their husbands made the decision about whether they would stay home. When asked whether a wife should simply take a job anyhow, over half the working women said they should, while only a third of the housewives agreed. Both groups believed that going against the husbands' wishes placed the marriage "at risk." Some said they would take the job anyway because it was their right. They believed that the marriage would be a bad one if such a decision could destroy it.

Over two-thirds of the housewives as well as the working women believed that women have an obligation to work outside the home when their assistance is needed to support the family, regardless of the husband's view.

Middle-aged Men at Work

Advantages. Most middle-aged men enjoy certain advantages at work. Ordinarily they have found their niche, and have at least worked out a reasonably agreeable style of work life. Often their wives work, too, now that the children are no longer young, so that money pressures

1978 © Sybil Shelton

By middle age most men have found a niche for themselves at work and have worked out an agreeable style of work life.

are not as great. A man may help out at home if the wife works, but the major homemaking responsibility is still hers, even after the husband retires, however unfair that may be. In fact in recent decades women's work life has lengthened, while men's has shortened. More women are working than ever before, and they are remaining in the work force until a later age. Meantime men are retiring at a younger age; only one in four men over 65 is still in the labor force (Neugarten, 1972).

Men also make more money than women who do the same work, and they fare better at the hands of hiring committees, yet not all men receive equal treatment. In one study married men were often aided in their search for jobs by wives they described as "gems" or "marvelous cooks" ("Only married men," 1976). Their wives, along with a "charming family" or "two fine sons," gave them a certain "aura of responsibility, maturity, and stability..." (p. 63). The single men, by contrast, were considered somewhat immature. The single women fared more poorly than the men but somewhat better than the married women, especially those with children.

Problems. Even married men with charming wives have their vocational problems, one being that men must earn their status on the job while women can attain status simply through marriage. Consider the high status of the presidents' wives who, with notable exceptions such as Eleanor Roosevelt, have achieved little on their own. Women have greater social mobility (both upward and downward) through marriage than men do through their occupations, and women more readily cross the boundaries of major status groupings.

Men also feel that their success as persons depends upon their vocational adequacy, and altogether too much of their happiness hinges upon it. In a study by Lowenthal, Thurnher, and Chiriboga (1975),

> the "main area which middle-aged men perceived as stressful was work (changing jobs; getting fired, hired, or promoted; or being without a job); nearly half reported changes in life satisfaction attributable to work. Work-related issues had less salience as a source of stress for the men in the pre-retirement stage than in middle age, no doubt because most of them expected to be well out of it soon; yet it was still a source of stress for one third of the older cohort" (p. 170).

Although almost three-fifths of the women in middle age and at pre-retirement worked, fewer than one in five reported feeling stress about work; this reflects its relatively low significance for them. For the men there wasn't a single other area apart from work that even a fifth named as stressful.

A devastating blow to men is unemployment, especially at middle age. Younger men are more resilient, but older ones find their age a handicap. The higher the worker's former status and the more sudden his fall, the greater the shock; and destructive effects are demonstrated in lower self-esteem and increased alienation. In one study of unemployed men, over half of whom had graduated from college, many had held managerial or engineering positions, and half were unemployed for the first time, after 20 years of steady work. These men felt that they had done socially worthwhile work during their employment, but now they felt insignificant. They felt ordinary for the first time in their lives, and a kind of dreariness permeated their daily existence (Braginsky & Braginsky, 1975).

Blue-collar workers have their own special problems. They usually work for others, and often feel manipulated. They find various ways to express dissatisfaction, including sabotage, fooling around, being absent, and in general showing little commitment to the job (Yankelovich, 1974b). Yet these people have little chance for mobility, for "the step ladder has been moved from the factory floor, and people now gain economic and social mobility through education, not by following the traditional Horatio Alger route" (p. 87). As a result the gap between the classes will inevitably grow. The alternative is for policy makers to devise creative modes of organization which will make these young blue-collar workers better satisfied and help them to fulfill their aspirations as human beings.

An especially poignant problem, most often experienced by white collar workers sometime during middle age, is the growing apprehension and ultimately the stark realization that they will never reach some long-held cherished goal. They have identified accomplishment of this goal with fulfillment as a person, as a male, and to abandon it is to lose a significant part of the self. Such a loss may precipitate a serious middle-age crisis and a desperate effort to fill the vacuum thus created with alternative goals and values. A man's devastation is greater when a colleague, often younger and less capable but with the right connections, is awarded the position that had been his goal.

Worker Satisfaction

Extent of worker satisfaction. Despite such problems, over the past decade almost 90% of all workers have been pretty well satisfied, especially those in the white-collar class (Quinn, Staines, & McCullough, 1974). Those who are dissatisfied are mostly in lower-status jobs, including nonfarm labor, factory work, clerical work, and so on. However,

Sussman declares that 15 to 20% of the current work force is unhappy, and that job dissatisfaction is on the rise ("Why millions," 1976).

This brings us to the question of what people consider being satisfied means to them. Certainly most workers can name features of their jobs that they dislike. The truth is that achieving vocational satisfaction is an extremely complex matter, and few ever really attain it, for "as Thoreau said, 'Most men live lives of quiet desperation'; the only difference, in modern terms, is the fact that young people are not so quiet in resigning themselves to a life of despair" (Story, 1974, p. 372).

In the following, several middle-aged adults indicate whether they find their work satisfying.

> Highly. It was my goal to be an elementary school teacher from the age of five on. I never did attain the desired degree of excellence, but perhaps satisfaction is primarily found in the striving. (*Female, age 62*)

> Yes. I waited until I was 50 years old to complete my education. I always wanted to be a nurse as early as my teens. I always tried to work around the sick and the elderly. (*Female, age 54*)

> No. I find it a bore. I get very tired of all the petty jealousies and selfishness of my coworkers and the pettiness of the bosses. I believe I do a good job, while receiving a minimum of appreciation. (*Female, age 63*)

> I enjoy my profession very much, particularly since I seem to have developed an aptitude for it. I am also able to help people in distress, which gives me a great deal of satisfaction. (*Male, age 51*)

Factors relating to satisfaction. According to some authorities, the critical test of satisfaction is whether the job makes maximum use of individual abilities; when people are "underutilized" they are generally not satisfied. It doesn't necessarily mean that they are bored. Workers may even accept a repetitive, uninspiring job by daydreaming or socializing with other employees. That sort of worker will put in eight hours on an assembly line, then go home to tackle jobs or hobbies that are interesting ("Why millions," 1976). Having a large salary is less important than other factors, and obtaining a raise may not bring about the desired satisfaction. If workers are dissatisfied with their pay, it is usually because they are making less than others with similar skills, abilities, and seniority.

Another factor that is important in modifying job satisfaction is whether workers continue to make satisfactory progress, in their own eyes, up the promotional ladder. As workers grow older, their jobs may bring their share of disappointments. Individuals accustomed to a succession of promotions and salary increases may ultimately find themselves on a plateau in which their salaries do not keep rising, and promotions may be awarded to persons younger than they. Hence middle-aged workers' salaries may not keep pace with rising consumer prices. As a result, in managerial occupations, career discontent may reach dramatic proportions. The middle-level executive, in particular, begins to feel inadequate in his efforts to compete, and harbors doubts regarding the value of competition (Marrow, 1972). In any case people are more dissatisfied in certain areas, especially in assembly-line work and clerical occupations. Generally the higher people are on the job scale, the happier they are; for example, those higher on the management scale find work challenging and have more opportunities to make decisions. Working conditions are also a factor. The sexes differ in degree of satisfaction, too, and men are better satisfied than women.

Worker satisfaction cannot be determined with accuracy at specific points in the career cycle. Often there are years of adjustment and readjustment before an individual decides to settle for a particular niche. As Story (1974) points out, it would be very hard to find even a "successful individual . . . whose early career was not a notorious series of false starts, often in totally unrelated fields" (p. 372). However by the time they reach their 40s, most people have settled down, and have a fairly clear idea of how contented they are.

In appraising worker satisfaction several factors are often overlooked. For one thing, the whole economy is so complex and such large numbers are involved, that a sizeable fraction of workers will always be dissatisfied. In addition it is easy to lose sight of the human tragedy of individuals when we cite numbers. It is of no satisfaction to an unemployed worker to know that more people are employed than ever before. It is also misleading to interpret job satisfaction as equivalent to job placement. The challenge is to have the sort of career that provides not only satisfaction, but the maximum opportunity for personal growth and making a contribution to society.

Improving Work Situations

A great deal of attention is being paid to improving work situations today. Above all, the former assumption that laborers will have no real part in determining their working conditions is losing ground. Instead working people at all levels, in all areas, are demanding a better deal (Story, 1974). In consequence efforts are being made to match workers to jobs, and to tailor jobs to people, or at least to structure those jobs so that they will be more challenging or interesting. For example, both Saab and Volvo in Sweden are utilizing autonomous work groups instead of conventional assembly lines to produce their engines and automobiles. Another idea that is being tried out, is organizing work according to work modules instead of continuous, day-long jobs. That is, the day would be broken into two-hour modules, each devoted to specific tasks, and workers could arrange or rearrange their sequence. Other ideas include staggered schedules and four-day work weeks, which may provide some relief from the uniformity of the 9-to-5 routine. In a similar vein, about a thousand industrial companies and government agencies are testing the European idea of flexi-time (flexible work time). For example, the clerical employees in the trust department at the First National Bank of Boston formerly began work at about 9 a.m. and quit at 5 p.m. However, beginning in 1973 they shifted to flexitime, in which they work their 8-hour day at any time between 7:30 a.m. and 6:30 p.m. They come in, eat lunch, and leave when they like, so long as they work the required number of hours each week and finish their assignments on time. The experiment proved so successful in this department that it spread to several other departments, with consistently favorable results: productivity increased, and overtime and absenteeism declined (Stein, Cohen, & Gadon, 1976).

Other solutions to present work dilemmas are more theoretical. One is that all should share society's more disagreeable tasks. Another possibility might be to get rid of jobs which make people unhappy or bored by designing machines that can perform them. A third idea is to try to make people like jobs that they have been unhappy about up to now. This might be achieved by giving them bonuses or special incentives.

It is certainly true that the lot of industrial workers in modern western countries is superior to that of their counterparts in other times and places. Despite the possibilities of improvement that we have discussed, it remains uncertain whether individual workers will acquire any greater control over their lives. Instead they may simply be directed in less obvious ways, or workers' participation in designing such plans may be more apparent than real. For example, workers' representatives who have managed to seize power within the hierarchy of labor may work out schemes with management that only appear to represent the best interests of the workers.

The Future

Looking ahead, certain trends in vocational adaptation can be anticipated. For one thing, more stress will be placed on finding work congenial to individual tastes and needs. The idea of a one-time job choice will be displaced by that of matching a changing self to changing jobs. Such a concept will require that seniority and other benefits be easily transferred from one job or place to another. Continuing job re-education will also be needed, but it will concentrate more on basic concepts than specifics, because specialties quickly become obsolete. For example, "the modern aerospace engineer is in the same plight as that of a hypothetical veterinarian who, after years of intensive preparation, finds that he has specialized in the unique diseases of extinct animals" (Story, 1974, p. 169). Increasing numbers of people will have a second career. After all, people are in better health and live longer than ever before. The notion of a single career may even become outmoded and replaced by a "serial career." In a recent study of middle managers, 70% of those surveyed, anticipated career changes sometime in the future, not because they were dissatisfied with what they were doing, but because they wanted to develop new interests (Leider, 1974).

Factors which could reverse the trend toward subordinating economic growth to worker satisfaction would be gross population or socialism in government. Either would place mass welfare ahead of individual autonomy. Already regionalism in social and cultural institutions is breaking down; and middle-sized businesses increasingly are being absorbed by large national or multinational corporations. Meantime the population is becoming more mobile. Bell (1973) insists that the United States is becoming a mass, postindustrial society communal in form, so that public mechanisms, instead of markets, allocate goods and services. Public decision rather than individual choice becomes the arbiter of such services, and claims of individuals are converted into claims of the community.

LEISURE

The Significance of Leisure

Definition. In general work involves obligation and efficiency, while leisure implies doing what one wishes at one's own pace (Gunter & Moore, 1975). We participate in leisure activities when we do not have to work to maintain our household or ourselves. That is, "leisure is doing what we don't have to do" (Neulinger, 1974, p. 186). Free time is not equivalent to leisure, but it does make leisure possible. Leisure "is a state of mind, it is a way of being, of being at peace with oneself and what one is doing" (p. 120). The way in which we determine how to use free time, can be called the leisure style.

Leisure activities may be classified as individual, joint, or parallel (Orthner, 1975). Individual activities demand no communication with others; in fact they may discourage any interaction. Joint activities involve a considerable degree of interaction and encourage communication. Parallel activities are essentially individual activities within group settings and require very little interaction between participants. In a study of upper-middle-class husbands and wives in a medium-sized urban area, it was found that the husbands spent 31% of their discretionary (free) time on weekends in individual activities, 34% in joint activities with their wives, and 27% in parallel activities with their wives. For their part, the wives spent 36% of their discretionary time in individual activities, 32% in joint activities with their husbands, and 25% in parallel activities with them (Orthner, 1975).

The growing significance of leisure. The topic of leisure is becoming increasingly significant. Ripley and O'Brien (1976) suggest that "how to live with leisure may become as important for tomorrow's generations as learning to live with work has been for yesterday's" (p. 56). Colleges and universities are already offering courses in leisure, and adult education courses in leisure-time activities are proliferating. Corporations that make leisure equipment such as boats, fishing tackle, and camping gear are thriving, and men's clothing manufacturers are expanding their range of leisure attire.

Leisure is considered significant for several reasons. Perhaps the most important is the need to compensate for the strains of high-pressure living. Unfortunately, many people must perform jobs which provide less than they might desire in terms of fulfillment; so fulfillment and happiness must be achieved for the most part through leisure activities. In addition leisure activities are often the glue that binds families together. The National Recreation Association has a slogan: "The family that plays together, stays together." While this slogan may be an exaggeration, certain trends have made family recreation more important. One is the family's transition to a more companionable institution (Orthner, 1975). On the other hand, recreation in itself is no guarantee of better family relationships. In a family of highly divergent personalities, joint activities may satisfy no one. At the other extreme family members may become so involved in individual pursuits that they ignore each other. In other words, while individual activities may prove satisfying for those involved, they may also involve commitments that interfere with communication and sharing. Hence a great deal of time devoted to individual activities reduces marital satisfaction (Orthner, 1975). On the other hand, activities which involve interaction, such as camping or games, contribute to family solidarity.

Leisure time activities help provide a sense of fulfillment and happiness that is often missing in a person's everyday routine.

Also enhancing the importance of leisure is its legitimization by society. Formerly it was perceived as wasteful; now it is regarded as a means of personal growth and fulfillment. Authorities believe it can become far more so when we learn to utilize it more effectively. The task will be to achieve this goal without meanwhile overstructuring it, and even making work of it.

One presumed reason for the growing emphasis on leisure–the increase in free time—may be more illusory than real. It is a myth, observes Butler (1975b), that almost all middle-aged persons have a great deal of leisure, for many of them moonlight. In addition housewives have increasingly assumed jobs outside the home, but they still have domestic responsibilities. When the time spent in commuting to work and performing jobs at home is also taken into account, the free time that remains is far less than is commonly believed.

Each sex has special reasons for developing leisure activities. For the woman there is the empty nest, which either strips her of her child-rearing function or blesses her with its absence, depending upon her outlook. Also, the chances are high that she will spend her later life alone because of death of her spouse (Sheehy, 1976). For the man leisure pursuits help to diffuse the tensions that build up from the job. These pursuits also become the focus of his life after he has retired. For both sexes leisure activities become important avenues of self-realization that were closed until now because of more pressing obligations.

Leisure Pursuits

Individual activities. In the following, several middle-aged persons answer the question: What are your chief, and most pleasant, forms of recreation or special interests?

Reading, travel, sewing, creating things, keeping in step with changes and applying them to my home and self. (*Female, 58, married, licensed real estate broker*)

At this age athletics and sports don't turn me on. I'm more interested in meeting and visiting with people, eating out, working for the church, knitting, and doing projects, etc. (*Female, 51, separated, office clerk*)

I like to travel. I like to dance (slow). I do a lot of different kinds of craft work. Working outside, especially with my flowers. (*Female, 54, widowed, LPN*)

I enjoy people most, but also visiting, cards, scrabble, social drinking, crocheting, knitting, sewing, decorating my own apartment and four others I rent. I also enjoy flowers, birds, etc. (*Female, 61, widowed, retired activity director*)

Outdoor sports, good conversation, creative achievements such as painting, cooking. (*Female, 41, married, teacher*)

Sports, music, boating, fishing, sailing. (*Female, 46, single, teacher*)

Piano playing, arts and crafts, grandchildren, being with my family, and music. (*Female, 53, married, housewife*)

Gardening, going to the lake in the summer, having the family come home, knitting, crocheting, and antiques. (*Female, 64, married, housewife*)

I have many special interests—of course, some are more special than others. I have little time to indulge them now; however, I expect to make up for lost time after I retire. They include, among others, the stock market, tennis, swimming, art, playing the organ, reading information books, travel, collecting old magazines, and rock hounding, and talking with really unusual or especially congenial people. (*Female, 62, single, college professor*)

Simply listing leisure pursuits provides no great insight into their significance, for a single activity has many facets, and may be employed by different people in varied ways. One adult may watch soap operas endlessly, looking for vicarious pleasures. Another may watch television selectively, ignoring all but the more sophisticated programs. A man may go camping in order to get away from the telephone and be outdoors, while his wife may go in order to strengthen the family.

Factors that relate to choice of leisure activities. The factors that determine the choice of leisure are many and complex; they include personal characteristics, family background, and age. In general adults' interests resemble those of their parents. Aesthetic parents have aesthetic children, and intellectual parents have intellectual children, although the specific areas of aesthetics or intellect that parents and their children follow may be quite different. Thus certain life styles and values become hallmarks of particular families. Even within the same family, individual differences in such traits as humanitarianism, aestheticism, practicality, and intellectualism may produce a variety of interest patterns. And whatever interests are developed in early years, stabilize between later adolescence and early adulthood. Later they either increase somewhat or remain stable throughout adulthood (Haan & Day, 1974). By their late 20s peoples' values and interests have also stabilized.

The degree to which age affects leisure activities is debatable. Gunter and Moore (1975) define adult, leisure life styles in terms of the way they differ from youth's: "Youth desire and seek out change and discontinuity; those in the establishment phase require order and continuity. The young people may want bright lights and loud music; their parents may require a more sedate setting—for example, bridge with friends or a dance" (p. 204). Troll (1975) attaches less importance to age as a determinant of leisure style, observing that changes in "the content of adult life from youth to middle age" seem to be more involved in narrowing of focus than in an actual change of interest. That is, with age, likes and dislikes become stronger and more stable. In general, however, the interests of adults vary more by sex, social class, and other group factors than they do by age" (p. 51). On the other hand, differences in interests and values according to sex are far less than is generally believed. Such sex differences as exist in youth tend to level out during adulthood, at least in the middle class (Haan & Day, 1974).

Among adults differences in choice of activity by both sex and age are more a matter of degree than kind. In a study by Lowenthal, Thurnher and Chiriboga (1975) of leisure activities among middle- and lower-middle-class adults, the large majority mentioned such pursuits as "radio listening, reading, household chores, shopping, visiting, being visited, and helping others. Those [activities] seldom reported included playing a musical instrument, dancing, solitary games, picnics, and physical exercise" (p. 6). The two older age groups were more selective about their activities than the younger ones. The middle-aged men had the least varied activities, and those anticipating retirement in the near future were doing what they could to improve their income before they retired. This factor, coupled with their decreased energy, resulted in fewer leisure activities such as club and church affiliations. They might still belong to certain groups, but their participation was erratic. The middle-aged women also engaged in fewer activities than younger women, but not for the same reasons as the men. True, half of them worked, chiefly to supplement the family income, but they were not preoccupied with their jobs, and focused their interests on the family.

Leisure styles. Collectively, the subjects in this study followed four main life styles. The first, or complex, type involved a variety of roles and activity patterns. Another, the simplistic type, was characterized by limited activities and few roles. The diffuse type included those who combined few roles with varied activity patterns, while the focused type had broad roles but few activities. Both newlywed men and women led a complex style of life, while middle-aged women led a simplistic one. Women at the pre-retirement stage followed activity patterns more like those of the men, with complex diffuse styles predominating, and simplistic and focused styles running a close second. In all four stages the men were about twice as likely as the women to pursue the focused life style, and twice as many of the women followed a diffuse pattern. In general, concluded the researchers, men and women differ somewhat in their use of leisure time. Men stress play while women engage in more social activities. Older men anticipate increased play and relaxation after they retire; and while their leisure activities become less active, they still display an "outdoor, athletic orientation."

Patterns also vary according to the stage of marriage. Before the children come, married adults engage in recreational activities similar to those they shared before marriage. But the most significant change in leisure patterns comes after the children are born (Kelly, 1975). There is a slight decrease in what are primarily companionship activities, and a slight increase in worklike activities. The change is from activities that are selected chiefly for their intrinsic satisfaction to those that relate to role expectations. That is, family roles tend to structure the parents' leisure style, and having children significantly limits their choice.

The postparental period, after the last child has left home and retirement begins, does not represent a complete return to the uncondi-tional activities of the pre-parental stage. Professionals shift slightly back toward work-related activities; and having children and grand-children in the vicinity does more to change the location of family activities than to decrease them. Meantime many activities associated with role expectations are exchanged for those related to personal satisfaction (Kelly, 1975).

Orthner (1975) discusses leisure in terms of the marital career. Certainly not all shared leisure activities have the same effect on marriage. And certainly more than merely physically being together is necessary to have a satisfying relationship. When a couple watches television or goes to a play, they are focusing on the activity rather than on each other. Perhaps only when the activity requires interaction are chances for communication and a better understanding increased. However, simply doing things together does not guarantee marital satisfaction either. What couples do, and how each partner feels about it, is important. If a particular pattern—whether parallel or joined—becomes dominant, other forms of activities are thereby reduced, and this shift may have an impact on their relationship.

Leisure-time activities vary in their influence over the marital career. In the earlier years of marriage, and after the children have left home, leisure activities are particularly important. In the first period a "relational identity crisis" occurs, and in the later period the dyadic relation between the two marital partners must be reaffirmed.

Between the first years of marriage and the empty-nest period, leisure activities bear little relation to marital satisfaction. During this period couples may define their personal satisfaction mostly in terms of their occupational and parental goals, thus placing their marital relationship "on hold" during the interim period. Thus it appears that the chief function of leisure for marital partners is to facilitate communication during periods of possible stress, and during changes in roles and interrelationships (Orthner, 1975).

The choice of leisure activities can be further modified by all sorts of situational and circumstantial factors, including the length of vacations, the amount of disposable income available, the climate, the local culture, or the type of housing people occupy. Leisure styles also become modified according to new roles, opportunities, associations, and such changes in geographical environment as moving from an apartment into a single-family house with a yard.

The significance of leisure activities. To date researchers have barely scratched the surface in determining the significance of leisure activities. And after individual leisure patterns have been analyzed, their overall significance in modifying the quality of life must be considered. For example, take a study of family vacations, which have become a common feature of family life. Then decide what, if any, significance such findings can have for people's overall leisure patterns. This study was made by Rosenblatt and Russell (1975), who observe that every year a great many families set out on vacations, often by car. Such a trip is a somewhat "delicate social event" that may involve certain problems (p. 209). For one thing, at home, where there is more space, family members are better insulated from each other. Also, there family members have worked out rules about territoriality or the use of space and objects. When traveling, the satisfactions and problems experienced vary according to several factors. The nuclear family members travel alone, so that grandparents, in-laws, and friends are not included. Besides, nuclear families, by contrast with other kinds of families, have already worked out a division of labor which may carry over, to a certain extent, to vacations. Oddly enough, couples who travel without children experience no more stress than those with children, perhaps because the children absorb frustrations that couples might otherwise direct at each other. Adults who travel with their parents experience less stress than traveling with unrelated persons; however, they do experience greater stress than traveling with marital partners or their own children. The problem that arises when adult offspring travel with their parents is that there are too many chiefs, and tensions arise over such decisions as when to stop for the night.

On the basis of their study Rosenblatt and Russell drew certain tentative conclusions. The fact that vacationers experience less stress in bad weather than good, they ascribed to the decrease in driving and the increase in lounging about and sleeping. Overall, vacationers experience less tension when they are on vacation than when they are not, and while problems do exist, vacations permit families to experiment in creative ways with their pattern of living. That is, when they are away from routines and rules, families may be free to try out new ways of relating to each other.

Rosenblatt and Russell (1975) also offer a few bits of advice to family vacationers. First, they must expect interpersonal difficulties. Second, they should be aware of problems that may occur when traveling with persons other than the immediate nuclear family. They note, too, that traveling with cars is risky, especially on long trips. Finally, they particularly recommend going to places that the family has enjoyed previously, taking a vacation that places people in familiar, houselike settings such as cabins with cooking privileges, or taking a camping vacation which permits settling down on a home base.

Social Relationships

Friendships at middle-age. Middle-aged adults spend much of their leisure time with friends, as distinct from the relatively large number of acquaintances they have among neighbors and colleagues on the job.

Adults have few close friends, and as they grow older they become less social (Haan & Day, 1974). These friendships last despite the passage of time or even physical separation. That is, once established, they tend to persist. The closeness of new friendships, however, is associated with the frequency of visits (Hess, 1971). Among the married, friends are chosen less in terms of age than for such factors as the ages of their children, their occupational status, or how long they have been married (Hess, 1972). Couples who are better off financially and have fewer children, have more family friends as couples. The couple nature of these friendships is proved by the fact that they become inconsequential if either couple has marital problems or if a member of either couple dies (Lopata, 1973).

Aside from friendships between married couples, close friends are usually of the same sex. Cross-sex friendships are potentially sexual, and are therefore discouraged in most societies (Hess, 1972). Such friendships are rare even in childhood, when they are sanctioned, though hardly encouraged; and also in old age, partly because of the uneven sex ratio (more women than men). They are only fully approved in marital and love relationships. Though numerically rare, they do exist, especially where the situation makes them unthreatening. For example, cross-friendship ties may exist between opposite-sex homosexuals or between men and women on the job who share the same interests but are not sexually attracted to each other.

Kaplan (1974) speculates regarding the alternate concepts of "intimacy overload" and "intimacy hunger." Perhaps all of us, in varying degrees, have an optimal number of personal attachments. Studies of friendship indicate that the majority of adults have only three or four best friends, and when people move they will substitute only three or four new close friendships for those that are no longer present (Hess, 1972).

Social class. Social relationships are quite different among white-collar and blue-collar adults. In one study (Marciano, 1975), material from Mirra Komarovsky's *Blue Collar Marriage* (1967) was used in order to determine blue-collar attitudes held by a friendship nucleus of five couples who had now attained a middle-class income, job status, and life setting. The results disclosed a high level of sex-role segregation and patriarchal patterns; little real communication between the couples; and the separation of the husbands' and wives' social lives. In pursuing the traditional sex roles the women had little time for mixing with others outside the home. By contrast the men had their own all-male cliques which reinforced their feelings of superiority and authority. Although the women had a college education the men believed them incapable of understanding business problems. Apparently couples with blue-collar backgrounds maintain traditional sex-role attitudes even after they have attained middle-class income and status.

Age and marital status. Marital status interacts with age in determining social relationships. In a study of patterns of close relationships among a random sampling in a large metropolis of 347 adults aged 18 to 65, younger single persons spent less time than older singles and married couples with intimates, had maintained these relationships over a longer period of time, and had come to know each other well. The married people involved more neighbors and kin in their network of close relationships. However, the latter categories of relationships were more limited than the former. The young singles were less likely to include their kin among their closest relationships, probably because they had nonfamilial concerns at this stage of their lives. Since they were involved in seeking companionship, finding a mate, and establishing a career, they associated more with agemates who possessed similar concerns. In general, when people arrive at the stage in life when their children and mates are the focus of their existence, they relate chiefly to kin and neighbors, in addition to some friends. At this stage the nuclear family provides much of their needed companionship; and fewer new friendships are established outside the family. Since close relationships require time and emotional energy, married persons have less time for intimate associations outside the family. Hence young couples have more friends outside the family than middle-aged married people (Shulman, 1975).

Of course there is much variation in the way individual adults interact socially. There are the loners and the extroverts, those with many superficial friends, and those with a few close ones. But the most common pattern among adults is to have a few close friends who share certain things in common, whether children, leisure activities, or personal traits.

SUMMARY

Work is still very important among middle-aged adults, a bit less for men and much more for some women, than formerly; nevertheless its meaning is changing. Today both sexes want something more than a job—they want a vocation that gives them a measure of fulfillment. They also expect to earn a high enough income to be able to afford the good things in life, including satisfying leisure activities. Both sexes still have their vocational problems, though working wives find such pursuits rewarding and both sexes are reaping the benefits of improved working conditions. Nevertheless men still feel devastated by unemployment, even when the wife's pay check plus his unemployment benefits can sustain the family.

While leisure is still less important in most middle-agers' life style than work, it is gaining rapidly in significance. These people engage in widely varied pursuits which are somewhat dependent on social class, education, sex, age, marital status, and individual tastes. People have their characteristic leisure styles that evolve over time, and change, to some extent, as the total life situation changes—for example, when the children leave home or retirement occurs.

SUGGESTED READINGS

Bould, S. Female-headed families: Personal fate control and the provider role. *Journal of Marriage and the Family,* May 1977, *39* (2), 339–349. A longitudinal study of female heads of families, ages 30 to 44, shows that women who are poor and/or must depend upon unstable or stigmatizing sources of income feel less able to plan for their lives. A general assessment is also made of the adjustment of female family heads and their dependents.

Burke, R. J. & Weir, T. Relationship of wives' employment status to husband, wife and pair satisfaction and performance. *Journal of Marriage and the Family,* May 1976, *38* (2), 279–287. Questionnaires submitted to 189 husband and wife pairs regarding their satisfactions at home and on the job, feelings of well-being, and inter-spouse communication, revealed important sex differences in how they felt about the wife working. In general working wives were better satisfied than nonworking wives, but husbands of nonworking wives were better satisfied than those of working wives.

Gordon, C., Gaitz, C. M., & Scott, J. Leisure and lives: Personal expressivity across the life span. In Binstock, R. H. & Shanas, E. (Eds.) *Handbook of Aging and the Social Sciences.* New York: Van Nostrand Reinhold Co., 1976, 310–41. Conceptions, meanings, and varieties of leisure are related to each major stage in the life span; and findings are presented from the Houston Life-Span Leisure Study.

Heath, D. H. Adolescent and adult predictors of vocational adaptation. *Journal of Vocational Behavior,* 1976, *9* (1), 1–19. A follow-up of almost 2,000 men, originally studied in 1964, 1966, and 1974 indicates that certain types are far more likely than others to react negatively to life cycle changes—for example, from work to retirement.

Hoffman, L. W. The employment of women, education, and fertility. *Merrill-Palmer Quarterly,* 1974, *20* (2), 99–119. The writer explores the reasons for the negative relationships between women's employment and fertility, and identifies those barriers which turn women toward maternity rather than professional employment. Evidence is presented that this condition is changing as both careers for women and childlessness become more acceptable.

Orthner, D. K. Leisure activity patterns and marital satisfaction over the marital career. *Journal of Marriage and the Family,* February 1975, *37* (1), 91–104. In this study of 216 husbands and 226 wives, leisure activity patterns are identified, classified according to marital stage, and related to marital satisfaction.

Pfeiffer, E. & Davis, G. C. The use of leisure time in middle life, pp. 232–243 in E. Palmore (Ed.) *Normal Aging II,* Durham: Duke University Press, 1974. (Originally published in *The Gerontologist,* 1971, *11* (3), 187–195) Data obtained from 261 men and 241 women aged 46 to 71, indicate how they spent their leisure time, both in everyday and vacation periods, and how they feel about such activities.

Psychology Today, Dec. 1976, *10* (7). See the brief articles, "Stress, Competition and Heart Attacks" (54–57, 134) by David C. Glass, and "How to Break the Vicious Cycle of Stress" (59–60) by Richard M. Suinn. In the first, Glass tells how hard-driving executives fight to achieve at the risk of heart disease. In the second, Suinn tells how different types of people can learn how to control their anxiety.

Rapoport, R. & Rapoport, R. N. (with Ziona Strelitz). *Leisure and the family life cycle.* London: Routledge and Kegan Paul, 1975. Basing their discussions on other research as well as on intensive interviews with individuals of various ages and social levels in English life, the authors stress the need for trained personnel that will help them to employ their leisure time effectively.

Seybolt, J. W. Work satisfaction as a function of the person: Environment interaction. *Organizational Behavior and Human Performance,* 1976, *17* (1), 66–75. A study of 926 male public employees indicated that more organizational inducements (pay, task variety, and complexity) are required to satisfy better-educated than less well-educated individuals.

Shelton, B. Feminism: Implications for employment counselors. *Journal of Employment Counseling,* 1976, *13* (3), 116–121. A review of the recent literature regarding women's counseling needs indicates that women experience role conflicts, institutional bias, and social hostilities that interfere with their vocational adjustment and achievement.

Sheppard, H. L. Work and retirement. In Binstock, R. H. & Shanas, E. (Eds.) *Handbook of Aging and the Social Sciences.* New York: Van Nostrand Reinhold New York, 1976, 286–309. This chapter deals with such varied aspects of work and retirement as women's growing participation in the labor force, work performance, unemployment among older workers, retirement decisions, and retirement age.

Wilkinson, M. W. Leisure: An alternate to the meaning of work. *Journal of Applied Rehabilitation Counseling,* Summer 1975, *6* (2), 73–77. Leisure is portrayed as providing time for self-actualization and the fulfillment of intrinsic needs, just as work provides for extrinsic needs. Various other distinctions between work and leisure, and their potential for satisfying personal needs, are explored.

IV
PART

Older
Adults

11 CHAPTER

Characteristics
of
Older
People

ESTABLISHING A FRAME OF REFERENCE

What Should Older People be Called?

There is no single accepted designation for the last stage of life. Many terms used for the aged evoke negative images, including the elderly, the retired, and even senior citizens and golden agers. Some terms are contemptuous and degrading. Older people may be described as " 'fading fast,' 'over the hill,' 'out to pasture,' 'down the drain,' 'finished,' 'out of date,' an 'old crock,' 'fogy,' 'geezer,' or 'biddy' " (Butler, 1975c, p. 2).

In the following, several persons over the age of 60 tell how they feel about the term "senior citizen," and what they think older people should be called. (Significantly, younger persons had no objection to the term senior citizen.)

Silly euphemisms usually amuse me. This one is no worse than "Interment Director," for "Undertaker," which I saw in a newspaper advertisement. (*Male, age 72*)

I can't think of a better term. (*Male, age 69*)

Yes, I object to it. Why use any special name? (*Female, age 73*)

Any term is agreeable to me. I just don't like for people to be always trying to "honor" us. (*Female, age 84*)

I dislike very much the terms "the aged" and "the elderly," and feel lukewarm about "senior citizen." I prefer "older persons" or "the long-living" better, but haven't encountered the ideal term as yet. (*Female, age 62*)

Butler advises that either the least objectionable of the common names—perhaps the old or the elderly—should be given a respectable status, or we should have a new name altogether. The Abkhasians in the Soviet Union simply describe older persons as the long-living, suggesting continuing life rather than approaching death (Butler, 1975c).

Whatever names older people may be called will inevitably become colored in the popular mind by the current status of this age group in society. Hence the best way to insure that names ascribed to older persons will be ego-building rather than ego-eroding will be to upgrade their status in society. The names ascribed to groups, and the images they conjure up, derive from the changing status of those groups in the total society.

Demographic Data

The elderly, as they are commonly called, are growing rapidly in number. In fact they are the fastest growing group in the United States. In 1900 only 4% of the American population was aged 65 or older. Now over 10% of the population is in that category and more than 100,000 are over age 100 (Kalish, 1975). By the year 2030, 17% of the population will be 65 or older if current birth trends persist. The growing numbers of the elderly reflect the rapidly increasing average life expectancy. In 1900 it was 47 years; now it is over 70. Considering the new medical advances and the declining birth rate, it is possible that the elderly will comprise a quarter of the whole population by the year 2000 (Butler, 1975c). It is simply a matter of more people reaching old age, for basic longevity has remained pretty stable. Claims that people in certain regions live to be about 130 are not well documented. They may live longer than the average person, but probably not as long as reported (Butler, 1975c).

Several factors account for the increase in the average individual's life span, most notably advancements in medicine and related sciences. Thus while we are seeing more physically young older persons, at the same time there are more severely sick and disabled old people. Another factor is the improved quality of life, although this has benefited persons in certain categories far more than those in others. Athletes and people in hazardous occupations such as coal mining or foundry work, do not live as long as the average; while farmers and executives live longer. Contrary to popular opinion, executives do not have any more stress-related diseases such as hypertension, than average individuals. In addition, while some authorities predicted that when women entered more stress-related jobs their mortality rates would be higher, this forecast has not come true.

What may lie ahead in the near, distant, or very distant future with regard to longevity, can only be conjectured. Major breakthroughs in the control of heart and vascular diseases and cancer might increase life expectancy by 10 or 15 years. The discovery of the basic causes of aging and ways to arrest it, might produce even more dramatic results. If one compares the cave man's knowledge of science with that of people today, what can humans be expected to achieve in a billion years, assuming that a neutron bomb does not reduce human life to zero? There may already be humanlike organisms on other planets, with quite different life spans from ours. In any case, in our own more limited time-and-space sphere, Butler (1975c) observes that simply "to extend the quantity [of life], but not its quality, is a macabre joke" p. 356).

When is One Old? Frames of Reference

Chronological age. Kalish (1975) raises the question, "When is old?" (p. 2). The answer depends upon one's frame of reference, as we discussed in chapter 1. From the chronological point of view, old age is most often considered to begin at age 65, but this is only because retirement commonly dates from that time. Nevertheless the same chronological years represent a different state today from in the past, just as people in the present may be quite different from those who have the same chronological age in the future. Moreover we continue to confine our operational concept of aging largely to calendar years, although no single approach is adequate. People who are psychologically and physically relatively young may be compelled to retire at 65; or they may be hard of hearing, for instance, at an early age.

Old age is sometimes divided into categories. Neugarten (1974) divides the older population into three categories. The young-old, between 55 to 75, are still working and at the peak of their social and vocational status. The middle-old, aged 65 to 75, constitute much of the retired population. The majority are in good health and have plenty of time for enriching their lives. The old-old, over age 75, are the frailest, loneliness, most impoverished, and unhealthiest. Ordinarily we refer to this group when we speak of the problem elderly and the deplorable status of the aged (Streib, 1976). On the other hand, one might as easily call those aged 55 to 65, the older middle-aged. For one thing, these people identify themselves as middle-aged, and for another, their health, life style, and activity, aside from vocation, more nearly resemble that of the middle-aged than of the elderly.

The definition of old age has changed over time. In societies where the life expectancy is only 35 to 40 years, an older person is much younger chronologically than in those places where the life expectancy is over 70 (Hauser, 1976).

Psychological age. Another approach to old age is psychological. It considers older persons' feelings, perceptions, and attitudes. Bailey (1976) says that the signs of approaching old age are "easily identifiable: the death or degenerative illness of a relative or close friend of approximately the same age; an increase in aches and pains; the tendency of others to mumble their words and of publishers of phone books to reduce the type size" (p. 39).

> For Mary Thompkins, social leader, it happened during her daughter's freshman year in college. Trim Mary—tennis playing, party giving, club going—looked into the lighted makeup mirror one morning and saw deepening lines from nose to mouth, shadows of other creases around her eyes, and three new grey hairs. . . . When is a person old? For Harrison Caldwell old age was still a future shadow on his 80th birthday. Although he had retired (and had the gold watch to prove it) when he was 65, the lumber company which he had served still used him as a consultant several days a month. Besides, he kept up his golf game and volunteered to help several young parolees (pp. 13–14).

Social age. Older persons' psychological age differs from their social age. Some individuals are psychologically ancient in their 20s; others are psychologically youthful in their 80s (Smith, 1973). That is, psychological age "is measured in terms of what a man is, how he experiences life" (p. 12). By contrast, "social age becomes that age which is gauged by social roles and habits. Forced retirement at 65 makes a social-role definition of old age" (p. 12). Hence older persons' social roles are defined by the way people at large perceive them. Thus the way individuals respond to people who have retired, defines their role in society.

Physical age. Aging may also be defined in physical terms with regard to body posture, hair color, voice, and the ability to see and hear. Physically an individual's body does not age in homogeneous fashion, for some parts of it may decline sooner than others. A man aged 70 may "retain a perfectly, smooth, unwrinkled face, a full head of black hair, and a heart performing like that of a man in his 50s—while his renal functioning may be like that of an 80-year-old" (Kalish, 1975, p. 5).

Developmental age. The alternative—as suggested in chapter 1—might be to have a developmental concept, but even this approach poses problems. Developmentally, aging would be viewed holistically—that is, in terms of all the processes and areas of behavior involved. It would be readily perceived that aging in different ways might proceed at different rates, and that regressions might occur. On the other hand, such an approach becomes increasingly complex because the older people become, the greater the asychrony of the aging process within their bodies. Besides, a more limited view might sometimes be more practical. For example, the physical criterion alone would be more appropriate in determining whether a man should retire from a construction job. It may be best simply to make clear the current frame of reference while always keeping clearly in mind all the options that exist.

Aging as pathology. The unusual "orderliness, predictability and apparently programatic character of senescence [aging]" has concerned biological theorists for a great many years (Medawar & Medawar, 1977, p. 57). The best known pathological theory of aging, which treats aging as a diseaselike process, was set forward by a Russian zoologist, Elie Metchnikoff. According to this concept, aging results from "cumulative self-poisoning—auto [self]-intoxication–by the toxins of bacteria normally resident in the gut" (p. 57). Although this theory has not proved popular, Metchnikoff deserves recognition for first treating aging as "an epiphenomenon of life—something superimposed upon the normal processes of living—rather than as a phenomenon somehow entailed by the life processes themselves" (p. 57). Another theorist, Leslie Orgel, views aging as resulting from "accumulated errors of information processing in the body. Among dividing cells such errors may of course arise in the nucleic acid information source itself, but in addition mistakes are bound to occur in the transcription and translation of genetic information into bodily constituents; and if these happen to be enzymes, then the products whose manufacture they make possible will be awry as well" (p. 57).

Thus far neither these views regarding aging nor any others have gained firm support. On the other hand, there has been some concern expressed about the possible negative consequences if scientists find ways to greatly prolong life. Overpopulation, and other problems arising from tampering with the natural order, might result. After all, death is the way nature has of removing successive generations to make room for those to come. Almost all medical advances in the field of aging serve to prolong life, and it is difficult to discriminate between socially constructive research and that which may disturb the natural order. With regard to "all life-saving and life-prolonging measures, the real mischief arises from their being adopted piecemeal and haphazardly, instead of being part of a well thought out program" (p. 57).

Perspective on aging. Whatever one's frame of reference with regard to age, certain observations should be kept in mind. It is difficult to determine the effects of aging because older persons differ so much from each other. Some individuals change far more than others, and aging proceeds at different rates in different parts of the same body. Apparently aging does not function as an independent variable, but as a function of other variables. Individual differences in the changes that occur over the years involve the interaction of diverse factors, including life experiences, psychological well-being, and alterations in physical status, including those caused by smoking, illness, and disease.

Attitudes Toward Aging

Variations according to culture and the times. Attitudes regarding later life are highly variable, ranging from positive to neutral to negative, but heavily skewed in the unfavorable direction. The Japanese have a strong awareness of aging and are preoccupied with changes, especially of seasons and years. For them, character improvement is a goal that comes close to being a national religion (Rohlen, 1976). Yet their attitude toward the elderly as such is neither strongly positive nor negative. In this country, researchers until recently simply accepted the concept of irreversible decrement (decay) and interpreted behavioral age differences—which typically favored the young—as irrefutable proof that functions decrease with age (Schaie & Gribben, 1975). The majority of people in the U.S. believe aging is somewhat sad and that it is accompanied by inevitable decline. Those who view aging positively, at least in this country, are the exception. One of these, Ewald (1972), perceives in retired persons the pioneers of the future, demonstrate for the general population by their own varied patterns of leisure, solutions to the problems involved in shifting from a work to a leisure economy.

Following, several persons over 65 tell how they feel about growing older.

1978 © Sybil Shelton

One of the great joys of old age is the time spent with one's grandchildren.

My former employer says I'm already old. I don't feel as though I am and am not at all concerned about it so long as I still command respect from my fellows. (*Male, age 65*)

Aging is just another genetic factor influenced by the interaction between an individual and his environment. One does not like or dislike a process of this sort; you accept it. If much worrisome thought is given to the process this becomes the means for changing life into a worrisome thing. (*Male, age 72*)

I am, and have always been, a fatalist, with no fear of the future, including my advancing age. (*Male, age 65*)

I dislike the limitations that ill health could bring about as a result of aging. I also dislike being dependent on anyone. (*Female, age 73*)

There are times when the prospect does not seem entirely pleasant; but, for the most part, aging does not occupy my mind. The prospect of the loss of my faculties would be difficult to take. (*Female, age 71*)

The times as a factor. At any one time, attitudes toward the aging are related to the economy's potential for supporting its population (Berman, 1975). Whenever the population outgrows the economy's capacity to support it, the weaker elements of humankind, including the aged, the infirmed, and the handicapped, become vulnerable. Life becomes relatively cheap and the basic need for self-preservation, as demonstrated in the law of survival of the fittest, produces attitudes and practices that operate subtly to deplete the older population. Certainly if there are excessive numbers of old people in the society while overwhelming numbers of younger ones are struggling for survival, it would be easier to rationalize turning off life-giving machines or cutting social security payments to the point of endangering older people's survival. Perhaps improved birth control methods have come along just in time to prevent a burgeoning population from having the catastrophic consequences suggested here. In heavily populated portions of the world, where birth control has thus far failed to balance the intake of new population with the exit of the old, suffering is already widespread, especially among the old.

Variations in views by age. Older and younger generations vary somewhat in the way they perceive the elderly. In a study of young, middle-aged, and older persons, all three age groups indicated that the death of a 75-year-old was less tragic than that of a younger person of any age (Kalish & Reynolds, 1976). In another study, Cameron and Cromer (1974) determined generational preferences by sampling three groups: young adults, middle-aged persons, and older persons. The two oldest generations expressed a next-younger generational preference, thus demonstrating an anti-old and/or pro-young preference. In addition, the young-adult generation was the most, and the older generation the least, preferred. The verdict is clear: as we age we find ourselves successively less desirable and acceptable.

How older people view themselves. The fact that older people do not devaluate themselves as much as younger people, does not mean that they view themselves positively. Most elderly Americans have negative attitudes toward aging, toward themselves, and toward life in general. Moreover when older people speak of others their own age, they hold the same kinds of stereotypes about aging as the general public: they consider themselves to be all right, but see others as old fogies (Moore, 1975).

It is uncertain to what extent these attitudes are a function of aging or of the unpleasant situations in which the elderly find themselves. Such negative feelings may actually represent a quite accurate perception of their situations; or those who regard themselves as old after they reach 65 may simply be defining themselves according to the socially accepted definition of age. Since there are no relevant longitudinal studies, it is uncertain whether the aged view themselves more negatively than they did when they were young. In general it appears that these negative attitudes have been less influenced by their age than by some of the concomitants of aging, especially poor health, inactivity, isolation, and institutionalization (Bennett & Eckman, 1973). It might be expected, therefore, that given improved situations for the elderly, more positive attitudes would emerge (Bennett & Eckman, 1973).

The elderly have developed various defense mechanisms to offset the negative stereotypes assigned them. They may try especially hard to behave in more acceptable ways; or they may refuse to accept themselves as elderly at all, concealing their age both from themselves and others. In one study (Tuckman & Lorge, 1954) of persons aged 20 to 80, those under 30 thought of themselves as young, and those between 30 and 60 as middle-aged. At age 60 only a few thought of themselves as old, and at 80 slightly over half called themselves old. A small percent of the 80-year-olds insisted on describing themselves as young. In general the older people are, the later they think old age begins. Hence there is a gap between their self-image and the image others hold of them (Rosow, 1974).

In the following, several older adults react to the questions: How old do you feel? Why do you feel older or younger than your age?

> Age as such does not bother me, since I am still able to garden, travel, and entertain whenever I wish. I guess I feel younger than my age. (*Female, age 73*)

I do not know how one feels in terms of number of years. At times I feel much younger, at times the reverse. (*Female, age 71*)

I do not feel old. I try to think young and be around young people as much as possible. I think I feel much younger than my years. I am usually taken for being younger than I am. (*Female, age 74*)

I feel like myself which is how I've always felt. I am aware that I can't do some things that I did at age 50 but it is silly to spend time thinking of such things, and I don't. (*Male, age 72*)

I guess about age 75—oh well, sometimes age 80. (*Female, age 92*)

I am stronger and feel younger than my age. I think it's because I have good health, a good attitude, like people, and have so many things I like to do. (*Male, age 69*)

I still feel young at heart except when my physical problems become untenable. (*Male, age 65*)

These peoples' apparently distorted views of their own aging may sometimes be quite realistic, at least in the psychological or physical sense. It is easily apparent that aging is highly variable in all but the chronological sense—and while it has been tacitly assumed that it is healthy to confront one's aging, which age are we talking about?

Current status of the image. Of late there have been signs that the image of the elderly may be improving (Seltzer & Atchley, 1971). In a national survey, Louis Harris and Associates (1975) found little evidence of ageism (negative feelings about old people) in public attitudes generally, and found too that the elderly portrayed their life situations—including social interaction, economic status, and self-perceptions—as far more positive than they are commonly assumed to be. Indeed some persons—for example, Cain (1974)—suggest that older people in America today are being awarded economic advantages that place them in a favorite status compared to other age groups.

It is important to remember that older people are highly heterogeneous and that some of them constitute a "contented leisure class" (Neugarten & Hagestad, 1976, p. 39). They are helped "by the greater permissiveness toward the new life styles of the retired and by a change in national values from instrumentality to expressivity and from a work ethic to a leisure ethic" (p. 39). Nevertheless this elderly leisure class, to whatever extent it currently exists, may vanish at some future date. If a no-growth economy persists, and the relative number of older persons continues to increase, the participation of older individuals in the labor force may again become necessary, a situation already being forecast for the United States in the decades following 2020 (Neugarten & Hagestad, 1976).

Upgrading the stereotype. Certain already apparent trends may succeed in modifying the negative stereotype of the elderly. The growing popularity of the life-span developmental approach, and of courses on adulthood and aging, may help young people to perceive themselves from the life-span point of view. From this perspective all of us are all ages, which in effect minimizes age-stage barriers. We all have in us aspects of the child and youth we once were, and the forces that will inevitably project us into later stages. Perhaps we will shift from the "I-We" or "others perspective," to the "us-all perspective," the collective point of view (Christoffersen, 1974). As Smith (1973) points out, the aging are all of us—if not now, certainly in time, if we live long enough. As he states it, "We have spoken of the old. We have spoken of ourselves. We ask not for whom the bell tolls for we know that the bell of aging tolls for us all, and that it is up to us to help bring about the changes which are needed for older people in our culture today and then for those of tomorrow" (pp. 194–195).

Whatever improvements are made in the lot of the elderly, or in the elderly themselves, will also reduce the negative stereotype. For example, the practice of retiring people from the labor force at 65, and barring them from various occupations even sooner, has generated a concept of the aged as useless and senile (Hareven, 1976). Besides, the aged have been viewed as doomed to continuing decline and a host of unfortunate disabilities. However, recent studies suggest that many phenomena associated with aging, that have been considered irreversible, can be reversed.

CHARACTERISTICS OF OLDER PEOPLE

Personality Characteristics

The validity of certain popular concepts. Commonly held views of personality in later years are often erroneous, while a few rest on more solid grounds. It is a myth that the elderly inevitably grow inflexible and conservative. Some people continue to change until the very end of their lives. Some individuals become more politically conservative, simply because of such factors as runaway inflation and job discrimination (Butler, 1975a). Another myth is that older people are unproductive. While decreases in productivity do occur, they may be more a result of diseases and other circumstances than of the process of aging itself. Besides, some older individuals are as productive as ever. Women whose energies may have been tied up for many years in nurturant activities may even become more so.

Older people are more autonomous and less nurturant than often believed. Ahammer and Baltes (1972) asked persons in three age groups (adolescents, adults, and older persons) to evaluate the desirability of certain behaviors from their own point of view and those of the other two generations. The adolescents and adults both saw the elderly as placing more value on nurturing behavior and less on autonomous behavior than older persons actually did. It seems, therefore, that the elderly are less willing to surrender their freedom and play a nurturant role than other age groups recognize. This conclusion seems justified: "the elderly are being told, in essence, 'take it easy; be a little passive and be loving, like grandparents should be,' whereas the elderly resist being molded into this structure" (Kalish, 1975, p. 75).

Older people are often viewed as feeling lonely and rejected by younger generations. It is true that there is a social barrier between the generations, and close friendships do not often develop between the very old and the very young. However, age segregation may be as much the preference of older as of younger people. Perhaps the old enjoy talking with others their own age because they have lived through the same periods and they can share recollections and talk over common problems (Kalish & Reynolds, 1976).

Some older people do perceive themselves as losers, as is commonly believed. A study of gambling and aging suggests that old people expect to lose while the young anticipate winning, the difference perhaps being locus of control (Stone & Kalish, 1973). However this attitude may derive from realistic appraisals of obstacles that society puts in the way of older persons rather than from any pessimism inherent in the aging process.

As often presumed, people do indeed become wiser with age as a result of their experiences (Butler, 1975a). Old age is the only time when one can attain an individual sense of the entire life cycle. This involves a subjective awareness of death, a sense of the unfolding process of change, and an understanding of human time as distinct from objective time. At this time people also understand what life is about; they have accumulated factual knowledge of what to expect during different phases of the life cycle, and they have certain concepts of those stages and phases.

Later years are also characterized by a review and awareness of past experience and unresolved conflicts. This has important consequences: people resolve guilt feelings and psychic conflicts; they also transmit values to the generation that follows (Lewis & Butler, 1974). The aged also have a nostalgic attachment to familiar objects, perhaps their home, pets, and keepsakes. They have a sense of legacy, too, a need to leave something behind when they die, whether it is money, jewelry, or furniture. Another important task of later life is the trans-mission of power, or knowing when to give up power, because it can be given up too late or too early.

A sense of satisfaction with one's life is perhaps more common than most realize, but not as common as it might be. Feelings of wisdom and serenity may derive from a sense that one has done one's best, or perhaps survived against great odds. The capacity for surprise, change, creativity, and curiosity does not necessarily decline over the years. Creativity can be found not only among famous people, but also among quite ordinary ones. In fact older persons may first become creative in later years, after other burdens have lessened.

It is also believed that the elderly decline in terms of how mascu-line or feminine they feel, and that they become somewhat neutral sexually. Indeed people appear to be relatively more or less feminine at different stages throughout life. Both young and middle-aged adults are judged to have "genderness" or strong characteristics of masculin-ity or femininity, while older males are not. Masculinity and femininity are commonly believed to peak during the middle years, and become somewhat more diffuse in old age. It is felt that after middle age, masculinity "plummets." Femininity apparently increases more slowly and then decreases more gradually. Older females are perceived as having less overall femininity than in earlier years. However, Cameron (1976) found no evidence that adult females had any weaker gender identifica-tion than did males. For either sex, genderness, once established in early childhood, is maintained at a constant level throughout life.

Certainly older peoples' self-perceptions stand in sharp contrast to the common stereotype of asexuality in old age. While all age groups in Cameron's study agreed that old men were the least masculine, older mens' self-ratings were not correspondingly low. It seems that older people have certain beliefs about their own generation in the abstract, but still other judgments about themselves in reality.

This writer believes that the discrepancy between older persons' self-perceptions and the cultural stereotype can easily be explained. People establish a concept of themselves as masculine or feminine, in varying ways and degrees, in early life, and this psychological percep-tion of self persists. However, the way people appear to others in later years suggests less genderness, particularly for males. For their part, older women appear less feminine in that their voices are a bit deeper, their faces hairier, and their busts flabbier. Nor do they have the physi-cal attractiveness that is portrayed as the feminine ideal. They have gone through menopause, and their life tasks are no longer dedicated to such traditionally feminine preoccupations as caring for the children. Older men appear less masculine since their voices are not as deep as they were before; nor do they possess the degree of strength or the capacity for vigorous activity that is associated with maleness. Furthermore many of their activities are less masculine than before. For one thing, after they retire, they help more often with household tasks, including cooking. They also become more sedentary and passive, which are characteristics associated with females.

Common characteristics of the elderly. There is no such thing as an aged personality type or even several distinct ones (Dibner, 1975). Instead older people may have typical adjustive reactions because of problems attached to the current status of old age. In general, however, personality is far more continuous than discontinuous through life, and "at any point in time, a person is more like he has always been than he is like peers of his age group" (Dibner, 1975, p. 80).

Nevertheless there are some characteristics that are found more commonly among older people than younger ones, one being preoccupation with the self. Such inner orientation, which Neugarten (1968) calls interiority, begins in middle age. As time goes on, "older people move toward more egocentric, self-preoccupied positions and attend increasingly to the control and satisfaction of personal needs" (p. 140). Perhaps this orientation is more a response to the growing bodily needs which focus attention on the self, rather than to any basic change in personality. Older people are presumed to be more conservative—that is, they are characterized by an attitude of maintaining the status quo rather than favoring change. This tendency takes the form of "behavioral rigidity, unyieldingness, and greater consistency in social and political attitudes" (Dibner, 1975, p. 82).

A related characteristic, cautiousness, undoubtedly stems from a decreased ability to cope. On the other hand, older people often manifest a certain disregard for what is socially proper. They may be outspoken to the point of bluntness, or show utter disregard for style or custom. Perhaps this as yet researched characteristic derives from older persons' growing isolation from their surroundings and an accompanying insensitivity to them. Such isolation may produce a reliance on internal rather than external standards of behavior.

Explanations of personality changes. Apparently most psychological changes associated with age derive from such nonuniversal biological causes as illness, or such life events as retirement or widowhood. Genetically programmed changes appear to be subtle and are rarely universal. Various theorists, including Flavell (1970), believe that genetics are of little significance after people pass the age of greatest reproductive potential. Instead changes that occur in adults derive chiefly from their own interaction with the environment, and the slowing down that characterizes older persons is simply evidence of basic alterations in the organism. As a result older people come to prefer simplicity to complexity. Younger persons, with their high energy and abundant resources, "adapt to the environment through seeking complexity, stimulation, and novelty . . . . However, in states of illness or fatigue, even the young organism will evidence preference for simplicity. Preference for simplicity [serves a definite purpose] in the case of waning energy and lessened resources" (Dibner, 1975, p. 86). Simplicity, in turn, permits the conservation of energy and easier adaptation at a stage when motor skills are deteriorating and the senses growing less acute.

This point of view, that older persons behave as they do because they find it prudent to adapt, reveals them "not as structurally different, as permanently or progressively incapable," (Dibner, 1975, p. 88) but as motivated by different needs. Thus the preference for simplicity is inherently characteristic of older people. While it correlates with age, it is independent of it, because younger persons too, when incapacitated or sick, seek simplicity.

Disengagement theory. Older people are often described as increasingly disengaged or detached from others and society. The process of social disengagement involves the mutual withdrawal by aging persons and those in their social environment from each other. Psychological disengagement concerns how much an individual is "affectively involved in living, for example, the ability to perceive oneself as vigorous and active, to be concerned with feelings, to rise to challenging or conflicting situations. [Social disengagement] is measured by the number of interactions and of roles maintained by the individual" (Kalish & Knudtson, 1976, p. 177).

This process arises, not from some mysterious function of aging, but from conditions that often relate to it. As individuals age, those people and objects they were attached to, gradually disappear as parents, uncles, aunts, and friends die. These significant persons in their lives drop off one by one, and even their familiar surroundings, including the childhood home, the neighborhood, and the community, die in the sense that they disappear or change beyond recognition. As people grow older they necessarily turn away from their social environment to their inner resources. Kalish and Reynolds (1976) asked a large sampling of persons what they would do if they only had a half year to live. Older persons were far more likely to focus on developing inner resources by such activities as meditation or prayer, while younger ones talked in terms of active participation in the world—they wanted to "live it up" or travel. Consequently most older people experience a growing sense of vulnerability and isolation. Such feelings become even more intense for those who become institutionalized and realize that death is near at hand.

Adults may feel a special anxiety after the death of their parents, somehow seeing themselves as next in line. Since parents usually die before their children, adult children may feel "invulnerable" as long as their parents live. But once the parents are gone, they often feel, "I am next."

Older people may cope with the situation in various ways. One is to establish certain new attachments, perhaps to welfare workers, physicians, or nurses, all of whom provide care instead of true emotional support. Still others—for example, a senior center director—may provide them with feelings of self-worth and competence. Such attachments are certainly weaker than those earlier in life. Moreover these persons may threaten whatever feelings of mastery older people have if they cater to their growing dependency rather than help them make it on their own. Both children and old people feel dependent; but old people, unlike children, cannot look forward to a time when their control over their lives will increase. Instead they know that further decrements will occur.

Some older people, left to their own inadequate devices, manipulate those who care for them as a last resort. They may behave like children, and begin exercising control by returning to childlike helplessness because that is the only way that they can get other people to help them. Acting like this may represent an unconscious return to a mechanism that worked well in childhood. But though older people may be as helpless as infants, they do not arouse in others the same feelings of tenderness. Instead, in order to protect their own autonomy, younger people may unconsciously withdraw from the elderly. Still other older people cling stubbornly to the shreads of their independence by refusing to ask for assistance, even when it is badly needed.

Older people may also seek to establish attachments that will transcend their physical death. Those whose religious views rule out attachment with heavenly beings, speak in terms of continuous attachment through their own accomplishments, having children, being remembered by others, or identifying with some cause or ideology that will live after them (Kalish & Knudtson, 1976).

Perspective on Personality in Later Years

Individual differences. In order to place the foregoing discussion in perspective, certain observations should be made or underscored. First, older people differ greatly as individuals; and they become increasingly varied rather than more homogeneous with advancing years.

Thus we see "extraordinarily young 80-year-olds as well as old 80-year-olds" (Butler, 1975a). In fact physiological factors vary more widely among old people than in any other age group, and the same is true of personality. In life styles, attitudes, beliefs, mode of dress, speech—all the ingredients that make up life—older people come in infinite varieties, in many cases resembling other age groups more than each other.

The complexity of personality factors. It is extremely difficult to state definitive principles of personality, because of their complex interaction and the subtle tortuous processes through which they function. As just one example, consider a study in which psychologist Norma Haan compared personalities of well-adjusted young and middle-aged adults to those of well-adjusted older persons. The younger and older groups had similar personalities but they relied on different traits at successive stages in life. Both the young and middle-aged well-adjusted adults valued intellectual pursuits, and characterized themselves as objective, interesting and having high intellectual aspirations. They were also socially poised, verbally fluent, and interested in many subjects and activities. While they also described themselves as sympathetic, warm, and giving, they valued these characteristics less (Casady, 1975a). The older subjects, those in their 60s and 70s, stressed other characteristics in themselves. They had come to care less about intellectualism and more about intimate personal relationships. The older individuals placed a higher value on gregariousness, cheerfulness, and sense of humor; and they were more protective of other people.

There were some differences according to sex coupled with age. The older men were more self-satisfied and had more consistent personalities than the younger ones. However they admitted that they were perhaps more conventional and less insightful. Both older and younger men placed a high value on independence. The older women were both more gregarious and responsive to humor than either the younger men or women. However they were less introspective, had lower aspirations, cared less for power, and were more uncomfortable with uncertainty.

Thus we see how many factors—including sex, age, and individual personality—interacted to determine adjustment within a relatively homogeneous sampling of economically secure, middle-class adults. The problems in drawing conclusions are compounded when one studies more heterogeneous populations.

Intellect

Cross-sectional data. Most of the research regarding adult mental function derives from cross-sectional studies. Mental abilities have been presumed to decline so slowly as to be imperceptible in middle age, and then more rapidly, depending somewhat on the specific ability or individual concerned. Intellectual factors which depend directly on speed of response tend to decline relatively early (Cunningham & Clayton, 1973). Those that involve decrements in verbal meaning, space concepts, reasoning, and number may not decline until people reach their late 60s (Schaie & Labouvie, 1974). More extreme declines may derive from senility or terminal drop, a phenomenon recognized only recently. The latter signifies that individuals who show an accelerated decline in any of various areas of cognitive performance are more likely to die within a few years than those who manifest no special change (Riegel & Riegel, 1972).

In general, both verbal and nonverbal problem-solving ability declines over the years. At one time psychologists ascribed these growing deficiencies to "rigidity and loss of abstractive ability." More recent theory suggests that decreasing problem-solving abilities derive from "difficulty in organizing complex material, in short-term memory, in making fine discriminations among stimuli and in withholding responses, even though [one] may think they are wrong" (Dibner, 1975, p. 78). Even when older people are given more time to solve a problem, their ability to do so is less than in the past.

Perhaps the most significant aspect of aging involves changes in the brain which account for the large number of elderly persons in nursing homes and mental institutions. With the increasing years, neurons die, the number of synaptic connections decreases, and "in the older animal the cellular response made to stress is less appropriate. One might say that the information available to an older cell for an appropriate response is either absent or is garbled in transmission. Since the primary information available to a cell is coded in its DNA, DNA seems like a good place to begin a biochemical study of aging" (Sinex, 1975, p. 35).

The earliest signs of senility often include impaired judgment and slowed thought processes. This condition, called senile dementia, is produced by a loss or shrinkage of nerve cells, which is sometimes associated with aging. It is characterized by such symptoms as disorientation in time, some speech disturbance, emotional disorders, poor memory (especially for recent events), and even delusions (Horn, 1974). While hardening of the arteries, or arteriosclerosis, may be a contributing factor in senility for one case in six, additional causes account for the others. The dementia of most older people relates to an organic disease of the nerve cells, the synapses and neurites. It is possible that biological research on tissue may, at some not too distant date, produce ways of preventing the lesions that produce senile dementia. The dementia in aging may be either chronic, deriving from cardiovascular disease—the natural concomitant of aging, or it may be acute, involving treatable conditions such as benign tumors, intoxication, infection, or nutritional defects (Sinex, 1975). There are certainly some elderly people in mental institutions whose dementia derives from treatable conditions.

Even among the elderly, dementia is the exception, not the rule. The chances at birth of ever being categorized as demented in later years is very small, possibly 2.3% for females and 1.8% for males. However, for persons after the age of 90 the chances become over 50%. The potential for becoming demented exists at any age, but becomes significantly greater at around 55 (Gaitz, 1971).

It should always be kept in mind, too, that older people vary greatly in mental characteristics. Some subjects, regardless of how old they may be, never show measurable memory impairment (Botwinick, 1973). It is more accurate to think of a decline in memory and other functions as descriptive of more and more individuals as they grow older, rather than as descriptive of all aging persons.

Longitudinal data. Except in instances of terminal drop and senility, recent longitudinal data present a far more encouraging picture of intellect in later years than has emerged before. While Piaget (Flavell, 1963) hypothesized that the final stage of intellectual growth (formal operations) is reached by about age 12, researchers are reporting consistent gains in conceptual development of young adults and older subjects (Papalia, 1972; Storck, Looft, & Hopper, 1972). In fact various studies reveal little or no age decrement except in very old people or during the period shortly before death (Jarvik, Eisdorfer, & Blum, 1973). For example, in one important study Baltes and Schaie (1974) found "no strong age-related change in cognitive flexibility. For the most important dimension, crystallized intelligence, and for visualization as well, we see a systematic increase in scores for the various age groups, right into old age. Even people over 70 improved from the first testing to the second" (p. 36). Crystallized intelligence refers to cognitive performance (perceiving relationships, reasoning, etc.) in which culturally acquired skills are used. By contrast, fluid intelligence connotes cognitive performance relatively independent of those skills.

Reconciling discrepancies. Several factors account for the overly pessimistic reports of earlier researchers. For one thing, the differential results of cross-sectional and longitudinal studies can only be appreciated if cohort differences are analyzed with reference to the changing conditions of society as well as changing biological conditions within the subjects involved (Riegel & Riegel, 1972). Changes in cognitive functioning may not result from aging per se but from the changes in physical health that often accompany aging (Kalish, 1975). Besides, the poor performance among the elderly in some studies may be due to a lack of formal education, and the fact that in the past, schooling relied more on memorization than on problem solving (Baltes & Schaie, 1974). It is significant that the specific age of decline is greater with successive generations (Schaie & Labouvie, 1974). Also, despite an apparent regression of cognitive functioning during advanced years, no longitudinal study has proved conclusively that specific abilities, once present, deteriorate in old age (Bielby, 1974). Deficits observed by researchers may reflect differences in performance rather than a decreased ability to learn (Schaie & Gribben, 1975).

Sociocultural factors may also distort the truth regarding mental and sensory performance in later years. In fact in short-term longitudinal studies, sociocultural differences have proved more important than age in accounting for differences in test results (Rudinger, 1972). And while hearing decreases with age, the effect is less significant in some cultures than others (Rosen, Olin, & Rosen, 1970). Anyhow the magnitude of auditory deficiencies in later years may be overestimated. Older people may hesitate to make a response for fear of making the wrong one, and thus cautiousness may contribute to what are thought to be performance deficiencies (Schaie & Gribbin, 1975).

The performance of the elderly also varies according to test content and the way tests are conducted (Furry & Baltes, 1973). For example much of the data about cognitive performance comes from intelligence tests whose contents are aimed primarily at the young (Baltes & Schaie, 1974). Besides, most of the tests are timed, and older people have learned through experience to be cautious.

Bielby (1974) observes that any of various combinations of reasons may be responsible for the apparent regression of cognition in any particular elderly individual. One reason may be only a measure of the differences between cohorts rather than true age differences. In the second place, regression may reflect a true neurological decrement which is inherently a part of aging, and whose nature is yet to be determined. In the third place, decrements in performance may result from the older person's isolation from social, occupational, and education experiences. Finally terminal drop, or proximity to death, may explain individual differences in the performance of elderly persons. Or perhaps all may contribute in different degree to cognitive decline. Certainly the lack of a stimulating environment may be a major reason for the decreasing cognitive performance of the elderly. Overall, the available research on aging suggests that there are some areas of decrement that cannot be helped, others that are remediable, some possible gains, and many individual differences that affect adaptation.

Recommendations. The Task Force on Aging of the American Psychological Association (APA, 1973), among others, recommends that much greater attention be given to understanding and eliminating unnecessary causes of decline in intellectual functioning. Schaie and Gribbin (1975) agree, declaring that the earlier concept of irreversible decrements in intelligence is incorrect. Given favorable environments there may be gains in particular intellectual functions, even in quite advanced years.

Already gerontologists have begun to consider the extent to which intellectual performance can be enhanced; and the results so far, although still somewhat meager, are promising (Baltes & Schaie, 1974). An individual's response speed, which is so significant on many intelligence tests, has been interpreted as a function of biological well-being which declines with aging. Nevertheless the response of elderly subjects has improved dramatically, as much as 20 to 35%, among women 65 to 80 years of age, after as little as two hours of training. In addition,

the breathing of concentrated oxygen for extended periods, to increase oxygen supply to the brain, seems to improve memory for recent events . . . Treatment of hypertension . . . also seems to be promising. . . .

In view of the positive results already obtained, it seems plausible that breakthroughs in research may ultimately produce far more dramatic retardations or regressions in the decrements of aging than we can even imagine today. What is necessary is persistent dedicated effort on a broad scale, involving researchers from a number of disciplines (Baltes & Schaie, 1974, p. 38).

Physical Status

Appearance. Troll (1975) summarizes changes that take place in appearance during adulthood. In the early years there is little change followed by gross transformations in middle age. There is some tendency to put on weight, and fat is redistributed. While body fat is a mere 10% of one's total weight in adolescence, it becomes at least 20% by middle age, with the majority of it focused around the waist. The chest or bust diminishes, while the hips and abdomen enlarge. The portion of the face that changes most is the bottom third. The distance between the bottom of the nose and the chin decreases because of changes in muscle, bone, teeth, and connective tissue. Because of a certain stiffening of the joints and decreased muscular resilience, posture becomes less erect and movements less fluid. Meantime the skin becomes less elastic, and wrinkles appear. The pouches and dark circles which often appear under the eyes become more apparent because the remainder of the skin lightens.

The most visible change is in the hair; during their 40s, peoples' hair thins, their hairline recedes, and baldness increases, especially in men. Also in the 40s, greyness appears and increases so that by their 50s, the majority of Americans are greyhaired, and a few are even white-haired. Certain less obvious hair changes include diminished facial hair in men and increased facial hair in women; stiff hair in the eyes, ears, nose, and eyelashes of men, and on womens' chin and upper lip.

Differences in appearance that come with age vary according to social class, sex, and the individual. On the individual level, differences among people of the same age are obvious. Middle-class people show the effects of aging far less than lower-class persons because they are often engaged in less physically strenuous activity and have more time and money to spend on their appearance. Women remain younger looking than men because they expend more effort, and use more aids (such as cosmetics), to enhance their appearance. Indeed from the onset of adulthood until old age, women's concern about their attractiveness increases (Nowak, 1974). Nevertheless they prize an appearance of youthfulness even more than they do attractiveness in general.

Sensory and perceptual abilities. The levels of sensory, perceptual, and motor abilities in later years are as follows. (It is important to keep in mind, however, that wide variations exist from one individual to another.) In terms of vision, more time is required to recover from exposure to glare or to adapt to the dark, so that night driving becomes harder after middle age. On the other hand, color vision is maintained very well throughout middle age, although more light may be required to fully distinguish colors. Vision itself does not decline significantly during adult years because retinal changes rarely occur prior to age 60. In general, visual acuity peaks at around age 20 and remains somewhat constant until the 40s, after which a very gradual decline begins (Timiras, 1972).

Hearing deficiencies are very common among older persons. Hearing changes during adulthood are so subtle and so constant, albeit slow, that many individuals possess a hearing loss of which they are not aware. As we stated earlier in this volume, losses in hearing appear mostly in the upper frequencies, and the decline begins at about age 10. The older the adult, the poorer the perception of high-frequency sounds (Dibner, 1975).

The senses of smell and taste are hard to measure, but such studies as exist indicate a decline in sensitivity to sugar and salt taste, and a slight decline in the number of taste buds, from the ages of 20 to 70, with a sharp drop after 70. Although most people are unaware of the loss of the sense of smell, marked changes also occur there (Dibner, 1975).

There is little modification in taste sensitivity until around age 50. After this time there is little difficulty in discriminating the four basic tastes of sour, bitter, salt, and sweet, although the ability to make finer distinctions in taste declines. After childhood the number of taste buds diminishes, and those remaining become less sensitive. Hence foods that may be relatively tasteless to adults may have plenty of flavor for children. After about age 40, the olfactory sense declines slightly, and this change may also modify taste sensitivity while at the same time giving people who live in a polluted atmosphere, a certain advantage (Timiras, 1972).

In general, body sensations become strongly diminished over time. For instance, older people may report no pain after contracting such diseases as peritonitis or pneumonia. People are more sensitive to touch, but have a lower tolerance for hot and cold. Presumably older persons' bodies are less capable of maintaining reasonably steady states under varying temperatures. Finally the tactile senses become generally less sensitive, especially in the hands and feet (Dibner, 1975).

People generally sleep the same number of hours each night (Thompson & Marsh, 1973); but after they reach their 40s, they awaken more often during the night, and their sleep is progressively less deep. Hence they may spend more time in bed as they grow older, but not feel as rested in the morning.

Changes in psychomotor performance also occur with age. There is a gradual loss in muscular strength after the 20s, and there are especially noticeable effects after unusual or continuous exertion. Since older people inhale less oxygen and exhale less carbon dioxide, their bodies are not prepared for strenuous work (Dibner, 1975). The factors most important in affecting motor performance are health, motivational states, and speed of response (Botwinick, 1973).

Changes also occur in perception, a "phenomenologic process where stimuli are not sensed as a chaos of independent events, but are rather given meaning" (Dibner, 1975). Such changes are especially important because perceptions mold behavior. While individuals may turn up the volume of a television set to compensate for poor hearing, they cannot change the manner in which the central nervous system organizes the sounds produced by the set.

In various ways older persons' perceptions become increasingly different. They become more susceptible to distorting illusions, have growing difficulty in distinguishing stimuli from the context in which they occur, and make judgments more slowly. Of course it is difficult to distinguish slower reactions due to aging from those produced by the wariness older people feel because of their reduced physical control over the environment.

The nervous system. With regard to the nervous system, Timiras (1972) cites data which indicate a reduction of conductivity across synapses and in peripheral nerves. Those changes in the nervous system which accompany the aging process reflect a general slowing down of practically all bodily processes and functions. Although this process is gradual, it occurs throughout the body. It is significant because "if you read more slowly and write more slowly, walk more slowly and jump away from danger more slowly, talk more slowly and follow what others are saying more slowly, you are literally on another 'wave length'" (Troll, 1975, p. 24).

Emotional Health

Conflicting stereotypes. Two opposite views exist about emotional adjustment. Each is partly false and partly true. One view is that the elderly become serene, living in a sort of "adult fairy land," as suggested by pictures of carefree grandmothers and "rocking-chair" grandfathers beloved by younger members of the family. The other is that older people are inevitably sad, dejected, and rejected, and are just waiting to die. Each stereotype is partly true. Older people do experience greater stresses than any other age group, strains that can prove devastating (Butler, 1975c). Skolnick (1973) reports a decline over the years in "companionship, demonstration of affection, including both kissing and intercourse, common interests, common beliefs and values, beliefs in the permanence of marriage, and marital adjustment" (p. 218). However there are many exceptions to this dismal picture. In a study of healthy, socially autonomous community residents, researchers found some surprising results. In general "psychological flexibility, resourcefulness and optimism characterized the group . . . rather than the stereotype of rigidity" (Butler, 1975c, p. 370).

The truth is that stress is a function of one's situation, and not an inevitable concomitant of aging. A study of 210 people in Detroit, who were ages 60 to 94, indicated wide variations in feelings of loneliness. It was not the degree of isolation per se which produced those feelings, but the way it compared with former social involvement. There was a discontinuity in social engagements called "desolation" (Gubrium, 1974, p. 107). In this group 64% of the widowed, 73.3% of the divorced, 59.1% of the single, and 22.8% of the married reported often being alone. A few from each group frequently felt that there was no point in living. Those who reported often feeling lonely included about a quarter of the widowed and divorced, and about 10% of the single and married people. Nearly half of the single and married people, about a third of the widowers, and a quarter of the divorced, felt satisfied with their lives. Those who were not content included about 10% of the widowed, divorced, and married, and about 5% of the single. On the whole, the single and the married felt less desolate than the widowed and divorced (Gubrium, 1974). Obviously no overall description of mental health can correctly describe all categories of older persons.

Characteristics of successful aging. A number of authorities have identified characteristics that apparently relate to successful aging. According to DeCarlo (1974), successful aging is correlated with physical and mental health, and intellectual performance. Moreover the active pursuit of leisure activities is critical to satisfactory adjustment, both in retirement and aging. Age and marital status are also significant. Eisdorfer and Lawton (1973) declare that the unmarried, most of them widows, are in by far the worst situation. The younger aged, those 65 to 70, are considerably better off than those 75 or older; and the distance between the two groups is widening.

On the basis of his far-ranging experience with the elderly, Robert Butler (1975b) has concluded that there is no "secret of life." However, certain things may help. For instance, "having a partner is very crucial to survival" (p. 32). Some emotional involvement may help to keep people alive. For another thing, it is good to have someone with you when you are ill. It is also important to have a continuing involvement in activities, including particular tasks and goals, with certain things to do each day. People who do so, seem to live longer. A third factor is maintaining physical fitness, although it is still unclear just how such activity relates to the process of aging. Other aids to survival are resourcefulness, flexibility, and the capacity to continue learning. Perhaps heredity is important, too; however, people can compensate for genetic weaknesses by taking good care of themselves.

It is sometimes suggested that in order to be emotionally healthy, older people must not deny to themselves, the fact that they are growing old. In the following, several persons over 60 answer the question: "Is it better to retain a youthful image of yourself or to accept your age?"

I find it most satisfying to try to maintain the most youthful image I can without artificial means or any attempt to hide my real age. (*Male, age 65*)

It's better to accept your age. Playing youthful roles can be pathetic. (*Male, age 67*)

I believe it is better to think and feel young, in the psychological sense. If you accept your aging, other people perceive you that way, too, with all the negative attitudes that the social stereotype of the aged suggests. It's even better to dye your hair, because white hair causes others to perceive you as old, and before you know it, you're acting that way. (*Female, age 63*)

Data from longitudinal studies suggest that certain types of individuals have more favorable prospects for their later years than others do. In one such study a 5-year follow-up of an original sample indicated that nonsurvivors (those who had died in the course of the study) demonstrated a greater incidence of arteriosclerosis and included more chronic cigarette smokers, than the survivors (Granick & Patterson, 1971). The former had adapted less well psychologically, had more often become widowed, more often disliked their current living situations, and had poorly defined goals. On the other hand, survival related to an individual's healthy view of self, feelings of continued usefulness, and good health, as well as to planned new contacts, self-initiated activity, and personal involvement. The organization of behavior as demonstrated by the survivors, tended to dispute the so-called disengagement theory, which states that an older person's withdrawal from outside contacts is natural and normal.

On the basis of studying 65 older people in San Francisco, Hochschild (1973) identified six general themes that constitute a basis for successful aging: (1) sufficient independence to allow continued feelings of integrity; (2) pleasant, satisfying relationships with other people, some of whom are willing to provide assistance when needed, without in the process showing a disrespect for older persons; (3) a reasonable degree of emotional and physical satisfaction and a comfortable physical environment; (4) stimulation of the mind in ways that are not too strenuous; (5) sufficient mobility to be able to experience varied environments; and (6) some type of intense life interest or involvement, at least partly to avoid preoccupation with thoughts of death.

While the foregoing data and views appear convincing, the picture is not clear-cut. As a result of following elderly people in Pennsylvania over a 19-year period (Britton & Britton, 1972), investigators concluded that while some participants actually gained and others lost personal strength over the years, "the positive-change people could seldom be distinguished from the negative-change people" (p. 153). That is, there were no distinguishable patterns that differentiated the two groups, which indicates how difficult it is to predict personality among older persons over an extended time span.

One reason for the inconsistency of research findings is the differential criteria used for defining successful aging. Erikson defines integrity-versus-despair as the psychosocial issue of old age. However, observes Butler (1975c), old people's anger and despair in not accepting their fate may be healthy. Again the very active person may look on rocking-chair types as unsuccessful examples of aging, yet those types may feel relatively content. Or is it justified to look upon people who were once very active and then withdrew from community life, as somehow in a state of decline? It may simply be that they have deliberately and consciously chosen a new way of life. Those people who judge the aged are typically young or middle-aged, and may therefore define "success" according to the way they think they will want to live when they are old.

Comprehensive Portraits

A summary description. Some authorities have attempted more global characterizations of older people. On the basis of his comprehensive study of older people, Butler (1975c, p. 408) constructs the following image of aging.

> Older people are as diverse as people in other periods of life, and their patterns of aging vary according to the range they show from health to sickness, from maturity to immaturity, activity to apathy, useful constructive participation to disinterest, from the prevailing stereotype of aging to rich forms of creativity.
>
> Ninety-five percent of older people live in the community and are not institutionalized or in protective settings. Physical illnesses are frequent and often chronic and limiting. This period of life is characterized by complex changes that are multiple, occur rapidly and have profound effects. Some people are overwhelmed. Others can come to accept or substitute for the loss of loved ones, prestige, social status and adverse physiological changes.
>
> "Old age" and "brain damage" alone do not account for the changes seen or the modes of adaptation of older people. Diseases, life experience, socioeconomic and other forces along with the subjective experience of growing old and approaching death, all interweave to contribute to the picture of old age.
>
> Older people are apt to be reflective rather than impulsive. Having experienced a great deal and having been "burned often," they think before acting. Under suitable circumstances, the present remains very much alive and exciting to them; but they also turn to a review of their past, searching for purpose, reconciliation of relationships and resolution of conflicts and regrets. They may become self-centered or altruistic, angry or contrite, triumphant or depressed.
>
> Those old people who are optimistic and resourceful may at the same time be painfully aware of the brevity of life and its tragedies. Optimism

is tempered by a more balanced view of the joys and sadnesses of life. The old continue to learn and change in response to their experiences and to human relationships. They are not often overwhelmed by new ideas for they recognize how few of them there are. Many are employable, productive and creative. Many wish to leave their mark through sponsoring the young as well as through ideas and institutions.

THEORY AND RESEARCH REGARDING THE ELDERLY

Theoretical Framework

What emerges in terms of images of aging also depends on one's frame of reference, or the molds into which the data are cast in order to interpret or explain them. For example, several models have been proposed to account for the decrements attached to aging. (1) The ecological model attributes the causes of aging primarily to factors within aged peoples' environment (Eisdorfer & Lawton, 1973). Provided that their needs are cared for and they are given opportunities for leading an active, satisfying life, there is little or no reduction in psychological functions except those for which the biological substratum itself is in the process of decline. (2) According to the developmental model, the causes of aging are to be found in difficulties of adjusting to this new stage of life. Individuals must cope with new problems in aging, just as they must also learn the tasks of earlier age periods. (3) The learning theory model postulates that changes in behavior with aging are simply a matter of inadequate learning. For example, people learn to be old just as they learn anything else, through reinforcement. If they had different kinds of reinforcement they would not manifest the symptoms of aging ordinarily observed in this society. Even if older people suffer physiological decline they can nevertheless learn to cope with it. Therapy based on learning theories can help the elderly to reverse the negative consequences resultant from their failures to adapt. However institutionalization reduces functioning because of the constrictions of institutional life. (4) According to the genetic model, limitations in functioning of the aged derive from "built-in obsolescence"; which means that certain characteristics have been genetically inherited. Nevertheless heredity does not operate alone, but inevitably is influenced by environment. Therefore steps might be taken to encourage more favorable tendencies and to prevent more negative genetic tendencies from manifesting themselves. (5) Another approach, the internal environment model, hypothesizes sources of aging that result from changes in metabolic processes and contents of body fluids. (6) Finally the neurophysiological model hypothesizes that aging is a matter of information-processing mediated by the neurophysiology of the organism. As brain cells are lost, the usual processing of information diminishes. Aging in this sense is interpreted as caused by a "series of subtle cortical insults that interfere with information processing" (Zubin, 1973, p. 7). Any composite model which would attempt to embrace the special functions of each of the foregoing would probably be too unwieldy to be practical.

The Inadequacies of Personality Research

We should be alert to the still-immature status of personality research. Much of the older literature regarding both personality and intelligence is shot through with methodological flaws. Entire theories, such as that of disengagement, may be constructed on "methodological artifacts" (Schaie & Gribben, 1975, p. 79). While significant improvements are being made, much research is still pretty weak, or relatively thin, in terms of depth and replication. As a result there is as yet little understanding of personality structure beyond that of the college-aged (Schaie & Marquette, 1972).

If we return to our original question of who are the old, we can answer: all of us and none of us—all of us in the sense that we are older persons-in-the-becoming, and none of us in the sense that no overall categorization fits. The task is to find models among older people who are sufficiently flexible to reflect the major and minor categories of persons in an increasingly pluralistic society, yet who are not so fluid and fragmented that they have no functional value.

Another common deficiency of aging studies is the presentation of data without meaningful interpretation. For example, mortality tables provide no information about functional losses preceding the events leading to death, and not even averages truly reflect individual experience. After all, death is removing progressively more subjects from samples of the aging after the period in which an acutely declining function may occur. Hence reliable data can only be derived from longitudinal research in which the aging processes of individuals are followed. In this manner "we can learn whether the average decline in renal function with age is occurring acutely in some individuals or gradually in most individuals" (Sinex, 1975, p. 24). Again we may be misled by the fact, for instance, that many persons past 90 are hypotensive, or manifest lower than average tension. Yet one cannot conclude that merely through the aging process do peoples' reactions become less intensive. By age 90 the hypertensive individuals, whose blood pressure increased along with their age, are no longer around to study.

CONCLUSION

The concept of age is somewhat confusing, and varies with one's frame of reference. While the chronological frame of reference is common, others—such as social, physiological, temporal, and cultural—are often implicit in attitudes toward older persons. Aging itself is an almost meaningless concept, because people vary so much in any age grouping.

Older people undoubtedly do have to cope with exceptional problems of a different kind and degree from those encountered at other ages. They are assigned negative stereotypes which are fortunately diminishing. They experience progressively greater physical and mental decline and disorders as the years go on, although such conditions vary greatly from one person to another, and many change little, physically or mentally, until old age. To what extent the degenerative or pathological conditions associated with aging might be prevented, mitigated, or reversed, given more favorable conditions and breakthroughs in relevant sciences, is uncertain.

A similarly confused picture exists regarding the personality characteristics associated with the elderly. Older people are often stereotyped as inherently unproductive, asexual, and cautious; however, such traits, when manifested in persons who showed these same traits earlier in life, reflect their changing circumstances. Besides, older people have highly varied patterns of characteristics, depending mostly on what they were in earlier years. Anyhow the more negative features of the stereotype are grossly exaggerated; most older people have quite positive traits such as mellowness, kindliness, etc. Even their present status is far less gloomy than is frequently presumed. Granted a more favorable environment, their adjustment will be correspondingly improved.

SUGGESTED READINGS

Aldag, R. J. & Brief, A. P. Age and reactions to task characteristics. *Journal of Employment Counseling,* 1976, 13 (3), 109–114. A comparison of older and younger workers refuted the popular notion that older employees attach more importance than younger ones to extrinsic rewards, such as high pay and job security.

Alpaugh, P. K., Renner, V. J., & Birren, J. E. Age and creativity: Implications for education and teachers. *Educational Gerontology,* 1976, 1 (1), 17–40. An analysis is made of the current literature on the cognitive aspects of creativity as related to aging, along with their implications for education. Research regarding creativity in general is also discussed, and its relationship to various types of education.

Ames, L. B., Metraux, R. W., Rodell, J. L., & Walker, R. N. *Rorschach responses in old age.* New York: Brunner/Mazel, 1973. After reviewing the literature concerning Rorschach responses of older subjects the researchers report the results of testing 200 men and women between the ages of 70 and 100. The results are analyzed for various subgroups according to age, socioeconomic status, occupation, sex, and mental condition.

Binstock, R. H. & Shanas, E. (Eds.) *Handbook of aging and the social sciences.* New York: Van Nostrand Reinhold Company, 1976. This book, written by authorities in their respective fields, evaluates and interprets research, concepts, and theories from the perspective of the various social sciences. It treats the social aspects of aging, aging and social structure, and aging as it relates to social systems, interpersonal behavior and social intervention.

Birren, J. E. & Schaie, K. W. (Eds.) *Handbook of the psychology of aging.* New York: Van Nostrand Reinhold Company, 1977. In stressing the psychological aspects of dying, the chapters in this volume, written by authorities in their respective fields, deal with a wide range of behavioral processes and phenomena.

Czaja, S. J. Age differences in life satisfaction as a function of discrepancy between real and ideal self concepts. *Experimental Aging Research*, 1975, *1* (1), 81–89. In a comparison of 10 women and 10 men from each of six age groups (20 to 25, 30 to 35, 40 to 45, 50 to 55, 60 to 65, and 70 to 75), significant differences were found among the groups with regard to real and ideal self concepts and life satisfaction.

Finch, C. E. & Hayflick, L. (Eds.) *Handbook of the biology of aging.* New York: Van Nostrand Reinhold Company, 1977. The chapters in this volume, written by authorities in their respective fields, explore in detail the biological changes that characterize aging in humans and other mammalian species. All the important organs and systems of the body are discussed.

Hochschild, A. R. Disengagement theory: A critique and proposal. *American Sociological Review*, 1975, *40* (5), 553–569. The classic disengagement theory—that it is normal for the aging gradually to withdraw from activities—is portrayed as a somewhat simplistic concept. Such disengagement as occurs is highly variable, and results from many factors, including the character of society and the individual's social position.

Kilty, K. M. & Feld, A. Attitudes toward aging and toward the needs of older people. *Journal of Gerontology*, 1976, *31* (5), 586–594. Attitudes toward aging of two age groups, one under and one over 60, derived from their opinion statements, are compared and analyzed.

Meier, E. L. & Kerr, E. A. Capabilities of middle-aged and older workers: A survey of the literature. *Industrial Gerontology*, 1976, *3* (3), 147–156. A survey of the literature indicates that middle aged and older workers function effectively on the job; and they have greater job stability, fewer accidents, and lose less time from work than do younger workers.

Mental Aging, Chapter 4 in Erdman Palmore (Ed.) *Normal Aging II.* Durham: Duke University Press, 1977. The articles in this chapter, written by various authorities, represent reports regarding the relationship between certain physical characteristics of the aging and their mental function. In general, these reports refute the common view that cognitive functioning inevitably declines with age.

Neugarten, B. L. Personality and aging. In Birren, James E. & Schaie, K. Warner (Eds.) *Handbook of the Psychology of Aging.* New York: Van Nostrand Reinhold Co., 1977, 626–649. A noted authority on aging reviews research relevant to personality in later years, with regard to the various dimensions and structure of personality, the range of individual differences and changes over time.

Oster, C. Sensory deprivation in geriatric patients. *Journal of the American Geriatrics Society,* 1976, 24 (10), 461–464. The effects of sensory deprivation on degenerative changes normally associated with aging are discussed, along with ways to maintain and even strengthen the aging individual's social values, and morale.

Payne, B. & Whittington, F. Older women: An examination of popular stereotypes and research evidence. *Social Problems,* April 1976, 23 (4), 488–504. Stereotypes of elderly women, on such topics as health and longevity, marital status, family roles and leisure activity indicate them to be based on considerable distortion and misinformation.

Pfeiffer, E. Survival in old age. In Erdman Palmore (Ed.) *Normal Aging II.* Durham: Duke University Press, 1974. This second volume offers additional information, from an interdisciplinary perspective, regarding the Duke University longitudinal studies of aging. It summarizes findings which build upon and extend the research presented in the first volume, including new findings about the older longitudinal panel and the first findings on a middle-aged panel.

Schaie, K. W., & Schaie, J. P. Clinical assessment and aging. In Birren, James E. & Schaie, K. Warner (Eds.) *Handbook of the Psychology of Aging.* New York: Van Nostrand Reinhold Co., 1977, 692–723. Clinical assessment of older people is discussed in terms of aims, diagnosis, techniques and the relation of assessment data to the life prospects of elderly clients.

Siegler, I. C. The terminal drop hypothesis: Fact or artifact? *Experimental Aging Research,* 1975, 1 (1), 169–185. Data from eight longitudinal studies are analyzed in order to clarify the concept of terminal drop.

12 CHAPTER

Life Styles
in
Later
Years

TYPES OF HOUSEHOLDS

Living Alone

Reasons for being alone. Each major grouping of older persons has its characteristic problems, tasks, and life styles. One such category, those who live alone, totals about 81% of people over 65 (Butler, 1975b). There are two main reasons that there are so many living alone. One is that women live longer than men; the other is that older people want to stay in their own homes. Even when it means financial deprivation, they prefer the freedom of living alone (Brotman, 1972). Meantime the current trend toward self-actualization, which involves more concern with oneself than in the past, contrasts with the more old-fashioned ideal of helping others. This is reducing the sacrifices that children make for their aging parents (Kalish, 1975).

Another reason that such a large number of people live alone is the decreasing number of births. If there is zero population growth, fewer older people will have living children or siblings. Indeed even more older Americans will be without families; they will have neither living children, siblings, nor relatives. And since there will also be fewer children and relatives to provide services for them in case of illness or incapacity, there will be more old people living alone, more couples without children living in age-segregated communities, and more people living in institutions (Shanas & Hauser, 1974).

The older never-marrieds. About 8% of the over-65 population, the never-marrieds, often live alone and are generally better adjusted than widows of that age. For one thing, the singles do not experience the disruption of having a spouse die. People who have typically been isolated report less loneliness than those only recently isolated. In fact older never-married singles are no lonelier than the married, while the widowed are twice as lonely.

Significant data regarding the adjustment of older singles comes from a study (Gubrium, 1975) of 22 such persons in Detroit. When asked how they thought of themselves in terms of age, they avoided locating themselves in any particular period of life; and they indicated that life was pretty much what it always had been. Here are some of their answers:

316

I don't think of it at all. I'm pretty good. I have never compared it. In our Scottish way, we don't like to analyze ourselves. I don't give it much thought.

I feel pretty good for 73. I feel equal to most others. (Gubrium, 1975, p. 33)

In general these single people denied ever being lonely.

I need 8 days in the week. I'm so busy now. I'm not unhappy. They are stupid questions, aren't they?

Never lonely! You can put that down twice! I've been the same right through! At 45 I was still the same. I'm satisfied. I was all satisfied and I'm still satisfied! I didn't change at all. (p. 33)

When asked if they missed any particular person it was usually a brother or sister, parent or friend. They would say that they missed someone, not that they were lonely. They were rarely as sorrowful as widows about missing someone.

All my life I never felt lonely. Oh, once in a while when it's kind of quiet. I don't feel lonely most of the time. It just comes once in a while. You feel you want to talk to your own relatives. I put the radio on. I never feel very lonely at any time.

These people also denied that their later lives were new or especially different, or that the quality of their lives was significantly deteriorating.

It's not down hill. It seems to me it stays about average. It's about the same. I don't think its down hill. You're not making it up hill, but I don't think you're down. As long as you're able to get up and around a little bit, it's a struggle, but I get by. I'd say its another experience. So, its continued personal growth. It's not necessarily decline (p. 35).

Sometimes singles miss someone very much, perhaps a friend with whom they have lived for a number of years.

I miss my friend, Lois. We lived together. Well, with Lois, we used to do everything together. We had nice trips together. We lived together for over 30 years (p. 34).

In general the elderly single believed their futures would simply be an extension of the past. They didn't worry about it, which suggests that they thought things wouldn't change very much. They looked on death as simply one more event in a chain of ongoing experience. When asked if they feared death, some responded as follows:

> No I don't. I don't know what it will be. Nobody knows. I don't think there's any use worrying. I have no fears.

> I know where I'm going to be buried—near my parents. We all have tombstones that match each other. My cousin has put up my tombstone. It has my birth date on it and all it needs now is the date of my death. So, there's a place for me (p. 36).

The older singles look upon their status as just another way of life. They do not perceive themselves as deviant or abnormal. Their lives are just as acceptable to them, as they imagine having a spouse is, to married persons.

> I'm very satisfied. I wouldn't know about that, not having been married. I learned a long time ago to be contented and I am.

> I think that half the married people have children to keep—even when they are old. I have nobody to keep but me. I have no complaints.

> A married man—he is going through the same maneuvers everyday. A single man can meet many people. A single man has a free hand. He can go and come as he pleases (p. 37).

It is clear that these people value their independence. They don't have the burden of dependents, especially children, although some of them said that they had never married because they were responsible for ailing parents. With regard to social relationships, they had often associated more with friends than with relatives when they were younger.

They do visit with others occasionally; however, compared to older married persons they engage in more solitary activities, and say that they are satisfied with them.

> Do knitting and watch TV. Visit with my neighbors. I watch TV in the morning and in the evening.

> Sometimes I knit, sometimes I play solitaire. In the morning I straighten out my clothes. After lunch, I sometimes read or take a nap. Evenings I watch TV and read the paper.

> I usually take a walk and have a glass of beer nearly every day. I do a lot of reading. I love reading. It's a good pastime when I'm home (p. 38).

The widowed. By far the largest category of older persons living alone is the widowed, who number about 10 million in the United States, or slightly over 12% of all women over the age of 14 (Bureau of the

Census, 1973). Their large numbers derive from the differential longevity of the sexes—a woman's life expectancy is seven years greater than a man's—and the practice of marrying men older than themselves.

Widows typically share certain major problems. One is the difficulty of finding a new mate. Unlike older men, widows face social sanctions against choosing a younger spouse, and hence the great majority remain alone. Another common problem is money, for most widows did not work outside the home until after their children were grown, and then only in low-paying jobs. Six out of ten elderly widows have incomes below the poverty level, and only 2% of those whose husbands were covered by a pension are receiving benefits ("Bleak future," 1975). The negative effects attributed to widowhood often stem more from socioeconomic factors than from the status of widowhood itself (Harvey & Bahr, 1974).

Both widows and widowers share certain troubles, and both rate themselves lower in life satisfaction than the marrieds (Hutchison, 1975). The original, and immediate, problem is to cope with grief after losing their mates (Parkes, 1972). This factor, coupled with increasing illness and a narrowing circle of friends, increases their social isolation. As the years roll on their close friends drop out one by one; and after one's spouse dies, the problem is doubled. As we noted earlier with regard to younger couples, interpersonal relationships represent long-term personal investments that couples have made jointly with others. That is, social relationships often involve the participation of both spouses. Therefore former routines and social activities are disrupted when pair relationships no longer exist. Meantime, without a spouse, the widowed lack someone with whom to share recreation, affection, and domestic tasks, as well as sexual satisfaction (Parkes, 1972). The temptation in such circumstances is to withdraw; and as the widowed progressively do so, others pull away from them too. Meantime as social patterns change, older persons' need to maintain good grooming, to fix good meals, or to keep an attractive house, may diminish.

Despite such problems, many of the widowed make a relatively good adjustment. They seem more content than the single or divorced people of any age, and they report the least stress and pressure of any other grouping despite their generally low incomes (A. Campbell, 1975). Since most of them are past retirement, they don't worry about work; and they are finished with childrearing. In cases in which the marital relationship was unproductive, or even tension-producing, the surviving spouse may embark upon a happier life than before (Parkes, 1972). However, the widowed often find their lives emotionally inadequate, as do single and divorced people (A. Campbell, 1975).

At least two programs have proved of some value to the widowed. In the widow-to-widow program, women who have adjusted to their own situations help those who are recently bereaved to work out a new life style and destiny in a positive fashion. The widow-helpers are trained in special programs, and to date, their efforts have met with considerable success (Silverman, 1972). Another approach, group therapy for widows, involves relatively homogeneous groups in terms of age and socioeconomic level; it has proved quite successful. Group members gain insight into their feelings and an understanding of the behavioral mechanisms involved. They also learn to give up old identities and establish new ones. However, not all the participants achieve these results. Certain ones find the experience depressing, or of no special value. Others complain that they want the group to serve a social rather than a therapeutic purpose. On the whole, however, group discussion can be effective for those who are able and willing to relate to other members (Hiltz, 1975).

Problems of being widowed. The statements below are typical of views expressed by widowed women when asked: "Do you experience special problems?"

Many, many, many! When you have had a good husband it is terrible to try to live without him. Loneliness, decisions, lack of escorts, lack of companionship, small tasks he used to do, and many others. (*Female, age 74*)

When one lives near a large city there's the fear of being alone at night. It limits attendance at symphony, opera, theatre, etc. (*Female, age 73*)

I miss my fine husband. (*Female, age 68*)

Living alone in the very late years. As time goes on, problems for all those who live alone become accentuated. Some give up and move to retirement or nursing homes, depending on their condition. Others hang on as long as they can, with varying degrees of assistance from younger generations—sometimes their families, sometimes close-knit neighborhoods and social groups. Some older persons are maintained for years in their own homes by their friends and neighbors. Ordinarily they have lived in the same community for a considerable period of time (Butler, 1975a).

Mr. Billings is 92 years old and totally blind, yet he lives alone, in his own home, in Minneapolis. He prepares some of his meals, and takes care of the house himself. Since he is familiar with the house and with household routines he manages very well, with the considerable assistance of relatives and neighbors.

The sort of stubborn determination and courage shown by this man are not at all unusual. A great many people prefer the risk of falls and broken bones to being placed in nursing homes. In terms of financial costs to society and morale of the persons concerned, community home-care services are the best solution for old people who live alone.

Living with Others in Primary Relationships

Those older persons who live with others fall into two main categories—those who live with a spouse, children, or a friend; and those living in some kind of group such as a nursing home or commune. Older women, especially, may live with a close friend, sharing expenses, household tasks, and companionship. Others live with a spouse, often enjoying a richer, fuller life than they did in middle age because they are free of the responsibilities of work and childrearing. Those with a reasonable income may travel, often in motor homes.

Living with one's children. Fewer older people than ever before live with their children, partly because society no longer demands that younger adults share quarters with their parents. In certain societies today, and in our own in the past, younger family members provided for older ones as a matter of course. However, today the cost of such care has grown, and greater numbers of people are living a longer time. Hence a family might have responsibility for grandparents and even great-grandparents (Butler, 1975a). In fact since 1920, the chance of a ten-year-old child having at least three living grandparents has risen from 1 in 10 to 3 in 8, and the chance of having all four has grown from 1 in 90 to 1 in 14 (Statistical Bulletin, 1972). Also people are increasingly mobile, and it is difficult to move units made up of several generations.

The small minority who do live with their children may have more cause for unhappiness than satisfaction. While they do have a certain security, and they are among people they love, still they often feel that they are an unwanted burden—and this is often the case. In addition most of their resources—money, space, and life routines—are largely controlled by their children. As J. D. Turner (1975) points out, family relationships may be thought of in terms of balance of power. In infancy and childhood there is a disproportionate balance of power because the children are dependent on their parents. Ultimately the parents change from being givers to receivers, and perceive their own status as dependent, in contrast with younger adults, who perceive themselves as low in receiving but high in giving. Over the years, as older individuals' exchange-power diminishes still further, they become increasingly dependent on their children. For this reason older adults make every effort to remain independent as long as possible, using their own assets and whatever pensions they may receive.

When these resources are no longer adequate, older parents most often turn to their children, and more often to the daughter than to the son. Perhaps because girls are less emancipated than boys, they have closer ties with their families. Hence it would seem more natural that parents would turn to their daughters in their own time of need. In general children support their parents because they feel a sense of duty.

Kinship support patterns. Even if they do not live with their children, aging parents usually maintain frequent contact with them. Indeed an important aspect of older parents' lives is interaction with their children, either in person or by mail and telephone. When aging parents and adult children live close together, they visit each other often, and engage in such joint activities as going to church, shopping, and pursuing various recreations. If they do not live close together, they may get together on special family occasions including holidays, weddings, funerals, and birthdays (Troll, 1975).

Kathleen Keer reports that the greater distance adults put between themselves and their aging parents, the more they invest of themselves in their children, who in turn cut off their own parents as they become adults. Meantime society helps to underwrite the growing emotional distance between aging parents and their children with programs that aid institutions even when families could afford to support their parents ("Generation chasm," 1977).

Support patterns within the kinship group take various forms, including gifts, advice, financial assistance, emotional support, or joint living arrangements. Surprisingly the proportion of older parents who help their children is greater than those who receive help from them (Kivett, 1976). Older parents have low expectations in terms of receiving assistance, especially money, from their children. Indeed only 7% of those over 65 receive regular financial help from relatives. By contrast 12% of older adults give financial or other support to their children, despite their own limited resources and declining health (Watson & Kivett, 1976). In general sons are more likely to receive monetary aid and daughters to receive services such as child care, from their parents.

If relationships between older parents and their children have generally been positive, affection may be maintained through the years. However if there are negative feelings, there develops a cyclical pattern involving anxiety, resentment, and guilt on both sides. Sons and daughters may resent the demands made on them by their dependent parents but feel guilty about having such negative feelings. At the same time parents try to lessen the burden that they impose on their children, and because they feel like a burden they too feel guilty, develop anxiety, and tend to withdraw. Yet they may also be disturbed that the sacrifices they made for their children have paid off with rejection (J. D. Turner, 1975).

The grandparent role. The great majority of older people, including both those who do and do not live with their children, become grandparents. In fact 70% of people over 65 have living grandchildren (Atchley, 1972). This fact takes on increasing importance as life roles— for example, that of worker—disappear or diminish. In addition since many mothers work today, grandparents often take care of the children. Meantime since their contacts with grandchildren require less responsibility than did their relationships with their own children, grandparents can afford to be more objective and relaxed. Hence the relationship is often quite satisfying, both to grandparents and grandchildren.

Nevertheless not all grandparents feel the same about their role, as a study by Neugarten and Weinstein shows. They interviewed grandmothers, most of them in their early 50s to middle 60s, and grandfathers a few years older. While the majority were satisfied with being a grandparent, about a third of the grandmothers and nearly that many grandfathers had reservations about it. Some of them felt too young to be comfortable in the grandparent role, because it suggests being old. The remainder who rejected the role simply had little interest in their grandchildren or were too involved in their own concerns. Among those who enjoyed the role a third said it provided a kind of biological renewal ("I feel young again") or biological continuity ("I see my life going on into the future through these children"). About a fourth thought it was an opportunity for a new emotional role, and that they intended to be better grandparents than they had been parents. About 30% said that being grandparents had little influence on their lives one way or the other.

Fewer than half of the grandparents conformed to the traditional grandparent stereotype, which included maintaining some control over the younger generation. The remainder represented two different life styles. The fun seekers (about a quarter of them) were something like playmates to the children; while the remainder were distant figures who emerged on birthdays, Christmas, and other special occasions. Those who had recently become grandparents perceived themselves as more youthful than their own parents had been at their age. Among the under-65 grandparents, about one-third were the more traditional type; another third were fun-seeking; and the last were distant. Among the grandparents over 65, over half were traditional, and nearly one-quarter were funseeking and the same number were distant (Horn, 1976).

In general the grandmother role is more valued and intensive than the grandfather role, partly because of the grandmother's experience with child care and her greater value to the younger mother. In addition, older widowed fathers are at a greater disadvantage than widowed mothers. They appear to be more vulnerable to social isolation, as well as to inattention from their children. The greater social isolation of widowers than of widows is believed to contribute to their higher suicide rate (Bock, 1972). In a study of 136 older fathers (Watson & Kivett, 1976), 18% lived in a household with a child; and almost all (90%) saw one or more children at least once a week, half of them daily. Most of these men rated their health as only fair to poor. With regard to religion, 79% considered it very important. Only 1 in 7 reported the present to be the happiest period in their lives.

The older father's role is less important than certain other variables in explaining differences in life satisfaction. Life satisfaction increases with social class and self-reported health; but it relates inversely to how many living children one has, perhaps because more children simply create more problems in old age, or it may be that large numbers of offspring characterize the lower social classes. These figures support the literature in general regarding the relation of social class and health to life satisfaction in later years.

Nursing Homes

Often there comes a time when people cannot take care of themselves and have no one to take care of them. Hence they must go to nursing homes. Most of them are women, simply because they live longer. Half of them have no living relatives and no direct relationships, even with a distant relative. Their average age is 78, and 60% to 80% are poor. Many have not always been so, but inflation has eroded their funds over the years. Eighty-five percent of them die in the nursing home after an average stay of 1.1 years. A third die within the first year, and another third live up to three years. While most people refer to all residential community facilities for the elderly as nursing homes, commercial nursing homes differ from homes for the aging. Commercial homes operate for profit, while homes for the aging, sponsored by various fraternal, religious or trust organizations, are nonprofit and voluntary, and are sometimes operated by federal, state, or municipal governments. The commercial homes receive more federal monies than the nonprofit ones, and they house about 80% of the institutionalized elderly. The care in most institutions of both types is very expensive, although Medicaid has helped considerably.

Deficiencies. It has been widely publicized that many nursing homes are severely deficient in a number of areas. They often have few or no nurses, and hardly qualify as homes. Robert Butler (1975c) often visited them, frequently disguising himself as a family member. Sometimes he saw "patients lying in their own urine and feces. Food is frequently left untouched on plates" (p. 263). On the basis of such observations Butler also lists "a grim catalog of medical deficiencies" (p. 264). In many cases drug prescriptions are wrongly administered, fundamental hygiene standards are neglected; and in order to keep down food costs, meals are often inadequate to the point of malnourishment. Few of the homes have social or therapeutic programs, and few are reimbursed by Medicare or Medicaid for putting such programs into effect (Gottesman, Quarterman, & Cohn, 1973). The employees are often grossly overworked, and just as grossly inefficient and untrained. The patients themselves are often treated in a highly authoritarian manner. Such care is no bargain at any price, and certainly not at the current high costs. Perhaps the worst abuses are at the commercial homes.

Sometimes patients are arbitrarily shifted from one facility to another, with little regard for the consequences. If elderly people voluntarily make a move which improves their living conditions, the results may be positive. On the other hand, those individuals who experience involuntary relocation, and who are financially dependent, indicate considerable life dissatisfaction (Smith & Brand, 1975). Such relocations often cut off contact with their only close friends and produce feelings of isolation. Any move, including going to a nursing home in the first place, is less traumatic when decisions are made in conjunction with other family members.

Individual reports. Answers to the following questions by several women who currently live in nursing homes afford a glimpse of what it is like to reside in such places.

Why did you come to the nursing home?

I was unable to live alone. (*Female, age 74*)

I had a partial paralyzing stroke; was unable to take care of myself. (*Female, age 77*)

Doctor's orders—I am too nervous to live alone and care for myself. (*Female, age 68*)

I was sent by the doctor. I lived alone, and had a broken thigh bone. The same hip was broken thirteen years before. I had no family left, no near relative in town. Also I knew of this home's good reputation. I was unable to care for myself. (*Female, age 86*)

What did you give up of special importance by coming to the home?

Home life, going on trips, going to church and stores, and visiting with relatives and friends. (*Female, age 74*)

Getting out. To church, friends' homes. Eating out with friends. I had to give up driving several months before, and was too lame to walk alone. I had enjoyed using my car, and took many trips with friends who had no car. I always had a friend who could help drive. I advise callers to keep going. I say, you'll enjoy memories of trips, travels, etc. (*Male, age 75*)

How do you spend your time, other than eating, sleeping, etc.? What activities do you engage in?

Taking care of myself, reading, writing letters to friends and relatives. Watching T.V., listening to the radio. (*Female, age 74*)

I work daily, Monday—Friday, in arts & crafts, mostly on hook rugs. I also go to all activities here, like Bingo, movies, sing-a-long, and to group activities. Also to holiday parties, picnics, boat rides, field trips, etc. & watch T.V., last but not least. I have bull sessions with two of the residents. (*Female, age 68*)

Because I walk very little (with a walker), I am very slow getting around. I wash own house daily and take entire care of my finances. I even order drugs from the Retired Persons' Pharmacy. I spend some time each morning waiting for help—to bring my dress (I keep underwear where I can reach it, to save time). I cannot wear elastic hose, so apply my own elastic bandage on my "good" leg. I have a severe foot and back ailment, so am unable to help out or play Bingo, etc. There's too little time to read or write much—I love both. (*Female, age 86*)

What do you like most about living in a nursing home?

Knowing you will be taken care of. (*Female, age 74*)

Making friends and keeping busy in doing crafts. (*Female, age 68*)

Feeling I'm cared for, not responsible for the care of a large house. I'm in a two-bedroom suite, and have made some fine new friends (roommates' families, etc.). Also I became very fond of two other residents, and am going to an annual birthday party of one's 92-93-94th. I found I could write "jingles," one each year. I also wrote a Christmas "Night before Christmas" for Home's "gazette." Institution food is not "like home."

What do you like least about living in a nursing home?

Missing my own home, and not be able to go out for rides, church, and lunches. (*Female, age 74*)

Having to give up my own home—and my own pace of living. (*Female, age 68*)

Constant (though unavoidable) change of employees—three shifts per day—and losing one or more who have come to seem like friends. In my case it means a lot that an aide can help dress my feet with various pads and bandages. The ones who do it most comfortably and quickly have had lots of experience. Both the aide and I get nervous when a new girl has to struggle against time. (*Female, age 86*)

What things worry you the most? What are your chief anxieties? Also, what do you rely on most to keep your morale up?

Worrying about a small house I still own. And wishing I was still there. My prayers and faith in God. (*Female, age 74*)

Not hearing from seven of my nine children. I rely on the activities program here to keep up my morale! (*Female, age 68*)

Retirement Parks, Communities, and Communes

At least until they become incapacitated, growing numbers of old persons are choosing to live in communities, apartment houses, or other places either restricted to, or catering especially to, older persons. Also communes for older persons are being developed—for example, one in Winter Park, Florida consists of 12 older people, all over 70. Other older persons enjoy living in mobile home parks which involve a life style and culture all of their own (Deck, 1972).

Some elderly people live in retirement communities, especially in California, Florida, and Arizona. Some of these communities are restricted to those over 50, although the rules vary considerably from place to place. Residents of these areas have more friends than the elderly in a general community, although they have fewer contacts with members of the family. While they may lack the stimulation of regular association with children and younger people, they apparently feel greater satisfaction in localities which cater to older people. In fact living among young adults and children can be tension-producing. Older people may find it difficult to adapt to younger peoples' life styles and behaviors, and the noise and inconsideration of children.

Living among their own age group pays other dividends as well. Arlie Hochschild (1973) became involved in a three-year participant-observation project among the residents of Merrill Court near San Francisco, a public housing project of senior citizens comprised chiefly of working-class widows. The group had developed its own norms and expectations of each other; and their own role models, reference groups, and positive self-images provided strong group support. In addition members were insulated from the unfortunate stereotypes of the outer world. Merrill Court became a true community of people who found a satisfying alternative way of life.

The question is sometimes raised: to what extent should older people in group-care facilities be helped, and at what point does such care produce a hospital atmosphere and result in over-dependence? In one

Many government subsidized nutrition programs have been a great help for low-income retired people.

study, elderly people in a retirement hotel and an apartment tower were provided little in the way of special services, but did not appear to miss them. At two other sites, a life-care home and a retirement village, the residents were provided with considerable services which nevertheless did not seem to create dependency. Instead they permitted the residents to be more independent by helping them to maintain themselves at "optimal levels" (Sherman, 1975).

Selection of Appropriate Facilities

As at any age, the choice of a place to live in later years is a highly individual matter, depending upon life styles and personalities. The old saying, one man's meat is another's poison, is certainly applicable in such situations. The important thing is that such facilities be expanded, upgraded, and constantly evaluated by government agencies, to prevent profiteering off the age group that can least easily afford it. There should also be readily available advisory services which may facilitate the dissemination of information and effect a favorable match between persons and facilities.

In the following, some people discuss where they would prefer to live in their later years.

In order of preference: my own home; with a family member; in a nursing home. (*Male, age 64*)

I want to remain in my own home as long as possible. I'd rather take chances on broken bones, etc., and stay there until I am helpless. Then I will go to a nursing home. I do not want to live with, and be a burden on, my children. (*Female, age 65*)

I want to stay in my own home; and I expect to leave enough money to employ a housekeeper, or nurse, or someone to take care of me there. (*Male, age 53*)

In my own home. I have no great desire to live beyond this. (*Male, age 65*)

In my own home. (*Male, age 67*)

Several of my friends (whom I have known for years) and I plan to form a small retirement commune and hire a nurse to live there to take care of any immediate medical needs. (*Female, age 63*)

RETIREMENT

The matter of retiring from work has come to affect increasing numbers of people. Years ago, a far higher percentage of the population was self-employed, and therefore continued to work almost all their lives. The average lifetime was shorter, so fewer people reached retirement age. Moreover increasing numbers are retiring at an earlier age than in the past, which increases the number of retired persons.

The Pluses and Minuses

Causes of stress. Retirement can produce stress for various reasons. The loss of a dominant social role, that of worker (Darnley, 1975), is one of them. In fact, observes Hochschild (1973), retirees lack status in a work-oriented society. Individuals who are retired must also cope with other aspects of retirement: the end of the work career, a decrease in income, increased awareness of the aging process, a greater potential for declining health, which will restrict activities, much more free time, changed interpersonal relations, and society's image of the retiree (Thurnher, 1974).

All of these can cause severe problems. Men's sexual interest may decline if they have difficulty adjusting to their new role—or nonrole. They are especially anxious if they have younger wives who are still working for they are not psychologically prepared for the role reversal in such cases (Troll, 1971). Those who doubt that they can create a satisfactory post-retirement lifestyle, suffer from the so-called "retirement syndrome," which includes gastrointestinal problems, irritability, and nervousness. The individual impact "is a function of economics, temperament, health, vigor, range of interest, all those factors that can effect individuals, whatever their age" (p. 73).

Yet responses to and problems experienced in retirement are highly variable. In Atchley's study (1975), not quite a third of retired persons had difficulty adjusting to retirement. Forty percent reported problems in adapting to a reduced income, which was by far the most frequently encountered problem. About one-quarter of the adjustment difficulties concerned missing work, and the other 38% involved such factors as the death of a spouse or declining health, both of which relate to retirement adjustment only in that they affect the overall situation.

It is commonly assumed that older men will have a more difficult time adjusting to retirement than women. However, in a study of 3,630 retired teachers and telephone company employees, Robert Atchley of the Scripps Foundation Gerontology Center found that the women were equally as work-oriented as the men, and had an even harder time giving up their jobs. The older women were also less likely to be married, and had a smaller income. The men, more than the women, suffered a certain anomie, and admitted that they were old; while the women were more often anxious, lonely, sensitive to criticism, and depressed. The men adjusted better to aging than the women; they simply realigned their energies and commitments. More of the women neither accepted social aging nor attempted to stall it off by continued engagement in activities. Instead they responded with greater levels of psychological stress ("Aging," 1976). However, these persons are a minority, for the overwhelming majority of both middle- and working-class men and women enjoyed retirement; and almost half adjusted to it very quickly.

Compensations. Retirement indeed can, and often does, yield a variety of satisfactions. It provides freedom from restricting routines, and time for pursuing special interests. The mental and physical health of persons whose occupations were unusually strenuous, boring or time-consuming, often improved. For retired persons in general, health improvement is more common than decline (Eisdorfer, 1972).

In a not very recent but interesting study (Reichard, Livson, & Petersen, 1962) which involved 87 men over 55, half of whom were retired and half still working, the findings indicated that those men who were both older and retired possessed greater ego strength, projected less hostility, were more open and trusting, had fewer obsessional defenses, were freer of overt anxiety, and had less hidden depression. The researchers concluded that the period of greatest difficulty is from 64 to

69, when transitions to new circumstances and roles are in progress, and that after the transition is complete, the situation improves.

In the following, some retired people discuss their feelings about retirement.

Since I'm retired I'm able to do what I please within the financial limitations of a retired person. (*Male, age 67*)

I have neither been happier nor the reverse [since retirement]. I miss my students but they continue to contact me and sometimes my colleagues invite me to lecture on favorite subjects. I don't run out of things to do. (*Male, age 72*)

If I could change my life style I would hope to find a totally satisfying employment that I could follow my whole life. (*Male, age 65*)

My feelings are mixed. I have felt the loss of prestige and feelings of worth. I feel relief from responsibility and criticism. I have many warm friends, old and new. (*Male, age 69*)

Since retiring I am very happy because I continue to do part-time work for a wonderful family during the summer. I'm active and have some time for travel. (*Female, age 68*)

I've been happier because I can do things I want to do and do not feel pushed. (*Female, age 74*)

I retired at age 54 and was young enough to travel in the United States, Europe, South and Central America and enjoyed every minute. (*Male, age 64*)

So far retirement has been the least rewarding period of my life. I have no competition and very limited satisfaction. (*Male, age 65*)

Factors that Influence Adjustment

Forced versus voluntary retirement. Whether retirement is positive or negative, for any particular person, depends on many factors. One of the most important is whether retirement is voluntary and planned or involuntary and precipitate. Some individuals simply have nothing to say about the age when they will retire, and worse still, may be completely uncertain when the axe will fall. Some big businesses are already forcing executives to retire at 60, or even as early as 55. Not surprisingly, the suicide rate for men climbs sharply between the ages of 55 and 65, a dramatic symptom that many male retirees feel they have been junked (Sheehy, 1976). Another factor in how people feel about retirement, is how they feel about work. Only when work has held a central position in an individual's life do feelings about it cause stress at retirement time (Fillenbaum, 1971). Still, even those who care less about work may have difficulty readapting their routines.

Individual differences. Personality factors are also important in retirement. For example far-sighted and flexible persons often enjoy the challenge posed by their new role, and are practically certain to make a good adjustment (Bynum, 1972). People also differ in the way they organize their time, and how much organization means to them. Some of the elderly find it hard to structure their time. By contrast, younger and middle-aged persons' time is usually structured for them. Some older people become disturbed at finding the days slipping away aimlessly. Others enjoy unstructured time, and spend it in casual activities.

Advance planning. Also of significance are certain pre-retirement factors, including advance adjustment and planning it. Those who have the most trouble adjusting are those who always had difficulty adapting to change, or who are faced with radically different changes (Atchley, 1975). The ways of adapting to the common vicissitudes of life remain relatively constant once they are established (Neugarten, 1973). Those who feel good about themselves and the world continue to cope well throughout their lives. Those who disintegrate at critical times such as retirement or death of a spouse, are those who have been falling apart all along (Troll, 1975).

The situation. Especially important is the total overview of retirees' lives. For example, the elderly living in retirement communities have a higher morale than those who live in age-integrated communities (Seguin, 1973). Other factors which promise good adjustment to retirement include a rich, fulfilling family life, good health, and satisfying avocations. Leisure activities of the aging may be thought of as prolonging and enriching life for them and their families (Staley & Miller, 1972). In sum, retirement adjustment involves the ways in which particular types of individuals operate in complex environments.

A cultural phenomenon that John Lozier and Ronald Althouse of West Virginia University call "retirement to the porch," demonstrates the importance of situational factors. This phenomenon occurs only in older communities because newer houses have only vestigial porches, and leisure life takes place in the back yard or on the patio. In any case, in certain older communities many retired men spend a good deal of time sitting on the porch, often swapping stories with passersby. While these men are healthy and active they help others and provide for themselves, thus establishing a basis for reciprocity in later years. After their health begins to fail they retire to the porch, drawing upon "social credit" that they have built up over the years. If they are customarily on the porch, and are suddenly absent, others express concern.

Not all older persons would have so pleasant a time on the porch. Those who have just recently moved into the neighborhood have only weak social networks. Besides, they often live in trailers or in dwellings without porches. There are others who have done nothing to build up reciprocity, and they would hardly receive much attention simply by sitting on a porch. What is needed for a successful old age, concluded the researchers, are neighborhood systems whereby an individual can store up credit over a lifetime. This history of good deeds reinforces the obligations of younger persons to them. Otherwise individuals who are helped may feel robbed of their dignity because they realize that others consider what they do for them to be charity rather than their due.

On the other hand, current conditions make this suggestion some-what impractical in most cases. The idea of reciprocity nowadays can hardly be on an individual basis. Older persons may, for some reason, have to move to another community; or the population of the com-munity itself may change and those who owe something to them have moved on. The new ideal must be for younger people as a generation coming to recognize their collective responsibility to the older genera-tions ("Retirement," 1976).

Retirement Activities

Typical patterns. The retired individual has many possibilities for rec-reation including reading, gardening, watching television, attending sports events, visiting friends and relatives, taking walks, pursuing creative interests, or taking special courses. It is not easy to evaluate the way elderly people spend their leisure time. Some may consider lonely an old man who spends much time sitting in a park; however, he may have been a loner all along.

Life style derives from all such activities, and is determined by the way they are patterned. In general such preferences are stable, and be-come more sedentary with the years. In one study the elderly were found to spend less time in certain leisure activities as they grew older, and about the same time in others. In general they spent less time listening, drinking, dancing, attending movies, traveling, hunting, reading, and in physical exercise. However, from their middle to older years they showed stable patterns in entertaining friends, watching television, cul-tural consumption (for example, listening to music) and cultural produc-tion (such as painting and playing music). Participation in clubs and organizations peaks during the ages of 40 to 54, discussions of im-portant issues by age 65, and observing spectator sports, either in public places or on television, by 40 (Rosenzweig, 1972).

Some older persons lead exciting, ever-changing lives, but the ma-jority retrench a bit. To some extent it may represent almost an unconscious adaptation to diminishing internal resources. Some of them, at least, find that simply getting up in the morning, getting dressed, eating, shopping, resting a bit, perhaps playing cards, or visiting, and going to bed, exhausts their physical resources. Hence the concept of time as being empty or filled depends on individual needs, satisfactions, and capabilities (Cath, 1975). Even unusually healthy people may choose to slow down simply because it is a good way to live. For years they may have lived at a breakneck pace governed by inflexible routines. Now they can pause in their walks to enjoy the birds and flowers, or simply sit in a rocking chair on the porch, reflecting deeply on ideas they only considered superficially before.

While the elderly engage in about the same range of activities as younger people, rarely do these two age groups participate in them together. Ordinarily there is a rather firm segregation in leisure activity— either because of generational preferences or fear of embarrassment— which causes older people to avoid situations where they might perform poorly (Miller, 1965).

In later years most people have more unstructured time than their past experiences or interests have prepared them to use properly. Unless they are ready for it, they may be unable to use their later years in a satisfying or effective manner. As a result some individuals may participate only minimally, which is hardly experiencing true leisure, for leisure is not merely time free from job demands. Some individuals may react by participating in work-related activities, some in pure relaxation, and others prefer merely to rest.

Hendricks and Hendricks (1976) raise the question of whether leisure assumes a different meaning when it is not related to the work cycle. For about 40 years, work structured life style, even for those who did not find their work life rewarding. During that period leisure activities may become a sort of "anticipatory socialization"—a preparation for the future use of leisure time (p. 249).

Participation in leisure activities is modified by many social, demographic, and personality variables. In the middle years, especially, women and men do not have equal opportunities for leisure activities. As the number of middle-aged women returning to work grows, the woman's disadvantage becomes even more conspicuous since she does most of the work at home, too; however, evolving sex roles may counterbalance this.

Even in later years a work orientation may persist, but increasing numbers of older people are finding equally significant values in other areas of life (Hendricks & Hendricks, 1976). By contrast, in future years older people will have had many years of exposure to mass media and commercial entertainment, and their leisure activities will undoubtedly reflect this. Moreover improvements in health care will enable them to participate more actively and satisfyingly in recreational activities, although passive leisure pursuits may be just as satisfying.

Individual life styles and activities. Below a number of older people relate their special interests and forms of recreation.

My family, my friends, bridge and traveling. (*Female, age 74*)

Good friends, gardening, music, reading, and traveling. (*Female, age 71*)

Church activities, singing in three choirs, visiting my son in Orlando, and enjoying recreation planned by the family. (*Female, age 68*)

Hobbies, and I find great joy in children. (*Female, age 73*)

Cards and T.V. (*Male, age 71*)

Membership in church clubs, the garden club, the writers' club, reading, and all major sports. (*Male, age 69*)

I play golf, bowl, and garden. I also do woodworking and dabble into digital electronics. My wife sews for both of us and we travel when possible. (*Male, age 64*)

Bridge, chess, poker, traveling, music, reading, bull sessions, cinema, and theater. (*Male, age 67*)

Bridge, fishing, trips, and occasionally going out for dinner or to the movies. (*Male, age 65*)

Conversations with my wife and my friends, studying psychology and genetics, writing, gardening. (*Male, age 72*)

Most older people enjoy television but are selective about what they watch.

Except for the New York State Market reports and Ticker Tape, TV is of no importance whatsoever, although I like travelogs and science programs, and occasionally watch a detective story. (*Male, age 64*)

I watch it two hours a night; the news on the Public Broadcasting System, situation comedies, and detective stories.

It's not important enough to make a color set necessary. I watch news, sports, and two or three family programs like "Mash," "Bob Newhart," etc. (*Male, age 65*)

I watch three hours daily, musicals, comedies, sports, and stories. (*Female, age 68*)

I watch three-quarters of an hour: news, special events, and the educational station. (*Female, age 73*)

The time I spend watching television is half spent because I can't sit idly and look at it. Seldom does it get my complete attention. I like good plays or movies, old fashioned music, and about half of the specials. (*Female, age 74*)

I probably average two hours a day. I like sports (basketball, football, baseball, Olympics), music (Lawrence Welk), some law enforcement programs, special programs, drama, and movies. (*Male, age 69*)

Categories of Life Style

Five typical life styles. Lowenthal (1972) outlines five life styles that influence adjustment in retirement. (1) Some people follow the obsessively instrumental life style, are task oriented, and even in their leisure, remain compulsively active. (2) There are persons with an instrumental, other-directed—doing little on one's own initiative—style who gain much of their satisfaction on the job from associating with others. After they retire, they ordinarily must find other ways to satisfy themselves. (3) Some individuals never develop networks of close personal relationships or a receptive nurturant style (p. 321). Retirement does not affect them much. However, it may hurt those for whom work has been a source of great satisfaction, including teachers, social workers, and psychotherapists. (4) People with an autonomous style are creative and can initiate activities. The loss of their work roles may interfere little with their lives because they are capable of filling new ones. (5)

Older people are very conscious of keeping up with the times and resort to continuing education or discussion groups to overcome this fear.

Self-protective people wish to disengage; indeed they may have had little to do with others over the years.

Middle-class fathers' life styles. In a similar study of men and women in California by Maas and Kuypers (1974), 47 middle-class fathers' life styles were seen as falling into four major clusters: family centered (19), hobbyist (11), remotely sociable (9), and physically unwell disengaged (8). The family-centered fathers' life styles focused on marriage, parenting, and grandparenting. They saw their children and grandchildren often and derived great satisfaction from their marriage and family relationships. These fathers were also quite active in clubs and informal groups.

For the hobbyist fathers, leisure-time activities and interests formed the basis of their lives. They engaged in a good deal of recreational pursuits, chiefly alone, and had developed more interests than they had had in their 40s and 50s. Generally these individuals were not very sociable, saw their grandchildren infrequently, and spent little time with their friends or at clubs. They expressed satisfaction with their children but spent little time with them. Nor did they interact very much with other members of their family or friends. They attended church more often than the other fathers.

The third grouping, the nine remotely sociable fathers, were concerned with interpersonal associations and large social issues. They were not especially involved in parenting and marriage. Over the years they had grown more remote from their children and had played little with their grandchildren. Nor did they have significant communication with their marriage partners. They had become increasingly involved in the political arena. They did not believe in an after life, and few had made plans for death. They concentrated instead on current issues and social networks. Of this group 56% scored very high in life satisfaction.

The smallest group, the eight unwell disengaged fathers, had poor health and perceived themselves as somewhat withdrawn from the world. They felt they could not count on their wives to do much for them, and they did little for their wives. They felt their marriages were changing for the worse, and they had few recreational interests. Over the years they had done less visiting, maintained fewer close relationships with members of the family, had attached less meaning to friendship, and were less involved in politics, than the other fathers. They expressed considerable dissatisfaction in the areas of parenting, marriage, and health.

Collectively, the majority of the fathers seemed quite pleased with their work or retirement situation, depending on which they had chosen. Eighty percent of those still working were very satisfied, and 70% of those who had retired were pleased with their status, the critical factor being that they had had the freedom to choose whether to work fulltime, part-time, or not at all.

Middle-class mothers' life styles. Among the 95 retired women interviewed in this study, six life-style clusters were found: the husband-centered (23), the uncentered (21), the visiting mothers (16), the work-centered mothers (12), the disabled and disengaging mothers (12), and the group-centered (11). The largest group, the husband-centered wives, did most things together with the spouse, and did not often see other members of the family. Their living pattern centered around the home, and they were satisfied with their neighborhood. Although their life style was rather limited, they found it quite comfortable. The uncentered mothers, by contrast, had an essentially negative life style. They had few recreational interests, no involvement with work, were dissatisfied with their finances, and did not find that retirement had improved their lives. They lacked any satisfaction or involvement with clubs and formal groups. They visited others often, chiefly in somewhat formal situations, such as for a bridge game or to go to spectator events. They often went to see their children and grandchildren. However, because they were dissatisfied with their health and finances, they did not see themselves as able to do much for others. The third group, the visiting mothers, were highly involved as hostess, guest, parent, and group member. They had frequent social interaction; close, meaningful relationships; many recreational interests; and a strong spiritual life. Still they looked on today's society with considerable disapproval. The work-centered mothers worked either part- or fulltime; 9 of the 12 were no longer married, did considerable visiting, and were satisfied with their health. The fifth group, the disabled disengaging mothers, were very dissatisfied with everything, and especially with their health. They made frequent trips to the doctor and had few personal involvements, except with their husbands and doctors. They played few other roles, such as that of guest, hostess, or grandparent. They had the lowest life satisfaction score of all the mothers' life clusters. Finally, the group-centered mothers spent much time at clubs or other formal, structured groups such as their church, perhaps because they were making up for the time that employment had interfered with such activities. There was a certain remoteness and formality about them; and they were not primarily wives, housewives, and mothers. They enjoyed their grandchildren, but did not see them often.

Several findings from this study of California parents are especially important. There was a wide range of life styles, so we can see that it is clearly inappropriate to stereotype the aged as though they are a homogeneous group. The array of life styles in later years is practically limitless, except in cases of ill health or disability. This study also provides significant insight into aging, at least for the type of population involved. According to popular stereotypes, aging brings progressive decrements in psychological functioning and a more closed mode of life. By contrast, most of these parents were still healthy, both physically and psychologically. The few who had unfortunate personality dispositions, had also had them as young adults. The diversity of life styles involved seemed limited only by the number of people studied. Certainly a more broadly-based study would have suggested a still wider range of possible ways of life. Even within these life style patterns, individuals demonstrated unique methods of interaction, satisfaction, and involvement; and expressed highly varied preferences for where they wanted to live. Since these groups were economically privileged, they were in general satisfied with the places where they had retired. Obviously, planning for the aged cannot be done in only one way; so the widely varied interests and capacities of aging individuals should be coupled with an equally broad diversity of opportunities and living arrangements (Maas & Kuypers, 1974).

The most remarkable finding of the study was the similarity in life style and personality in young adulthood and old age. Nor did old age necessarily bring new psychological problems. Instead, problems that have existed already were at worst exacerbated. The fathers' way of life was steadier than the mothers', perhaps because the mothers' adult life course involves greater discontinuities. It is as if "the trajectory" for the fathers' life style was established very early in their adult lives. By contrast, the mothers' life style sometimes changed quite radically in marital, parental, occupational, and other contexts.

For old age to be understood, it must be viewed as an integral part of the total life cycle, rather than simply as the final period, to be set apart from the rest of life. Hence societal planning must be done within the context of adulthood as a whole. The evidence also suggests that wives and mothers should expand their interests beyond the family and home if their later years are not to be stressful. This does not mean that extrafamilial activities should take the place of familial ones. Instead they should supplement and enrich women's lives, and help keep family problems in perspective.

Policies regarding Retirement

Many suggestions for improving the prospects for successful retirement are implicit in the foregoing; let us consider two additional ones. First, because of the diversity of life styles, and the complex dynamics of individual personality, business, government and personal policies regarding retirement must be flexible (Soileau, 1972). The idea of a fixed retirement age is contrary to the public interest, and is certainly not based on any scientific data (Schaie, 1975). The current trend is toward raising the retirement age. The Swedes have moved it up to 67; and ultimately mandatory retirement may vanish altogether.

Enforced retirement because of age has several negative effects. It deprives older people of the right to earn extra money to buy some luxuries, and it robs the country of very real skills and talents (Manpower administration, 1972). Those for whom work is important, suffer the most from forced retirement. Besides, older people are at least as productive as younger people. They are also reliable, and have a low job turnover and low absenteeism. Many of them are quite creative, sometimes more than when they were younger, partly because their responsibilities have diminished (Butler, 1975c).

A second way to improve old age is to introduce into educational curricula the information, skills, and concepts that prepare people for retirement. The concept of career education has already been accepted, and is even considered desirable, beginning with kindergarten. It is just as essential that people be prepared throughout their schooling for the non-work years to follow.

PERSPECTIVE ON LIFE STYLES OF LATER YEARS

As we have noted, older people have diverse, more or less satisfactory, life styles. While certain of the less desirable features of their way of living may derive from physiological changes, others reflect society's failure to date to adapt properly to older peoples' needs.

A persistent theme in the literature on aging is that activities developed early in life can be maintained throughout life, but only within supportive and unthreatening environments (Pfeiffer & Davis, 1972). Ideally every individual should develop and maintain resources, interests, and activities that give satisfaction even in later years. After the age of 70, health problems may increasingly interfere with all but sedentary leisure activities, but even these may be creative and personally satisfying (Gordon, Gaitz, & Scott, 1977).

SUGGESTED READINGS

Bennett , R. G. Retirement: The emerging social pattern. In Bier, William C. (Ed.) *Aging: Its challenge to the individual and to society.* New York: Fordham University Press, 1974, 119–133. Retirement is discussed in terms of such aspects as attitudes toward, and reasons for, adjustment to retirement.

Gubrium, J. F. (Ed.) *Time, roles and self in old age.* New York: Human Sciences Press, 1976. Articles by a number of authorities deal with such theoretical issues as the chronology of life, disengagement theory, role consistency, the single aged, and retirement roles.

Heath, D. H. Adolescent and adult predictors of vocational adaptation. *Journal of Vocational Behavior*, 1976, *9* (1), 1–19. A typology of work satisfaction and attitudes, applied to data obtained from 1922 males in 1964, and again in 1966 and again in 1974, suggests that certain types are more susceptible to adverse consequences of cycle change (e.g. work to retirement) than others.

Lowenthal, M. F. & Robinson, B. Social networks and isolation. In Binstock, Robert H. & Shanas, Ethel (Eds.) *Handbook of aging and the social sciences.* New York: Van Nostrand Reinhold Co., 1976, 432–456. Social relationships of the elderly are analyzed according to dyadic and multiple person networks (family, friendship, work and leisure) and their consequences in terms of involvement or isolation.

Masse, B. L., Scheiber, S., Lovely, M. L., Schwartz, H. A., & Bragman, R. The experience of retirement, pp. 167–183 in William C. Bier (Ed.) *Aging: Its challenge to the individual and society.* New York: Fordham University Press, 1974. Several individuals—a priest, a nun, a businessman, an executive, and a religious educator—describe their personal experiences with retirement.

Morgan, L. A. The re-examination of widowhood and morale. *Journal of Gerontology*, November 1976, *31* (6), 687–695. The effect of married status on morale relative to several variables (health, income, age, family interaction and employment) was determined for a population of 232 widowed and 363 married women aged 45 to 74. Factors associated with higher morale included being married rather than widowed, having frequent family interaction, and having good health.

Nahemow, L. & Lawton, M. P. Similarity and propinquity in friendship formation. *Journal of Personality and Social Psychology*, 1975, *32* (2), 205–213. In a sociometric study of the friendship network among 270 residents in a city housing project which includes many elderly tenants, issues of propinquity (nearness) of residence and similarities in age, sex, and race between chooser and chosen were analyzed according to a theory of social space.

Peppers, L. G. Patterns of leisure and adjustment to retirement. *Gerontologist*, 1976, *16* (5), 441–446. An analysis was made of patterns of activities of 206 retired men (median age 68.8), most of whom had been either owners, partners, or managers in small businesses or farm ventures, or lower-level government officials.

Robertson, J. F. Significance of grandparents: Perceptions of young adult grandchildren. *Gerontologist*, 1976, *16* (2), 137–140. The significance of grandparenthood is examined in terms of responses obtained from 86 18- to 26-year-old grandchildren. In general the grandchildren perceive their grandparents as having real significance and as having responsibilities toward them.

Social roles and self concepts. Chapter 6 in Erdman Palmore (Ed.) *Normal aging II.* Durham: Duke University Press, 1974. The several articles in this chapter concern the social-psychological aspects of aging and relationships between self concepts, social roles, and life satisfaction.

Sussman, M. B. The family life of old people. In Binstock, Robert H. & Shanas, Ethel (Eds.) *Handbook of aging and the social sciences.* New York: Van Nostrand Reinhold Co., 1976, 218–243. After defining and analyzing various family and kin networks in both historic and current perspective, the author considers how they impinge on the quality of life for older persons.

Thomae, H. (Ed.) *Contributions to human development: III. Findings from the Bonn longitudinal study of aging.* Basel, Switzerland: S. Karger, 1976. Findings from a 1965-to-1973 longitudinal study of aging in 220 adults born between 1890 and 1895, focus on changes in cognitive function, psychomotor performance, personality, social roles, and leisure behavior, as well as on patterns of successful aging.

Treas, J. & Vanhilst, A. Marriage and remarriage rates among older Americans. *Gerontologist,* 1976, *16* (2), 132–136. There has apparently been no great increase in either first marriages or remarriages among older Americans in recent years. Those older Americans most likely to marry include men, the divorced, the young-old (close to 60 years of age) and those living in western and southern states.

13 CHAPTER

Problems of Later Years

OLD AGE IN AN AGE-GRADED SOCIETY

Later Years in the U.S.

The lowest-status age stage. In terms of developmental stage theory, old age is distinctive in several ways. Unlike other age stages it has a clear-cut and identifiable beginning, age 65, at least as far as working life is concerned; many people retire and begin to collect social security (Hareven, 1976). From this time on, older peoples' social value declines sharply. As Butler (1975c) aptly states it: "In America childhood is romanticized, youth is idolized, middle age does the work, wields the power and pays the bills, and old age, its days empty of purpose, gets little or nothing for what it has already done" (p. xii). Nor can people at this stage look forward to things to come; for this age stage is the only one from which there is no exit except death.

> The general tragedy of old age in America is that we have shaped a society which is extremely harsh to live in when one is old. The tragedy of old age is not the fact that each of us must grow old and die, but that the process of doing so has been made unnecessarily and at times excruciatingly painful, humiliating, debilitating and isolating through insensitivity, ignorance and poverty (Butler, 1975c, p. 3).

Ageism

Definition. The problems associated with later years are not so much inherent in aging itself as the result of ageism, the process of systematically stereotyping and discriminating against people simply because they are old. As we know, older people are often viewed as inflexible in thought and manner, senile, and old-fashioned in their skills and morality. Of course ageism is not confined to the elderly. Young people may not trust anyone over 30, and those over 30 may not trust those younger than they (Butler, 1977b). Nevertheless the term is most often used to describe negative attitudes toward the elderly.

Expressions of ageism in this sense cover a broad range of phenomena, including myths and stereotypes, "outright disdain and dislike, or simply subtle avoidance of contact; discriminatory practices in housing, employment and services of all kinds; epithets, cartoons and jokes"

(Butler, 1975a, p. 12). Another instance of ageism is the unfortunate attitude of many health practitioners. In general such persons give lower priority to the elderly than to younger groups. Moreover few young people indicate any real enthusiasm about pursuing careers in geriatric medicine, geriatric social welfare, or other services for the elderly.

Older people must also cope with numerous myths and inaccurate stereotypes which are hardly calculated to improve their self-concepts or feelings of security. They are portrayed as slow-moving, poor learners, and unchangingly conservative. They are also perceived as looking backward rather than forward, involved in a second childhood, increasingly egocentric, and as something of a caricature of their earlier personality. In addition, it is believed that they become irritable, cantankerous, shallow, and over-talkative; and that their minds wander aimlessly as they forever reminisce. They are pictured as often being sick, restricted in movement, and without interest in or capacity for sex, for their bodies have shrunk and their minds do not function the way they did. Thus "feeble, uninteresting, [the old person] awaits his death, a burden to society, to his family and to himself" (Butler, 1975a, p. 7). The truth is that older people vary more in personality than any other age group, and become increasingly diverse with later years, so that there are very young 80-year-olds as well as old ones.

Stereotypes of the elderly take root when we are very young. In one study (Hickey, Hickey, & Kalish, 1968, p. 224) over 200 third-graders were asked to write about an old person. The most common characteristic ascribed such a person was "kind," but oddly enough, the second most common rating was "mean." Certain of their comments follow:

> My sister and I like to walk down to the corner with old Mr. Smith, but we have to walk slower when we are with him.
>
> They always ask you to talk louder.
>
> Old people usually die, or lose a leg or an arm.
>
> Old people are mean, and they don't let you walk on their lawn.
>
> Old people are funny.

As people grow older, their view of the elderly becomes progressively more unpleasant, although recent articles and television programs are portraying them in a more positive way. What effect such presentations will have, remains to be seen.

Factors that produce ageism. A major factor contributing to ageism is our nation's youth cult, with its consequent devaluation of age. While older persons evaluate later years more positively than younger ones do, being old is always rated as less desirable than being young. In a study of young, middle-aged, and older adults (Kalish & Reynolds, 1976), all age groups said that the death of a 70-year-old was less deplorable than that of younger or middle-aged persons. A second factor in producing negative attitudes toward the elderly is their relative isolation. These developments include shifts in proportions of age groups due to a rising reduction of deaths in infancy and early years, the decline in fertility and increasing life expectancy, the change from a rural to an industrial economy, and the corresponding decrease in productive roles of older people, as well as the denigration of later years (Hareven, 1976).

Unfortunate effects. The effects of ageism are often subtle, but always damaging. Like all prejudices, it affects older persons' views of themselves. Thus they tend to adopt the very stereotypes that serve them so poorly; in so doing they reinforce them. Meantime younger people try to avoid old people, who remind them that their day, too, will come. Ageism is simply a defense mechanism which makes it easier to ignore the plight of older people. By ignoring them we can, at least for a time, avoid reminders of the reality of our own future aging and death. In societies that venerate the elderly there is no need to shunt the aged aside.

PROBLEMS WITH INTERPERSONAL RELATIONSHIPS

Conflict between Generations

Certain of the elderly's interpersonal problems reflect generational friction. This conflict derives from several major factors, one of which is the increasing burden older people impose on younger ones. By the year 2000 the number of individuals over age 65 will have grown by 50%, even if there is no change in current life expectancy (Eisenberg, 1977). This dramatically growing minority will place still heavier burdens on societal and support systems. Meantime medical advances themselves will increase the number of those chronically ill by decreasing the incidence of mortality from acute illnesses (Eisenberg, 1977).

The middle-aged, especially, will find this burden hard to bear. It is their own parents who are the aged, and for whom they feel a deeply personal responsibility. Meantime they must also care for the young, both individually and collectively. Often such responsibilities "trap them in their careers or life styles until the children grow up or their parents die" (Butler, 1975c, p. 15). Hence the middle-aged may become somewhat ambivalent toward both the young and old, because both groups serve as reminders of their own fading youth. Moreover the responsibilities of the middle-aged will increase in the future as more of their parents and grandparents live longer.

The old, in self-defense, adopt certain prejudices against the young. Perhaps they are somewhat jealous of the younger generation's greater vigor, sexual prowess, and physical attractiveness. They may also be anxious regarding the dramatic changes they perceive in the world about them, for which they may condemn the younger generation. They may be resentful that only a brief time is left to them, and envy those who still have most of their lives left (Butler, 1975c). The elderly strike back in the only ways available to relatively powerless persons: "They complain, nag, criticize, become irritable and petulant, and alternate between assertions of independence and obvious manipulations to permit dependence" (Kalish, 1975, pp. 74–75). Still, these people are in the minority, for astonishingly enough, many of the elderly, even the very poor, have a healthy morale and high life satisfaction.

Age segregation. Some authorities believe that greater association between the generations would facilitate communication and reduce conflict. In their Report to the President of the Panel on Youth, James S. Coleman (1973) and his colleagues strongly recommended ending age segregation. While they were discussing the integration of youth into society, the principle is the same. Butler (1977b) specifically opposes the isolation of older people, particularly in terms of housing and activities. He believes in a certain mixing of age groups, and that children can only understand the realities of aging by associating with the elderly.

On the other hand, some degree of age segregation may be both natural and healthy. There is a tendency for people to be attached to those similar to themselves. Often those older people who live in retirement villages with others their own age are happier than those who live in mixed-age groups. They do not have to tolerate ever-present ageism, and their friends and neighbors are experiencing the same problems they are.

Family Problems

Older people, especially those whose spouses have died, often receive help from their adult children, although they get less than their counterparts of generations past. For reasons we discussed in the last chapter—greater longevity, and the tendency of younger people to focus on themselves—aging individuals try to maintain themselves without seeking help. No longer, as in colonial times, do they take their children's assistance for granted (Kalish, 1975).

Hence while relationships with kin persist, fewer old people reside with them. In a study of persons aged 65 to 85 who resided in communities ranging from rural towns to large cities, 82% lived alone and the remainder were with a member of the family. The majority were extensively involved with family, neighbors, and friends. Over half saw their children at least once a week and had five or more neighbors whom they visited; only 5% did not know their neighbors.

Arling's (1976b) research suggests that contact with adult children does not necessarily produce greater life satisfaction. While parents and children are concerned about each other, they may be unable to share experiences or empathize with each other. Adult children have their own household affairs and jobs to attend to, while aging parents may be restricted by health and financial considerations. Usually aging parents, after a lifetime of increasing autonomy, must somewhat abruptly adapt to diminishing self-sufficiency. This reduced autonomy is hard in a society in which individuality and self-efficiency are stressed.

When older parents live in a home, roles are reversed as parents become dependent on their children. Older persons' autonomy can only be maintained by providing them with financial assistance, helping them to cope with their physical disabilities, and teaching young people to respect the elderly as individuals who have their own special qualities.

Marriage Problems

Marriage in later years. One of the most difficult problems of the widowed in later years is finding another mate. Some older people do marry, occasionally for the first time, and undoubtedly more would, given the opportunity. Indeed, the older that singles of either sex become, the less their chances of marriage or remarriage. Moreover the chances grow progressively slimmer each year. A woman between 65 and 69 is twice as likely to marry as one between the ages of 70 and 74.

The sexual double standard is especially apparent, for older men are six times more likely to marry than older women. For one thing, society portrays women as sexually unattractive at an earlier age than men, and accepts the marriage of younger women to older men. In addition, there are three single women for every single man over 65. In the case of the widowed of either sex, heirs. children, and even the memory of the departed spouse may interfere with remarriage.

Old people in the south and west remarry twice as often as those in the northeast and north central states. In those parts of the country, retirement communities facilitate finding a mate, especially for those who are relatively healthy and well-to-do. Those who do marry are quite romantic; they favor religious ceremonies and June weddings.

Sex relationships. These couples, as well as those who live together without being married, may be confused or misled by recent counseling. Older couples have been urged to try for "a second honeymoon" marriage, and to continue to have a sex life. However the new norms may be as unhealthy as the old ones, if they encourage older couples to believe that they can maintain youthful sexual patterns throughout life —a physiological impossibility. In this sense the recent new sexual norms are as unfair to the aging as the more traditional norms, because they suggest that "youthful sex is the only good sex" (Cleveland, 1976, p. 236). The most realistic and healthy goal, suggests Cleveland, is "to gain intimacy, joy, and fulfillment through a broad spectrum of sensual sexual interactions" (p. 236). This ideal is constructed on the basis of the physiological fact that people continue to be capable of sexual response, but it also acknowledges that physiological changes do occur.

Social Relationships

Significance. With support from adult children weakening, friends nowadays assume correspondingly greater importance. Friendship constitutes a vital source of a stable self-image and of emotional support, as well as being a way to integrate oneself into the larger society (Hess, 1972). Similarly Lowenthal and Haven (1968) reported that old people who consistently have at least one close relationship, can cope with the severe emotional losses inherent in aging that may prove devastating to more friendless, isolated persons.

Older people naturally feel more comfortable with those their own age; they correctly feel somewhat unwanted in groups of younger people. They also get along better with persons who have shared the same period of early socialization and who have lived through the same historical times. They "share recollections of the same ball players, movie actors, automobiles, and politicians; they remember dancing the same dances, using the same slang, fighting in the same wars, wearing the same clothing styles" (Kalish, 1975, p. 87).

Isolation. As the years pass, such rewarding relationships may diminish as various forms of isolation increase. Aging people feel cut off from their social and material environment, because their senses are failing. They also sense that they have been placed out of the way on the shelf, just because they are old. In addition, they are cut off because they are no longer in the work world. Becoming unable to drive is especially damaging, since almost any satisfying life style involves much going and coming.

Also, as individuals get older they have less control over their social relationships, including the ability to maintain contact with friends. Their adult children may indiscriminately move them from here to there for practical reasons. Perhaps they may be relocated to new neighborhoods because of urban renewal; or sometimes they may be uprooted from their own homes because they are no longer able to take care of themselves. It is difficult to make friends in their new environment, partly because they have less mobility. In addition new neighbors and friends rarely provide the same feelings of security as old ones (Kalish, 1975).

Death produces an especially painful form of isolation as friends or family, especially a spouse, die. While marriage has become an integral part of the social structure, society has done little to afford adequate solutions to fill the gap when marital partners are no longer available. Consequently the surviving spouse not only suffers grief due to loss, but a disorganization of life style produced by the spouse's absence. As one heartbroken man confessed after his wife of 47 years had died: "I hardly know how much of my feeling of devastation derives simply from losing my wife and how much is sheer selfishness, not having her wait on me in the many little ways that I had come to take for granted." The death of a spouse produces loss of a sexual relationship, and of a significant other with whom to share work and leisure as well as loneliness (Parkes, 1972).

PROBLEMS OF PERSONAL COPING, HEALTH, AND ADJUSTMENT

Coping Problems

Age-related limitations. Another reason for older persons' growing isolation is their failing sensory, motor, and sometimes mental capacities. Over ten times as many older persons as younger ones are unable to read ordinary newsprint; and of the 500,000 legally blind persons in this country, about half are over 65 (White House Conference on Aging, 1972). Hearing impairments are even more common than visual problems; they involve 13% of those 65 to 74, and 26% over the age of 75 (Riley, Foner, et al., 1968). Visual deficiencies arise either from disease or naturally occurring "deteriorative processes," and to some extent from accidents, while hearing losses more often involve such environmental variables as noise pollution (Kalish, 1975).

Problems relating to time, space, and movement. Other coping problems can be broad, including time, movement, and space. Readaption to problems of space grows harder as peoples' movements become increasingly hampered by such difficulties as arthritis, general weakness, and failing senses. The elderly may have trouble driving because of failing sight or other problems, while public transportation may be expensive and inconvenient (Kalish, 1975). While only a small fraction of automobile accidents involve elderly drivers, their accident rate is high indeed if it is based on the number of miles they drive. In fact, accident rates of persons from 70 to 79 are about equal to that of teenagers, while for drivers 80 and older, it is even higher (Riley, Froner, et al., 1968). Older drivers' errors most typically include failing to yield the right of way, turning improperly, and running red lights. Rarely do their accidents result from speeding.

Adaptation with regard to time can also be a problem, for "on the one hand, time is running out; on the other hand, time may pass slowly, for available activities and relationships perhaps are not so stimulating or challenging or enjoyable as they once were" (Kalish, 1975, p. 91). Or an older person may simply be unable to engage in activities that were absorbing in earlier years. A former tennis buff is no longer able to run; the avid reader may lack the vision for sustained reading; the hearing-impaired individual who once spent much time in social groups may now avoid them because it is difficult to communicate with them.

Older persons' decreased capacities have far-reaching ramifications. Those who are handicapped are less likely either to engage in physical activities that they formerly enjoyed, or to increase their associations with others. Individuals suffering from impaired hearing or arthritic conditions may find walking, or even dressing, difficult. Although older people may adapt pretty well to these problems, and even find compensations for their loss, they may prove ego-threatening, partly because this society attaches great importance to continuing personal growth and physical integrity. Besides, the gradual realization that one can no longer expect to improve in certain ways can be quite devastating, particularly because it often coincides in time with other losses, including the death of friends and the realization that there will be no further job promotions.

Utilization of potential. Despite their handicaps, older people possess important potential both for personal growth and contributions to society, which has been too long ignored. As early as 1874, psychologist George Beard was researching the limitations of age, and reported that 70% of the world's creative works are completed by age 45, and 80%

by age 50. Within this time period he named ages 30 to 45 as life's most creative and productive years (Hareven, 1976).

However, older people need not be unproductive—indeed we can give dramatic examples of highly productive older people. Among creative octogenarians are Georgia O'Keefe, who continues to paint; and Pope John XXIII, who revitalized his church. Examples of creative septuagenarians are Duke Ellington, who continued to compose and had a full concert schedule until his recent death; and Golda Meir, who served as Israel's prime minister. Some older people express their creativity for the first time in their late years, when they finally have enough leisure time to develop their talents. When productive incapacity does exist, it ordinarily derives from various losses, diseases, or circumstances rather than any "aging process" (Butler, 1975c).

In general men's coping capacities fail more rapidly than women's. In the late 1950s the percentage of males over 65 who were unable to perform common retirement activities, such as gardening, traveling, was twice that of females; and in the 1970s the gap had widened so that four times as many men were seriously limited in their activities. This is especially peculiar because the population of females over age 65 is greater than the population of older males (Verbrugge, 1976). On the other hand, the proportion of such persons to all the aging is miniscule. Since society has failed to provide outlets for self-actualization among the elderly, those individuals who are psychologically simplistic appear best able to adapt. Those who are most able, and are even in quite good or moderately good health, often become preoccupied with health problems simply because they lack satisfactory outlets for their abilities.

Attempting to take first-time measures in later years will not work. It is necessary instead to assume "a life-course orientation in all of our social educational and economic institutions" so that as people approach their later years they will be prepared to continue developing their potential. Such a perspective would be strengthened by life-span oriented education. As Albert Bandura, former president of the American Psychological Association, said: "Life-long learning may eventually take precedence over degree-seeking as our population undergoes still further changes" (1974, p. 2).

Physical Health Problems

Type and incidence of physical disorders. In order of importance, the chief causes of limited activities in later years are heart condition, arthritis and rheumatism, orthopedic impairment, and mental and nervous conditions. Every year approximately 15% of 45- to 65-year-olds are hospitalized, compared with 25% of those over 65 (USDHEW, 1971).

Certain observations may help to place these figures in perspective. For one thing, as we have stated before, some systems and organs of the body begin to fail earlier than others (Kalish, 1975), so that we cannot measure decline by age alone. For another thing, older people, as opposed to younger ones, suffer more from chronic disease than from acute illness. Often the disabilities cannot be expected to improve, so older people must somehow adjust to them. On the other hand, older people who use whatever strength they have to remain physically active, make the best of the physical facilities they do have.

Improving physical health. Attempts to improve the health of older persons must take place on both the individual and professional level. Aging people should be educated about what constitutes good health care, including whatever modifications are required by aging. Changes in the body over the life span necessitate corresponding psychological adaptations, or maladjustments will result. For example, an older man who has always perceived himself as the epitome of strength and health may tax himself unduly, and precipitate a heart attack.

Professionals must keep abreast of the latest developments, particularly in the area of adult disease. A panel of the National Cancer Institute has warned that too many women under 50 are undergoing X-ray examinations for breast cancer in spite of the possibility that the risks of these X-rays may outweigh the benefits. It has been recommended that routine X-raying of the breasts (mammagraphy) be discontinued in women under 50 who are not in high risk categories, because it is feared that X-rays may cause cancer ("Women under 50," 1977).

Where cancer and other serious diseases are concerned, there also remains much to be done on the psychological level. Patients not only must cope with their own fears of the disease, but with other peoples' attitudes as well. It may be that the patients' own revulsion toward the disease is reflected and magnified by those close to them, which increases their own difficulties in adjusting to it. Although the chances of cancer being cured are about 50%, people view it as a killer, and the person who contracts it "as someone scheduled to be executed." Friends and relatives even experience the loss before it occurs, and sometimes seem to withdraw from the patient before he or she dies. Since everyone is affected by the major diseases of adulthood, either as a patient, or as a friend or relative of one, it would seem important to educate the public about them. Nevertheless the social and psychological problems associated with cancer and other major diseases have been neglected (Severo, 1977).

Perspective on physical health. Both professionals and laymen should modify their concepts of physical aging, for much of what we view as aging nowadays is actually caused by illness and disease rather than by physical aging. This generalization relates to mental, physical, and emotional conditions among older persons. Eventually the chief diseases of later life will become preventable, or at least treatable. Already acute brain syndromes and the mental depression experienced by old people, are "treatable and reversible." We have learned that physical appearance will deteriorate much less if people avoid excessive exposure to the sun and cigarette smoking, because both cause skin wrinkles. Eventually even such physical changes as loss or graying of hair may become controllable. Older persons' physical health is already much better than is generally known. Over 81% of those over 65 are completely ambulatory and move about independently (Butler, 1975c).

Physical self-image. One problem of aging is adapting to a revised physical self-image. Sometimes older people make such statements as, "When I look into the mirror, I see the face of an old person. It isn't me—I have the spirit of a young person" or, "I am a prisoner of my body. It's not really me with arthritis, with sagging breasts and loose skin—it's someone else" (Kalish, 1975, p. 58). On the other hand, such attitudes are not universal. An individual's physical self-concept does not relate to age per se, but rather reflects particular life circumstances (Plutchik, Weiner, & Conte, 1971).

Individual testimony. Many old people describe their health as good, and then go on to name their various ailments. They are generally quite aware of the importance of health, and take various precautions to stay well.

> I have good health and a good physician who takes care of my health problems. (*Female, age 83*)

> I'm healthy. I visit the doctor, get rest and exercise, and eat properly. (*Female, age 68*)

> My health is good. I take medication for high blood pressure, but only when pain is present. (*Female, age 73*)

> I am not able to do what I want to do. The mind and heart are willing but the flesh is weak. I'm not complaining—just thankful I can do as much as I can. (*Female, age 73*)

> Physically I can't do some of the things I could when I was fifty. I have a problem with glaucoma that requires regular treatment and for this reason it is a nuisance, but I don't worry about it. (*Male, age 72*)

I've always had poor health, but somewhat better as I've grown older. I've had little strength or extra reserve, but have used what energies I have for volunteer community work. (*Female, age 70*)

I take aspirin for sinus and mild arthritis. Occasionally something for sinus relief and sleep. A little nitroglycerine occasionally (it's prescribed) for heart and muscle relaxation. (*Male, age 69*)

Nutrition. Despite their growing concerns about health, older people often eat poorly and unwisely. When the body is aging, it needs whatever support it can get. For example, symptoms which suggest a serious organic change in the brain sometimes result from nutritional deficiency, and pathological symptoms disappear as proper diet is provided. Yet the diets of the aging poor are often not adequate for maintaining mental and physical health; and even those who are more affluent may experience nutritional deficiencies because they have faulty eating habits.

A broad range of factors contribute to poor nutrition in the elderly. For one thing, their decreased mobility can make it difficult to prepare a meal. They may have to shop by telephone and are thus unable to be selective. Poor hearing and consequent isolation at the table may also contribute to reduced appetite. Sometimes they eat little—or too much— because they are lonely or depressed. When older people join community groups, make friends, or do volunteer work, they often have an easier time eating (Marble & Patterson, 1975).

Nutritional help for older individuals and groups may assume various forms. People may be encouraged to join nutrition classes, or they may be counseled individually, so that all an individual's qualities—including his or her likes and dislikes, as well as the nutritional quality of the food that he eats—are taken into consideration. For those who cannot cook for themselves, meals that are not only nutritious, but also appealing, should be provided.

Alcohol, the fourth leading killer in the United States (after liver diseases, highway and other accidents, and crime), poses significant problems for older people. For one thing, more people with histories of alcoholism survive into later years than in the past because there are more effective treatments for it, including antibiotics and proper nutrition. Some people also become alcoholics for the first time in old age because they frequently experience grief and loneliness. Sometimes alcohol is too casually prescribed for older people to help them sleep or to improve their appetite. Alcohol, in turn, "blocks reaction time, impairs coordination and fuzzes mental abilities, especially memory. Serious falls and misjudgments can result" (Butler, 1975c, p. 363). In addition, alcoholism and its accompanying malnutrition often account for memory impairments in old age which may be wrongly attributed to a hardening of the arteries. On the other hand, older people who have long been moderate drinkers, may benefit from cocktails, especially when they are shared with friends. Indeed they seem to profit somewhat both physically and emotionally from what can be pleasant experiences.

Major Mental Health Problems

Definition and incidence. All the problems already discussed, and more, contribute to the disproportionate number of older persons with major mental health problems. About 10% of the population of the United States is 65 or older, while over 30% of the patients in mental hospitals are in that age range (Simon, 1971). However, such estimates are tentative because there are many older people who are mentally ill and are cared for by their families. Furthermore, many who are institutionalized as mentally ill are actually suffering from some physical ailment, perhaps extreme malnutrition, which only makes them appear to be mentally ill. For another thing, many of the quite disturbed elderly are in nursing homes instead of mental institutions. More older women than men are institutionalized, partly because of the stresses of widowhood and the fact that older women ordinarily do not have a spouse able to take care of them. By contrast, older men more often have younger wives who are caring for them.

The mental disorders of later years fall in two main categories: those that are organic, and those that are related to individual personality and experience (Kalish, 1975). Many older people grow senile and incompetent for social reasons rather than because of factors inherent in aging. Nevertheless some do have a brain disease, with its accompanying personality change, memory loss, and depression. The organic disorders, also termed organic brain syndromes, may either be chronic or reversible. Reversible brain syndromes can frequently be treated. By contrast, chronic brain syndromes, which derive from permanent damage to the brain, as in senile brain disease or cerebral arteriosclerosis, may be treated symptomatically but never reversed. Functional disorders include various kinds of neuroses, psychotic disorders, personality disorders, and psychophysiological disorders.

Acute reversible brain syndromes represent "major psychiatric medical emergencies," and afflict over half the geriatric patients admitted for mental illness. If properly treated, a significant proportion of such persons improve sufficiently to return to society. Nevertheless many mentally confused older people are returned home untreated, even when they are suffering from "reversible confusional states," which are often caused by anemia, alcohol, malnutrition, or undiagnosed physical ailments such as infections, congestive heart failure, and even fecal impaction. In other cases such conditions may be induced by drugs, perhaps by tranquilizers prescribed by doctors.

Attitudes and therapy. Immediate diagnosis and treatment of emotional and mental disorders is critical, especially with regard to reversible brain disorders. Otherwise these conditions may become chronic and irreversible, though they may be subject to some improvement. Older people have fewer emotional reserves and coping skills than younger ones, and may require prompt assistance so they will not be overwhelmed with anxiety.

Oberleder (1969) recommends a positive approach to the problem of senility. Emotional breakdowns attributed to senility are similar to breakdowns at any age. If the "normal props" of living were restored to elderly people senility might very well disappear. We have been misled by presumably very limited explanations of senility so that we ascribe it to such conditions as chronic brain syndrome and arteriosclerosis of the brain. We are reminded that millions of neurons are lost every day from the brain cells, producing irreversible changes in later years. Such ideas have become so ingrained that even when startling research reveals no relationship between actual brain damage and function among older people, we simply ignore such results. Instead, we should pay more attention to the trauma involved in apparently ordinary situations. For example, older people who lose their teeth and must eat without dentures may experience real trauma, so that it brings on senility almost "overnight." "Instant senility" may also be brought on when one is advised to wear a hearing aid. Such "harbingers of old age" can produce severe breakdown in some persons, especially those who have always prided themselves on being healthy and intact. In short, the ideal is that senility be treated as a curable mental disorder, that positive attitudes and therapeutic programs be developed, and that we abandon the fatalistic concept of irreversible changes in the brain.

Financial Problems

Financial problems are a major cause of stress in later years. Far more older than younger people have serious financial problems. Family heads over 65 receive slightly over half the income of younger ones, and for older persons not living with their families the proportion is only 48% (Kalish, 1975). Over a third of older persons have difficulty paying for their housing, and over half do not always have enough money to pay their expenses (Institute for Interdisciplinary Studies, 1971). When asked what their greatest needs are, older people most often mention money for goods and services. In addition, the diminishing of financial resources occurs as other resources decrease too. Younger people might walk in order to save the cost of transportation, but older ones may have trouble walking. Younger persons can borrow money against future prospects, but older ones can rarely look forward to an increase in their future income. Younger individuals can often increase their income by moonlighting, while older ones have difficulty obtaining any work at all. They may be arbitrarily retired, and experience bias when they attempt to get jobs. Moreover no job training programs are concerned with the elderly, so they have little chance to learn new skills (Butler, 1975b). They may not be physically able to work, or they may be compelled to work (if they find any) at a marginal job with very low pay. If they earn too much money, they must sacrifice half their social security benefits, even though an equivalent income from private pensions or other assets involves no such penalty. Social security benefits for those who worked for a lifetime at low wages, often with periods of unemployment, are below the poverty line, and these persons are the least likely to have any additional income. Many older people are not covered by private pensions, and only a fraction of those who are, will ever collect. For most people, the margin is narrow between income and expenses over the working years (Fitzpatrick, 1975). To sum up: "Improving the economic status of the aged is not a cure-all for physical pain, bereavement, loneliness, or disengagement—yet a little money for an occasional treat might lessen these burdens of old age" (p. 131). Yet many older Americans have to give up even modest pleasures because they lack funds.

Worry over financial problems in later years is a function of both income and, to some extent, the personality of the individual involved. Often such worries are quite realistic, as illustrated in the following testimony and are produced by continuing inflation rather than the failure to lay up a nest egg.

> After I made the decision that I could get along without the million-dollar yacht that attracted me at age 18 I have had no overwhelming financial problems. We have coped by matching plans with incomes. (*Male, age 72*)

> I do have serious financial problems and cope by careful budgeting. (*Male, age 71*)

> I have no problems because I budget. (*Female, age 82*)

ENVIRONMENTAL AND SOCIAL PROBLEMS

The Environment

A commonly ignored or overlooked problem of older people is that imposed by an environment largely planned by and for younger persons. They can easily become disheartened by an endless succession of frustrations and obstacles that would be no problem to younger persons: high bus steps, the need to cross wide, busy streets to catch a bus, fast-changing traffic lights, high curbs, and inadequate building labels (Birren, 1977). There are multiple examples of such problems.

Older persons also share the same environmental problems of younger ones, and often feel their impact more keenly. They must endure the pollution, the crowding, and the excess noise so common today. Often they live in neighborhoods where even "good" children treat them with little respect, make too much noise, and race their bikes about in such a way as to unnerve them.

Crime

Violent crime. Another environmental hazard is crime, which more often victimizes older than younger persons. Not just the old, but the middle-aged, are quite vulnerable to violent crime, especially robbery. As a result many of the elderly become so anxious that they practically become prisoners within their own homes. In addition, many thousands of social security checks each year are stolen, usually from mail boxes. People are subject to various kinds of "terrorism," especially in lower income areas. Stones may be thrown through their windows, clothes stolen from the wash lines, and their gardens trampled. Mysterious phone calls and letters also upset them (Butler, 1975c). Often after being criminally assaulted, older people never quite recover. Various factors including loss of hearing, poor vision, slower motor and mental responses, and poorer physical coordination enhance older persons' vulnerability to crime. Problems of isolation are hard enough to cope with anyway because people are already confronted with widowhood, the death of friends, poverty, mandatory retirement, transportation problems, and physical impairments. When the actual fear of crime is added to these other factors, it causes many older people to remain locked in their homes day and night.

Crimes of violence against the elderly are committed by all sorts of people, including those in need of drugs, armed robbers, gangs, and muggers, most of them youthful. Much of this crime is never reported because the elderly fear retaliation, or they may fear the expense of hiring a lawyer and taking the case to court. Even among crimes reported by persons of all ages, only 12% culminate in arrest, 6% in convictions, and 1% in imprisonment—figures that hardly constitute a deterrent to crime. When older people resist assault, their chances of death and injury increase. Ten percent of all robbery victims are killed, and another 10% are seriously injured.

Inner-city crime. A large fraction of crime against the elderly is in the inner cities, although just recently crime has also risen sharply in the suburbs. Senator Harrison Williams of New Jersey reports that "elderly tenants in private and public housing in many of our big cities are the most vulnerable victims of theft, violence, rowdyism, and outright terrorism" (Butler, 1975c, p. 302).

Older people become "trapped" in high-crime urban centers because of their low incomes and unwillingness to move out of a neighborhood they have lived in for years, even though it may be decaying. Often their anxiety about change is even greater than their fear of crime. Frequently they simply cannot afford to move anywhere else.

One often overlooked byproduct of crime in inner cities is the reluctance of various service groups to visit there and of physicians to practice there.

Measures against violent crime. The victims of crime ought to be compensated for losses they have incurred, including medical and legal costs, and property damage. They should be protected against reprisal by alert neighbors and friends, and by increased police surveillance. Their buildings should be provided intercom systems to announce the arrival of visitors, locked mailboxes, sturdy door locks, and in apartment houses, doormen or TV monitors. Lighting should be improved in the streets, parks, and any other places especially conducive to assault. Special protective measures are required in elevators, laundry rooms, and subway stations. Especially in high crime communities, or in any areas where there are rowdy young adolescents, escort services should be provided. Older people could organize in order to monitor their buildings, report the presence of strangers, and check the functioning of such security devices as locks and alarms. Police protection would be more adequate if officers were educated about the sociology of crime and how to take care of vulnerable persons, especially the mentally ill and the elderly. They should receive such advice as: don't carry money;

walk close to the curb; and go in groups, especially at night. Wherever older people are concentrated, special police protection should be provided. Finally, older people should attend survival and defense classes especially designed for them.

Another and recent tactic for discouraging crime against the elderly is to make examples of offenders. Often a group of elderly people will sit in the courtroom during trials of those who have hurt one of them, in order to exert silent pressure that sterner sentences be meted out to offenders. Recently as twenty elderly persons looked on, a 19-year-old youth who had beaten and robbed an 82-year-old woman of $2.00, was denounced as a fiend and predator, and received the maximum prison sentence, 8½ to 25 years. The defendant had become "the focus of a public outcry against lenient treatment of youthful offenders after he had jumped bail of $500 set beside his long record of attacks on elderly persons, a record the judge did not know about" (Perlmutter, 1977, p. 1). In pronouncing the sentence, the judge said: "He is a predator in the dirtiest sense of the word—preying on the helpless. We cannot continue to countenance teenage predators taking advantage of the elderly" (p. 1).

Fraudulent schemes. Often older people are victimized in other ways too. Door-to-door salesmen offer them "bargains" that prove to be worthless. Persons with poor vision may be cheated when change is made. Funeral directors may exploit them, especially after a loved one dies, for the bereaved may feel that any effort to reduce costs would be equivalent to downgrading the value of the deceased. In other cases quack doctors prey upon the elderly, peddling all sorts of cures and anti-aging schemes, capitalizing on their intense desire to improve their physical condition. One of the most widespread areas of fraud is that of medical misrepresentation.

Older people may also fall prey to the "loneliness industry," which offers all sorts of lures ranging from lifetime dancing lessons to dating services. Other fly-by-night operators offer such get-rich-quick schemes as selling franchise rights to vending machines. These people take their money and vanish forever. Because older people wish to find an ideal retirement home, they prove easy prey for high-pressure land salesmen. Lots may be described as ready for building, yet will lack a source of water or other vital facilities. Buying condominiums carries particular risks, for while they do offer certain tax advantages and services, buyers may be assessed later to pay for a garden, a pool, or other amenities. Often older people simply have not counted on such expenses, and with their fixed incomes, cannot afford them.

Rapid Change

Another, and often overlooked, problem of older people is change; and while everyone is affected by it, for better or for worse, the most negative impact has probably been on the elderly. For one thing, the growing exclusivity of the nuclear family has weakened the kin network, so that it is no longer the place where social activities take place. The increased job mobility has tended to remove nuclear families from the geographic locations of their parents and relatives. Young and middle-aged couples have been attracted to the suburbs because of their greater benefits for children, while the older generation is left in the central city. Meantime rapidly changing times have caused the values of older people to become more quickly outdated, and they themselves are therefore less adequate guides for the young.

Fast change also helps to account for the cult of youth, because the older generations' ways of living and thinking go so quickly out of style. As youthful ways of life are considered more appropriate for a fast-changing society, so do their physical and behavioral traits become the norm. Hence physical features and characteristics associated with

1978 © Sybil Shelton

The weakening of the nuclear family has left many of the aged homeless and on the streets in our central cities.

the over-the-hill generation are negatively viewed, while those associated with youth emerge as the ideal.

In addition, "suddenly there are large numbers of [the elderly] and no one knows quite what to do. In each succeeding decade the proportion of elderly to young in the population increases. Anticipated breakthroughs [on] major killers like cancer and heart disease may swell the ranks of the old even more" (Butler, 1975c, p. xi). Indeed, over 10% of Americans are now over age 65, and by the year 2000 this figure may well reach 20% (Butler, 1975c). Until society can devise flexible policies which will satisfy the changing demands produced by demographic trends and evolving needs, the elderly generation will suffer.

PERSPECTIVE ON LATER LIFE PROBLEMS

General Considerations

For a better perspective on problems of the elderly, the following points are pertinent. In the first place, we all have problems, usually one after another, but rarely in bunches. Yet the elderly often have to continuously cope with a wide variety of problems, without breathing spells between them, at that stage in life when it is hardest to cope. On the other hand, most of them do very well for a variety of reasons (Kalish, 1975). One is sheer necessity—that is, everyone has just two alternatives, either to "live old or to die young" (p. 21). Neither seems exhilarating, but many old people manage to cope with their problems anyway, and "to enjoy life as much as, and often more than, younger persons" (p. 21). Also, they are often less susceptible than younger people to "certain anxieties and vanities and social pressures" of earlier years, so that they "can be more free to be themselves, to do what is important to them."

In any case, the anticipation of the decrements of old age is actually more foreboding than the reality proves to be. Declines occur quite gradually, so that aging individuals are continually adapting without realizing it. In any case, older people often continue to enjoy life and adjust to chronic problems that appear overwhelming at first. These areas of decline are only one aspect of an individual's life and, if other parts of it prove satisfying, the importance of particular deficits shrinks. To some degree people prepare themselves for what life may be like in the future, and hence develop a certain readiness for dealing with these problems when they do occur. Since the anticipation is often worse than the reality, the problems of adaptation are correspondingly less. This is not to say that mental and physical decrements lack significance. They do pose serious problems which are often enhanced by other difficulties associated with aging, including the death of close friends and family members, a sharply reduced income, increasing social isolation, and changing family and social roles. The point is, says Kalish (1975), that older people do indeed have resources that permit them to function with "amazing effectiveness" despite multiple losses; and persons who work with the elderly should make every effort to help them compensate with whatever residual strengths they have, rather than dismissing their problems as the inevitable outcome of aging.

In the following, several older people relate what has helped them most in making life adjustments. People most often mention remaining active, being religious, and having certain attitudes toward life. Even in later years they are used to coping somehow; and they are rarely defeatist.

> I get along by keeping active in church work, home, and the community. *(Female, age 68)*

> I have a natural optimism. *(Female, age 73)*

> I've got common sense and a faith in God. It is fundamental that you make the best of the situation in which you find yourself if you cannot better it. *(Female, age 74)*

> I cope by deciding what is necessary to do and what is possible to do. *(Female, age 71)*

> I pay attention to what I am doing instead of to myself doing. *(Male, age 72)*

> I'm keeping busy, mostly doing garden work. *(Male, age 71)*

> My religious faith and helping to build a better world keep me going. *(Male, age 69)*

> I have the belief in my own ability to cope, which I developed as a child. My own self-confidence plus an exceptionally wide range of abilities developed over the years, has always carried me over the bumps without undue stress. *(Female, age 65)*

> My religion sees me through so that I feel I can cope with practically anything. *(Female, age 92)*

SUGGESTED READINGS

Butler, R. N. *Why survive? Being old in America.* New York: Harper & Row, Publishers, 1975. This book covers a wide range of topics regarding the elderly, including their most common problems.

Campbell, R. J. Psychopathology of aging. In Bier, William G. (Ed.) *Aging: Its challenge to the individual and to society*, New York: Fordham University Press, 1974, 96–116. Psychopathology in later years is discussed in terms of contributing factors, type of disorder, and distinction between normal and pathologic aging.

Denes, Z. Old-age emotion. *Journal of the American Geriatrics Society*, 1976, 24 (10), 465–467. In this study of one-hundred 60- to 94-year-olds' emotional status, the chief factors relating to emotional sterility were retirement, loneliness, and decline in sensory and motor functions. Suggestions are made for preventing emotional "emptiness" before it produces psychological impairment.

Fischer, D. H. *Growing old in America*. New York: Oxford University Press, 1977. A historian traces the changing status of the elderly in America from an exaltation of age in colonial times to their sorry state today, and suggests the causes of such changes. He dwells at some length on the changing political fortunes and vicissitudes of the elderly.

Kreps, J. M. The economy and the aged. In Binstock, H. & Shanas, E. (Eds.) *Handbook of aging and the social sciences*, New York: Van Nostrand Reinhold Company, 1976. The impact of the economy on the aging is considered in terms of such factors as inflation, employment, and consumer problems.

Matthews, S. Old women and identity maintenance: Outwitting the grim reaper. *Urban Life*, 1975, 4 (3), 339–348. Because of their multiple current and future problems, older people find it difficult to project a desirable self-image into the future. They employ various strategies to maintain their desired identity, even in the process of dying.

Miller, D. B., Lowenstein, R., & Winston, R. Physicians' attitudes toward the ill aged and nursing homes. *Journal of the American Geriatrics Society*, 1976, 24 (1), 498–505. A survey of 302 physicians in a medium-sized city in New York state indicates a general disinterest in the care of sick elderly patients in institutions. It is concluded that both the government and medical schools should give more attention to the needs of chronically ill elderly patients.

Our surplus citizens: How America wastes its natural resources. *Saturday Review*, August 7, 1976, 6–26. In this special report consisting of nine articles, problems relating to retirement are explored.

Payne, B. & Whittington, F. Older women: An examination of popular stereotypes and research evidence. *Social Problems*, April 1976, 23 (4), 488–504. After comparing common notions about older women with actual data, Payne and Whittington concluded that such women are devoted and unfairly stereotyped as sexless, sick, alone, and uninvolved, except in church work.

Pfeiffer, E. Psychopathology and social pathology. In Birren, James E. & Schaie, K. Warner (Eds.) *Handbook of the psychology of aging*. New York: Van Nostrand Reinhold Company, 1977. This chapter concerns the more common forms of intrapersonal and interpersonal pathology found in later years, including commentary and research on such topics as adaptive tasks and processes, functional psychiatric disorders, organic brain syndromes, and social pathology.

Ross, H. E. & Kedward, H. B. Demographic and social correlates of psychogeriatric hospitalization. *Social Psychiatry*, July 1976, *11* (3), 121–126. Groups who have a high-risk rate for future psychogeriatric institutionalization include widowed and separated men, older persons living alone, residents of old age and nursing homes, and women with smaller than average families. Overall it seems that the most significant factor leading to such institutionalization is social isolation.

Savage, R. D., and others. *Intellectual functioning in the aged.* London: Methuen & Co., 1973. The investigations reported here are categorized according to intellectual functioning in the aged and the mentally ill aged, changes in intellectual functioning in the elderly, the structure of intellectual functioning in the aged, and problems relating to intellectual impairment in the aged.

14
CHAPTER

Policies
and
Programs

There are two main categories of programs in which older persons are involved. One includes adults of all ages, and the other is for specific subgroups of older people (Havighurst, 1973). Those for adults in general are wide-ranging, and include such activities as study or discussion groups, continuing education, group therapy, and training for leisure pursuits (Havighurst, 1973). Other programs are designed for older persons, or even more specifically for subgroups of the elderly, according to their special interests and needs. Thus social security and Medicare programs involve all the elderly, while part-time job programs would only concern those who desire or need to continue working.

ELDERLY ACTIVISM

Volunteer Work

All across the country older people are becoming increasingly involved in a large variety of volunteer organizations. Not only do these programs enrich the lives of the volunteers; they also tap a rich reservoir of vital resources for society. Certain of these programs are countrywide; others are less well known. Everyone is familiar with volunteers in the hospital and schools. Another important though not widely known program, is the Senior Volunteer Program (RSVP). Programs like this one are locally planned, operated, and controlled; and involve all kinds of work, so long as it does not displace someone who would ordinarily receive pay for it, and so long as it is not "made" work. Volunteers work in such places as libraries, museums, schools, daycare centers, and hospitals ("Program Information Statement," 1973). Members of the Service Corps of Retired Executives (SCORE) possess skills that they are willing to share with others. For instance, they provide free counsel to small businesses already in existence or to individuals who are planning new ventures. Project Find, developed by the National Council on Aging, involves learning about the lives of the elderly poor, attempting to identify their greatest needs, and then locating resources to help them. The Senior AIDE Program (Alert, Industrious, Dedicated, Energetic), officially called the Senior Community Program, is designed to improve the low-employment, low-income status of many of the elderly poor often by finding part-time employment for them. A Dial-A-Listener Program in Davenport, Iowa permits elderly persons to talk with others of their own age by dialing a particular number, and ten elderly professional people answer their calls. Such a service helps to dispel the anxiety that many old people feel about possibly suffering an injury or falling without having anyone to contact for help.

Political Activism

Future prospects. The elderly are not prone to becoming involved in politics. It has often been suggested that they might constitute a powerful political force if they would but develop a consistent policy, stick together, and assume an active role on their own behalf. However, observes Maddox (1974), there is little chance of a gerontocracy in Western civilization, partly because in later years interest in social and political problems usually declines. Older people also lack the prestige that comes from working and being economically affluent (Rosow, 1974). In addition, they are more heterogeneous than other minorities, and therefore have trouble developing a program on which they can agree. While most minority groups are strongly held together by certain shared significant characteristics such as religion or race, older people cut across all the varied subgroups and strata of society. Hence they possess little sense of "we-ness" as a group. Only recently has this situation been changing, at least in the sense that social programs have been developed and legislation passed on their behalf (Kalish, 1975).

Organizations that represent the elderly. Certain organizations have been formed to represent their interests, the best known of which is the Association of Retired Persons (AARP). This Association has drafted a declaration of aging rights which includes the following:

> To live with sufficient means for decency and self-respect; to move about freely, reasonably, and conveniently; to pursue a career or interest without penalty founded on age; to be heard on all matters of public interest; to maintain health and well-being through preventive care and education; to receive assistance in times of illness or need or other emergency; to peace and privacy as well as participation; to protection and safety amid the hazards of daily life; to act together to seek redress of grievances; to live life fully and with honor—not for their age but for their humanity (Offir, 1974a, p. 40).

The AARP has also developed a broad variety of services and programs. Some are concerned with keeping older people mentally active, including bringing library books to those who cannot get out, and arranging two-week vacations on college campuses. They also make available through themselves or related agencies, drugs, travel, and insurance at reduced cost. And they produce a newsletter at a minimal subscription rate through which AARP members can keep abreast of news and activities about their age group.

By contrast the Grey Panther Movement is not a service organization, but "a grass-roots movement of social activists trying to take control of their lives" (Offir, 1974a, p. 40). One 23-year-old Grey Panther says that young people are also affected by this movement, since they "see that they are being denied a future, because when they get older the youth culture won't worship them anymore" (Offir, 1974a, p. 74). The Grey Panthers ascribe problems of aging to deficiencies in the American society, which defines people in terms of economic production instead of the types of human beings that they are; and they call "this production-line ideology the Detroit syndrome" (p. 40). They claim that the obsolescence of both things and human beings is simply built into this society.

Butler (1976) proposes a grass-roots organization with chapters throughout the country, which would have no other business than to represent the interests and needs of older people. Not only older persons, but the middle-aged and children would become involved. Since the middle-aged must support people at both ends of the life span, part of their burden would be reduced by whatever was done for the elderly. They would also gain information and support regarding their own task in caring for older people. This organization would have many lobbying functions on behalf of older persons with regard to both foundations and federal agencies. Study groups would be formed in which persons would gain solid knowledge concerning the field of aging, so that efforts on their behalf would be positive and effective.

HELPING OLDER PEOPLE HELP THEMSELVES

Vocational Assistance

The economic hazard of retirement. Most people prefer to retire by age 65, especially those employed in heavy labor, assembly-line jobs, or other tedious work (Sheppard & Hendrick, 1972; Terkel, 1974). Adequate provision for persons who have worked for a specific period of time, should be made. Both social security and company retirement plans are important steps in that direction, but they remain inadequate. Perhaps the biggest problem is inflation, which makes pay checks smaller and smaller. Another hazard is the uncertainty of company pensions, especially in less stable industries. Unionized workers fare better than others, but they are still in a minority.

Discriminatory policies. There are those who do not wish to retire, but would rather work, either in a full- or part-time capacity; and there is a growing feeling that age-mandatory retirement is unsound and unfair. At 65, some individuals are in sounder health mentally and physically than others are at 50. Besides, by forced retirement, society loses the contributions of a large fraction of its best-trained citizenry. Even in situations in which retirement by reason of age is not mandatory, age-discriminatory policies often exist. Older people are often among the last hired and the first fired. Nevertheless this problem is gaining increased recognition, and will undoubtedly diminish as the number of older people increases.

Special employment programs. Several concrete suggestions are being made for helping older people cope with their employment problems. One is that older persons be provided with training to update obsolescent skills. Special assistance should be given to less efficient and handicapped persons, for their personal and financial needs are often greater than average ("Work in America," 1972). Pending reform in the private sector, Butler (1975) believes that the government should provide jobs for those older persons who desire, need, or have the ability to work either part- or fulltime. One example is the foster grandparent program, in which persons over 60 who are below the poverty level, assist with deprived or neglected children who have no close personal relations. Such children include the physically handicapped, the disturbed, and the mentally retarded. Another organization, called Operation Mainstream, includes the Green Thumb Program for men and the Green Light Program for women. These people plant trees, beautify parks, make highway rest areas, and reconstruct historic sites. In the Green Light Program, older women serve in community programs helping the handicapped, the sick, the shut-ins, and very old people. Unfortunately such programs are still often designated specifically for one sex. Instead it should be clearly stated, not simply assumed, that all programs are for qualified persons of either sex. Some women, even older women, would far rather plant trees, for instance, than assist in a hospital.

Developing positive attitudes toward retirement. The writer believes that the most important, though difficult, objective regarding employment in later years is to rear and educate people throughout their lives in such manner as to have them eagerly anticipate job retirement, not so much because they should rest as because they can expand and enrich their lives in ways they could not while still employed. To date, our institutions, including the government and the schools, have failed to recognize the need for a massive effort to educate people in the creative use of free time. While social scientists are already aware of the problem, and society itself is making some adaptations (classes in leisure-time activities, bowling clubs, and so on), a large social lag remains. The potential for early retirement, coupled with long-term creative training for the use of leisure, could make later years the richest period of life. However, even given such a situation, flexibility of choice should be the ideal, and ultimately become the reality. Even given optimum alternatives some persons will choose not to retire because they are highly talented, or ego-involved in a particular vocational skill.

Educational Programs

The need. Educational programs for older persons should serve two basic purposes: to compensate for earlier educational deficiencies, and to enrich life. Many older people would enjoy and profit from courses which update earlier learning or open new vistas. A minority have not acquired even basic learning skills, and are in effect functional illiterates. As Sweetser (1975) points out,

> There is a quality which can be called sophistication, and which is manifest by the ability to manage one's everyday affairs so as to avoid being victimized, to take advantage of rights and opportunities, and to make reasonable judgments about events in the world at large. Some minimum amount of formal education seems necessary for the development of this quality. . . . Better educated old people, therefore, mean more sophisticated old people (p. 103).

Andragogy. In order to be effective, the processes of teaching the elderly must be adapted to their capacities and needs. By contrast with pedagogy, which is the art and science of teaching children, andragogy may be defined as "the art and science of helping adults to learn" (DuBois, 1975). The concept of andragogy is based on certain assumptions regarding adult learners: first that adults are self-directing and do not require that others make decisions for them. Second, adults bring with them to the learning experience a broad experiential background, including previous formal and informal education, widespread reading, and travel. Third, the developmental tasks and social roles that adults are called upon to perform provide a strong readiness to learn. Finally, adults have a particular time perspective in which they expect to utilize their new learnings at once, by contrast with the youth's perspective, which suggests postponing application until some future time (DuBois, 1975).

Educational programs for the elderly should also be varied, and include vocational education. They should be available throughout adulthood. For one thing, times are changing so rapidly that intermittent, lifelong education is viewed as increasingly essential. At the same time it would help to reduce the gap between generations, both in personal effectiveness and interpersonal compatibility. In the current older generation, the majority has had far less educational opportunity than younger people. However, they are capable of making up their deficiencies, because learning capacity need not decline as a result of aging until the very last years (Bailey, 1976). Besides, continued learning will help to retard any intellectual deterioration that otherwise might occur (APA Task Force, 1973).

Educational offerings and opportunities should be designed to meet the special interests and needs of older persons. They should involve developing leisure activities, general intellectual enrichment, and practical matters such as consumer education, protection from crime, and mental and physical hygiene. Meantime conditions must be such that people can avail themselves of such opportunities. Prerequisites for particular courses should be flexible; classes should be held in convenient places, including nursing homes; and motivation by the teacher should be positive and ego-building. Many of these people have been away

1978 © Sybil Shelton

Education programs for the elderly are being geared toward career-oriented courses rather than the "no credit" enrichment or do-it-yourself courses offered previously.

from formal education for many years; and apparent deficiencies may be a result not of intellectual impairment, but of unfamiliarity with newer teaching methods, "rusty" learning skills, and a lack of self-confidence. When the learning situation is modified to take such factors into account, older students do amazingly well. Mercedes Spotts, now in her 40s, earned her bachelor's degree in sociology and is now working on her master's degree. Because of her improved credentials she has received a promotion in her job at the Municipal City Court ("Graying of the Campus," 1977). Elmir Ricketson, age 65, has won three degrees, and has taken many postgraduate courses across the years, including several in the past decade. Her postgraduate studies have included extensive work in accounting and interior design. John Rogers, bank president and lawyer, age 52, decided to return to college to pursue a long-time interest in art, and he has already produced a considerable number of paintings. In 1975, 34% of all those enrolled in college, 3.7 million adults, registered for college courses.

The colleges themselves are enthusiastically supporting this movement ("Graying of the campus," 1977) because there are fewer younger students, and the end of this trend is not in sight. By 1995 it is estimated that the 18- to 24-year-old population will have dropped by 20% from 1980, and by the year 2000 there will be 81% more adults aged 35 to 44, than at present.

One effect of the changing student population will be a shift in emphasis in order to meet the needs of these older students. Some institutions, it is forecast, will become "three-tiered," serving traditional students, middle-aged students, and retirees. The overall trend in adult education is toward career-oriented credit courses, and not the "no-credit 'enrichment' and do-it-yourself courses (such as yoga and home-repairing) that some colleges have offered for years" ("Graying of the Campus," 1977, p .1).

GOVERNMENT POLICIES AND PROGRAMS

Some Basic Considerations

Realistic appraisal of need. For several reasons it is essential that the government make a large-scale commitment to helping older people, one being that a great deal of money is needed. Such funding will require a drastic change in policy. At present less than 1% of the National Institute of Health's funding goes to studying the aged, and only 3 to 5% of the National Institute of Mental Health's budget goes toward the study of older people's mental problems (Butler, 1976).

The government must also make up for what individuals and families will no longer do. Kalish (1975) suggests that the recent emphasis on individual self-development which we have mentioned, has diverted attention from helping the elderly. As a result, the elderly have few advocates who will look out for their needs. Such service organizations as exist usually neglect elderly people (Bloom, 1973). Moreover the elderly are often treated in a patronizing fashion and lose considerable independence when they are given assistance. The sheer magnitude of the problem also requires macro-programs that only the government can undertake. In earlier decades there were few older people to be concerned about, partly because the life span was shorter, and partly because there were many immigrants to the U.S. whose parents were often left behind in Europe. However, persons over 65 will comprise at least 17% of the total American population by early in the next century. If there is a breakthrough in one or more major diseases, that percentage could be much higher. Yet we have hardly begun to learn how to deal with the elderly among us.

In order to meet such great need, advises Butler (1975c), the national policy on aging should be broad-ranging and include the following points: (1) All high-risk groups, including children, the disabled, the sick, and the elderly, should be given priority in government programs. (2) Poverty should be defined in realistic terms, taking into account the current cost of living. (3) Property taxes should be drastically reduced for the aged in order to permit older people to keep their homes. (4) Older persons should be allowed to work as long as their health permits. They could also be incorporated into a national senior service corps, foster grandparent, or other service programs. (5) Programs for continuing, lifetime education should help the elderly to build new skills and thus allow them more flexible choices. (6) Aspects of elderly persons' environment, including parks, transportation facilities, crime protection, health clinics, and the like, should be adapted to meet their needs. For example, sick elderly people should not have to await their turn for hours in doctors' office or in clinics. (7) Other priorities should include the construction of nonprofit nursing homes, the right to mental health care, and adequate basic and applied research.

Funding research. Another policy should be the funding of significant studies. Research proposals should be very carefully screened to insure that maximum benefits will be derived from the all too inadequate funds currently available. One worthwhile five-year research project funded by a grant to the University of Southern California involves a team of sociologists, psychologists, social workers, urban planners, and anthropologists who have been attempting to develop a brand-new flexible policy for older Americans. It is based on data obtained both from other countries and different groupings within this country. Researchers are finding how very different the anxieties and life styles of aging "black, Anglos, Mexican-Americans and East European Jews living in a sprawling metropolitan environment are from the problems facing old people in Europe, Mexico and Africa" (Kessler, 1976, p. 56). Most programs at present are based on the only data available, which are derived largely from studies of "middle-class, native-born white Americans . . . and they are therefore hardly representative of the pluralistic society of our contemporary United States" (p. 56).

Among the aims of medical and biological researchers on aging are: to distinguish the aging process from chronic diseases associated with aging; to learn how to prevent and control diseases that have the effect of decreasing "inherent life expectancy"; to define in detail the normal aging processes in humans and other species, and to determine how to postpone, modify, temporarily reverse, or even bring to a halt, each step in the process (Berman, 1975). Ultimately biological data on molecular engineering, or biochemical modification of the genetic material involved in aging, may have significant applications and help the elderly to maintain a state of "complete physical, mental and social well-being, and not merely the absence of disease or infirmity" (Berman, 1975, p. 2).

Social Security

Background. By far the most important and sweeping form of assistance for older persons is the social security program. When the Social Security Act was first passed in 1935, various categories of persons, including the self-employed, were excluded, but by the 1970s, over 90% of those over 65 were eligible for social security benefits, although some of them chose to continue working and to postpone or reduce those benefits (Fitzpatrick, 1975).

It is sometimes argued that social security benefits are intended only to provide basic income, which is to be supplemented by private savings or other types of public and private employment-related pension plans. However, as Thomas R. Donahue, former Assistant Secretary of Labor, points out:

> In all too many cases the pension that was promised shrinks to this: "if you remain in good health and stay with the same company until you are 65 years old, and if the company is still in business, and if your department has not been abolished, and if you haven't been laid off for

too long a time, and if there is enough money in the fund, and if that money has been prudently managed, you will get a pension" (U.S. Senate Hearings, 1970, p. 1541).

Nor can the elderly rely on their savings because during most of their working years, wages were much less than they are today, and the buying power of what they have managed to save has been progressively reduced by inflation. On income-tax forms in the early 1970s, married couples over 65 reported having less than $2,000, and two-thirds of the unmarried had less than $1,500 in financial assets, including government bonds, stocks, or savings (Murray, 1972).

Most people support those legislators who contribute to the ever-growing national debt in order to fund currently popular programs. The result of continually dipping into the public coffers over the decades has been a continuing and dangerous rate of inflation which may do more than anything else to create poverty among the elderly. If present-day, younger middle-aged adults tighten their belts in order to prevent this borrowing, they can reverse the rate of the inflation spiral and create a far better economic foundation for their own later years.

Social security currently covers most workers; and it is ordinarily paid for by both workers and their employers. Self-employed individuals make their own social security contributions each year when they pay their income tax, and these contributions provide four major kinds of protection: retirement benefits, survivors benefits, disability benefits, and medicare health-insurance benefits.

Retirement benefits. Workers become eligible for full retirement benefits at age 65, or they may retire at 62 with 80% of full benefits. The nearer they are to 65 when they begin to collect benefits, the larger the fraction of full benefits received. The amount of the retirement benefit that recipients are entitled to at 65 is the key to benefits under other programs (Golenpaul, 1976). Workers who delay taking their benefits until after they reach 65, receive 1% over what they would have received for each year that they do not claim those benefits. A minimum benefit is provided for persons under social security systems. In 1975, average monthly earnings of $500, or $6,000 a year, would give a worker $323.40 a month in social security. In general the largest retirement check that could be paid to a 65-year-old worker in 1975 was about $341.70 a month; the maximum to the family of the retired worker was about $619.90. If the wife is also 65, she would obtain half that amount, or $161.70. On the other hand, if the wife is between 62 and 65, she may obtain a reduced benefit, depending on how long before age 65 she begins receiving checks. She will obtain this amount for the rest of her life unless her husband dies first, in which case she would get a widow's benefit. If the wife is eligible to receive retirement benefits based on her own earnings, she can get whichever is larger, her husband's or her own. When the woman worker receives a retirement benefit and has a dependent husband aged 62 or over, he may draw a benefit similar to that of the wife that begins at age 62. Children of a retired parent cease receiving benefits at 18 unless they are still in school, in which case they can continue until age 22. On the other hand, disabled children may continue to obtain benefits as long as their disabilities continue to match the definition within the law.

Survivors' benefits. With survivors' benefits, the family is provided with life-insurance protection which could amount to $100,000 or more, after a period of years. The amount of protection depends upon what the worker would have been entitled to at 65. These benefits include a cash payment to help cover burial expenses, and a lump-sum death payment. A survivor benefit is paid to children until they reach 18, or until they are 22 if they are in school; or at any age if they are disabled before the age of 22. An eligible child receives 75% of the basic benefit. The widow or widower also receives a survivor's benefit if the children are under 18 or disabled, but this benefit is generally only 75% of the basic benefit. In 1975 the total family survival benefits could go as high as $848.70 a month.

Disability benefits. Disability benefits are paid to three groups. The first is insured workers under 65 who have severe disabilities. These individuals collect the same amount as they would if they were 65. Meantime eligible dependents of such workers receive the usual benefits. Permanently disabled children of workers receiving retirement or disability benefits, or who have died, can collect benefits after age 18; and in such a case the mother can also obtain benefits if the children are under her care. Disabled widows, dependent widowers or, in some situations, the surviving divorced wife of a worker who worked long enough under social security, may receive benefits as early as age 50 if they become disabled. The majority of people over age 65, and many under that age, who have been entitled to disability checks for at least two years under Medicare protection, also receive disability benefits. Medicare helps pay the costs of inpatient hospital care, as well as certain types of follow-up care. Medicare also helps to defray the cost of physician services, outpatient services, and certain other medical items.

Limitations on earnings. In 1975 persons under 72 could earn up to $2,520 without forfeiting their social security benefits. In these cases only earned income is counted. Dividends, pensions, and so forth, are not. Those who earn more than that amount in a year forfeit one dollar of benefits for each two dollars earned in excess of that amount. After individuals reach 72, they may earn any amount and still obtain full benefits.

HELP WITH MAJOR PROBLEMS

Mental Health

Prevention. Assistance for older people with psychological and physical problems must be both preventive and therapeutic, and must consider both minor and major difficulties. Even among the well-adjusted, such simple adaptive behaviors as life review can be a helpful defense mechanism—that is, reminiscing is a creative self-therapy which reduces fears and anxieties. Mental health personnel who resist listening to older patients' soliloquies are thereby suppressing an important source of reintegration (Butler & Lewis, 1973).

Many older people may also profit from various forms of group therapy. Butler and Lewis (1973) are conducting age-integrated psychotherapy groups composed of 8 to 10 members ages 15 to 80, and even older, in each group. All the persons in the group are experiencing crises which may be related to divorce, parenthood, widowhood, illness, education, adolescence, or impending death. The groups are balanced in terms of personality, sex, and age. Within these groups the elderly have contributed, in particular, models for aging, the creative use of reminiscing, a sense of development through life, and solutions for grief and loss. The results have demonstrated the possibilities for personal and psychological growth, even until the very end of life.

More serious problems. Patients with more serious disorders are usually placed in inadequate mental-health centers or foster homes. Even the community mental-health centers of the National Institute of Mental Health fail to meet the needs of the poor, the old, and the chronically mentally ill (Chu & Trotter, 1974). The aged and infirm mental patients are in even worse condition in most so-called foster homes, where a mere pittance is paid for their care, and the homeowner makes a profit even from that. The facilities are notoriously inadequate, and psychiatric care is almost wholly lacking.

Decent psychiatric facilities for the elderly require at least three things: adequate funds, changed attitudes, and facilities geared to the patients' special needs, which can be determined by research. All too often such people are considered beyond help. After they are put away they become a case of, "out of sight, out of mind." Perhaps the most essential task here is to educate the public to care about them; otherwise support to supply the necessary facilities will not be forthcoming. In order to coordinate suitable programs and establish standards, Butler (1975c) believes that a government commission on mental health and illness of the elderly is essential. The costs of such programs, while admittedly great, would save money in the long run because so many people would be restored to reasonably good physical and emotional health.

The attitude that something can and should be done for senile patients is especially important, for many people feel negatively toward them. Folsom (1972) has achieved quite dramatic reversals of senility among VA hospital patients. He describes the case of a 77-year-old man who had had two heart attacks and several strokes. "When we got him," recalled Folsom,

> his family was convinced he would die. In three months, they had taken away all of his bodily functions (by enemas and the injection of a catheter) except breathing and eating. He had no purpose in living and was in a desperate state.
>
> First we threw away the pages of instructions from the family. Then we started to bombard him with facts: his name, the date, time, his room number. We showed him the bathroom and started him on exercises. Two months later he was able to go home. But the family had ruled out his return psychologically. So he had furloughs at home until they got used to him again.
>
> He subsequently got back to his vegetable gardening again and keeps the freezers of two families well-stocked (Folsom, 1972).

Physical Problems

Prevention. Physical, like mental, problems involve prevention as well as therapy. Preventive medicine is concerned with such matters as nutrition, smoking, physical activity, the excessive use of drink and drugs, and styles of life that are endangering. For example, how personality and life styles cause heart attacks, is under scrutiny (Butler, 1975b). Prevention also involves the research required to head off or minimize the effects of disease. Especially deserving of attention are the chronic degenerative diseases such as strokes and heart attacks, which strike men with greater frequency than women. More effort should also be made to prepare people for longer survival and for leisure in later years.

It is probably important for the elderly to become more active, although evidence on this point is not conclusive. Older persons whose health practices involve regular physical activity, have a health status (in terms of medical consultations and hospital admissions) equal to that of most people 20 years younger (Belloc & Breslow, 1972). Palmore (1970) reported that four times as many inactive older persons reported poor health as those who engaged in regular physical activity. While such research suggests that health benefits derive from physical activity, it is possible that poor health may have been the reason for cutting down on physical activity in the first place.

There is at least some evidence that elderly subjects show significant gains in health after training (Sidney & Shephard, 1977). In one study, a group of men and women over 60 had a relatively inactive life. The women spent more time than the men in light physical effort, but neither sex spent much time in heavy physical work. However, after a year of programmed exercise, favorable changes were observed in body composition as well as in life style, including an increase in physical activity and a diminished use of their car.

Another important aspect of preventive medicine is diet. In general older people need about the same amount of minerals, vitamins, and proteins as adults of all ages. However the total number of calories required may be less because of lowered metabolic requirements, as well as decreased activity (Marble & Patterson, 1975). In practice older people need a "meal guide" based on their own living habits and preferences. Nutrition for the elderly should also take into account conditions that are especially common at that age. For example, missing teeth, sore gums, and poorly fitting dentures may hinder eating, while a new set of teeth or a visit to the dentist may contribute to a better diet. For instance, when poor oral conditions exist, softer foods might be the answer. For older persons with chronic diseases, a modified diet should be a part of their routine medical care. Such diets are based on their regular eating habits, which are modified only to meet their current medical needs (Marble & Patterson, 1975).

Research. Certain significant research is being pursued by government agencies and universities. The National Institute on Aging, a division of the National Institute of Health, has a major biomedical program concerned, for example, with attempting to learn why aging produces decreasing resistance to disease, why cells age and die, and so on. Institute researchers also intend to make in-depth studies of the life experiences of people from their early years until old age, in order to find out how and why they age the way they do. In addition they are trying to find out how best to deliver mental and physical health care to older people. At the University of Southern California's Gerontology Center, psychologists Diana Woodruff and David Walsh are trying to exploit ways of learning in which the elderly may do better than the young ("New tricks," 1975). Dr. Woodruff speculates that by using brain wave biofeedback, the elderly could be taught to produce brain waves like those of younger people, and to lower their blood pressure. Either of these things may enhance their intellectual performance. Youth today places a good deal of stress on body awareness, and the old may even be more adept in this regard. As a result of these and other programs progress is being made. For example, "major breakthroughs in the treatment of cancer, stroke, and heart disease are anticipated in the not very distant future" (Butler, 1975c, p. 174).

Needs. Collectively such programs should meet particular criteria. For one thing, professionals who deal with older people should be equipped by temperament and training to do so. All too many people simply exploit the aged, and give them minimal time for maximal fees. William Schofield (1974) describes the YAVIS syndrome, the psychotherapists' preference for treating Young, Attractive, Verbal, Intelligent, Successful (well-paying) individuals. These personnel should aim to help older people gain a "sense of activity and strength" rather than giving them drugs for subduing their feelings (Butler, 1975c, p. 236). Instead many psychiatrists cope with older persons' mental and emotional problems by "chemical straightjacketing," that is, by giving them tranquilizers and antidepressants. Similarly attempts are made to reduce the elderly's problems merely through simplification, which is the path of least resistance. While such an approach may initially remove some of their frustrations, it may also reduce their capacity to adapt. Hence the tension-reducing environment indirectly becomes a tension-producing one. The vulnerability of the elderly has been increased because everything is done for them and they have no chance to do anything for themselves. Ideally they need some challenge, although not that which is beyond their capacity to cope (Lawton & Nahemow, 1973).

Professionals should treat older people as if they have value, which of course they do. The attitude all too often is: they have little time left, so they are hardly worth large expenditures of time and money. As a result they are often denied appropriate preventive medicine in favor of "simplistic diagnoses of senility; and prognoses of chronic or irreversible [are made]" (Butler, 1975c, p. 174). Findings indicate otherwise, and they suggest that custodial care be displaced by refurbished treatment programs with more flexible procedures. Elderly people, like many others, should have the right to refuse particular types of care. They must also have the right to treatment, and not merely abandoned in custodial institutions.

Long-term Care

Home care. Whenever possible, people who cannot take care of themselves should be maintained at home (Shore, 1972). Hence there should be home care, hospitals, daycare centers, and care programs related to individual needs in order to prevent unnecessary institutionalization. To date, however, the vast majority of the incapacitated elderly are placed in nursing homes.

Nursing-home care. Various authorities have outlined their own conceptions of what nursing homes should ideally be. Dr. Kübler-Ross (1974) insists that they be made as much like homes as possible; "and that means that you include children, not only for visiting, but for residing there at least during the day in day-care centers so that the old people can help with the little ones. The elderly can perhaps plant a little garden and do some woodwork and all the other things that used to make life meaningful at home" (p. 148).

Butler and Lewis (1973) go into somewhat more detail in describing the ideal nursing home. It should be truly homelike and lively, "not sterile, antiseptic, and reminiscent of a motel" (p. 295). Public monies should be diverted from the commercial nursing home industry to creating "multi-purpose centers or galaxies" operated as cooperatives. Older people themselves would participate in their control, or at least serve as board members. Programs should also be realistic and adequate for chronic care. These galaxies, in turn, would be functionally linked to other units of the nation's care system, including social agencies, hospitals, and mental health centers. Competent inspectors would make frequent unannounced visits; and a national personal health care corps would perform the duties now inefficiently discharged by home health aides and visiting nurses. The latter would provide many services, including shopping for elderly persons' drugs and groceries, and listening to and talking with them. Such services would permit many of the elderly to stay at home. Families would be provided with financial assistance in order to be able to maintain older relatives at home if they so desired.

A legally enforceable bill of rights could be devised to protect both personal and property rights of the elderly. Custodial care, when inevitable, would "signify the highest quality of personal, social and health care" (p. 298). Ideally such facilities should become places for rehabilitation, "nurturing the sense of hope and self esteem which can make the last, and often most difficult, years of life worthwhile, up to the moment of death" (p. 299). For example, institutionalized persons should be provided with relationships with persons outside the institution.

Unfortunately nursing homes suggest houses of death, and "psychologically, many older people consider themselves buried alive when they enter such a home" (Butler, 1975c, p. 229). Indeed many commercialized facilities for the old in America have been described as "human junk yards" by Congressman David A. Prior and "warehouses" by Senator Frank Moss.

Personal testimony. In the following, several female nursing-home residents reply to the question: "If you were asked to design an ideal nursing home, what are some of the things that you would stress?"

Separate the troublemakers from the people who are easy-going. (*Age 68*)

I would recommend pleasant, comfortably furnished rooms as in this one; and as far as possible, residents should be regarded as persons. (*Age 86*)

I'd stress cleanliness, good food, and courtesy, both on the part of patients and the help. (*Age 87*)

All residents should have their own rooms, big enough to have a chair or table from their own home and a big enough place to bring some of the things they hate to part with. (*Age 74*)

I'd like a better variety of food. (*Age 77*)

The Environment

Some general principles. Only recently has the importance of ecological factors in relation to older persons been recognized. Ecology may be defined as "the study of natural systems, emphasizing the interdependence of one element in a system upon every other element" (Lawton & Nahemow, 1973, p. 619). The elderly undoubtedly experience the environment somewhat differently from the way younger persons do, a factor of importance to gerontologists, architects, planners and engineers.

Certain principles are especially relevant here. First, the effect of environments depends upon their significance for the individuals who live in or react to that environment. The aesthetic qualities on which architects often place special stress are rarely of primary importance to the elderly. Instead older people appreciate environments in which they feel free and unrestrained. For example, they especially value a neighborhood where they feel secure and can move about freely.

In the second place, older persons' environments, such as their local neighborhoods, are critical because they are less mobile than younger people. They are also more vulnerable to their surroundings because they are less capable of altering or manipulating them. For example, a neighborhood may change radically in terms of its population. In one study (Lawton, Kleban, & Singer, 1971) in which elderly Jewish residents in a deteriorating Philadelphia neighborhood were compared with similar residents of other communities, the former had lower morale, poorer health, and less contact with neighbors. The problem was that most of the Jewish residents had moved out, so that those who remained constituted a distinct racial minority.

Even among the elderly, many individual differences exist. People do not change their basic preferences with the passage of years. Some older people prefer rural, and others urban, environments. Some prefer quite traditional, others very modern, surroundings; and the same is true of younger persons. For some, flowers, pets, and possessions are especially important; others need contacts with friends and neighbors.

Environments serve to accentuate or alleviate the effects of other problems. In fact psychological problems often derive from an inhospitable environment rather than from the aging process itself. People at any age are vulnerable to such factors as "inadequate housing, deterioration of older neighborhoods, anti-therapeutic institutions, poorly located services, inadequate transportation, and architectural barriers to mobility. . . . " (APA Task Force, pp. x–xi, 1973).

Residential concerns. In the last chapter we discussed some residential problems of the elderly. Let us review certain principles which should improve this situation. First, the older person's neighborhood should be safe, attractive, and close to shopping areas. Those who prefer, and the great majority do, should be maintained in their own homes. Legal service organizations should make provision for the upkeep of older persons who cannot afford it. The same organizations, or perhaps interested friends or relatives, might also help to safeproof the house by installing fire alarms and locks, constructing railings for cellar stairs, and placing lights in dark corners where people might trip. Air conditioning is important because the elderly are vulnerable to severe heat. Housing might be planned to accommodate life's successive stages, including the childrearing, empty-nest, and retirement periods. In some cases campuslike arrangements might be devised to offer a variety of services and activities especially adapted to older persons' needs. Communities may also help older residents by providing reduced property taxes, or even subsidies, and free membership in food cooperatives. Transportation programs could include provisions for senior citizens, including reduced rates on transit systems during off hours. Various "adventures in learning" might be provided by such plans as the Institutes for the Elderly, which involve distinguished retired professors, idea exchanges, and special library and education extension services in retirement homes. These organizations might also provide recorded music, casette players, and film programs. Still another program already in existence is the driver refresher course for senior citizens, which is operated in Texas. For homebound or institutionalized persons, the Friendly Visitor Plan arranges for volunteers to visit, provide companionship, and perform such services as shopping and letter writing.

Finally it is important that older persons' housing situations permit opportunities for primary group relationships. In one study, people whose mean age was the early 70s, and who lived in a hotel remodeled into apartments, were highly satisfied with their housing, partly because it was a vast improvement over where they had lived before, and also because it provided an interactional network. Nevertheless 41% of the 63 persons interviewed sometimes no longer felt they were useful to others. Those who visited most with their adult children, most often expressed those feelings; whereas those who did much less visiting were bothered little by such sentiments (Hampe & Blevins, 1975). Apparently relationships with other elderly persons whose circumstances are the same, are more supportive of morale than those with adult children.

Miscellaneous services. Butler (1975c) suggests still other ways that the quality of life of the elderly may be improved. For one thing, they need the same basic services as other people, including tax assistance, health care, social service, recreation, and education; and when ill, they need home care. Families need help in caring for disabled members who are not hospitalized. Central referral and information services are necessary in order that the elderly and their families know where specific needs can be met. Assistance at home is especially essential, including health, dental, legal, nutritional, homemaking, and social services. In addition, outpatient care should be provided. Homemaker-home health aides can provide a variety of services including light housecleaning, light cooking, laundry, and patient hygiene (Butler & Lewis, 1973). Other vital services are physicians' housecalls, nutritional care and guidance, education concerning the use of drugs, and transportation and communication, including telephone, radio, television, and newspapers. For the elderly such services are not a luxury but a necessity, in order for them to keep in contact with the outside world. They also need protective services, especially in high-crime areas. In addition, free checking at banks, meals-on-wheels, at-home library service, and reduced prices at eating places are becoming increasingly common and are a very real help.

The age-segregation issue. Authorities' opinions differ about whether older persons do best in age-integrated residential settings. Dr. Kübler-Ross (1974) dislikes the segregation of older people, for that is not "what life is all about." She believes that older people fare better when they are involved with people of different generations. Robert Butler (1976) agrees, favoring a "life cycle" kind of community which involves all age groups. He recalls that, "My kids saw an older couple across the street go from their 70s into their 80s and finally die. It shows children the realities of what aging is. And it is just as important for older people to keep in contact with the young, to share in their mentality. But some people can't stand kids. They never could. If they prefer to live in a retirement community with their peers, they should have that right" (p. 32).

By contrast, Rosow (1974) suggests putting older people together in residential settings. There they can form strong friendship groups and be protected from the negative attitudes of the society at large. Under these conditions they develop their own norms and images, which differ from those of the larger social order. It is essential, however, that such concentrations involve suitable opportunities for healthy interaction. Under these conditions certain individuals become role models for others. In summary, "the crucial conditions are the anchorage of older people in a group of similar peers and the insulation from conflicting external norms and definitions" (p. 167).

CONCLUDING OBSERVATIONS

Certain points are generally relevant to all programs for older people. Old people should play a major role in whatever decisions are made concerning the services provided to be for them. They should also be educated concerning their own rights and how to procure them (Butler, 1975c). Sometimes those who are helping the elderly are not as sensitive and understanding as they might be; also, some people dislike having others meddle with their lives, regardless of how good their intentions might be. Intervention sometimes costs more in terms of time, energy, and emotional upset than if matters had simply been left to take their course (Kalish, 1975).

The problem, observes Horn (1976), is that "helper and helpee live in different skins . . . they can't get inside someone else's body and mind to see what his needs are" (p. 95). In order to overcome this obstacle, researchers at the University of Michigan's Institute of Gerontology have devised a so-called empathic model in order that they may experience sensory loss similar to that of people in their late 70s and older. They learn how difficult it is to pick out small traffic signs with "75-year-old eyes" (p. 95). In general the Institute's environmental studies program is concerned with the everyday problems that interfere with older persons' freedom and mobility. Using this model the researchers are evaluating home furnishings, street signs, public transit systems, and other features of the environment.

Certainly it would be a good idea to survey adults in general in order to determine what kind of programs they believe are needed. Below, a number of adults suggest how programs for older Americans should be improved.

Stop entertaining older Americans! Encourage them to give as long as they can, physically, mentally, and emotionally. (*Female, age 73*)

There should be more gerontology research and stricter standards by law for retirement homes and nursing homes. (*Female, age 71*)

Senior-citizen homes should have ground-level instead of high-rise apartments. (*Female, age 83*)

Programs could be improved by a change in thought patterns. To think of the elderly as assets rather than as liabilities would make them into assets. (*Male, age 72*)

Social security payments should not be affected by marriage. There should be no limit on work and no penalty for earning money. (*Male, age 69*)

Locally ways should be devised to bring recreation into these peoples' lives. A careful plan of field trips should take place. (*Female, age 43*)

Perhaps some of the newer carpeted nursing homes should have some rooms not carpeted so men that have chewed tobacco for years aren't forbidden to. So many of the elderly don't see well, and it seems it is more for show than for the senior citizen. I could write a book on this. (*Female, age 61*)

There ought to be more recreational activities and provisions for travel. (*Female, age 46*)

Happier and cheerier environments should be provided for them; and home care if possible—no nursing homes. (*Female, age 53*)

When they reach 75 years old, half price on telephone and lights. (*Female, age 58*)

Programs should be highly diversified in order to take care of the needs of the widely diverse types of older people. All programs should be open to members of both sexes. Above all, they should be aimed at helping older people to help themselves, especially by providing services that permit them to remain in their own homes. (*Female, age 62*)

Another important point is that all programs should take future trends into account. For example medical advances will make better health possible, which in turn will dictate more active programs for more active older generations. This kind of orientation also requires that the future older generation, the young people of today, receive "a life course orientation in all of our social, educational, and economic institutions, so that when they approach the 20- to 30-year post-parental stage, they will not be forced to project as empty a future as do most people who now make up the post-parental and retirement cohorts" (Lowenthal, Thurnher, & Chiriboga, 1975, p. 244). Besides, such education would teach young people how their present habits and life styles will affect their adjustment in later years.

One positive byproduct of such an education should be an increased identification with, and concern for, the current generation of older people. Lozier and Althouse (1975) tell of an elderly woman, isolated from her kinsfolk in an urban neighborhood, who does a great deal for people who are even older and frailer than she is. As she grows older and requires more help herself, she would like the community to recognize her past services. She wishes that she could count on her earned reward and thus retain a sense of dignity, but she fears that such will not be the case. The moral is this: it is not simply a matter of providing services for old people in order that aging be successful. Instead people should be able to store up credits over their lifetime which will force reciprocity by younger people. Otherwise the elderly, who earlier provided the past generation with help, will be denied their due because it will not be recognized that being served is not a matter of charity.

Certainly there is no point in keeping people alive longer, if they are not able to live satisfying, effective lives (Butler, 1975). Therefore a major research effort should revolve around not merely extending life, but creating a productive old age and reducing the period of disability before death. It is to be hoped that life-cycle education for youth will help them to appreciate their obligation.

Finally it should be stressed that quality of life is the major goal. All sorts of things may be done for the elderly which may alter or prolong their lives without truly improving their quality. Among factors which would make their lives better in later years are adequate income, good health, a high level of education, the possibility of part-time work, and preretirement planning (Schaie & Gribbin, 1975).

SUGGESTED READINGS

Beattie, W. M. Jr. *Aging and the social services.* In Binstock, Robert H. & Shanas, Ethel (Eds.) *Handbook of aging and the social sciences.* New York: Van Nostrand Reinhold Company, 1976, 619–642. Social services for the elderly are dealt with in terms of types of service, ideological perspective on developing such services, models of social service systems and future prospects.

Cain, L. D. Aging and the law. In Binstock, Robert H. & Shanas, Ethel (Eds.)

Handbook of aging and the social sciences. New York: Van Nostrand Reinhold 1976, 342–368. This chapter deals with age-law matters such as the legal status of aging, law and age status across the life course, the special legal status and legal problems of the elderly.

Carp, F. M. User evaluation of housing for the elderly. *Gerontologist*, 1976, *16* (2), 102–111. A study of the long-range effects of improved housing on 190 tenants indicated them to be generally satisfied with their surroundings. However, they had found especially inconvenient certain adaptations that had been designed especially to meet older persons' needs.

Compton, D. M. The untapped reservoir of human energy. *Journal of Leisurability*, 1975, *2* (3), 20–28. An outline is given of steps that may be taken by park, recreational and leisure agencies, to help special populations (the poor, the aged, the retarded and the handicapped) to develop their own resources.

Hudson, R. B. & Binstock, R. H. Political systems and aging. In Binstock, Robert H. & Shanas, Ethel (Eds.) *Handbook of aging and the social sciences.* New York: Van Nostrand Reinhold Co., 1976, 369–400. Three basic issues are dealt with here: how aging becomes manifest politically, distinctive patterns and consequences for political systems, and the response of political systems to aging as a social concern.

Huttman, E. Alternative methods of providing services for the elderly in independent and semi-independent living arrangements. *Journal of Sociology and Social Welfare*, 1975, *3* (2), 153–156. On the basis of a nationwide study of housing developments in Canada, including interviews with 301 elderly residents and 294 development managers, an assessment is made of the services that are provided, and of those that should be provided in the community.

Kagel, C. J. Community services to the aging. In Bier, William C. (Ed.) *Aging: Its challenge to the individual and to society.* New York: Fordham University Press, 1974, 236–246. The writer summarizes the nature of communities services that are essential for the aging. These services must be designed to meet such special needs of the elderly as nutrition, clothing, shelter, environmental safety, transportation, leisure, and legal protection.

Keith, P. M. Evaluation of services for the aged by professionals and the elderly. *Social Service Review*, 1975, *49* (2), 271–278. A comparison of evaluations of services by professionals and by elderly clients showed them to be generally congruent, except that the clients placed more stress on services that would enhance and extend their social and physical independence.

Labouvie-Vief, G. Toward optimizing cognitive competence in later life. *Educational Gerontology*, 1976, *1* (1), 75–92. Accumulating evidence is cited to indicate that widely-held views regarding pervasive decrements in later life are invalid, and that intellectual development in later years is characterized by plasticity rather than inevitable decline. Extended educational opportunities for adults should be modified to take into account such findings; and experiential mechanisms are proposed which may maximize results.

Ladan, C. J. & Crooks, M. M. Some factors influencing the decision of mature women to enroll for continuing education. *Canadian Counsellor*, 1975, *10* (1), 29–36. Questionnaires submitted to women, who had recently completed a class in a Canadian University after a lengthy period, indicated that they were seeking self-fulfillment and the satisfaction of personal needs in other than the affiliative area of their lives. Husbands were supportive of their wives' continuing education for a brief period, but became somewhat negative if they pursued their studies for a longer period.

Lakoff, S. A. The future of social intervention. In Binstock, Robert H. & Shanas, Ethel (Eds.) *Handbook of aging and the social sciences.* New York: Van Nostrand Reinhold Co., 1976, 643–663. Intervention for the aging is treated in terms of its future as a social concern, ideals of social justice, the post-industrial society, and warnings about forecasting.

Shanas, E. & Maddox, G. L. Aging, health, and the organization of health resources. In Binstock, Robert H. & Shanas, Ethel (Eds.) *Handbook of aging and the social sciences.* New York: Van Nostrand Reinhold Col., 1976, 592–618. Health care for the elderly is analyzed according to needs, health status of the elderly, and the organization and utilization of health care resources.

Wasserman, I. M. The educational interests of the elderly: A case study. *Educational Gerontology*, 1976, *1* (4), 323–330. A study of 166 registered voters over age 60 indicated their interest in a wide variety of college courses was low. The suggestion is made that efforts regarding educational programs should be focused on persons under 70.

15
CHAPTER

Death

CONCEPTS OF DEATH

Alternative Approaches

Until very recently the subject of death was avoided as much as possible in the U.S. Only of late have philosophers, psychologists, sociologists, and others begun seriously to consider its impact on personal development, social adjustment, and society ("Acceptance," 1975).

> Depending upon their frame of reference, these authorities view death in a variety of ways: biological (organic tissue dies throughout the life span and then ceases to exist entirely), psychological (the impact on the person and others who witness it), sociological (its meaning to society at all levels), theological (religious concepts of an after life), philosophical (why do humans die and what is the meaning of it), commercial (the cost and ritual of burial), and legal (the certificate attesting to death and the prolonged probating of willed property). Thus, dying is not simply the process of removal from life; rather it embraces a complex variety of situations and circumstances (Bischof, 1976, p. 357).

Death may also be considered in statistical terms, which supply us with significant figures and facts. Even though death most commonly occurs in later years, it may happen at any stage in life ("Acceptance," 1975). Accident and suicide are the major causes of death among younger persons, and continue to be so in later years, although their relative significance declines. Another leading killer in the United States, alcoholism, results in 85,000 deaths annually, by causing liver diseases, accidents, and crime (Butler, 1975c). Of the 1.7 million deaths each year of those over 65, 70% are from heart disease, stroke, or cancer, with the first-named accounting for 40% (Kalish, 1975). Fourth-ranked influenza and pneumonia rank fourth; each causes fewer than 5% of elderly deaths. Important causes of mortality for men are accidents and a related category of bronchitis, emphysema, and asthma. Among women, diabetes mellitus and arteriosclerosis occur more frequently (Bouvier, Atlee, & McVeigh, 1977). Often death is associated with some special psychological stress; it may be acute mourning, or an anniversary, or some particular loss of status or self-esteem.

Definitions of Death

How to determine the time of death is still at issue, even among professionals (Moody, 1975). The criteria of death vary not only among laymen, but also among physicians, and even from one hospital to another. Death is sometimes defined as the absence of certain clinically detectable vital signs. A person is dead "if his heart stops beating and he quits breathing for an extended period of time, his blood pressure drops as low as to be unreadable, his pupils dilate, his body temperature begins to go down, and so forth" (Moody, 1975, p. 101). This clinical definition has been used over the centuries, both by physicians and laymen.

More recently death has sometimes been defined as the lack of brain wave activity. This concept has resulted from the development of increasingly sensitive techniques for detecting biological processes, including those which cannot be observed overtly. For example, the electro-encephalograph (EEG) "is a machine which amplifies and records the minute electrical potentials of the brain" (Moody, 1975, p. 102). A recent trend has been to interpret true death as the lack of electrical activity in the brain, as demonstrated by flat EEG tracings. However, setting up an EEG machine is a complex task, and even experienced technicians may have to work with it for some time to obtain correct readings. Moreover it does not infallibly determine whether resuscitation is possible in particular cases, because overdoses of drugs may serve to depress the central nervous system.

Still others say that death can only be defined as a bodily state which represents an irreversible loss of vital functions and from which the individual cannot possibly be revived. Since many people have been revived after all hope has been given up, it is currently not possible, according to this definition, to determine exactly when death occurs. Certainly if resuscitation eventually takes place, a certain amount of "residual biological activity must have been going on in the cells of the body, even though the overt signs of these processes were not clinically detectable by the methods employed. In short, it seems that it is impossible at present to determine exactly what the point of no return is. It may very well vary with the individual, and it is likely not a fixed point but rather a shifting range on a continuum" (Moody, 1975, p. 103).

According to the concept of "terminal drop," death can be predicted from certain dramatic changes in cognitive function in the period preceding demise. That is, significant changes both in personal adjustment and performance may serve as indicators of impending death

(Riegel & Riegel, 1972). Apparently terminal drop may occur anywhere between one and five years prior to death.

Persons who have come back from the brink of death reject the so-called annihilation concept of death, which defines it as sleeping or forgetting. Instead they describe death as "a transition from one state to another, or as an entry into a higher state of consciousness or of being. One woman, whose deceased relatives were there to greet her at her death, compared death to a homecoming. Others have likened it to other psychologically positive states, for example, to awakening, to graduating, and to escape from jail" (Moody, 1975, p. 69).

The Experience of Death

Testimony from such persons has intensified the curiosity and apprehension people have always had about the experience of death. Humans have often wondered, usually with foreboding, what it was like to die—and such reports offer some reassurance. Persons who have journeyed to the threshold of death—like those cited above—generally say that there is much less terror and discomfort than is commonly believed; and some of them have even felt happiness or ecstasy. One individual's

> last violent reaction was fighting against the sense of dying, even though she was no longer afraid. She then gave in, knowing that she wanted it, death! Next she witnessed in rapid succession a great many scenes from her life. They began around the age of five and were marked by vivid impressions of color. She had the sense of a beloved doll and was impressed by how bright blue the glass eyes were. She also had a picture of herself on a bright red bicycle on an equally bright green lawn. Other scenes followed, not of her whole life, but of her early childhood, and she emphasized that the death scenes all made her ecstatically happy . . . (Holcomb, 1975, p. 256).

Other views about what it is like to die are more speculative, and usually reflect an individual's personal philosophy. Although the survival drive motivates people to avoid premature death, Keleman (1975) insists that the "orgasm of dying" is similar to the excitement experienced during one's life when one meets the unknown. He believes that humans have a natural genetic programming for dying which is an essential part of life's total development plan, and at impending death excitement can build up to the point of something resembling orgasm. However, such reactions become averted in a culture which encourages utilizing the body as a mere instrument of the mind. For this reason death is perceived as the grim reaper, ready to undermine the total life support system.

Keleman (1975) believes that concepts of life beyond the grave should not be regarded as pure fantasy. That is, he does not dismiss the idea of personal immortality. Humanist John Wren-Lewis (1975) agrees with Keleman, arguing:

> if the body experiences itself as psychic energy rather than inert matter, images of personal survival may well be the most valid way of approaching the mysterious transformation of that energy into death. This seems to me not only the most humanistic, but also the most truly scientific attitude, for to dismiss the unknown as nonexistent is sheer dogmatism. The death revolution will be stillborn if it starts out with any such premature closing of accounts with reality (p. 18).

DEATH IN CULTURES PAST AND PRESENT

Philosophical and Historical Views

In all ages and all societies death has been a matter of keen interest and speculation. The Bible contains little about events after death or the exact nature of the life that follows. Only two passages in the entire Old Testament (Isaiah, 26:19 and Daniel, 12:2) refer specifically to life after death. Isaiah declares that "Thy should live; together with my dead body shall they arise. Awake and sing, ye that swell in dust. . . . the earth shall cast out the dead". Plato, one of the greatest philosophers of all time, who lived in Athens from 428 to 348 B.C., portrayed death as the separation of the soul from the body. In several of his dialogues— especially in *Phaedo, Gorgias,* and the *Republic*—he treats the topic of physical death. Presumably, after separation from the body, the soul meets and talks with the departed spirits of others and is guided to the next life by guardian spirits. Some souls are met after they die by a vessel which transports them across water to another shore. Nevertheless Plato confessed that his own representations of life after death are at best probabilities (Moody, 1975).

A singular work, *The Tibetan Book of the Dead,* comprises the prehistoric teachings of wise men over the centuries in Tibet. These views were passed down through the generations by word of mouth, and finally set down in the eighth century. Dying is portrayed therein as "a skill—something which could be done either artfully or in an unbecoming manner, depending on whether one had the requisite knowledge to do it well" (cited in Moody, 1975, p. 84). After death the individual no longer has a physical body, and exists in a void. The dying individual experiences great contentment, and his whole life is reflected before him.

The Hindus' and Buddhists' concept of death differs sharply from the Western one of complete dissociation from life. They perceive death as "anything but the endless time of never coming back or the absence of presence" (Kübler-Ross, 1975, p. 53). Although death is viewed as unavoidable, it can be escaped by being reborn, the only real escape being the dissolution of all desires. The "conquest of death" involves "the cultivation of a disciplined mind and body. . . ." (p. 71). Once an individual has come to accept the reality of death, that person then begins to "transcend both life and death and to [come] into unity with the Changeless Absolute" (p. 71).

Views of Death in Modern Western Society

A grim view. Marcuse (1959) describes the contrasting ethics one can derive from the various interpretations of death in the history of Western philosophy. On the one hand, death may be glorified as that which

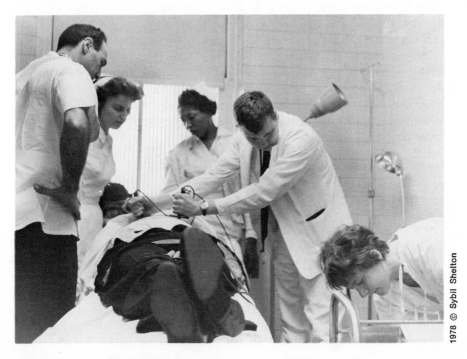

1978 © Sybil Shelton

The fear of death in Western society makes people put it out of their minds until the loss of a loved one.

gives meaning to life and is the precondition for the "true" life of man. On the other hand, death is accepted as inevitable. Another view in modern Western society, and certainly in the United States, is that death is grim and terrifying. Birth is a cause for celebration, but death is feared. In this sense "it lies in ambush and strikes unexpectedly from the side as it claims the young, the innocent, the high minded, and the frivolous . . ." (Holcomb, 1975). Death's "ultimate victory is in persuading us that the good God of all beginnings . . . is turned by the power of death into what James Joyce called . . . the hangman God and what C. S. Lewis called the cosmic vivisectionist" (pp. 275–276). Perhaps it is the certainty of death that makes people dread it so much. And perhaps those who fear it especially are accustomed to being in charge of their own existence. They feel a certain terror that they cannot manipulate the forces of death (Kübler-Ross, 1975).

Most people simply evade the reality of death, except when the demise of family or friends rudely forces it into our consciousness. Ordinarily we are too wrapped up in the business of living to waste time on what we can't ultimately prevent anyhow. We simply take living for granted, and we don't sit around congratulating ourselves that we are alive. It is only when death is imminent for ourselves or those we love, that we feel a certain life hunger (Imara, 1975).

In order to avoid facing such an unpleasant topic, says Herman Feifel, we retire the older generation to so-called leisure communities, telling ourselves that their lives are richer there. Actually we are relieved that we don't have to deal with their aging process. Rest homes and hospitals assume more than just the physical burden of dying. They allow the family to avoid the "impending specter of death" ("Acceptance," 1975, p. 216).

Decreasing emphasis on maintaining life regardless of circumstances. This negative view of death is parallelled by a corresponding de-emphasis on maintaining life for life's sake, resulting in part from the growing world population and our shrinking natural resources. Hall and Cameron (1976) observe Americans' growing support for capital punishment. In 1974 a Gallup poll found that 64% of the American people approved the death penalty, compared with 47% in 1957. Even suicide no longer repels us, and its rate is climbing, especially among young people and blacks. Psychologist Robert Kastenbaum believes that suicide may win society's approval and insists that, as we acknowledge the right to dignify death, suicide will become an ethical alternative, and "strengthen the social fabric" (p. 108). Theologian Richard Rubenstein defends suicides as examples of applying reasoning to human problems, and he argues that it is "irrational to prolong suffering, to keep alive the malformed or the unconscious, to support murderers at public expense, or to allow unwanted babies to be born" (Hall with Cameron, 1976, p. 108).

At a New Haven hospital, 43 deformed babies were permitted to die over a period of 30 months (Hall with Cameron, 1976). The doctors and the parents themselves decided that the children could hardly look forward to a "meaningful humanhood". In rare cases doctors may even go beyond the withholding of life, as in the case of a child who was determined prenatally to be without limbs. This story has been told to over 30 groups of people and there has not been a single expression of outrage. In other words, simply being alive is not enough today—life must also be meaningful. A neurosurgeon, Milton Heifetz, once wrote that "I treasure life, but I do not believe life is warranted if it cannot be lived with some measure of grace and dignity. A man who cannot speak, who cannot think, who would live as a vegetating mass of protoplasm without any hopeful recovery should not be forced to live" (Hall with Cameron, 1976, p. 106).

The foregoing quotation represents an emerging value in America. In Gallup polls in 1947 and 1950 a majority of Americans said they would not permit doctors to practice euthanasia. Only 36% would have allowed doctors to end the lives of persons suffering from incurable diseases, even if both the families and the patients requested it. However, in the mid-1970s almost three-fourths of Americans favored it; and almost 80% of the members of the American Association of Professors of Medicine who responded to a questionnaire replied that they had withdrawn treatment in response to the direct request of their patients. Among 125 terminally ill patients in cardiac and intensive care units, 20 of the patients were deliberately allowed to die, over half because medical treatment was withheld. The plug was pulled on the rest, either because there was no chance of recovery, or because another patient required the life-sustaining machine, or simply as an act of mercy. However, two of the cases were ethically unclear.

The happiness of the patient isn't always a deciding factor. In one case, the night before surgery was planned on a woman, her son-in-law called the doctor and reminded him that he had already performed almost the same operation on her and asked him not to perform it again. If the physician operated, the family's savings would be fully depleted; and they would be denied "a color TV, a second car, and a larger home" (Hall with Cameron, 1976, p. 106). Therefore the physician called off the operation, believing that the few extra years the patient would have from it, would simply not make up for the deprivation that the young family would endure.

Such problems are new, and are brought on by advances in medical technology. If there were enough machines in our hospitals, large numbers of people who would otherwise die would continue to survive and "the prospect of hospitals made up of bed after bed filled with terminal patients is chilling but possible" (p. 106). Moreover the cost of such care is rising astronomically. In the case of Karen Ann Quinlan, the 21-year-old woman with brain damage who had been in a coma for 5 months when her parents went to court to obtain legal permission to turn off the life-support machines which were keeping her alive, $100,000 had already been spent in medical fees. As the financial costs grow, "our eroded reverence for life may wear away entirely" (p. 108).

Many times we simply have no way of knowing before people become unconscious whether or not they would choose to have the machines turned off. In one case a technician who had hooked up 600 patients to machines indicated that 400 of them had been able to communicate their desires, and that not one of them had asked to be permitted to die. Generally they wanted to be attached to the machines as soon as possible (Hall with Cameron, 1976).

Hall and Cameron concluded by speculating that final solutions in some form of death may one day become at least partly acceptable. In 1975 over half of Americans under age 30, said that "incurable disease or continual pain confer upon a person the moral right to end his life" (p. 108).

> If this trend continues, we may one day institute the euthanasia parlors like those portrayed in the movie Soylent Green. In this picture of the future, people who wish to end their lives report to a government building, where beautiful girls welcome them and administer a legal drug. As they lie dying the volunteers watch movies of idyllic pastoral settings and listen to Beethoven's Ninth Symphony; and while Soylent Green is mere fiction, we must not forget that science fiction has been on target with many of its conjectures. Of course there are great dangers here. Ultimately, bureaucrats might decide that only certain people would be permitted access to medical technology; or mercy death might be the reward that people would receive on retirement, and the date of retirement would be arbitrary (Hall with Cameron, 1976).

Already one large city hospital has begun to purchase cheaper though less efficient respirators, thus further endangering lives.

Death as positive. Most current authorities on the subject perceive death as both natural and positive, especially in its impact on life. Imara (1975) believes that it is necessary to learn to die in order to learn to live. Sometimes becoming one's true self means dying in terms of the life which is prescribed by society; and new growth requires the death or throwing off of restricting shackles. That is, growth suggests a succession of dyings and rebirths in the manner that caterpillars become butterflies. People have the ultimate chance for growth when they face death, but growth should not be contingent upon this final crisis. Through understanding that dying possesses growth-producing qualities, an individual can learn to die and grow at any point in life. Those qualities that enable a person to deal positively with death when it ultimately comes, are the identical qualities that identify growing persons at any stage in life (Imara, 1975).

Kübler-Ross's views are similar, and she is convinced that her own experiences with the realities of death have enriched her life more than any she has ever had, because confronting death has challenged her to answer basic questions regarding the meaning of life. She believes that it is important to realize that life is quite short, so that whatever we do has meaning; and as we look back over our lives, we should perceive that we have truly lived (Kübler-Ross, 1975). In this sense, "death is not an enemy to be conquered or a prison to be escaped. It is an integral part of our lives that gives meaning to human existence. It sets a limit on our time in this life, urging us on to do something productive with that time as long as it is ours to use" (Kübler-Ross, 1975, p. x). Regardless of whether we die earlier or later in life, the important factor is whether we have lived fully and completely in the years we have had.

Function of fear of death. On the other hand, coming to view death as a friend might have unexpected consequences. Perhaps a "healthy fear" of death keeps us from taking undue chances and motivates us to live as healthy a life as possible in order to prolong it. In addition, Kastenbaum (1974) suggests that too little fear of death might result in a dangerously low level of procreation which would threaten the continuation of the species. In a study which included both tenth-graders and college undergraduates, young people perceived various alternatives for continuing themselves beyond death. This yearning for self-continuation is especially high among those who feel strong anxiety about death. Such individuals desire to postpone their death and "to keep the torch burning to the option of passing it on to the next generation" (p. 76). Others, however, perceive procreation as a satisfying way of reducing their concern over their personal mortality.

A changing concept. In general, evaluations of death vary according to place, time, circumstance, and individual philosophies. Certainly studies of death attitudes and ceremonials through the years and around the world indicate its significance to be highly fluid. We can only guess what its status would become if, as has been predicted, the life span should be extended by several decades, or if some eons from now, its length should become optional. A number of times the writer has posed the question to college undergraduates: If you could choose to live forever, and have good health and a body characteristic of whatever age you designate, throughout eternity, would you do so, or would you choose to have a normal life span? In addition, those questioned are told that once they have made the decision, they cannot change it. A large majority always settles for the normal life span.

Individual Feelings about Death

Typical views. Certain attitudes toward death are typical. Even when approaching death people ask, "Why me?" and wish to find a meaning for their suffering. This question cannot be answered in generalized terms because the meaning of life and death vary from one individual to another (Kübler-Ross, 1975). The act of dying itself may involve a certain amount of "anticipatory self grief," grief over the loss of one's own life—that is, fearing what it may be to lose one's self. In addition, fear of dying is often associated with unfounded beliefs that dying itself is quite painful, that one may be abandoned by everyone when dying, that death involves an ultimate aloneness, and "that there may be final medical procedures that will further dehumanize oneself by being turned into a sort of plumbing shop . . ." (Holcomb, 1975). The fear of pain can be relieved by a knowledge of modern pain-relieving processes. It can help to know that though dying is rarely pleasant, it is neither as painful nor as unpleasant as is often feared.

Fear of dying involves not only physiological, but psychological, factors. Pain is more easily dealt with than loneliness. It helps if the patient's family visits frequently, communicates openly, and gives constant assurance that the dying person will not be abandoned. About two-thirds of the dying are anxious about being a burden to others, and about half are anxious about separation from their loved ones; they are concerned about how their loved ones will get along after they die (Holcomb, 1975). Many also feel that life no longer has any real meaning.

Older person's attitudes toward death. Bischof (1976) summarizes the attitudes of older adults' feelings about death. They realize that they have already lasted longer than many of their earlier contemporaries. They have a strong belief that their lives should not be prolonged artificially. They think of life, not as the number of years lived, but in terms of the time that remains. Finally they desire to leave this world with respect and dignity.

In general the older the adult, the less important time becomes, so that death is less formidable to the very old than it is to the young

(Bischof, 1976). It is true that older people think about death more frequently, but they are also less afraid of it (Kalish & Reynolds, 1975). Many older persons come to accept, or even welcome, the idea of their own death. They may feel that they are ready; or they may wish to escape infirmity; or they may have religious convictions which convince them that their life will continue after death (Butler, 1975c).

Young people generally avoid thinking about death; and when it does intrude on their consciousness, they view it negatively. Yet even at this stage, individual views vary. In a *Psychology Today* questionnaire the typical respondent—a 20- to 24-year-old, single, caucasian, somewhat religious, Protestant, somewhat politically liberal, college graduate from a small family—had an ambivalent attitude toward death, both "risking death and loving life, wanting happiness and behaving in self-destructive ways; regarding death as taboo and insisting on a new permissiveness to talk about it. . . ." (Schneider, 1971, p. 44). Most of the respondents recognized death and dying as aspects of living. Almost half believed that most people participate consciously or unconsciously in their own death. Only 2% wanted formal funerals, and a third wanted none at all. Almost a third wished to donate their bodies to medical schools or to science. Almost none of them wanted to die in youth or in the prime of life. Two-thirds of them would have liked to live to old age, and more men than women wanted to live out their full life spans. Both sexes accurately placed the time of least fear of death in the years over 70.

Individual views of death. Here several adults on successively older age levels tell how they feel about death.

Thoughts of my own death scare me so badly I don't even like to talk about the subject. (*Male, age 33, research psychologist*)

Death is a part of life; we all have to come to it. I hope I will be able to face the deaths of my loved ones calmly, as grief is a private matter. I feel that those I love are better off because I believe there is a life after death. (*Female, age 33, housewife*)

I don't fear death. I believe in life everlasting and that heaven is better than life on earth. Maybe when the time actually comes, if I know it is near, I won't have quite as positive an attitude. But I still won't fear it. (*Female, age 34, hair stylist*)

Death is the gateway to heaven and hell. It's inevitable and in many cases it is kind. However, I'm not ready to meet mine. (*Female, age 58, teacher*)

I think a lot about my own in terms of preparedness, but honestly evade dwelling on the hereafter. As for my spouse going first, I cannot imagine how I'll be able to fill the void, but I'm sure I'd keep busy and involved. (*Female, age 58, real estate broker*)

One of the most shameful aspects of the human condition is that man's final moment is likely to be one of pain, and his final days, even years, ones of discomfort and helplessness, a soul abiding in a decaying carcass. One's greatest reward would be to go quickly and peacefully. Even so, the vista of a universe continuing for an eternity without being a part of it is intellectually appalling, incomprehensible, unacceptable. (*Male, age 59, journalist*)

It's unavoidable. I think things were planned right. I have seen elderly people ready. They were tired and I am confident there are things worse than death. I fully believe in a hereafter. (*Female, age 61, retired activity director*)

I think the way the life plan is laid out is really stupid, no matter what force or power is responsible for it. Why should one's only existence climax in pain, a wasting away of the body and death? Death is the worst force of all. You have a brief look at the world and then—poof—you're finished for all eternity. And you'll never know about all the exciting things that will happen a billion years from now. (*Female, age 62, college professor*)

If I should go to hell (which isn't likely) and find it didn't exist, I'd be relieved. If I go to heaven (as I expect to) and find there is no such place I'd be disappointed but I would not regret trying to live an upright Christian life. (*Male, age 69, retired college president*)

The death of a 17-year-old granddaughter, due to suicide following a drug episode, filled me with sadness. I like to think of death as being like welcome sleep when one is tired or ill. (*Female, age 73, widow*)

Factors that modify attitudes toward death. Feelings about death involve many factors, one of which is individual convictions about the worth of past accomplishments. Those who have not fully lived, who still have unsettled matters and unrealized dreams of accomplishment, who have not availed themselves of the significant things in life, such as loving, being loved, and contributing effectively to others' welfare, these people are the most unwilling to die (Ross, Braga, & Braga, 1975).

Religious persons typically view death differently from nonbelievers. To the religious person death is simply the last stage in earthly life; but it is not a complete death because only the body dies (Ross, Braga, & Braga, 1975). Most important is the quality of people's religion, and not merely their religious affiliation. Those who have truly integrated religion into their lives have the most positive feelings toward death, and Christians typically adjust better to it emotionally than non-Christians. The better educated are also better adjusted, perhaps because they are generally more financially secure and hence can leave their affairs in better order.

One's attitude toward death takes on special meaning in one's final days. An analysis of eight interviews indicated certain factors which were important for terminal patients' emotional adjustment. These included the "ability to cope with stressful situations in the past, a feeling of having lived a meaningful and fulfilled life, a warm and supporting relationship with one's spouse, hope of a joyful life after death, the ability to talk frankly about the meaning or consequences of one's illness, an explanation of one's position that combines tactful candor with assurance of support, and a feeling of concern from one's children and close friends" (Carey, 1975).

SOME PRACTICAL ISSUES

Treatment of the Dying

The best place to die. Dr. Melvin J. Krant, in "The Organized Care of the Dying Patient" (1972), observes that "helping someone to die well is one aspect of good health care." But what dying well signifies, depends on the person involved. Unless patients are mentally incompetent they should be part of whatever decisions are made about their welfare (Carey, 1975). Members of the family can help most by maintaining an environment which is comparable with the individual's preferred life style, as much as circumstances permit. All too often, at this stage people are simply handled like inert pieces of baggage, to be stashed wherever the caretakers decide.

Over two-thirds of the people in the U.S. die outside the home, in contrast with about half, three decades ago ("Acceptance," 1975). Yet patients often prefer to spend their last days at home, in the environment to which they are accustomed; and their will should prevail when circumstances permit. Instead of being in a "sterile hospital" they want "companionship, and relief from pain; hypnosis, drugs, wine and music. . . . (Huyck, 1974, p. 163). In a familiar environment they can face the inevitability of death "with the dignity befitting the [end] of a life marked by individuality and uniqueness as well as the common sharing of our humanity" ("Acceptance," 1975, p. 216).

Care of the dying. The terminally ill also need much tender, loving care, "for [while] they may be as helpless as a child . . . they seldom arouse tenderness" (Weisman, 1972, p. 144). They should be made to feel, even in their final days, that they are of value; and they should have people readily at hand with whom they can share their fears, feelings and anxieties (Kübler-Ross, 1974). In fact, everything possible should be done to relieve their feelings of isolation and insulation from others.

They have their own special concerns. One of these is death itself. Most of the elderly do not fear it, but often do want to discuss it, if their listeners are supportive and caring. They also enjoy reviewing their lives; and this reminiscing helps them to perceive their lives as a whole, and to reflect upon what they have done. Some of them even write their life stories, often at length, perhaps with a double motive: to leave a legacy for their descendants, and to review their own past (Kalish & Reynolds, 1975). Meantime they should be protected from excessive pain, for the greater discomfort individuals suffer on approaching death, the less able they are to retain a high level of positive emotion. On the other hand, they should not be drugged simply so that they will not be troublesome.

Many of the dying, with occasional exceptions—which should be respected—profit greatly from regular visits from a chaplain. They want to come to grips with such ultimate matters as finding the meaning of life and death (Carey, 1975). Those chaplains who come regularly to talk to patients are most helpful. Counseling is most needed shortly after an individual learns of having an incurable disease, and that death may be imminent. It is easier to prevent deeply unhappy feelings than it is to uproot them once they have taken hold. Whatever care is given should be accorded graciously and unobtrusively, so the patient will not feel guilty about being a burden (Carey, 1975). Even at this stage, patients can easily sense subtle forms of rejection.

An important issue which sometimes arises is whether patients should be told of their unfavorable prognosis. The majority say that they would like to know, and most of them do know, even if they are not directly told (Kalish & Reynolds, 1975). If they ask, they should certainly be informed that they are seriously ill; but they should also be told of all the treatment possibilities. They should not be told that they are going to die at a particular time because no one actually knows when they will die. Besides, such a definitive statement erases the patient's hope (Kübler-Ross, 1974) and many persons have lived far beyond medical expectations. Patients also need to know that their physicians will not simply give up, but will continue to make every effort to prolong their lives.

Since it is not always appropriate, or possible, to make one's wishes known in case of severe illness or deterioration, it is a good idea for intimates to share with each other their feelings about such matters as whether to be told that their prospects of survival are slim, whether they favor the use of life-sustaining machines, and how to take care of the funeral. Some individuals do not want to be told their condition is probably terminal; and it isn't easy to know, without asking, who these few are. Another question is just how long doctors should insist on keeping patients alive, especially after irreparable brain damage has occurred and there is no prospect of that person ever resuming a satisfying life.

When death is obviously at hand, intimates should be warmly supportive but should also muster all the strength they can to keep from falling apart themselves, to avoid making the dying person's last moments overwhelmingly anxious. Unless they can accept the necessity of letting go of the loved one, it will be more difficult for that individual to accept the reality of death (Carey, 1975).

On the other hand, people are often given up for dead long before death has actually occurred. As Butler (1975c) points out, "we are so preoccupied with defending ourselves from the reality of death that we ignore the fact that human beings are alive until they are actually dead. At best, the living old are treated as if they were already half dead" (p. xi). Especially in case of the terminally ill, relatives and friends may write them off. Perhaps dying persons fare best whose loved ones provide the ultimate in attentiveness without displaying uncontrolled grief.

The right to die. One issue of growing importance, because of the increasingly sophisticated life-maintaining equipment available, is the right to die. Passive euthanasia connotes letting patients die naturally instead of exercising dramatic means to keep them alive, when their life would simply involve a vegetative existence or continuous suffering. Active euthanasia suggests the deliberate killing of persons who are presumed to be hopelessly and helplessly disabled or ill. Doctors themselves often support the biological preservation of the individual, even at the price of the patient's loss of dignity (Warren, 1972). However, passive euthanasia is receiving some consideration as a medical practice under carefully safeguarded circumstances, including the individual's own wish to die.

Most authorities oppose artificially keeping a patient alive after extensive and irreversible brain damage has been done. They also believe that while our minds are still clear we should make known our wishes about our last days—including whether we would prefer medical intervention simply to preserve "technical life" (Huyck, 1974, p. 163).

The majority of laymen, too, oppose maintaining a person indefinitely who has no future prospect but pain and who has expressed a will to die. Mark and Dan Jury (1976) tell the poignant story of their grandfather, an old miner who, after his retirement, was afflicted with various infirmities commonly associated with old age. His habits gradually changed; he stopped hanging around the local garage, which had become a ritual ever since his retirement; and he lived in his own mind, indulging in all sorts of fantasies. At night he would get up, tear his room apart, and strew the bedclothes all around, sometimes totally losing control of his bowels during the process. One day he simply decided to stop eating, and he adamantly refused food despite his family's coaxing. His family rejected the only alternative, which was to resort to hospitalization and intravenous feeding. They felt that to strap this man to a hospital bed, "with tubes protruding from his arms was completely alien to the sort of person he had always been" (p. 61). They decided that it was Gramp's right to determine his own destiny and to die through his own will if he so desired. As he told his daughter, "I'm just going to lay here until it happens" (p. 61). His family felt that this was the way he would want it and that he should not be denied his right to die. Meantime, he wanted someone around him all the time and "his bony but still strong fingers clutched the hand of whoever was with him" (p. 63). Finally after three weeks, Gramp died, and Mark wrote: "I felt no sense of relief after Gramp was gone. There was a tinge of emptiness. I thought: 'You pulled it off, Gramp. You really pulled it off'" (p. 63).

Undoubtedly this issue will grow even more heated as life-maintaining machines grow still more sophisticated and as more people make so-called "living wills." Will laws be passed to validate these wills? And who will become the ultimate arbiters? Butler (1975c) advises that there should be panels for each case, including doctors, family members, attorneys, clergymen, social workers, and representatives of the state.

The rights and tasks of the dying. According to Noyes and Clancy (1977), the fatally ill person has certain rights and tasks. One chore is to accept reality, which includes cutting back their former freedom; and they must also stick to necessary rules and routines imposed by their caretakers. Yet fatally ill persons should also remain independent to whatever extent possible—for example, they should be willing, if able, to feed themselves.

Dying persons also have certain rights. Ultimately they must be freed from the expectations of others, except when these involve cooperating and maintaining physical functions, as in eating and eliminating. Dying persons also have the right to be cared for by society or their families; and while families cannot be obligated to respond to these needs, the elderly are entitled to respect, status, and care. Dying persons are making room on earth for others, and in the process they should impose as small a burden as possible. In return they are entitled to continuing care and concern from intimates and community.

Another right of dying persons is to continuity of care, so that there are no disconcerting disruptions and abrupt changes in services. While programs should be flexible, there should be a degree of continuity, coordination, and communication. In larger communities especially, because of the geographical isolation of families, and the many clinics and large number of personnel involved, communication may be fragmented and inadequate. It is essential that federal standards be developed for the care of such patients.

Dying persons should also be accorded certain privileges. One of these is the right of disengagement. As their physical health and energy decline, they lose interest in the world around them, and turn their interests to the disordered functions of their bodies. Families that resist this disengagement and cling to dying persons, place an emotional burden upon them. The dying role also carries with it the right to a certain dignity and status within the community. Instead dying persons have had little respect or esteem in our society. Finally the dying person has the right to be protected from abuse, for all too often these people receive inadequate care (Noyes & Clancy, 1977).

Putting Death in Perspective

Death as the natural culmination of life. Ideally, declare most authorities on the subject of death, we should view death as both natural and positive. Typically an individual's normal state is presumed to involve the best of health, while death is viewed as the ultimate "calamity," observes Katchadourian (1976, p. 52). Perhaps if "medicine could convey the notion that illness and death are part of life rather than aberrations imposed upon it, conceptual and practical gains in understanding the life cycle would be considerable" (p. 52). The most important message that Kübler-Ross (1974) tries to convey is that death doesn't have to be a completely destructive experience. Instead it can be "one of the most constructive, positive, and creative elements of culture and life" (p. 2). It may be that if we realize that ultimately everyone will share the same fate, we will also be able to comprehend that in life we should become "as one, aware and appreciative of our differences, and yet accepting that in our humanness, we are all alike" (p. 3). Such attitudes, by contrast with dread and fear, would not only improve the quality of life but also the quality of dying ("Acceptance," 1975).

Developing healthy attitudes toward dying. Authorities advise that everyone consciously seek to develop healthy attitudes toward dying. While dying individuals have no choice over when death will occur, it is within their control to determine the quality of that experience—whether it be life-affirming or life-denying (Imara, 1975). Such an attitude, suggests Kübler-Ross (1974), requires an acceptance of the idea of death, for those who do so achieve a "very outstanding feeling of equanimity and peace" (p. 34). She herself no longer denies the reality of death, although it took a long time for her to work it through in this death-denying society; and "once you have faced your own finiteness and have accepted it, you will see that life becomes much more meaningful and more valuable" (Kübler-Ross, 1974, p. 21). Perhaps one reason that people fear death in this society is that they lack familiarity with it, because it usually occurs in a hospital.

Another common suggestion for developing a good attitude is that people become better acquainted with death. Mrs. Rose Marie Smith, founder of the Journey's End Foundation Fund, a nonprofit organization working to transform the image of death, says we have kept death in the closet for too long. She says that death is often a real friend, for it releases an individual from suffering. Also, it is simply the natural conclusion of life ("Attitudes toward death," 1975).

In a similar vein, Kübler-Ross advises that people try to experience death and relate to it in various contexts, including viewing people in the dying process, attending their burial, or perhaps interacting with the body. She believes that we err in sheltering children from death and the dying, and that we are depriving them of an experience with which they should become familiar. After an individual dies we try to make the body appear natural, and we assist the bereaved ones by doing many things for them. Participating in the process will actually help those who grieve, advises Kübler-Ross and later it will help them to face their own death.

Stanley Keleman's (1975) view is similar, and it is also somewhat novel. He comments on Plato's reputed death-bed aphorism that the secret of the good life is to "practice dying." Keleman advises that people resolve any ambivalent feelings they have in all the "little dyings" that they experience, from the actual death of loved ones to the demolition of treasured self-images, all of which can become significant rehearsals for the final "big dying."

People may also resolve anxiety about death through philosophy and religion. Religious sentiments may help one to have confidence in God's caring and may give one a firm belief in a life after death. Nevertheless religion in the conventional sense is not essential to an acceptance of dying. Perhaps a "shared identity, by which an individual identifies with all mankind becomes his best defense against death" (Erikson, 1976, p. 16). Imara (1975) tells of a woman who was an agnostic; she neither believed nor disbelieved, for the matter of divinity was simply not relevant to her concept of the world. As she herself became more loving, she became more positive regarding her experiences with others, but the concept of divinity itself was still not relevant. What Imara observes is that the religious question concerns our need for being committed to something on which we can focus our lives. It permits us to do what we believe is good, and this activity helps us to expand our potential as individuals.

An individual can also get help from others who have achieved, or are themselves seeking to achieve, wholesome attitudes toward death. One can talk to others who face terminal illness with inner calm (Carey, 1975). Or those who reside in group living facilities such as retirement villages, can collectively devise ways of preparing themselves for impending death. In any case, one should keep one's affairs in order; and if one is the family breadwinner, plan ahead so that dependents will be secure.

Coping with the death of loved ones. Death not only affects the dying but also the loved ones who are left behind. Perhaps the hardest task of those who remain, is the process of letting the dying go. In such cases grief can be lessened by assuring the dying person that the survivors will carry on whatever unfinished work that person leaves, and that the family will continue to cope effectively with life's tasks (Holcomb, 1975). A mother whose only son, a young adult, died of cancer, felt first a shock and then a certain numbness; and as she progressed through later stages of grief she experienced certain psychosomatic symptoms. Finally she concluded that "grief cannot be hurried, but eventually an emotional balance returns . . . you cannot bring back the one you love but you have to face reality. A change has occurred in my life, and my life must now have more meaning. I watched our son fight to live and stood by as he accepted death. He knew there was not much hope for him and became very brave. I could not disappoint him and I had to be strong for him" (Mise, 1975, p. 101). In other words, the best way to pay tribute to the one who dies, is to make one's own life thereafter, significant.

Grief cannot be defined simply, for it is a type of emotion that has "psychologic, physiologic, and existential (spiritual) elements or dimensions, which interpenetrate with each other. . . . Grief work is the process of working through the disengaging process, becoming freed from the relationship that existed, and reinvesting emotional capital, plans, and energy in new dimensions of life" (Holcomb, 1975, p. 251). This practice will involve "working through" a whole complex of distressing emotions, and re-establishing one's ongoing life course without the presence of the person, thing, or relationship that no longer exists. In order to illustrate the processes of normal grief work, Holcomb describes reactions to the unexpected loss by death of a significant, though older, person. Even when the loss of that person was not completely unexpected, the first reaction is often one of denial. Although it may not be verbally expressed or recognized by the individual as such, there is an unconscious need to somehow undo the reality of the event itself. Later, after accepting the reality of death, the grieving person experiences a clearcut syndrome of somatic disturbances which may last from a few minutes to an hour or so in extreme form, and for several hours or even days, with diminishing severity. Such symptoms include shortness of breath, tightness in the throat, an empty feeling in the abdomen, chills, dull headaches, and prickly feelings along the spine.

Grief, especially among the aging, involves not merely the death of others, but many forms of bereavement, including the anticipation of one's own death; the anticipated or actual loss of some body functions such as sexual potency, sight, hearing; or of some organ such as a leg, lung, or kidney; or even the loss of physical beauty or a beautiful figure; the loss of professional or vocational status through retirement; economic conditions; a loss of social or economic status which is closely related to an individual's self-perception; the loss of significant relationships as those that occur through divorce or separation; or losing close friends who have for some reason become alienated; and the loss of certain significant possessions such as financial resources or one's home (Holcomb, 1975).

The reaction to others' death depends on several factors, one of which is an individual's feelings about the death of that specific person. One might feel differently when a young person dies, from when an older individual, or one who is in pain with no chance of recovery, dies. Another element in the reaction to death is the degree of devotion felt toward the dying person. After all, watching a stranger die is not the same as seeing a loved one pass on. Also involved are matters of dependence and distance—whether one has been constantly caring for the dying person, or physically removed from the place of death (Bischof, 1976).

These first reactions to death will be followed by feelings of tiredness and general weakness. The psychological, as distinct from the somatic, syndrome includes "general irritability, whether expressed verbally or not; a feeling of hostility, often expressed toward the deceased in such statements as, "Why did he do this to me?" or, "Why did God do this to me—two ways of saying the same thing—I'm damned mad at my husband/wife (or whomever) and at God for leaving me alone" (Holcomb, 1975 p. 263). At times, individuals may assume blame themselves, even if nothing could have been done for the individual. They may have a desire to talk more than usual, especially about the deceased; or feel a restlessness about going through meaningless motions; and they may experience a general feeling of being alone and bewildered. These early psychologic manifestations are displaced by new patterns, as bodily functions revert to normal. There may still be some tiredness and loss of appetite, coupled with feelings of irritability and guilt. There is a need for catharsis of both negative and positive feelings, as well as for a working through of guilt feelings. The work of normal grief has been called "the illness that heals itself." In this sense it represents a "pain with a purpose." Gradually the mourner comes to accept the return to normal routines without the loved one. At this stage the grieving individual may feel disloyal to the dead person for becoming increasingly emotionally detached from him or her. Yet this emancipation is a requirement for reestablishing a healthy hold on life.

Usually the most intense period of bereavement is immediately after the significant person has died. However, two more intense periods involve preparation for, and participation in, the funeral service or memorial ceremony; and coming home afterward to one's home. The funeral or memorial service itself may provide a catharsis for deep feelings, helping the individual to achieve a reintegration and restablization of the self. Even after the funeral or memorial service is over, there is much to do in working through grief. There is the matter of coping with the meaninglessness of simple daily routines because they are no longer shared with the deceased. Sometimes grief work is neurotic; it either persists too long or is delayed, and appears long after the death itself. The pain of the grief work is very great, and may not result in healing, but instead in sadistic actions toward others, or masochistic self-punishment.

Another task when someone dies, is taking care of the details of the final rite of passage—including finding out family preferences, individual desire, and religious affiliation. The donation of bodies to medical research, and cremation are increasingly common. Contributing to worthy causes instead of lavishly displaying flowers is also common. In most cases, burial is taken care of by professionals, including religious persons and funeral directors (Bischof, 1976). And memorial services are coming increasingly to be preferred over funeral services, because they can be simple, dignified, and economical (E. Morgan, 1973).

Holcomb (1975) calls it a myth that only professionals, such as psychiatrists and ministers, can properly counsel bereaved persons. Many sensitive and emotionally mature adults, given a reasonable amount of training and some ongoing supervision, can often be of even more help to persons in crisis than professionals can. For one thing, they are helping out of general concern, and not for money. Whether they be professionals or laymen they must have a real concern for others, able to listen and to "share long silences, to let happen what needs to happen in meaningful relationships" (p. 274). In the process of having to "reach deep into their own spiritual being to help another in distress, if only to suffer meaningfully in silence alongside a fellow human, they find and develop those spiritual resources needed to meet their own needs in times of stress and distress" (p. 274).

A CLOSING COMMENT

Significant changes are taking place in society's attitudes and practices regarding death. The subject itself is no longer taboo, and a host of psychologists, philosophers, and other professionals are engaged in a furious ferment, sorting out and debating the significant issues. A look at history and a glance around the world readily discloses that views and practices relating to death derive, often in obscure ways, from the total context of a culture; and they inevitably evolve at varying speeds, according to the rapidity of change within society itself.

In the main it seems that attitudes and practices in this society are becoming healthier, to a considerable degree because we are looking at them squarely and beginning to do something about them. As a case in point, consider the decision by many persons to dispense with such costly traditions as purchasing fine caskets or having funerals. Nevertheless we must realize that death cannot be turned into a wholly rational matter, because it represents the loss of a self that one deeply values, even for those who believe it may assume another form in eternity.

Society has yet to take large measures for prolonging the life span or even for ultimately transcending death altogether. While this final triumph over death seems impossible for centuries to come, and may not occur at all, certain respected scientists believe that given adequate funding, life could be lengthened even within our lifetime.

SUGGESTED READINGS

Agich, G. J. The concepts of death and embodiment. *Ethics in Science and Medicine*, 1976, *3* (2), 95–105. Certain of the best known criteria of death are defined and criticized.

Bok, S. Personal directions for care at the end of life. *New England Journal of Medicine*, 1976, *295* (7), 367–369. The functions of living wills are discussed and suggestions are made for drawing up more effective documents.

Bugen, L. A. Human grief: A model for prediction and intervention. *American Journal of Orthopsychiatry*, April 1977, *47* (2), 196–206. An alternative is presented to the prevalent model of grieving based on stages of bereavement. Two dimensions—the closeness of the relationship and the mourner's perception of the preventability of death—are named as the chief predictors of the duration and intensity of bereavement.

Chown, S. M. Morale, careers and personal potentials. In Birren, J. E. &

Schaie, K. Warner (Eds.) *Handbook of the psychology of aging*. New York: Van Nostrand Reinhold Company, 1977, 672–691. This chapter reviews relevant research regarding common reactions to the frustrations of later life, and analysis made of their impact on self-assessment and morale.

Hall, E. & Cameron, P. Our failing reverence for life. *Psychology Today*, April 1976, 9 (11), 104–108; 113. The world's growing population problem is related to societal attitudes toward such diverse topics as euthanasia, suicide, abortion and homosexuality. Since all of these serve to help to control population, society may come to assume a more positive attitude toward them.

Kalish, R. A. Death and dying in a social context. In Binstock, Robert H. & Shanas, Ethel (Eds.) *Handbook of aging and the social sciences*. New York: Van Nostrand Reinhold Company, 1976, 483–507. An authority on the subject considers death in terms of definition, its meaning, attitudes toward it, the process of dying, and coping with the death of others and, ultimately, of self.

Koestenbaum, P. *Is there an answer to death?* Englewood Cliffs, New Jersey: Prentice-Hall, 1976. The writer discusses individual attitudes regarding death, consciousness and immortality, and suggests ways of improving such attitudes.

Kübler-Ross, E. (Ed.) *Death: The final stages of growth*. Englewood Cliffs, New Jersey: Prentice-Hall, 1975. An outstanding authority on the subject of death presents a collection of essays on issues regarding this topic, along with her own insightful commentaries.

Lofland, L. H. *Sage contemporary social science issues: XXVIII. Toward a sociology of death and dying*. Beverly Hills, California: Sage Publications, Inc., 1976. This reprint of seven articles from *Urban Life* deals with various aspects of death, including the physician's role, the state execution, coroner's strategies, and practices in institutions that house the elderly.

Marshall, V. W. Socialization for impending death in a retirement village. *American Journal of Sociology*, March 1975, 80 (5), 1124–1144. The life cycle is portrayed as involving adaptation to new social roles at successive life stages which involve countless major and minor adjustments, the last being preparation for death. Congregate living facilities are suggested as providing the best settings for this type of socialization, for there residents devise means of collective socialization for impending death.

Rupert, M. K. Death and its definitions: Medical, legal, and theological. *Michigan Academician*, 1976, 8 (3), 235–247. An analysis is made of various definitions of death, and the problems that arise when such concepts are applied to actual cases.

Schneidman, E. S. *Death: Current perspectives*. Palo Alto, California: Mayfield Publishing Company, 1976. This collection of recent essays reflects current thinking on death from the orientation of philosophy, religion, history, medicine, literature and sociology. Death is treated in terms of diverse cultural definitions, its differential effects on segments of society, its effects on the persons most directly involved, and its significance on the individual level.

Veatch, R. M. *Death, dying, and the biological revolution.* New Haven: Yale University Press, 1976. In this critical survey of medical, ethical and legal aspects of dying, the author appraises the various philosophical, practical, and social issues involved. Such controversial topics are treated as technologies for extending life, decisions regarding keeping terminally ill persons alive, what to tell dying persons, dying persons' rights, and public responsibility.

V
PART

Conclusion

16
CHAPTER

Perspective
on
Adulthood

SOME GENERALIZATIONS

Similarities and Differences

The foregoing survey of the adult life-stages yields certain general conclusions. First of all, our humanness dictates a certain commonality within our lives, while the unique blending of individual heredity and patterns of experience create infinite variations within them. To a certain extent we all remain, in varying degrees, out of synchrony with each other. While the fundamental principles that govern development bind us all, we may be grappling with different tasks at somewhat different stages in our development.

The Unevenness of Progress through Life

In a way, progression across the life span is uneven, like broken-field running. It is inaccurate to think of gradual and equal decline in each decade between the ages of 20 and 70. Decline may be focused in one or two decades, while plateaus or even improvements may be the rule during others. In other words, changes in behavior do not follow a straight line across the years. Nor do changes in the body proceed at a homogeneous pace.

The Predictability of Personality

Despite this unevenness, development does not proceed in a random fashion. Instead, within broad limits, individuals grow along paths that are predictable from earlier points in their lives and from knowing something about their personality structure, ways of coping, success in adapting to earlier life events, and expectations of life (Neugarten, 1971). In order to understand people it is important to be familiar with their previous life experiences (Lowenthal & Chiriboga, 1973).

Individual variations in certain characteristics, especially, appear to persist over the years—for example, activity level. In general, active, quick-moving babies become highly active adults (Haan & Day, 1974). Individuals may slow down somewhat over the years, but they will tend nevertheless to remain in the same position relative to their age-peers, throughout life. Another characteristic which is persistent over the years, is degree of conventionality. Unconventional thought is one of the most stable characteristics from early adolescence to late adulthood, as are the related traits of rebelliousness and sex-typed behaviors (Haan & Day, 1974). Although adolescent girls are a bit more conventional than adolescent boys, they become less conventional by young adulthood; and in middle age, even less so than men (Haan & Day, 1974).

Certain other life-style characteristics, such as humanitarianism, intellectualism, aestheticism, and practicality, tend to become more important from late adolescence to early adulthood and to remain stable or even increase a bit over the adult years (Haan & Day, 1974). By their late 20s most people have established core interest and value patterns, which in general resemble those of their parents.

Although a degree of consistency is the rule in most peoples' lives, their earlier characteristics do sometimes appear to change. In one project, the Grant Study, at least half the men who as adolescents had appeared quite colorless and bland, became quite interesting and full of life in their mid-40s (Vaillant, 1977). One such individual took up deep-sea diving; another had an exciting love affair; and still another, a frightened, mother-dominated boy in adolescence, became a well-known scientist who had unusual autonomy and prestige.

The Divergence of Physiological and Psychological Development

To a certain degree, humans also manage to transcend their physical limitations. Psychological health and physical vigor certainly interrelate, but they are not locked in tandem. For most people life is not all downhill after they have passed their physical peak. Instead people move "toward greater comfort, candor, and an objective sense of self as displayed by now 40- and 50-year old people who have been followed over a period of time" (Haan, 1976, p. 64). Even in the young-old, and often in the old-old years, large numbers of people continue to grow, arriving at successively higher stages of self-actualization.

Viable Alternatives

Over and over, life histories demonstrate the legitimacy of highly varied life styles. In Ross Firestone's book, *The Success Trip* (1976), 34 people who have been successful in a variety of fields, including such diverse persons as Albert Ellis, Howard Cosell, and Mike Wallace, describe in what manner they achieved success. The predictably common denominators were driving ambition, intelligence, and hard work. Otherwise there was no pattern, because some were rich and some poor; some were pushed to achieve when they were children, and others did not find their niche until they were well into adult years. Many of them indicated that sheer luck had much to do with reaching the top, but the majority added that one must have the potential for taking advantage of this luck.

CAUTIONS REGARDING STAGE THEORY

As we discussed earlier in this volume, the value of stage theory is that it establishes a certain order to the life experience. However, it often suggests a precision that may not actually exist. For example, the woman's life cycle is commonly viewed as a sequence of inflexible stages: "home-centered activities in childhood, work before and after marriage, bearing and rearing children, caring for the retired husband, widowhood, and death" (Movius, 1976, p. 57). These hypothetical stages do not take into account such life discontinuities as returning to school, or developing new interests (Lopata, 1971).

Also consider the stage theorist's common observation that individuals must successfully discharge the tasks of each age if they are to be ready for the next ones. As an example of someone who did not do so, consider an older person who may be "only a child in old man's skin, for the petulance or demands of old age may be simply [remains] of the selfish wishes of a young child. . . . (Smith, 1973, p. 186). Or take a middle-aged male who at 18 got married and settled down to a dead-end job; he may feel dissatisfied because he was denied the testing of alternatives that belong to the late teens and 20s. On the other hand, people can, and often do, make reparations, even at a late date. Those who continue to grow over the years, develop new aspects of personality that they might earlier have considered foolish, or suppressed (Sheehy, 1976).

According to society's own conception of stages, people are assigned age roles. As a result most people unfortunately submit to the age stereotypes foisted upon them. Instead, insists Montagu (1977), people should remain forever young in spirit. They should preserve "the spirit of a child, of youthfulness, of inquisitiveness—an open-mindedness that is free to consider everything, a sense of humor, playfulness—all these are qualities we are designed to develop rather than outgrow" (p. 46).

Finally, particular characteristics of development can be too closely linked with a particular stage, which makes some people believe that those qualities must inevitably be a part of that stage. For instance, characteristics ordinarily associated with aging may either partially or wholly derive from factors other than biological aging. It is difficult to determine to what extent differences between younger and older persons are due to the effects of aging or to differences between those born at different times in history (cohorts) (Neugarten, 1973). Different cohorts are influenced by different sociocultural conditions and in consequence may react differently. Fortunately new research techniques are being devised that will help to differentiate cohort and age differences.

Neugarten (1973) summarizes the results of studies concerned with differences in personality, according to age. She concludes that there is neither an overall decrease in the competency of performing adult social roles, nor a diminution of social interaction, at least until peoples' mid-60s or early 70s. On the other hand, there is an increase in turning inward that begins in one's late 40s or early 50s. Since the inward orientation begins well before the changes associated with aging, which we have mentioned above, this attribute appears to be truly developmental.

Differences in social adaptation are relatively independent of age in persons between 50 and 80 (Neugarten, 1973). Instead factors such as health, financial resources, work status, and marital status, are far more important than chronological age in determining the adjustment of people of this age. As for social interaction, its decline in peoples' late 60s and early 70s may or may not have developmental components.

A FEW RECOMMENDATIONS

Research Needs

If the most is to be made of adult life, certain kinds of research should be done. For one thing, the life styles of people who age successfully should be studied. In a longitudinal study of aging begun in 1958 by Dr. Nathan W. Shock, Director of the Gerontology Research Center in Baltimore, a panel of over 1000 men, ages 20 to 103, have been seen at least once, and over 100 of them, at least four times. They are somewhat homogeneous in terms of social characteristics, and all have advanced degrees. While they are not representative of the entire population, they do portray aging under the best conditions (Tobin, 1977).

Cross-cultural and subcultural studies are both needed; each can lend perspective to the other. Such studies, says Kessler, have already taught us certain things. For one, growing old does not necessarily mean a succession of losses, for in certain cultures older people are the winners. This means that old age can bring influence and power. On the other hand, such studies also show us that dramatic discontinuities in the life span can set age groups apart from and against each other (Kessler, 1976). Each age stage should be studied within the broader framework of the entire life cycle, since no stage is an independent part of life. While each age has its distinctive characteristics, it can only be appreciated in terms of what has gone before and what may be anticipated in the future.

Careful attention should also be paid to the significance of research findings. For example, consider the finding that in later years, simpler persons, those less sensitive to the external environment, are somehow insulated from stress. While they may have fared more poorly in their younger years, when people who are highly active and creative are rewarded, they improve in mental health in later middle age, and presumably after that too. By contrast, highly complex people may feel more stress as time goes on, partly because they become frustrated with their increasing limitations (Troll, 1975). Is it safe to assume, on the basis of such evidence, that complex individuals must necessarily sustain stress in later years? As medical science reduces the physical limitations of later years, and as society becomes more supportive of the lifelong development of human potential, they will find this stage in life more satisfying.

Finally, research regarding adulthood must greatly increase in quantity and improve in quality if significant theories are to emerge. A common theme among researchers "is the apparent absence of convincing findings on the nature of developmental processes in adulthood and the observation that directionality of age changes is in considerable doubt" (Schaie, 1973, p. 151). As the pieces fall into place, and gaps are closed, a more meaningful psychology of adulthood will emerge.

Unfortunately, observes McCall (1977), most present-day psychologists are taught that only through the experimental method can cause-effect conclusions be reached. The experimental method has yielded much worthwhile information; however, developmental psychologists have embraced this attitude so strongly that they have ignored "the process of development as it naturally transpires in children growing up in actual life circumstances . . . " (p. 334).

Fortunately many authorities are urging that developmental psychologists become more concerned with naturalistic ecology. Certainly "the description of relationships in naturalistic environments, while not sufficient to establish that factor X does cause factor Y, is necessary for such a conclusion. Yet historically, description is not one of the psychologist's delights—it is a second-class method of study . . . because it does not permit one to infer causality" (p. 336).

Need to Improve Relations between Age Groups

Much has been made of the need to improve relationships between youth and their parents. The need to improve the relations between middle-aged and older persons is as great or greater. In a study of three generations, Kalish and Johnson (1972) found that the middle-generation mothers felt more negative about older people and more anxious regarding the aging process than either the daughters or the grandmothers; and that the grandmothers held the most positive views toward aging and the elderly. Perhaps the middle-aged women were resentful of caring for aged parents while at the same time perceiving undesirable symptoms of aging in themselves.

Tensions may also arise between young and middle-aged adults, or between the young-old and the old-old. Often middle-aged workers are bypassed for promotion in favor of younger ones. Or young adults may resent middle-aged ones for clinging too long to society's reins. The young-old may avoid the old-old, who represent what they realize with dread they will shortly become, and with whom they are unwillingly lumped into the same general category.

Remedial measures for these tensions must be based on a careful analysis of their causes. Lack of mutual understanding can be helped by making life-span psychology and education an integral part of education at all age levels and by arranging experiences in which people of different ages participate. Such work may assume the form of continuing education classes, workshops, volunteer work on social projects, and

The relationship between youths and their parents has improved over the years.

so on. Other measures are more controversial, such as incorporating teenagers earlier into the world of work, as suggested by the Coleman II Panel on youth; or deliberately arranging housing that mixes the old and the young.

Bronfenbrenner (1970) believes that segregation by age is the most "intensive" type of segregation in America, and that the wall between age groups should be broken down. Children, he declares, require people of other age groups if they are to become human. By contrast, the socialist countries of eastern Europe are quite conscious of the importance of mixing age groups. In the Soviet Union, places of business adopt children's groups from a school or hospital ward or community center; and people within the place of business get to know the children as friends.

The writer believes that intermingling should be encouraged, not forced, and probably for brief rather than permanent periods, unless cultural factors make such extended association natural and satisfying.

Life-span Education

Fortunately the life-span education courses recommended here are now being given in some colleges and medical schools. Our immediate task is to recognize the urgency of universalizing this form of education and to foster the quantity and quality of research that would provide causes with the substance they need.

Various recommendations for such programs are already being made. Bailey (1976) suggests that education about the stresses of middle age be studied in high schools and colleges through various courses and modules, which will lead to increased communication and understanding of parental behavior by adolescents and young adults. Persons going through the climacteric might profit from educational offerings in the form of informal seminars, perhaps at womens' and service clubs. Specialists who deal with people at this age, including doctors, psychiatrists, and social workers, need training regarding the stresses of this period. All such efforts should become part of an overall educational strategy that embraces people at all ages, from early childhood on.

In other words, education for all of life should run like a thread through all education. Perhaps young people, accustomed to projecting themselves into the future, would become more responsible about such present habits as smoking or drinking. Young people often live in a manner that makes successful life in the future more difficult. The emphasis in education should be on making the most of one's potential, not merely on avoiding or curing·pathology. As we gain greater insight

into the ways that people develop more effective coping skills throughout their lives, a reservoir of useful information can be made available
to all students of developmental psychology.

Environmental Control and Social Engineering

It is increasingly recognized that the environment can be so exploited as to work for or against us. For one thing, the varying impact
of particular environments on different age groups and kinds of people
should be determined. A part of life-span education should be learning
to select and control environments to suit diverse individual needs. In
addition, the tempo and conditions of adult life should become properly
related to the physiological processes of that life. One reason for the
increase in psychosomatic ailments and life stresses is that the socially
defined pace of life in industrial societies is "out of phase with its basic
metabolic rhythms" (Katchadourian, 1976, p. 51).

An important component of self-image, from the lifetime perspective, is the degree to which people feel in control of their lives (Brisset,
1972). A sense of internal control is more characteristic of men than
women, and it increases from childhood to age 60 (Staats, 1974). Yet,
as population density grows, so does the complexity of human interrela-
tions and of the governmental bureaucracy intended to cope with them.
In such a situation, it becomes essential that the architects of the society
safeguard against excessive regimentation and the undermining of
individual initiative.

Social engineering, which could change our environment, might
take many forms. Butler (1975a) recommends diverting the money now
spent on spectator sports to facilities that encourage physical recreation
for the entire population. He feels that the large chunks of public park
space now "gobbled up by golfers could be more equitably divided
among hikers, swimmers, and other sports enthusiasts" (p. 367).

Butler also advises that life tasks become less age-specific. Ordinarily we associate youth with education, the middle years with work,
and the later ones with retirement. However, these three aspects of life
should run concurrently and continuously throughout life. Youth could
work and travel as well as attend college, while middle-aged persons
would take time off for creation and study; and 70-, or even 80-year-
olds could enjoy work, study, and leisure.

If we apply what we are learning about exercise, nutrition, the
environment in general, and the reorganization of our life styles, we
may ultimately be able to restrict deterioration and senescence to a brief

time at the end of our years. It is certainly not worthwhile lengthening our lives unless we also learn how to make them more satisfying (Troll, 1975).

LOOKING AHEAD

Anticipatory planning and imaginative forecasting should become an integral aspect of government, social and educational programs, and research. Even now, although the dim outlines of the future are just emerging, contingency programs subject to continuing modification, should be devised. Here are a few possibilities.

Changes in the Family

As in the past, the family will be a basic element of adult life styles in the future. Pickett (1977) summarizes several predictions concerning its future:

(1) Harry and Joan Constantine (1973) believe that ultimately, lifetime partners who have sex only with each other will constitute a minority who will nevertheless involve substantial numbers of people. Most families will center around pairs who "share a primary but not exclusive commitment." Instead the family will be permeable, allowing new members of other families to join it.

(2) James Ramey (1976) foresees an increase in multiadult households, a situation which will afford an enriched environment both for children and adults, all of whom will relate easily to each other, regardless of kinship.

(3) Jessie Bernard (1975) believes that marriage in the future can only succeed on an egalitarian basis. Many women have come to realize that traditional marriage favors their husbands. They reject unequal marriage, holding a job outside the home while doing most of the work in the household as well. Some women will marry but refuse to have children; others who have children will insist that parenting and child rearing be shared.

(4) Other authorities foresee a two-step marriage: the first phase will be legal cohabitation, and in the second, permission to have children will be granted. Among the young the de facto two-step marriage often exists already, but the first step is not legal.

(5) Pickett (1977) himself predicts, on the basis of projections derived from U.S. Census Bureau data, an increase in premarital sex, divorce, singlehood, and female-headed households; and a slight decline in the marriage rate and the population growth. Such factors, along with

The future of the family is of concern for many authorities due to such factors as longevity.

the smaller proportion of people marrying, the later age at marriage, the greater similarity in age of marriage partners, and the delay in having children, will produce a progressive reduction in family size.

(6) On the other hand, most authorities reject any idea of either widespread promiscuity or a further sharp reduction in the numbers of children being born. While "casual sex between strangers will probably increase, most sex will involve a concern for the other person. As for children, there will always be those adults who will not see their lives as complete until they become parents" (p. 332). In short, the family of the future will involve varied "family profiles. The traditional family, as we have known it, will survive in a smaller, more flexible form, but it will be joined by other forms which were once considered deviant" (p. 332). Furthermore, the boundaries of marriage will shift and change, with continued variations. Future marriages will contain forms as contrasting as traditional unions and homosexual marriages. For "those who like kaleidoscopes, the future is beautiful indeed. Those who prefer a still life may find it less to their liking" (p. 332). Pickett concludes by observing that most social scientists' future projections are based on current findings, and forecasting almost never takes into consideration

the inevitable "dramatic scientific achievements or the sudden events which change the course of history" (p. 332).

Potential for Increasing the Life Span

Far more dramatic changes may be in store for us regarding the life span. In the future we may know enough about aging to modify the process directly—perhaps by altering the body chemistry—or indirectly, through health care and improved nutrition. Also, genetic factors which cause such changes as loss of hair or graying may be modifiable. Perhaps, too, certain chronic and acute diseases now common among the aged, may be identified and controlled, if not eliminated. While humans may never be able to live forever, as a result of future breakthroughs "they can live much longer and more comfortably, mostly free from the violent ravages of disease, with perhaps a gradual and fairly predictable decline toward eventual death" (Butler, 1975c, p. 17).

Strehler's conjectures regarding longevity. More dramatic changes in longevity may occur. If an institute on aging were properly funded, declares Strehler (1977), by the year 1983 we might well understand, in depth, the details of cellular and bodily aging (p. 54). However, if no special research effort is made, the date for controlling aging will be delayed until the beginning of the next century, which is certainly too late to help most of us living today. Some opponents of such research believe that the world would become populated with "decrepit, patched up, wizened, senile people, perhaps fed through tubes and moving with the aid of electronic prostheses" (p. 54). Such a picture is simply not true, because the life span can hardly be increased if the body's overall condition is not improved. Persons who lived 150 years would be correspondingly healthy for most of their life span, and even those of a less advanced age would have bodies like those of much younger persons.

The potential impact of a greatly expanded life span is remarkable to contemplate; it would produce a revolution in human societies. Because of the vastly better health and the greater time available to assimilate the world's wonders and wisdom, future mentality would be more advanced than that of today. And since the healthy middle years of life would at least double, people would have more time to contribute to society. Professionals today require many years for their training; if their post-training years doubled, they could make a far greater contribution than at present. On the other hand, many people would probably move from one occupation to another, which would require periodic retraining. With so much time available, people might take off a year or two to learn new skills or to update older ones. Meantime, as machines take over more of the burdensome, repetitive tasks, human beings, with their vastly increased physical resources, will be able to experience more creatively the varied worlds of music, art, poetry, and entertainment. However, such a utopia will be made possible for the readers of this book only if society provides far greater support for aging research than it does at present.

Population Control

The quality of life in the future will be related in no small measure to the number of persons on this planet, and to what kind of people they are. Dr. Kingsley Dunham, a geologist, forecasts a "world-wide emergency . . . based on systems analysis of the future population growth, consumption of natural resources, and resulting pollution" ("Population proliferation," 1973, p. 6). He notes that the world's resources are "nonrenewable and finite" and that unless population growth can be curbed, famine and/or pollution could lead to mass death within a few decades (p. 6). In consequence, adds Dunham, people must be called upon increasingly to control their own personal parenting desires for the good of society.

To date, such matters have been mostly allowed to drift; there have been only isolated and sporadic efforts at establishing planned parenthood programs. It will be difficult to cope with the widespread paranoia that any kind of governmental restrictions on an individual's choice to have children would evoke. Most people reject even more strongly any recommendations of quality control, such as through sperm banks stocked with contributions from superior donors. Yet if, at some future time, humans' use of essential resources outruns their ingenuity in developing them, the question may arise: who will have the right to reproduce, and in what numbers?

Relationships between the Generations

The current greying of America, or the increasing average age of our population, may have several affects. In time increasingly larger numbers of older people must be maintained by smaller numbers of younger ones. Moreover, because of their larger numbers, the elderly's demands for special benefits will have greater power effect. Consequently, warn some sociologists, there may develop "a war between the ages that [will] make the generation gap of the 1960s seem tame ("End of youth culture," 1977).

As the proportion of younger to older people declines, the nation's preoccupation with matters of youth may decrease. There may be fewer fans of pop music, and less juvenile programming on television. After decades of stress on very active sports which chiefly involve young people, recreation may focus on less energetic pursuits. There has already been a revival of some of the more sedate, leisurely pastimes such as ballroom dancing and taking cruises on ocean liners.

Older people can also be expected to have more sophistication and power in the future. They are becoming increasingly better educated, and are gaining more income and acquiring greater experience in promoting their concerns. One group alone, the American Association of Retired Persons, has over 12 million members ("End of youth culture," 1977).

The Contributions of Futurism

The growing emphasis on futurism should afford better perspective on the matters we have been discussing. Futurism focuses most often on comprehending and anticipating technological and scientific advances in order that controls may be designed to make the most of their effects (Spekke, 1976). For example, researchers at the Hudson Institute and the Aspen Institute for Humanistic Studies have concluded that the future may be brighter than many people think. After reviewing the Institutes' research, The London Times concludes that we may not, because of overpopulation, be "inexorably driving ourselves towards a ravished earth on which we are doomed to watch each other starving to death on color television sets" (Spekke, 1976, p. 605). As people climb the socioeconomic ladder and gravitate toward urban areas, women's status changes, reasons for producing large families diminish, family-planning technologies become more accessible, and the fertility rate declines. Moreover as societies evolve, so do patterns of consuming resources. In more prosperous societies people devote their extra funds not so much to increased quantity of goods as to quality, and beyond that to "symbolic consumption" (p. 605).

The Science of Adulthood

Some of the most exciting future developments will be in the science of adulthood itself. When Muson (1977) inquired of Vaillant what were "the biggest surprises" in his Grant Study of male adults he replied:

I think the recovery process per se, for people who were in various kinds of pain at one point or another in their lives, but who turned it into success in another form, would be one surprise. I think another was that in studying health, I expected to find people who were in no trouble at all. I didn't know people like that, but I assumed that around the corner, over the hill, were people whose lives were like the quarterback in high school whom the girls all wanted—and there was no one like that. There was nobody whose life wasn't at time filled with enough pain to send him to a psychiatrist [if he had been so inclined]. Life is difficult for everyone, and that is not readily apparent.

Another surprise was that there were no bastards. If you know enough about someone, the views they have that you think of as selfish or politically and morally reprehensible fall into place in terms of their lives. It is very hard to do this work and not sympathize (pp. 42, 48).

A science of adulthood cannot simply be extrapolated from psychologies of earlier stages. While much can be learned from them, assumptions about adults derived from them must be tested throughout the life span. Until recently most longitudinal studies originated in child research, which focused on personality traits and psychoanalytic theories, and suggested that the consequences of what happened in the early years would be with a person forever. However, as subjects in such studies grew older, it became apparent that changes can occur (Lowenthal, 1977).

It is difficult, but important, to distinguish between conclusions about human development that have a firm empirical base and those that in large measure reflect the special philosophical bias of the author. For example, Lawrence Kohlberg's theories of moral development are often presented uncritically, as though they were fact. While Kohlberg's theories have held up pretty well empirically, his proposed stages are not entirely progressive. Some people may continue to progress to higher stages, and some stabilize at a relatively immature stage. Many people regress at critical stages, and for some, regression becomes the norm. Cross-sectional studies of value have disclosed regressive tendencies both at middle age and the preretirement stage (Lowenthal, Thurnher, & Chiriboga, 1975). After such views as Kohlberg's have become firmly entrenched in textbooks and supported by the prestige of the persons who formulated or publicized them, they take on a certain sanctity. Considering the constantly changing environments in which humans interact, replications of earlier research are desirable and maintaining a permanently tentative attitude becomes necessary.

In any case, considering the brief history of adult psychology, tremendous gains have been made already. Undoubtedly the growing focus on this area will disclose a wealth of data and give us insights impossible to imagine at present. The challenge is to find effective ways to convert this information into potentially more rewarding life styles at all stages of aging.

SUGGESTED READINGS

Bakker, C. B. Why people don't change. *Psychotherapy: Theory, Research and Practice*, 1975, *12* (2), 164–172. The concept that humans resist change because of genetically based structures is rejected in favor of the view that stability results primarily from continuities within an individual's environment, and that needed changes can be effected through environmental modifications.

Elder, G. H. *Children of the great depression: Social change in life experience.* Chicago: University of Chicago Press, 1974. This longitudinal study of a cohort, a group of boys and girls born in 1920–21, demonstrates the impact of change within families and between generations. Elder traces the impact of the depression on his subjects' lives from preadolescence in the 1930s through middle age in the 1960s.

Francoeur, R. T. & Francoeur, A. K. The aesthetics of social sex: A revolution in values. *Journal of Operational Psychiatry*, 1975, *6* (2), 152–161. After reviewing historical and current attitudes of the United States towards sexual and other human relationships the authors predict an eroticized society which will embrace sexual relationships as an approved means of social and interpersonal communication.

Hauser, P. M. Aging and world-wide population change. In Binstock, R. H., & Shanas, E. (Eds.) *Handbook of Aging and the Social Sciences.* New York: Van Nostrand Reinhold Company, 1976. Aging and increasing longevity are considered in terms of world population trends. Demographic factors regarding aging are analyzed for individual countries, and comparisons are made between more and less well developed countries.

Lesse, S. Factors influencing sexual behavior in our future society. *American Journal of Psychotherapy*, 1976, *30* (3), 366–384. Predictions for the next several decades are made about the probable effects on the family, sexual relationships and leisure, of such factors as social and political forces, population increase, automation, and cybernation.

Lowenthal, M. F., Thurnher, M., Chiriboga, D., & Associates. *Four stages of life.* San Francisco: Jossey-Bass Publishers, 1976. In this study of adults at four life stages (high school seniors, young newlyweds, middle-age parents, and an older group about to retire), characteristics conducive to successful coping at different periods in life are identified. Part One provides an indepth description of the subjects at each stage, while Part Two concerns "the sense of time as continuity, discontinuity or intrusion." In general the book provides perspective on changes across the life span.

Monge, R. H. Structure of the self-concept from adolescence through old age. *Experimental Aging Research*, 1975, *1* (2), 281–291. A study that involved 4,540 persons in five age groups (9 to 19, 20 to 34, 35 to 49, 50 to 64, and 65 to 89) indicated a substantial continuity in self-concept across the life span. That is, self-regard varied little by age group, despite the varying problems and social attitudes experiences at different stages of life.

Muson, H. The lessons of the Grant study. *Psychology Today,* 1977, *11* (4), 42; 48–49. The author raises questions about interpretations made by Vaillant as reported in the annotation below. In particular he takes issue with Vaillant's criteria of mental health, and observes that his sample was limited to the middle class.

Neugarten, B. L. Adaptation and the life cycle. *Counseling Psychologist,* 1976, *6* (1), 16–20. After considering ways that social change and historical setting affect the timing of major life events and consequent social expectations with regard to age appropriate behaviors, Neugarten observes that certain regularities in the life cycle are apparent, including increased interiority (preoccupation with inner life), changed time perspective, and personalization of death. The psychology of the life cycle becomes not so much one of crisis behaviors as a psychology of timing, because crises are caused by occurrences that upset the rhythm of the life cycle.

Vaillant, G. E. How does the best and brightest come of age. *Psychology Today,* 1977, *11* (4) 34–41. In this preview of a lifetime study published later in book form (*Adaptation to Life,* Little, Brown and Company), the author tells what happened to a group of men chosen for their superior characteristics in college during the 35 years that followed their graduation. It tells about how the men copied styles, and how some of them dealt creatively with challenges and succeeded, while others made little progress or even regressed.

Valentine, J. H., Ebert, J., Oakey, R., & Ernst, K. Human crises and the human environment. *Man-environment Systems,* 975, *5* (1), 23–28. A study of the relationships between 3 environmental factors (weather, pollution, and news events) and human crises and their resolution, indicated that such factors collectively account for differential effects according to such variables as sex, age, and marital status, of the persons affected.

Wilder, J. Male and female: The significance of values. *American Journal of Psychotherapy,* 1977, *31* (1), 11–18. Because of rapid technological and educational expansion in recent decades, certain of women's values have changed. These values will in turn tend to produce still further technological and social changes which will then produce still newer values.

References

Acceptance of the idea of mortality. *Intellect*, 1975, *103* (2362), 215–216.

ADAMS, D. L. & deVRIES, H. A. Physiological effects of an exercise training regimen upon women aged 52 to 79. *Journal of Gerontology*, 1973, *28*, 50–55.

ADAMS, G. R. & HUSTON, T. L. "Social perception of middle-aged persons varying in physical attractiveness." *Developmental Psychology*, 1975, *11* (5), 657–658.

ADLER, N. E. Emotional responses of women following therapeutic abortion. *American Journal of Orthopsychiatry*, 1975, *45* (3), 446.

Aging—Feminine and masculine. *Human Development*, 1976, *5* (11), 47–48.

AHAMMER, I. M. & BALTES, P. B. "Objective versus perceived age differences in personality: How do adolescents, adults and older people view themselves and each other?" *Journal of Gerontology*, 1972, *27*, 46–51.

ALLON, N. & FISCHEL, D. Urban courting patterns: Singles' bars. Paper presented at the annual meeting of the American Sociological Association in New York City, August, 1973.

American family remains strong despite fear of depression. *Intellect*, 1975, *104* (2369), 140–150.

ANASTASI, A. *Differential psychology*. New York: Macmillan, 1958.

ANTHONY, S. *The discovery of death in childhood and after.* New York: Basic Books, 1972, 182.

ANTONUCCI, T., "Attachment: A life-span concept. *Human Development*, 1976, *19*, 135–142.

APA Task Force on Aging. Recommendations to the White House Conference on Aging, ix–xiv in C. Eisdorfer and M. Powell Lawton (Eds.) *The psychology of adult development and aging.* Washington, D.C.: American Psychological Association, 1973.

ARIES, P. The family, prison of love. *Psychology Today*, 1975, *9* (3), 53–58.

ARLIN, P. K. Cognitive development in adulthood: A fifth stage? *Developmental Psychology*, 1975, *11* (5), 602–606.

ARLING, G. Resistance to isolation among elderly widows. *International Journal of Aging and Human Development*, 1976, *7* (1), 67–86.

——— The elderly widow and her family, neighbors and friends. *Journal of Marriage and the Family*, 1976, *38* (4), 757–768.

ATCHLEY, R. C. *The social forces in later life: An introduction to social gerontology.* Belmont, California: Wadsworth Publishing Co., 1972.

——— *The sociology of retirement.* Cambridge, Mass.: Schenkman, 1975.

Attitudes toward death. *Intellect*, 1974, *103* (2366), 488.

BAILEY, S. K. The several ages of learning. *Change*, 1976, *8* (4), 36–39.

BAILYN, L. Family constraints on women's work. *Annals of the New York Academy of Science*, 1973, *19* (208), 82–90.

BALTES, P. B. & SCHAIE, P. B. On the plasticity of intelligence in adulthood and old age: Where Horn and Donaldson fail. *American Psychologist*, 1976, *31* (10), 720–725.

────── The myth of the twilight years. *Psychology Today*, 1974, *7* (10), 35–40.

BANDURA, A. Editorial. *APA Monitor*, 1974, *5*, 2.

BARAN, A., SOROSKY, A., & PANNOR, R. The dilemma of our adoptees. *Psychology Today*, 1975, *9* (7), 38.

BARDWICK, J. M. Evolution and parenting. *Journal of Social Issues*, 1974, *30* (4), 39–62.

────── Psychological factors in the acceptance and use of contraceptives. In J. Fawcett (Ed.) *Psychological perspectives of population*. New York: Basic Books, Inc., 1973.

────── *Psychology of women: A study of bicultural conflicts*. New York: Harper & Row, Publishers, 1971.

BASILE, R. A. Lesbian mothers. *Women's Rights Law Reporter*, 1974, *2* (2).

BAUER, F. C. Fact and folklore about adolescents. *National Association of Secondary School Principals Bulletin*, 1965, *49* (299), 172–182.

BAUMRIND, D. Coleman II: Utopian fantasy and sound social innovation. *School Review*, 1974, *83* (1), 69–84.

────── Early socialization and adolescent competence. In S. E. Dragastin and G. H. Edler (Eds.) *Adolescence in the life cycle*. Washington, D.C.: Hemisphere Publishing Corp., 1975, 117–143.

BELL, D. *The coming of post-industrial society*. New York: Basic Books, 1973.

BELLOC, N. B. & BRESLOW, L. Relationship of physical status and health practices. *Preventive Medicine*, 1972, *1*, 409–421.

BEM, S. L. Androgyny vs. the tight little lives of fluffy women and chesty men. *Psychology Today*, 1975, *9* (4), 58–62.

BENGTSON, V. L. & STARR, J. M. Contrast and consensus: A generational analysis of youth in the 1970s. *Youth, 74th Yearbook of National Society for the Study of Education, Part I*. Chicago: University of Chicago Press, 1975, 224–266.

BENNETT, R. & ECKMAN, J. Attitudes toward aging: A critical examination of recent literature and implications for future research. In C. Eisdorfer and M. P. Lawton (Eds.) *The psychology of adult development and aging*. Washington, D.C.: American Psychological Association, 1973.

BERGIN, A. E. Psychotherapy can be dangerous. *Psychology Today*, 1975, *9* (6), 96–100, 104.

BERLAND, T. Maintaining the male. *Generations in the middle*. Chicago: Blue Cross, 1970.

BERMAN, H. J. Prologue to aging: Societal structure and the aged. In M. G. Spencer and C. J. Dorr (Eds.) *Understanding aging: A multidisciplinary approach*. New York: Appleton-Century-Crofts, 1975.

BERNARD, J. *The future of marriage*. New York: Bantam Books, Inc., 1973.

────── *The future of motherhood*. New York: Penguin Books, 1975.

BIELBY, D. & PAPALIA, D. E. Moral development and perceptual role taking egocentrism: Their development and interrelationship across the life-span. *International Journal of Aging and Human Development*, 1975, *6* (4), 293–308.

BIRD, D. The case against marriage. In L. K. Howe, (Ed.) *The future of the family.* New York: Simon & Schuster, 1972.

BIRREN, J. E. The abuse of the urban aged. In S. H. Zarit (Ed.) *Readings in aging and death: Contemporary perspectives.* New York: Harper & Row, Publishers, 1977, 128–131.

BISCHOF, L. J. *Adult psychology (2nd ed.).* New York: Harper & Row, 1976.

BLAKE, J. Coercive pronatalism and American population policy. In R. Parke, Jr. and C. F. Wistoff (Eds.) *Aspects of population growth policy.* Washington, D.C.: Commission on Population Growth and the American Future, 1973, 85–109.

Bleak future for elderly women. *Intellect,* 1975, *103* (2363), 282.

BLOOM, J. E. Revenue sharing and the elderly: How to play and win. Washington, D.C.: National Council on the Aging, 1973.

BLUMBERG, P. M. & PAUL, P. W. Continuities and discontinuities in upper-class marriages. *Journal of Marriage and the Family,* 1975, *37* (1), 63–76.

BOCK, E. W. Aging and suicide. The significance of marital kinship and alternative relations. *The Family Coordinator,* 1972, *21,* 71–79.

BOTWINICK, J. *Aging and behavior.* New York: Springer Publishing Co., Inc., 1973.

BOUVIER, L., ATLEE, E., & McVEIGH, F. The elderly in America. In S. H. Zarit (Ed.) *Readings in aging and death: Contemporary perspectives.* New York: Harper & Row, 1977, 28–36.

BOUWSMA, W. J. Christian adulthood. *Daedalus,* 1976, *105* (2), 77–92.

BOWER, T. Repetition in human development. *Merrill-Palmer Quarterly,* 1974, *20* (4), 303–318.

BRACELAND, F. J. Emotional accompaniments of cardiac surgery. *Postgraduate Medicine,* 1974, *55* (3), 130.

BRAGINSKY, D. D. & BRAGINSKY, B. M. Surplus people: Their lost faith in self and system. *Psychology Today,* 1975, *9* (3), 69–72.

BRANDWEIN, R. A., BROWN, C. A., & FOX, E. M. Women and children last: The social situation of divorced mothers and their families. *Journal of Marriage and the Family,* 1974, *36* (3), 498–514.

BRAUN, P. & BENGTSON, V. Religious behavior in three generations: Cohort and lineage effects. Paper presented at the annual meeting of the Gerontological Society, San Juan, Puerto Rico, 1972.

BRAUNGART, R. G. Youth and social movements. In S. E. Dragastin and G. H. Elder (Eds.) *Adolescence in the life cycle.* Washington, D.C.: Hemisphere Publishing Corporation, 1975, 255–290.

BRISSETT, D. Toward a clarification of self-esteem. *Psychiatry,* 1972, *35* (3), 255–263.

BRITTON, J. H. & BRITTON, J. O. *Personality changes in aging.* New York: Springer Publishing Co., 1972.

BRONFENBRENNER, U. Developmental research, public policy, and the ecology of childhood. *Child Development,* 1974, *45* (1), 1–5.

———— *Two worlds of children: U.S. and U.S.S.R.* New York: Russell Sage Foundation, 1970, 477–481.

BROTMAN, H. B. Facts and figures on older Americans (An overview 1971). Washington, D.C.: Department of Health, Education, and Welfare, 1972.

BUREAU OF THE CENSUS. *Current population reports,* series P-20. No. 255. Marital Status and Living Arrangements, March 1973.

BUSSELEN, H. J., Jr., & G. K. BUSSELEN. Adjustment differences between married and single undergraduate university students: An historical perspective. *The Family Coordinator,* 1975, *24* (3), 281–287.

BUTLER, R. N. Age-ism, another form of bigotry. In S. N. Zarit (Ed.) *Readings in aging and death: Contemporary perspectives.* New York: Harper & Row, 1977, 132–134.

———— A life-cycle perspective: Public policies for later life. Chapter 5 in F. Carp (Ed.) *Retirement.* New York: Behavioral Publications, 1972.

———— a. "Man does not die,' he kills himself. *International Journal of Aging and Human Development,* 1975, *6* (4), 367–370.

———— b. Psychiatry and psychology of the middle-aged. In A. M. Freedman, H. J. Kaplan, & B. J. Sadock (Eds.) *Comprehensive textbook of psychiatry (2nd ed.),* Baltimore: Williams & Wilkins, 1975, 2390–2404.

———— Successful aging and the role of the life review. In S. H. Zarit (Ed.) *Readings in aging and death: Contemporary perspectives.* New York: Harper & Row, 1977, 13–19.

———— Toward a psychiatry of the life-cycle: Implications of sociopsychologic studies of the aging process for the psychotherapeutic situation. In S. H. Zarit (Ed.) *Readings in aging and death: Contemporary perspectives.* New York: Harper & Row, 1977, 213–224.

———— We should end commercialization in the care of older people in the United States: Some thoughts. *International Journal of Aging and Human Development,* 1976, *7* (1), 87–88.

———— c. *Why survive? Being old in America.* New York: Harper & Row, Publishers, 1975.

———— & LEWIS, M. I. *Aging and mental health: Positive psychosocial approaches.* St. Louis: The C. V. Mosby Company, 1973.

BYNUM, J. E., Jr. An exploration of successful retirement adjustment: The formulation of hypotheses. Ph. D. Dissertation. Washington State University, 1972.

CAIN, L. D., Jr. The growing importance of legal age in determining the status of the elderly. *The Gerontologist,* 1974, *14* (2), 167–174.

CAMERON, P. Masculinity/femininity of the generations: As self-reported and as stereotypically appraised. *International Journal of Aging and Human Development,* 1976, *7* (2), 143–151.

———— Social stereotypes: Three faces of happiness. *Psychology Today,* 1974, *8* (3), 63–64.

———— & CROMER, A. Generational homophyly. *Journal of Gerontology,* 1974, *29,* 232–236.

CAMPBELL, A. The American way of mating: Marriage si, children only maybe. *Psychology Today,* 1975, *8* (12), 37–42.

CAMPBELL, C. Economic reality—intruder on the American dream. *Psychology Today,* 1975, *9* (1), 36–37.

CAPEL, W. C., GOLDSMITH, B. M., WADDELL, K. J., & STEWART, G. T. The aging narcotic addict: An increasing problem for the next decades. *Journal of Gerontology,* 1972, *27,* 102–106.

CAREY, R. G. Living until death: A program of service and research for the terminally ill. In E. Kübler-Ross (Ed.) *Death: The final stage of growth.* Englewood Cliffs, N. J.: Prentice-Hall, Inc., 1975, 75–86.

CARTER, H. & GLICK, P. C. *Marriage and divorce: A social and economic study (2nd ed.).* Cambridge, Mass.: Harvard University Press, 1976.

CASADY, M. Character lasts: If you're active and saucey at 30, you'll be warm and witty at 70. *Psychology Today,* 1975, *9* (6), 138.

———— The pinch of stepping out of stereotype. *Psychology Today,* 1976, *9* (9), 102–103.

———— Where have the radicals gone? *Psychology Today,* 1975, *9* (5), 62–63; 92.

CATH, S. H. The orchestration of disengagement. *Journal of Aging and Human Development,* 1975, *6* (3), 199–213.

CHILMAN, C. S. Some psychosocial aspects of female sexuality. *The Family Coordinator,* 1974, *23* (2), 123–131.

CHRISTOFFERSEN, T. Gerontology: Towards a general theory and a research strategy. *Acta Sociologica,* 1974, *17* (4), 393–407.

CHU, F. D. & TROTTER, S. *The madness establishment.* New York: Grossman Publishers, 1974.

CLAVAN, S. & VATTER, E. The affiliated family: A continued analysis. *The Family Coordinator,* 1972, *21,* 499–504.

CLEVELAND, M. Sex in marriage: At 40 and beyond. *The Family Coordinator,* 1976, *25* (3), 233–240.

COHLER, R. J. et al. Social relations, stress and psychiatric hospitalization among mothers of young children. *Social Psychiatry,* 1974, *9* (1), 7.

COLE, S. G. & BRYON, D. A review of information relevant to vasectomy counselors. *Family Coordinator,* 1973, *22* (2), 213–221.

COLEMAN, J. C. *Abnormal psychology and modern life (5th ed.)* Chicago: Scott, Foresman and Company, 1976.

COLEMAN, J. S. *Youth: Transition to adulthood.* Report of the Panel on Youth. President's Science Advisory Commission. Chicago: University of Chicago Press, 1974.

CONSTANTINE, L. L. & CONSTANTINE, J. M. *Group marriage.* New York: Collier Books, 1973.

CONSTANTINOPLE, A. An Eriksonian measure of personality development in college students. *Developmental Psychology,* 1969, *1* (4), 357–372.

Coping with stress. *Human Behavior,* 1976, *5* (5), 38.

COWING, D. E. Sexual behavior in college students. *American Journal of Orthopsychiatry,* 1975, *45* (2), 284–285.

COX, H. Why do Americans want a child god? *Intellectual Digest,* 1973, *4* (4), 17–19.

CRAIG, J. J. *Human development.* Englewood Cliffs, N.J.: Prentice-Hall, Inc., 1976.

CROAKE, J., KELLER, J., & CATLIN, N. *Unmarried living together: It's not all gravy.* Dubuque, Iowa: Kendall/Hunt Publishing Company, 1974.

CUBER, J. F. & HARROFF, P. B. *The significant Americans.* New York: Appleton-Century-Crofts, 1965.

CUNNINGHAM, W. R. & CLAYTON, V. "Fluid" and "crystallized" intelligence in the elderly. Proc. 81st Ann. Conv. APA, 1973.

CURTIN, S. Aging in the land of the young. In S. H. Zarit (Ed.) *Readings in aging and death: Contemporary perspectives.* New York: Harper & Row, 1977, 87–97.

DARNLEY, F., Jr. Adjustment to retirement: Integrity or despair. *The Family Coordinator,* 1975, 24 (2), 217–226.

DAVIS, E. E. Are adolescent's anti-society oriented? October 1973, 102 (2351), 62–64.

DeCARLO, T. J. (Ed.) Recreation participation patterns and successful aging. *Journal of Gerontology,* 1974, 29, 416–422.

DECK, J. *Rancho paradise.* New York: Harcourt Brace Jovanovich, Inc., 1972.

Depression and disillusionment. *APA Monitor,* 1976, 7 (5), 13.

DIBNER, A. S. The psychology of normal aging. In M. G. Spencer and C. J. Dorr (Eds.) *Understanding aging: A multidisciplinary approach.* New York: Appleton-Century-Crofts, 1975.

DONNELLY, C. A free-spending, job-squeezed, house-proud future. *Money,* 1976, 5 (5), 96.

DOUVAN, E. Sex differences in the opportunities, demands and development of youth. *Youth. 74th Yearbook of National Society for the Study of Education, Part I.* Chicago: University of Chicago Press, 1975, 27–45.

DRAGASTIN, S. E. & ELDER, G. H. *Adolescence in the life cycle: Psychological change and social context.* New York: John Wiley & Sons, Inc., 1975.

DREEBEN, R. Good Intentions. *School Review,* 1974, 83 (1), 37–47.

DREYER, P. H. Sex, sex roles, and marriage among youth in the 1970s. *Youth 74th Yearbook of National Society for the Study of Education, Part I.* Chicago: University of Chicago Press, 1975, 194–223.

Drive for rights of children. *U. S. News & World Report,* 1974, 77 (6), 42–44.

DuBOIS, E. E. Adult education and andagogy: New opportunities for the aging. In M. G. Spencer and C. J. Door (Eds.) *Understanding aging: A multidisciplinary approach.* New York: Appleton-Century-Crofts, 1975.

DUBOS, R. The despairing optimist. *The American Scholar,* 1976, 45 (2), 168–172.

DUVALL, E. M. *Family development (4th ed.)* Philadelphia: Lippincott Company, 1971.

EDWARDS, M. & STINNETT, N. Perceptions of college students concerning alternate lifestyles. *Journal of Psychology,* 1974, 84, 143–156.

EHRLICH, H., SOKOLOFF, N., PINCUS, F., & EHRLICH, C. *Women and men: A socioeconomic factbook.* Baltimore, Md.: Research Group One, 1975.

EISDORFER, C. Adaptation to loss of work. In F. Carp (Ed.) *Retirement*. New York: Behavioral Publications, 1972, 245–265

———— & LAWTON, M. P. (Eds.) *The psychology of adult development and aging*. Washington, D.C.: American Psychological Association, 1973.

EISENBERG, L. On the humanizing of human nature. *Impact*, 1977, *23* (3), 213–224.

———— The search for care. *Daedalus*, 1977, *106* (1), 235–246.

ELDER, G. H. Jr. Adolescence in the life cycle. In S. E. Dragastin and G. H. Elder, Jr. (Eds.) *Adolescence in the life cycle*. Washington, D.C.: Hemisphere Publishing Corp., 1975, 1–22.

End of youth culture—Changes it will bring. *U. S. News & World Report*, October 3, 1977, 54–56.

ERIKSON, E. *Childhood and society*, (2nd ed.). New York: W. W. Norton, 1963.

———— Identity and the life cycle. *Psychological Issues*. Monograph, 1., 1959.

———— Reflections on Dr. Gorg's life cycle. *Daedalus*, 1976, *105* (2), 1–28.

———— Reflections on the contemporary youth. *Daedalus*, 1970, *99* (1), 144–157; 172–175.

EWALD (1972) cited in F. Darnley, Adjustment to retirement: Integrity or despair. *Family Coordinator*, 1975, *24* (2), 217–226.

Executive woman, January 1975. Cited in G. Sheehy, *Passages*. New York: E. P. Dutton & Co., Inc. 1974, 223.

FASTEAU, M. F. The high price of macho. *Psychology Today*, 1975, *9* (4), 60.

FEIN, R. A. Men's entrance to parenthood. *The Family Coordinator*, 1976, *25* (4), 341–348.

FELDBERG, R. & KOHEN, J. Family life in an anti-family setting: A critique of marriage and divorce. *The Family Coordinator*, 1976, *25* (2), 151–159.

FELSON, M. & KNOKE, D. Social status and the married woman. *Journal of Marriage and the Family*, 1974, *36* (3), 516–521.

FENGLER, A. P. & WOOD, V. Continuity between the generations: Differential influence of mothers and fathers. *Youth and Society*, 1973, *4* (3), 359–372.

FERREE, M. M. The confused American housewife. *Psychology Today*, 1976, *10* (4), 76–78; 80.

FILLENBAUM, G. G. On the relation between attitude to work and attitude to retirement. *Journal of Gerontology*, 26, 2, 244–248.

FIRESTONE, S. *The dialectic of sex: The case for feminist revolution*. New York: Bantam Books, Inc., 1972.

FISHER, E. O. A guide to divorce counseling. *The Family Coordinator*, 1973, *22*, 55–61.

FITZGERALD, J. M., NESSELROADE, J. R., & BALTES, P. B. Emergence of adult intellectual structure: Prior to or during adolescence? *Developmental Psychology*, 1973, *9*, 114–119.

FITZPATRICK, B. Economics of aging. In M. G. Spencer and C. J. Dorr

(Eds.) *Understanding aging: A multidisciplinary approach.* New York: Appleton-Century-Crofts, 1975, 105–133.

FLAVELL, J. H. Cognitive changes in adulthood. In L. R. Goulet and D. B. Baltes (Eds.) *Life span developmental psychology.* New York: Academic Press, 1970, 248–257.

———— *The developmental psychology of Jean Piaget.* New York: Van Nostrand, 1963.

FLEMING, J. D. What mother knows best: If one baby's nice what's wrong with two? *Psychology Today,* 1975, *8* (12), 43.

FOLSOM, J. C. Simple physical activities for the elderly and disabled. *Gerontologist,* 1972, *12,* 139.

FOZARD, J. L., NUTTAL, R. L., & WAUGH, N. C. Age-related differences in mental performance. *Aging and Human Development,* 1972, *3,* 19–43.

FREEDMAN, M. Homosexuals may be healthier than straights. *Psychology Today,* 1975, *8* (10), 28–32.

Freeing up after forty. *Human Behavior,* 1976, *5* (5), 50–51.

FRIED, B. *The middle age crisis.* New York: Harper & Row, Publishers, 1967.

FRIEDMAN, R. Response No. 1 to Dr. Kagan's article. *Journal of Youth and Adolescence,* 1976, *5* (2), 131–144.

FURRY, C. A. & BALTES, P. B. The effect of age differences in ability-extraneous performance variables on the assessment of intelligence in children, adults and the elderly. *Journal of Gerontology,* 1973, *28,* 73–80.

GAITZ, C. *Aging and the brain.* A symposium at the University of Texas Medical Center, Houston, Texas. New York: Plenum Publishing Corporation, 1971.

GALLAGHER, B. J. An empirical analysis of attitude differences between three kin-related generations. *Youth and Society,* 1974, *5* (3), 327–349.

GALLAGHER, U. M. What's happening in adoption? *Children Today,* 1975, *4* (6), 11–13; 36.

GARDNER, B. B. The awakening of the blue collar woman. *Intellectual Digest,* 1974, *4* (7), 17–19.

GAYLIN, J. Don't blame the divorce rate on working wives. *Psychology Today,* 1976, *16* (2), 18.

———— Executives vs. the career woman. *Psychology Today,* 1976, *9* (8), 22.

———— His legs are lovely, but can he type? *Psychology Today,* 1976, *9* (10), 21.

———— Jobs cool student protest. *Psychology Today,* 1976, *10* (2), 30.

———— Love and labor: Happy wives, working mothers. *Psychology Today,* 1976, *10* (5), 44; 46.

———— More men than women still turn on to nudes. *Psychology Today,* 1976, *10* (3), 19.

GELLES, R. J. Abused wives: Why do they stay. *Journal of Marriage and the Family,* 1976, 659–668.

———— Demythologizing child abuse. *The Family Coordinator,* 1976, *25* (2), 135–141.

Generation chasm. *Human Behavior,* 1977, *6* (2), 36.

Generation in the middle. *Report by Blue Cross,* 1970, *23* (1), 11.

GILDER, G. *Naked nomads.* New York: Quadrangle, 1974.

GILL, B. D. Kappans respond to the walkabout idea. *Phi Delta Kappan,* 1974, *56* (1), 63–64.

GILMARTIN, B. G. That swinging couple down the block. *Psychology Today,* 1975, *8* (9), 54–58.

GLASS, D. C. Stress, competition and heart attacks. *Psychology Today,* 1976, *10* (7), 54–57; 134.

GLENN, N. Psychological well being in the post-parental stage: Some evidence from national surveys. *Journal of Marriage and the Family,* 1975, *37* (1), 105–110.

GLICK, P. C. A demographer looks at American families. *Journal of Marriage and the Family,* 1975, *37,* 15–36.

———— Some recent changes in American families. *Current Population Reports,* P-23, (52), 1975.

———— The life cycle of the family. U.S. Bureau of the Census.

———— Updating the life cycle of the family. *Journal of Marriage and the Family,* 1977, *39* (1), 5–13.

———— & NORTON, A. J. Perspectives on the recent return in divorce and remarriage. *Demography,* 1972, *10* (3), 301–314.

———— Perspectives on the recent upturn in divorce and remarriage. U.S. Bureau of the Census, U.S. Department of Commerce, 1972.

GOETHALS, G. W. Adolescence: Variations on a theme. *Youth. 74th Yearbook of National Society for the Study of Education, Part I.* Chicago: University of Chicago Press, 1975, 46–60.

GOLDSTEIN, J. On being adult and being an adult in secular law. *Daedalus,* 1976, *105* (4), 69–87.

GOLENPAUL, A. (Ed.) *Information please almanac: Atlas and yearbook 1976.* New York: Information Please Almanac, 1976.

———— *Information please almanac (31st edition).* New York: Simon & Schuster, 1977.

GOODMAN, N. & FELDMAN, K. A. Expectations, ideals, and reality: Youth enters college. In S. E. Dragastin and G. H. Elder (Eds.) *Adolescence in the life cycle.* Washington, D.C.: Hemisphere Publishing Corporation, 1975, 147–170.

GORDON, C., GAITZ, C. M. & SCOTT, J. Value priorities and leisure activities among middle-aged and older couples. *Diseases of the Nervous System,* 1973, *34* (1), 13–16.

GOTTESMAN, L. E., QUARTERMAN, C. E., & KOHN, G. M. Psychosocial treatment of the aged. In C. Eisdorfer and M. P. Lawton (Eds.) *The psychology of adult development and aging.* Washington, D.C.: American Psychological Association, 1973.

GOULD, R. Adult life stages: Growth toward self-tolerance. *Psychology Today,* 1975, *8* (9), 74–78.

GRANICK, S. & PATTERSON, R. D. *Human aging II: An eleven-year biomedical and behavioral study.* Washington, D.C.: Government Printing Office, 1971.

GRAUBARD, S. R. Preface to the issue "Adulthood". *Daedalus,* 1976, *105* (2), v–viii.

Graying of campus: Adult students alter face of U.S. colleges. *The Wall Street Journal,* January 24, 1977, 1, 20.

GRINDER, R. E. The concept of adolescence in the genetic psychology of G. Stanley Hall. *Child Development,* 1969, *40,* 355–369.

GRUBER, H. E. Courage and cognitive growth in children and scientists. In M. Schwebel and J. Raph (Eds.) *Piaget in the classroom.* New York: Basic Books, Inc., 1973.

GUBRIUM, J. F. Being single in old age. *Aging and Human Development,* 1975, *6* (1), 29–41.

——— Marital desolation and the evaluation of everyday life in old age. *Journal of Marriage and the Family,* 1974, *36* (1), 107–113.

GUNTER, B. G. & MOORE, H. A. Youth, leisure, and post-industrial society: Implications for the family. *The Family Coordinator,* 1975, *24* (2), 199–207.

GUTTMANN, D. The new mythologies and premature aging in the youth culture. *Journal of Youth and Adolescence,* 1973, *2,* 139–155.

HAAN, N. ". . . change and sameness . . ." reconsidered. *International Journal of Aging and Human Development,* 1976, *7* (1), 59–65.

——— Personality development from adolescence to adulthood in the Oakland growth and guidance studies. *Seminars in Psychiatry,* 1972, *4* (4), 399–414.

——— Personality organizations of well-functioning younger people and older adults. *International Journal of Aging and Human Development,* 1976, *7* (2), 117–127.

——— & DAY, D. A longitudinal study of change and sameness in personality development: Adolescence to later adulthood. *International Journal of Aging and Human Development,* 1974, *5* (1), 11–39.

HALAS, C. M. Sex-role stereotypes: Perceived childhood socialization experiences and the attitudes and behavior of adult women. *Journal of Psychology,* 1974, *88,* 261–275.

HALL, E. People plan their lives in terms of imaginary systems: Nobody lives in the real world. *Psychology Today,* 1974, *8* (2), 61–70.

——— with CAMERON, P. Our failing reverence for life. *Psychology Today,* 1976, *9* (11), 104–108, 113.

——— & POTEETE, R. A. Do you Mary, and Anne, and Beverly and Ruth, take these men—A conversation with Robert Rimmer. *Psychology Today,* 1972, *5* (8), 57–64, 78–82.

HALL, G. S. *Senescence: The last half of life.* New York: Appleton-Century-Crofts, 1922.

HAMPES, G. D. & BLEVINS, A. L. Primary group interaction. *International Journal of Aging and Human Development,* 1975, *6* (4), 309–320.

HAREVEN, T. K. The last stage: Historical adulthood and old age. *Daedalus,* 1976, *105* (4), 13–27.

HARRIS, L. and ASSOCIATES. *The myth and reality of aging in America.* Washington, D.C.: National Council on the Aging, 1975.

HARRIS, T. G. As far as heroin is concerned, the worst is over. *Psychology Today*, 1973, *7*, 68–71.

HARTUP, W. & LEMPERS, J. A problem in life-span development: The interactional analysis of family attachments. In P. Baltes and W. Schaie (Eds.) *Life span developmental psychology: Personality and socialization.* New York: Academic Press, Inc., 1973.

HARVEY, C. D. & BAHR, H. M. Widowhood, morale, and affiliation. *Journal of Marriage and the Family*, 1974, *36* (1), 97–106.

HAUSER, P. M. Aging and world-wide population change. In R. H. Binstock and E. Shanas (Eds.) *Handbook of aging and the social sciences.* New York: Van Nostrand Reinhold Company, 1976, 59–86.

HAVENS, E. M. Women, work, and wedlock: A note on female marital patterns in the United States. *American Journal of Sociology*, 1973, *78*, 975–981.

HAVIGHURST, R. J. A cross-cultural view of adolescence. In J. F. Adams (Ed.) *Understanding adolescence (2nd ed.)* Boston: Allyn & Bacon, Inc., 1973.

———— Charlotte Bühler: December 20, 1893–February 3, 1974. *Human Development*, 1974, *17*, 397–398.

———— *Developmental tasks and education (3rd ed.)* New York: McKay, 1972.

———— Youth in crisis. *School Review*, 1974, *83* (1), 5–10.

———— Youth in social institutions. *Youth. 47th Yearbook of National Society for the study of Education, Part I.* Chicago: University of Chicago Press, 1975, 115–144.

———— NEUGARTEN, B. L., & TOBIN, S. S. Disengagement and patterns of aging. In B. L. Neugarten (Ed.) *Middle age and aging.* Chicago: University of Chicago Press, 1968.

HENDRICKS, J. & HENDRICKS, C. D. *Aging in mass society: Myths and realities.* Cambridge, Mass.: Winthrop Publishers, Inc., 1977.

HENLEY, J. R. & ADAMS, L. D. Marijuana use in post-college cohorts: Correlates of use, prevalence patterns, and factors associated with cessation. *Social Problems*, 1971, *14*, 125–131.

HERTEL, B. & NELSEN, H. M. Are we entering a post Christian era? Religious belief and attendance in America 1957–1968. *Journal for the Scientific Study of Religion*, 1974, *13* (4), 409–419.

HESS, B. Amicability. Unpublished doctoral dissertation. Rutgers University, 1971.

———— Friendship; in Riley, Johnson and Foner, *Aging and society, vol. 3*, Russell Sage Foundation, New York, 1972.

HICKEY, T., HICKEY, L., & KALISH, R. A. Children's perceptions of the elderly. *Journal of Genetic Psychology*, 1968, *112*, 227–238.

High cost of kids. *Newsweek*, January 10, 1972, 42–43.

HILTZ, S. R. Helping widows: Group discussions as a therapeutic technique. *The Family Coordinator*, 1975, *24* (3), 331–336.

HIRSCH, G. T. Non-sexist childrearing: Demythifying normative data. *The Family Coordinator*, 1974, *23* (2), 165–170.

HITE, S. *The Hite report: A nationwide study of female sexuality.* New York: Macmillan, Inc., 1976.

HOBBS, D. F., Jr. & COLE, S. P. Transition to parenthood: A decade replication. *Journal of Marriage and the Family,* 1976, *38* (4), 723–731.

HOCHSCHILD, A. R. *The unexpected community.* Englewood Cliffs, N.J.: Prentice-Hall, Inc., 1973.

HOFFMAN, L. W. Effects of maternal employment on the child—a review of the research. *Developmental Psychology,* 1974, *10* (2), 204–228.

―――― The employment of women. Education and fertility. *Merrill-Palmer Quarterly,* 1974, *20* (2), 99–119.

HOFFMAN, M. L. Developmental synthesis of affect and cognition and its implications for altruistic motivation. *Developmental Psychology,* 1975, *11* (5), 607–622.

HOLCOMB, W. L. Spiritual cases among the aging. In M. G. Spencer and C. J. Dorr (Eds.) *Understanding aging: A multidisciplinary approach.* New York: Appleton-Century-Crofts, 1975, 234–278.

HORN, J. Retirement—a dirty word, a depressing time. *Psychology Today,* 1975, *9* (1), 95–96.

―――― Senility: Some glimmerings of hope. *Psychology Today,* 1974, *8* (1), 110.

―――― The new grandparents—Cool and distant or fun-loving. *Psychology Today,* 1976, *9* (12), 30–31.

HORN, P. A new teenage course: Learning to be parents. *Psychology Today,* 1975, *8* (10), 79—80.

How many children? *Children Today,* 1972, *1* (3), 26.

HUNT, M. Sexual behavior in the 1970's. *Playboy,* 1973, *20* (10), 84–88.

―――― *Sexual behavior in the 1970s.* Chicago, Ill.: Playboy Press, 1974.

―――― Survey of sexual behavior. Reported in *The Detroit Free Press,* Robin Adams Sloan column, July 1974.

HUTCHINSON, I. W. III. The significance of marital status for morale and life satisfaction among lower-income elderly. *Journal of Marriage and the Family,* 1975, *37* (2), 287–293.

HUYCK, M. H. *Growing older.* Englewood Cliffs, N.J.: Prentice-Hall, Inc., 1974.

IMARA, M. Dying as the last stage of growth. In E. Kübler Ross (Ed.) *Death: The final stage of growth.* Englewood Cliffs, N.J.: Prentice-Hall, Inc., 1975, 147–163.

Institute for Interdisciplinary Studies. Older Americans speak to the nation—a summary. (White House conference on Aging, background papers). Minneapolis, Minnesota, 1971.

JACOBY, S. 49 million singles can't be all right. *The New York Times Magazine,* February 17, 1974.

JARVIK, L. F., EISDORFER, C., & BLUM, J. E. (Eds.) *Intellectual functioning in adults.* New York: Springer Publishing Co., Inc., 1973.

JENCKS, C. & RIESMAN, D. The war between the generations. *Teachers College Record,* 1967, *69* (1), 1–21.

JENSEN, M. S. Role differentiation in female homosexual quasi-marital unions. *Journal of Marriage and the Family,* 1974, *36* (2), 360–367.

JONES, D. Sex differences in the friendship patterns of young adults. Unpublished paper, 1974.

JORDAN, W. D. Searching for adulthood in America. *Daedalus*, 1976, *105* (4), 1–11.

JUNG, C. G. The stages in life. In *The Collected Works of C. G. Jung*, Vol. 8 New York: Julian Press, 1960.

JURY, M. & JURY, D. Gramp. *Psychology Today*, 1976, *9* (9), 57–65.

KAGAN, J. Exploring childhood. *Children Today*, 1973, 2 (2), 13–14.

KALISH, R. *Late adulthood: Perspectives on human development*. Monterey, Calif.: Brooks/Cole Publishing Company, 1975.

———— & JOHNSON, A. Value similarities and differences in three generations of women. *Journal of Marriage and the Family*, 1972, *34*, 49–55.

———— & KNUDTSON, F. W. Attachment versus disengagement: A life-span conceptualization. *Human Development*, 1976, *19*, 171–181.

———— & REYNOLDS, D. K. Death and bereavement in a cross-ethnic context. Unpublished manuscript, 1975.

———— & REYNOLDS, D. K. *Death and ethnicity: A psychocultural study*. University of Southern California Press, Los Angeles, 1976.

KANGAS, J. & BRADWAY, K. Intelligence at middle age: A thirty-eight year follow-up. *Developmental Psychology*, 1971, *5*, 333–337.

KAPLAN, H. *The new sex therapy*. New York: Quadrangle, 1974.

KAPLAN, J. An editorial: Alternatives to nursing home care: Fact or fiction. *The Gerontologist*, 1972, *12*, 114.

KASTENBAUM, R. Fertility and death. *Journal of Social Issues*, 1974, *30* (4), 63–78.

————, DERBIN, V., SABATINI, P., & ARTT, S. The ages of me: Toward personal and interpersonal definitions of functional aging. *Aging and Human Development*, 1972, *3* (2), 197–211.

KATCHADOURIAN, H. Medical perspectives on adulthood. *Daedalus*, 1976, *105* (2), 29–56.

KAY, E. *The crisis in middle management*. New York: American Management, 1974.

KEEBLER, N. Family therapy: A profusion of methods and meanings. *APA Monitor*, 1976, *7* (5), 4–5; 12.

KELEMAN, S. *Living your dying*. New York: Random House, 1975.

KELLY, E. L. Consistency of the adult personality. *American Psychologist*, 1955, *10*, 659–681.

KELLY, F. J. & BAER, D. J. Physical challenge as a treatment for delinquency. Cited in W. Kilpatrick, Identity, youth and dissolution of culture. *Adolescence*, 1974, *9* (35), 406–411.

KELLY, J. R. Life styles and leisure choices. *The Family Coordinator*, 1975, *24* (2), 185–190.

KEMPLER, H. L. Extended kinship ties and some modern alternatives. *The Family Coordinator*, 1976, *25* (2), 143–149.

KENISTON, K. Prologue: Youth as a stage of life. *Youth. 74th Yearbook of National Society for the Study of Education, Part I*. Chicago: University of Chicago Press, 1975, 3–26.

KERCKHOFF, R. K. Marriage and middle age. *The Family Coordinator*, 1976, 25 (1), 5–11.

KESSLER, J. B. Aging in different ways. *Human Behavior*, 1976, 5 (6), 56–60.

KIEV, A. *A strategy for handling executive stress.* Chicago: Nelson-Hall Publishers, 1974.

KILPATRICK, W. Identity, youth and the dissolution of culture. *Adolescence*, 1974, 9 (35), 407–412.

KIMMEL, D. *Adulthood and aging.* New York: John Wiley & Sons, Inc., 1974.

KINKADE, K. Commune: A Walden Two experiment. *Psychology Today*, 1973, 6 (9), 71–82.

KISKER, G. W. *The disorganized personality (3rd ed.)* New York: McGraw-Hill Book Company, 1977.

KIVETT, V. R. The aged in North Carolina: Physical, social and environmental characteristics and sources of assistance. Technical Bulletin No. 237, Raleigh, N.C.: Agricultural Experiment Station, 1976.

KLEIBER, D. A. & MANASTER, G. J. Youth's outlook on the future: A past-present comparison. *Journal of Youth and Adolescence.* 1972, 1 (3), 223–232.

KOCH, J. & KOCH, L. Sex therapy: Caveat emptor. *Psychology Today*, 1976, 9 (10), 37.

KOHLBERG, L. The cognitive developmental approach to moral development. *Phi Delta Kappan*, 1975, 51 (10), 670–673.

KOLBENSCHLAG, M. Dr. Estelle Ramey: Reclaiming the feminine legacy. *Human Behavior*, 1976, 5 (7), 25–27.

KOMAROVSKY, M. *Blue-collar marriage.* New York: Random House, 1967.

―――― Cultural contradictions and sex roles: The masculine case. *American Journal of Sociology*, 1973, 78 (4), 873–884.

KRANT, M. J. The organized care of the dying patient. *Hospital Practice*, 1972, (7), 101–108.

KÜBLER-ROSS, E. *Death: The final stage of growth.* Englewood Cliffs, N.J.: Prentice-Hall, Inc., 1975.

―――― *Questions and answers on death and dying.* New York: Macmillan, Inc., 1974.

LAMPE, P. E. Adultery and anomie. *Human Behavior*, 1976, 5 (1), 14–15.

LASSWELL, M. E. Is there a best age to marry? An interpretation. *The Family Coordinator*, 1974, 23 (3), 237–242.

LAUDICINA, E. V. Toward new forms of liberation: A mildly utopian proposal. *Social Theory and Practice*, 1973, 2 (3), 275–288.

LAWTON, M. P. & NAHEMOW, L. Ecology and the aging process. In C. Eisdorfer and M. Powell Lawton (Eds.) *The psychology of adult development and aging.* Washington, D.C.: American Psychological Association, 1973.

LAWTON, M. P. KLEBAN, M. H. & SINGER, M. The aged Jewish person and the slum environment. *Journal of Gerontology*, 26, 231–239.

LEAF, A. Getting old. *Scientific American*, 1973, 229 (Sept.), 45–52.

―――― Threescore and forty. *Intellectual Digest*, 1974, 4 (7), 70–71.

LEE, P. C. & GROPPER, N. B. Sex-role culture and educational practice. *Harvard Educational Review*, 1974, *44* (3), 369–410.

LEIDER, R. J. Why a second career? *The Personnel Administrator*, March–April, 1974.

LeMASTERS, E. E. *Parents in modern America*. Homewood, Ill.: Dorsey Press, 1973.

LeSHAN, E. J. *The wonderful crisis of middle age*. New York: David McKay, 1973.

LEVINGER, G. & SNOEK, J. D. *Attraction in relationship: A new look at interpersonal attraction*. Morristown, N.J.: General Learning Press, 1972.

LEVINSON, D. The mid-life transition: A period in adult psychosocial development. *Psychiatry*, May 1977, *40*, 99–112.

────── The psychological development of men in early adulthood and the mid-life transition. Minneapolis: University of Minnesota Press, 1974.

────── *The seasons of a man's life*. New York: Alfred A. Knopf, 1978.

────── Toward a conception of adult development. In progress, 1974.

LEWIS, M. I. & BUTLER, R. N. Life review of therapy. *Geriatrics*, 1974, *29*, 165–173.

LIONELLS, M. & MANN, C. H. *Patterns of midlife in transition*. New York: William Alanson White Institute, 26 page monograph, 1974.

LONDON, P. The psychotherapy boom: From the long couch for the sick to the push button for the bored. *Psychology Today*, 1974, *8* (1), 63–68.

LONG, I. Human sexuality and aging. *Social Casework*, 1976, *57* (4), 237–244.

LONG, L. H. (Ed.) *The world almanac*. New York: Doubleday, 1970.

LOPATA, H. Z. Living through widowhood. *Psychology Today*, 1973, *7* (2), 86–92.

────── *Occupation: Housewife*. London: Oxford University Press, 1971.

LOWENTHAL, M. F. Psychosocial variations across the adult life course: Frontiers for research and policy. *The Gerontologist*, 1975, *15* (1), Part 1, 6–12.

────── Some potentialities of a life-cycle approach to the study of retirement. In F.M. Carp (Eds.) *Retirement*. New York: Behavioral Publications, 1972, pp. 307–336.

────── Toward a sociopsychological theory of change in adulthood and old age. In J. E. Birren and K. W. Schaie (Eds.) *Handbook of the psychology of aging*. New York: Van Nostrand Reinhold Co., 1977, 116–127.

────── & CHIRIBOGA, D. Social stress and adaptation: Toward a life-course perspective. In C. Eisdorfer and M. P. Lawton (Eds.) *The psychology of adult development and aging*. Washington, D.C.: American Psychological Association, 1973.

────── Transitions to the empty nest: Crisis, challenge, or relief? *Archives of General Psychiatry*, 1972, *26*, 8–14.

────── & HAVEN, C. Interaction and adaptation: Intimacy as a critical variable. *American Sociological Review*, 1968, *33* (1), 20–30.

──────, THURNHER, M., CHIRIBOGA, D., & ASSOCIATES. *Four stages of life: A comparative study of women and men facing transitions*. San Francisco: Jossey-Bass, 1975.

LOWY, L. Social welfare and the aging. In M. G. Spencer and C. J. Dorr (Eds.) *Understanding aging: A multidisciplinary approach.* New York: Appleton-Century-Crofts, 1975, 134–178.

LOZIER, J. & ALTHOUSE, R. Retirement to the porch in rural appalachia. *Aging and Human Development,* 1975, *6* (1), 7–15.

LUCKEY, E. B. What I have learned about family life. *The Family Coordinator,* 1974, *23* (3), 307–313.

LYELL, R. G. Adolescent and adult self-esteem as related to cultural values. *Adolescence,* 1973, *8* (29), 85–92.

LYNESS, L. L., LIPETZ, M. E., & DAVIS, K. E. Living together: An alternative to marriage. *Journal of Marriage and the Family,* 1972, *34* (2), 305–311.

MAAS, H. S. & KUYPERS, J. A. *From thirty to seventy.* San Francisco: Jossey-Bass, Inc., Publishers, 1974.

MACCOBY, E. E. & JACKLIN, C. N. What we know and don't know about sex differences. *Psychology Today,* 1974, *8* (7), 108–112.

MACE, D. R. What I have learned about family life. *The Family Coordinator,* 1974, *23* (2), 189–195.

———— & MACE, V. C. Marriage enrichment—Wave of the future? *The Family Coordinator,* 1975, *24* (2), 131–135.

MACKLIN, E. D. Heterosexual cohabitation among unmarried college students. *The Family Coordinator,* 1972, *21* (4), 463–472.

MADDOX, G. L. "Is senior power the wave of the future?" Paper presented at the 140th Annual Meeting of the American Association for the Advancement of Science, San Francisco, February, 1974.

MAINARDI, P. The politics of housework. In J. S. and J. R. Delora (Eds.) *Intimate life styles.* Pacific Palisades, Calif.: Goodyear Publishing Co., Inc., 1972.

MALIA, M. E. Adulthood refracted Russia and Leo Tolstor. *Daedalus,* 1976, *105* (2), 169–183.

Manpower Administration. U.S. Department of Labor. *Back to work after retirement.* Washington, D.C.: U.S. Government Printing Office, 1972.

MARBLE, B. B. & PATTERSON, I. M. Nutrition and aging. In M. G. Spencer and C. J. Dorr (Eds.) *Understanding aging: A multidisciplinary approach.* New York: Appleton-Century-Crofts, 1975, 195–208.

MARCIANO, T. D. Variant family forms in world perspective. *The Family Coordinator,* 1974, *24* (4), 407–420.

MARMER, S. S., PASNAU, R. O., & CUSHNER, I. M. Is psychiatric consultation in abortion obsolete? *International Journal of Psychiatry in Medicine,* 1974, *5* (3).

MARROW, A. J. (Ed.) *The failure of success.* New York: Amacom, 1972.

MAY, R. Values, myths, and symbols. *Review of Existential Psychology and Psychiatry,* 1974, *13* (3), 267–273.

McCALL, R. B. Challenges to a science of developmental psychology. *Child Development,* 1977, *48* (2), 333–344.

McMORROW, F. *Midolescence: The dangerous years.* New York: Strawberry Hill Publishing Company, 1974.

McQUADE, W. What stress can do to you. *Fortune,* 1972, *85,* 102–107.

MARSH, G. R. & THOMPSON, L. W. Effects of age on the contingent negative variation in a pitch discrimination task. *Journal of Gerontology,* 1973, *28,* 56–62.

MEDAWAR, P. B. & MEDAWAR, J. S. Revising the facts of life. *Harpers,* 1977, *254* (1521), 41–61.

MEDLEY, M. L. Marital adjustment in the post-retirement years. *The Family Coordinator,* 1977, *26* (1), 5–11.

MEDVED, M. & WALLECHINSKY, D. *What really happened to the class of '65?* New York: Random House, Inc., 1976.

MENDES, H. A. Single fathers. *The Family Coordinator,* 1976, *25* (4), 439–444.

Menstrual myths. *Human Behavior,* 1977, *6* (2), 62.

MILLER, S. J. The social dilemma of the aging participant. In A. M. Rose and W. A. Peterson (Eds.) *Older people and their social world.* Philadelphia: F. A. Davis Company, 77–92.

MIZE, E. A mother mourns and grows. In E. Kübler-Ross *Death: The final stage of growth.* Englewood Cliffs, N.J.: Prentice-Hall, Inc., 1975, 97–104.

MONTAGU, A. with COLEMAN, D. Don't be adultish. *Psychology Today,* August 1977, *11* (3), 46–55.

———— The pill, the sexual revolution, and the schools. *Phi Delta Kappan,* 1968, *49* (9), 480–484.

MOORE, P. What we expect and what it's like. *Psychology Today,* 1975, *9* (3), 29–30.

MOODY, R. A., Jr. *Life after life.* Atlanta: Mockingbird Books, 1975.

MORGAN, E. *A manual of death education and simple burial.* Chicago: Celo Press, 1973.

MORGAN, M. *The total woman.* Old Tappan, N.J.: Fleming H. Revell Co., 1973.

MORIYAMO, I. M. Problems in the measurement of health status. In E. B. Sheldon & W. E. Moore (Eds.) *Indicators of social change.* New York: Russell Sage Foundation, 1968.

MOUSSEAU, J. The family, prison of love. *Psychology Today,* 1975, *9* (3), 52–54; 56–58.

MOVIUS, M. Voluntary childlessness—The ultimate liberation. *The Family Coordinator,* 1976, *25* (1), 57–63.

MURRAY, J. Home ownership and financial assets: Findings from the 1968 survey of the aged. *Social Security Bulletin,* 1972, *35* (8), 3–5.

MUSON, H. The lessons of the Grant study. *Psychology Today,* 1977, *11* (4), 42; 48–49.

MUUS, R. E. Puberty rites in primitive and modern societies. *Adolescence,* 1970, *5* (17), 109–128.

NAFFZIGER, C. C. & NAFFZIGER, K. Development of sex role stereotypes. *The Family Coordinator,* 1974, *23* (3), 251–258.

National Center for Health Statistics, Health Services and Mental Health Administration, Rockville, Maryland, *Services and activities offered to nursing home residents,* Vital and Health Statistics, 1972, Series 12 (17), 1–42.

NEUGARTEN, B. L. A developmental view of adult personality. J. E. Birren (Eds.) *Relations of development and aging.* Springfield, Ill.: C. C. Thomas, 1964.

—— Age groups in American society and the rise of the young old. Ann. Amer. Acad. (September) 1974, 187–198.

—— (Ed.) *Middle age and aging.* Chicago: University of Chicago Press, 1968.

—— Patterns of aging: Past, present, and future. *Social Service Review,* December 1973, *47,* 574.

—— Personality and the aging process. *The Gerontologist,* 1972, *12,* 9–15.

—— The 1971 Robert W. Kleemeier Award Lecture delivered at the 24th Annual Meeting of the Gerontological Society, Houston, October 28, 1971.

—— & DATAN, N. Sociological perspectives on the life cycle. In P. B. Baltes and K. W. Schaie (Eds.) *Life-span developmental psychology: Personality and socialization.* New York: Academic Press, 1973.

—— & GUTMAN, D. L. Age-sex roles and personality in middle age: A thematic apperception study. In B. L. Neugarten and associates. *Personality in middle and late life.* New York: Atherton Press, 1964, 44–89.

—— & HAGESTAD, G. O. Age and the life course. In R. H. Binstock and E. Shanas (Eds.) *Handbook of aging and the social sciences.* New York: Van Nostrand Reinhold Company, 1976, 35–55.

NEULINGER, J. On leisure. *Behavior Today,* April 29, 1974, 120.

NEWMAN, B. M. & NEWMAN, P. R. *Development through life: A psychosocial approach.* Homewood, Ill.: Dorsey Press, 1975.

New tricks to teach the old. *Intellect,* 1975, *104* (2369), 147.

NORTON, A. The family life cycle updated. In R. F. Winch and G. B. Spanier (Eds.) *Selected studies in marriage and the family (9th ed.).* New York: Holt, Rinehart and Winston, 1974.

—— & GRYMES, R. Marital status and living arrangements. Washington, D.C.: U.S. Department of Commerce, March 1973.

NOWAK, C. Concern with youthfulness and attractiveness in adult women. Unpublished Master's thesis. Wayne State University, 1974.

NOYES, R., Jr. & CLANCY, J. The dying role: Its relevance to improved patient care. *Psychiatry,* 1977, *40,* 41–47.

NYDEGGER, D. N. Middle age: Some early returns—a commentary. *International Journal of Aging and Human Development,* 1976, *7* (2), 137–141.

NYE, F. I. Emerging and declining family roles. *Journal of Marriage and the Family,* 1974, *36* (2), 238–245.

OAKLEY, A. *The sociology of housework.* New York: Pantheon Books, Inc., 1975.

OBERLEDER, M. Emotional breakdowns in elderly people. *Hospital Community Psychiatry,* 1969, *20,* 21.

OFFIR, C. At 65, work becomes a four-letter word. *Psychology Today,* 1975, *7* (10), 40–42, 76–80.

———— Beauty does as beauty is: How looks influence liking. *Psychology Today*, 1974, *8* (3), 30; 34.

———— What are little girls made of? Puppy dogs' tails too. *Psychology Today*, 1974, *8* (3), 43; 113.

O'LEARY, V. E. & DEPNER, C. E. Alternative gender roles among women: Masculine, feminine, and androgenous. *Intellect*, 1976, *104* (2371), 313–315.

O'NEILL, N. & O'NEILL, G. *Open marriage: A new life-style for couples.* New York: Avon Books, 1972.

Only married men need apply. *Human Behavior*, 1976, *5* (5), 63.

ORTHNER, D. K. Familia Ludens: Reinforcing the leisure component in family life. *The Family Coordinator*, 1975, *24* (2), 175–183.

OSMOND, M. W. & MARTIN, P. Y. Sex and sexism: A comparison of male and female sex-role attitudes. *Journal of Marriage and the Family*, 1975, *37* (4), 744–758.

PALMORE, E. Health practices and illnesses among the aged. *The Gerontologist*, 1970, *10*, 313–316.

———— (Ed.) *Normal aging II.* Durham, North Carolina: Duke University Press, 1974.

———— & LUIKART, C. Health and social factors related to life satisfaction. *Journal of Health and Social Behavior*, 1972, *13*, 68.

PAPALIA, D. E. The status of some conservation abilities across the life span. *Dissertation Abstracts International*, 1972, *32*, 4901.

PARKES, C. M. *Bereavement: Studies of grief in adult life.* New York: International Universities Press, 1972.

PECK, E. *The baby trap.* New York: Pinnacle Books, 1972.

PERLMUTTER, E. Maximum term given attacker of woman. *The New York Times*, March 3, 1977, 1c; 33c.

PFEIFFER, E. & DAVIS, G. Determinants of sexual behavior in middle and old age. *Journal of the American Geriatrics Society*, April 1972, *20*, 157.

PICKETT, R. S. Tomorrow's family. *Intellect*, 1977, *105* (2383), 330–332.

PIKUNAS, J. *Human development (3rd ed.).* New York: McGraw-Hill Book Company, 1976.

PLECK, J. H. & SAWYER, J. (Eds.) *Men and masculinity.* Englewood-Cliffs, N.J.: Prentice-Hall, Inc., 1974.

PLUTCHIK, R., WEINER, M., & CONTE, H. Studies of body image, body worries, and body discomforts. *Journal of Gerontology*, 1971, *26*, 344–350.

POPENOE, P. Problems of working mothers. *Family Life*, 1976, *36* (2), 1–4.

Population proliferation and pollution. *Intellect*, 1973, *102* (2351), 6.

PRINGLE, BRUCE M. Family clusters as a means of reducing isolation among urbanites. *The Family Coordinator*, April 1974, *23* (2), 175–179.

Program information statement (1972) cited in B. K. Smith *Aging in America.* Boston: Beacon Press, 1973.

QUINN, R., STAINES, G., & McCULLOUGH, M. Job satisfaction: Is there a trend? U.S. Department of Labor, Manpower Research Monograph No. 30. Washington, D.C.: Government Printing Office, 1974.

RADL, S. *Mother's day is over.* New York: McKay, 1973.

RAMEY, J. Multi-adult households: Living groups of the future. *The Futurist,* 1976, *10,* 79–83.

RAO, S. N. Academic achievement and anxiety. *Psychological Studies,* 1974, *19* (1), 38–42.

RAPOPORT, R. & RAPOPORT, R. N. *Leisure and the family life cycle.* London: Routledge and Kegan Paul, 1975.

Recreation for all is latest goal in cities. *U.S. News & World Report,* May 23, 1977, 72–73.

REICHARD, S., LIVSON, F., & PETERSON, P. G. *Aging and personality: A study of 87 older men.* New York: John Wiley & Sons, Inc., 1962.

REINER, B. S. & R. L. EDWARDS. Adolescent marriage—Social or therapeutic problem? *The Family Coordinator,* 1974, *23* (4), 383–390.

RESTAK, R. The danger of knowing too much. *Psychology Today.* 1975, *9* (4), 21–23; 88; 92–93.

Retirement to the porch. *Human Behavior,* 1976, *5* (3), 45.

RIEGEL, K. F. & RIEGEL, R. M. Development, drugs, and death. *Developmental Psychology,* 1972, *6* (2), 306–319.

RILEY, M. W., FONER, A., & ASSOCIATES. *Aging and society (Volume I) An inventory of research findings.* New York: Russell Sage Foundation, 1968.

RIPLEY, T. & O'BRIEN, S. Career planning for leisure. *Journal of College Placement,* 1976, *36* (3), 54–58.

Rising divorce rate. *Intellect,* 1975, *103* (2366), 488.

ROGERS, D. *Psychology of adolescence (3rd ed.).* Englewood Cliffs, N.J.: Prentice-Hall, Inc., 1977.

ROGERS, K. Crisis at the midpoint of life. *New Society,* April 1936, 39.
———— The mid-career crisis. *Saturday Review of the Society,* 1973, *1* (1), 37–38.

ROHLEN, T. P. The promise of adulthood in Japanese spiritualism. *Daedalus,* 1976, *105* (2), 125–143.

ROLLINS, B. C. & CANNON, K. L. Marital satisfaction over the family life cycle: a reevaluation. *Journal of Marriage and the Family,* 1974, *36,* 271–283.

ROSEN, S., OLIN, P., & ROSEN, H. V. Dietary prevention of hearing loss. *Acta Otolaryngol,* 1970, *70,* 242–247.

ROSENBERG, S. D. & FARRELL, M. P. Identity and crisis in middle aged men. *International Journal of Aging and Human Development,* 1976, *7* (2), 153–170.

ROSENBLATT, P. C. Behavior in public places: Comparisons of couples accompanied and unaccompanied by children. *Journal of Marriage and the Family,* 1974, *36,* 750–755.

ROSENBLATT, P. C. & RUSSELL, M. G. The social psychology of potential problems in family vacations. *The Family Coordinator,* 1975, *24* (2), 209–215.

ROSENZWEIG, M. R. Keep that brain busy. *Parade Magazine,* May 7, 1972.

ROSOW, I. Old People: Their friends and neighbors. *American Behavioral Scientist,* 1970, *14* (1), 59–69.

———— *Socialization to old age.* Berkeley, Calif.: University of California Press, 1974.

ROSS, K., BRAGA, J., & BRAGA, L. D. Omego. In E. Kübler-Ross (Ed.) *Death: The final stage of growth.* Englewood Cliffs, N.J.: Prentice-Hall, Inc., 1975, 164–166.

RUDINGER, C. Determinants of intellectual performance: Results from the Bonn Gerontological Longitudinal Study. *Archives of Psychology,* 1972, *125,* 23–38.

RUDOLPH, S. H. & LLOYD, J. R. Rajput adulthood: Reflections on the Amar Singh diary. *Daedalus,* 1976, *105* (2), 145–168.

RUSSELL, C. S. Transition to parenthood: Problems and gratifications. *Journal of Marriage and the Family,* 1974, *36,* 294–302.

SCANZONI, J. Sex role change and influences on birth intentions. *Journal of Marriage and the Family,* 1976, *38* (7), 43–58.

SCHAIE, K. W. A reinterpretation of age-related changes in cognitive structure and functioning. In L. R. Goulet and P. B. Baltes (Eds.) *Life-span developmental psychology: Research and theory.* New York: Academic Press, 1970, 486–508.

———— Developmental policies and aging. In L. R. Goulet and M. P. Lawton (Eds.) *The psychology of adult development and aging.* Washington, D.C.: American Psychological Association, 1973.

———— Reflections on papers by Looft, Peterson and Sparks: Towards an ageless society. *The Gerontologist,* 1973, *13,* 31–35.

———— & GRIBBEN, K. Adult development and aging. In M. R. Rosenzweig and L. W. Porter (Eds.) *Annual review of psychology, Vol. 26,* Palo Alto, Calif.: Annual Reviews, Inc., 1975, 65–95.

———— & LABOUVIE-VIEF, G. Generational versus onteogenetic components of change in adult cognitive behavior: A fourteen-year cross-sequential study. *Developmental Psychology,* 1974, *10* (3), 305–320.

———— & BUESCH, B. Generational and cohort-specific differences in adult cognitive functioning. *Developmental Psychology,* 1973, *9* (2), 151–166.

———— & MARQUETTE, B. Personality in maturity and old age. In R. B. Dreger (Ed.) *Multi-variate personality research: Contributions to the understanding of personality in honor of Raymond B. Cattell.* Baton Rouge: Claitor's Publishing, 1972, 612–632.

SCHNAIBERG, A. & GOLDENBERG, S. Closing the circle: The impact of children on parental status. *Journal of Marriage and the Family,* 1975, *37* (4), 937–953.

SCHNEIDMAN, E. S. You and death. *Psychology Today,* 1971, *5* (1), 43–45; 74–80.

SCHOFIELD, W. *Psychotherapy: Purchase of friendship.* Englewood Cliffs, N.J.: Prentice-Hall, Inc., 1974.

SCHWARTZ, M. & BADEN, M. A. Female adolescent self-concept: An examination of the relative influence of peers and adults. *Youth and Society,* 1973, *5* (1), 115–128.

SEGRE, R. Senescence of the voice. *Eye, Ear, Nose, Throat Monthly,* 1971, *50* (6), 223–227.

SEGRE, S. Family stability, social classes and values in traditional and industrial societies. *Journal of Marriage and the Family*, 1975, *37* (2), 431–436.

SEGUIN, M. M. Opportunity for peer socialization in a retirement community. *The Gerontologist*, 1973, *13*, 208–214.

SELTZER, M. M. & ATCHLEY, R. C. The concept of old: Changing attitudes and stereotypes. *The Gerontologist*, 1971, *11* (3:1), 226–230.

SELYE, H. Stress. *Intellectual Digest*, 1974, *4* (10), 43–46.

SEVERO, S. Cancer: More than a common disease for many patients an uncommon silent stigma. *The New York Times*, May 4, 1977, 1; 48.

SHANAS, E. & HAUSER, P. M. Zero population growth and the family life of old people. *Journal of Social Issues*, 1974, *30* (4), 79–91.

SHEEHY, G. *Passages: The predictable crises of adult life.* New York: E. P. Dutton & Co., Inc., 1976.

SHERMAN, S. R. On-site services in retirement housing. *Aging and Human Development*, 1975, *6* (3), 239–247.

SHEPPARD, H. & HERRICK, N. *Where have all the robots gone? Worker dissatisfaction in the 70's.* New York: The Free Press, 1972.

SHORE, H. Institutional care for the aged: Letter to HEW secretary Elliott Richardson. *The Gerontologist*, 1972, (2), 114.

SHULMAN, N. Life-cycle variations in patterns of close relationships. *Journal of Marriage and the Family*, 1975, *37* (4), 813–821.

SIDNEY, K. H. & SHEPHARD, R. J. Activity patterns of elderly men and women. *Journal of Gerontology*, 1977, *32* (1), 25–32.

SILVERMAN, A. & SILVERMAN, A. *The case against having children.* New York: David McKay Co., Inc., 1971.

SILVERMAN, P. R. Widowhood and preventive intervention. *The Family Coordinator*, 1972, *21*, 95–102.

——— Widowhood and preventive intervention. In S. H. Zarit (Ed.) *Aging and death: Contemporary perspectives.* New York: Harper & Row, Publishers, 1977, 175–182.

SILVERMAN, R. E. *Psychology (2nd ed.).* Englewood Cliffs, N.J.: Prentice-Hall, Inc., 1974.

SIMON, A. Mental hygiene. In *Physical and mental health.* (White House Conference on Aging background paper) Washington, D.C., Government Printing Office, 1971.

SIMON, W., GAGNON, J. H. & BUFF, S. A. Son of Joe: Continuity and change among white working class adolescents. *Journal of Youth and Adolescence*, 1972, *1* (1), 13–34.

SINEX, F. M. The biochemistry of aging. In M. G. Spencer and C. J. Dorr (Eds.) *Understanding aging: A multidisciplinary approach.* New York: Appleton-Century-Crofts, 1975, 21–39.

SKOLNICK, A. The intimate environment. Boston: Little, Brown, and Company, 1973.

SMITH, B. K. *Aging in America.* Boston: Beacon Press, 1973.

SMITH, M. B. with COLIN CAMPBELL. Are you an iceberg, a mirror or an island? Our many versions of the self. *Psychology Today*, 1976, *9* (9), 74–79.

SMITH, R. T. & BRAND, F. N. Effects of enforced relocation on life adjustment in a nursing home. *Journal of Aging and Human Development*, 1975, *6* (3), 245–259.

SMITHSON, W. S. Emotional maturity. *Mental Hygiene*, 1974, *58* (1), 9–11.

SOILEAU, F. The implications of early and career socialization for social and leisure patterns among the elderly. Ph.D. Dissertation. Louisiana State University, 1972.

SPEKKE, A. A. America: The next 200 years. *Intellect*, 1976, *105* (2376), 49–50.

SPINDLER, G. D. The education of adolescents: An anthropological perspective. In E. D. Evans (Ed.) *Adolescence: Readings in behavior and development*, Hinsdale, Ill.: Dryden Press, 1970.

SPREITZER, E. & RILEY, L. E. Factors associated with singlehood. *Journal of Marriage and the Family*, 1974, *36* (3), 533–542.

SROLE, L., LANGNER, S., MICHAEL, S. T., OPLER, M. K., & RENNIE, T. A. C. *Mental health in the metropolis: The midtown Manhattan study*. New York: McGraw-Hill Book Company, 1962.

STAATS, S. and the 1972 Experimental Psychology Class. Internal versus external locus of control for three age groups. *International Journal of Aging and Human Development*, 1974, *5* (1), 7–10.

STAFFORD, R., MACKMAN, E., & DIBONA, P. The division of labor among cohabiting and married couples. *Journal of Marriage and the Family*, 1977, *39* (1), 43–58.

STALEY, E. J. & MILLER, N. (Eds.) Leisure and the quality of life: A new ethic for the 70's and beyond. Washington, D.C.: The American Association for Health, Physical Education, and Recreation, 1972.

Statistical Bulletin. *Metropolitan Life Statistical Bulletin*, 1972, *53*, 8–10.

STEGNER, W. The writer and the concept of adulthood. *Daedalus*, 1976, *105* (4), 39–48.

STEIN, A. H. & BAILEY, M. M. The socialization of achievement orientation in females. *Psychological Bulletin*, 1973, *80* (5), 345–366.

STEIN, B., COHEN, A., & GADON, H. Flextime: Work when you want to. *Psychology Today*, 1976, *10* (1), 40–43; 80.

STEIN, P. J. *Single*. Englewood Cliffs, N.J.: Prentice-Hall, Inc., 1976.

——— The Jung triangle. *Human Behavior*, 1976, *5* (5), 17–23.

STOLMER, F. H. The intimate network of families as a new structure. In H. A. Otto (Ed.) *The family in search of a future*. New York: Appleton-Century-Crofts, 1970.

STONE, K. & KALISH, R. Of poker, roles and aging: Description, discussion, and data. *Aging and Human Development*, 1973, *4*, 1–13.

STONE, L. J. & CHURCH, J. *Childhood and adolescence (3rd ed.)* New York: Random House, 1973.

STORCK, P. A., LOOFT, W. R., & HOOPER, F. H. Interrelationships among Piagetian tasks and traditional measures of cognitive abilities in mature and aged adults. *Journal of Gerontology*, 1972, *27*, 461–465.

STORY, M. L. Vocational education as contemporary slavery. *Intellect*, 1974, *102* (2356), 370–372.

STREHLER, B. L. A new age for aging. In S. H. Zarit (Ed.) *Readings in aging and death: Contemporary perspectives.* New York: Harper & Row, Publishers, 1977, 49–55.

STREIB, G. F. Social stratification and aging. In R. H. Binstock and E. Shanas (Eds.) *Handbook of aging and the social sciences.* New York: Van Nostrand Reinhold Company, 1976, 160–185.

STRIBLING, F. T. Annual report of the court of directors of the Western lunatic Asylum to the legislature of Virginia, with the report of the physician, for 1841. Richmond, Va.: Shepard and Conlin, 1842, 15–16.

SWEETSER, D. A. Sociologic perspectives on aging. In M. G. Spencer and C. J. Dorr (Eds.) *Understanding aging: A multidisciplinary approach.* New York: Appleton-Century-Crofts, 1975.

TARRANT, M. Thrifty, cautious, self-reliant and ahead of the game. *Money,* March 1976, *5* (3), 87–96.

TAVRIS, C. The experimenting society: To find programs that work, government must measure its failures. *Psychology Today,* 1975, *9* (4), 46–56.

——— Women: Work isn't always the answer. *Psychology Today,* 1976, *10* (4), 78.

TAYLOR, A. R. Habits, fears and desires of the genus graduate student. *Change,* 1976, *8* (4), 31–34.

TERKEL, S. *Working.* New York: Pantheon Books, Inc., 1974.

The economics of being single. *Money,* 1976, *5* (7), 32–38.

The emotional pain of mastectomy. *Psychology Today,* 1977, *10* (11), 98–99.

The social limits of fertility. *Human Behavior,* 1976, *5* (6), 24.

The television image of women. *Intellect,* 1975, *103* (2365), 424–425.

THOMPSON, L. & MARSH, G. Psychological studies of aging. In C. Eisdorfer and M. P. Lawton (Eds.) *The psychology of adult development and aging.* Washington, D.C.: American Psychological Association, 1973.

THOMPSON, V. D. Family size: Implicit policies and assumed psychological outcomes. *Journal of Social Issues,* 1974, *30* (4), 93–124.

THURNER, M. Goals, values, and life evaluations of the preretirement stage. *Journal of Gerontology,* 1974, *29,* 85–96.

TIDBALL, M. Study of American women achievers. *The Executive Woman,* February 1975.

TIMIRAS, P. S. *Developmental physiology and aging.* New York: Macmillan, Inc., 1972.

TOBIN, J. D. Normal aging—the inevitability syndrome. In S. H. Zarit, (Eds.) *Readings in aging and death: Contemporary perspectives.* New York: Harper & Row, Publishers, 1977, 39–47.

TORREY, E. F. The primal therapy trip: Medicine or religion? *Psychology Today,* 1976, *10* (7), 62–68.

TRILLING, D. Daughters of the middle class. *Harpers Magazine,* 1977, *254* (1523), 31–38.

TROLL, L. E. *Early and middle adulthood.* Monterey, Calif.: Brooks Cole Publishing Co., 1975.

———— Is parent-child conflict what we mean by the generation gap? *The Family Coordinator*, 1972, *21* (3), 347–349.

———— The family of later life: A decade review. *Journal of Marriage and the Family*, 1971, *33*, 274.

TROST, J. The family life cycle: A problematic concept. Paper presented at the 13th International Seminar on Family Research, International Sociological Association, Paris, France, 1973.

TSOI-HOSHMAND, L. Marital therapy and changing values. *The Family Coordinator*, 1976, *25* (1), 57–63.

TUCKMAN, J. & LORGE, I. Classification of the self as young, middle-aged or old. *Geriatrics*, 1954, (9), 534–536.

TURNER, J. D. Patterns of intergenerational exchange: A development approach. *Aging and Human Development*, 1975, *6* (22), 111–115.

TURNER, R. H. Is there a quest for identity? *The Sociological Quarterly*, 1975, *16* (2), 148–161.

U.S. Bureau of the Census. Household and family characteristics: March 1975. *Current Population Reports* (P-20, No. 291). Washington, D.C.: U.S. Government Printing Office, 1976.

U.S. Bureau of the Census. Number, timing, and duration of marriages and divorces in the United States: June 1975. *Current Population Reports* (P-20, No. 297). Washington, D.C.: U.S. Government Printing Office, 1976.

U.S. Department of Health, Education and Welfare (USHEW), Health in the later years of life: Selected data from the National Center for Health statistics. Washington, D.C.: Government Printing Office, 1971.

U.S. Senate hearings, Special Committee on Aging, 91st Congress, 2nd Session, Part 10A: Pension aspects of the economics of aging. Washington, D.C., 1970, p. 1426.

VAILLANT, G. E. How the best of the brightest came of age. *Psychology Today*, 1977, *11* (4), 34–41; 107–108; 110.

VEEVERS, J. E. The life style of voluntarily childless couples. In L. Larson (Ed.) *The Canadian family in comparative perspective.* Toronto: Prentice-Hall of Canada, 1975.

———— Voluntary childlessness and social policy: An alternative view. *The Family Coordinator*, 1974, *23* (4), 397–406.

VERBRUGGE, L. Sex differentials in morbidity and mortality in the United States. Paper presented at the Annual Meeting of the Population Association of America, 1975.

VINCENT, C. E. An open letter to the caught generation. *The Family Coordinator*, 1972, *21* (2), 143–150.

WALSH, R. H. The generation gap in sexual beliefs. *Sexual Behavior*, January 1972, 4–10.

WARREN, D. I. & WARREN, R. B. Six kinds of neighborhood. *Psychology Today*, 1975, *9* (1), 74–80.

WARREN, T. R. Senior researcher. The Kennedy Center for Bioethics testimony, U.S. Senate Special Committee on Aging, 1972.

WATSON, J. A. & KIVETT, V. R. Influences on the life satisfaction of older fathers. *The Family Coordinator*, 1976, *25* (4), 482–488.

WEI-MING, T. The Confucian perception of adulthood. *Daedalus*, 1976, *105* (2), 109–124.

WEINER, I. B. *Psychological disturbance in adolescence*. New York: Wiley-Interscience, 1970.

WEISSMAN, A. *On dying and denying*. New York: Behavioral Publications, Inc., 1972.

WEITZMAN, L. J. To love, honor, and obey? Traditional legal marriage and alternative family forms. *The Family Coordinator*, 1975, *24* (4), 531–548.

What future for the American family. *Changing Times*, 1976, *30* (12), 7–10.

When college graduates enter the real world. *U.S. News & World Report*. March 14, 1977, *82* (10), 79–80.

Where are the role models? *Psychology Today*, 1977, *6* (2), 60–61.

White House Conference on Aging. Aging and blindness. Special Concerns Session report. Washington, D.C.: Government Printing Office, 1972.

Why millions hate their jobs and what's afoot to help. *U.S. News & World Report*, September 27, 1976, 87–90.

WIREMAN, B. O. Crisis in authority. *College and University Journal*, 1970, *9* (4), 19–20.

WOLFARTH, G. A. An examination of family need fulfillment in an experimental extended family setting. Unpublished professional paper. Texas Woman's University, 1973.

Women under 50 are warned on the risks of breast X-rays. *The New York Times*, March 3, 1977, 16.

WOODRING, P. Why 65? The case against mandatory retirement. *Saturday Review*, August 7, 1976, 18–20.

WOODRUFF, D. S. & BIRREN, J. E. Age changes and cohort differences in personality. *Developmental Psychology*, 1972, *6*, 252–259.

Work in America. Report prepared for the Secretary of Health, Education and Welfare, by the Upjohn Institute for Employment Research, 1972.

YANKELOVICH, D. *The changing values on campus*. New York: Simon & Schuster, Inc., 1972.

———— *The new morality: A profile of American Youth in the 70s*. New York: McGraw-Hill Book Company, 1974.

———— Turbulence in the working world: Angry workers, happy grads. *Psychology Today*, 1974, *8* (7), 81–87.

YORBURG, B. The future of the American family. *Intellect*, 1973, *101* (2346), 253–260.

Youth. The 74th Yearbook of the National Society for the Study of Education, Part I. Chicago: University of Chicago Press, 1975.

Youth's attitudes. *Children Today*, 1975, *4* (6), 14–15.

ZABLOCKI, B. Urban communes project. Unpublished data, Columbia University, 1975.

ZARIT, S. H. Gerontology—Getting better all the time. In S. H. Zarit (Ed.)

Readings in aging and death: Contemporary perspectives. New York: Harper & Row, Publishers, 1977.

ZEITLEN, M. Corporate ownership and control: The large corporation and the capitalist class. *American Journal of Sociology,* 1974, *79,* 1073–1119.

ZIMBERG, S. The elderly alcoholic. *The Gerontologist,* 1974, *14,* 221–224.

ZUBIN, J. Foundations of gerontology—History, training, and methodology. In C. Eisdorfer and M. P. Lawton (Eds.) *The psychology of adult development of aging.* Washington, D.C.: American Psychological Association, 1973.

Glossary

aborigines: Natives; early inhabitants.

aestheticism: Sensitivity to art and beauty.

affiliative: Characterized by a close relationship to others.

ageism: The process of systematically stereotyping and discriminating against people on the basis of age.

aging: The process by which an organism progresses through the stages of immaturity, maturity, and deterioration from conception until death.

agnostic: One who believes it impossible to know whether or not there is a God or future life.

agrarian: Relating to agriculture or the land.

alternative family: Any of the family living styles other than the traditional two-parent nuclear family.

amniocentesis: Perforation or tapping, as with a needle, of the innermost membrane of the sac enclosing the embryo.

amphetamines: Synthetic drugs customarily used as inhalants, as sprays for head colds, hay fever, etc., and as diet pills. Amphetamine sulfate is a white, odorless powder that acts as a stimulant to the nervous system.

androgynous: Characterized by both masculine and feminine characteristics.

annihilation concept: The view of death as a state of total unawareness or nothingness.

anomic: Rootless and lacking a sense of identity.

anomie: A state of normlessness characterized by feelings of personal and social demoralization and disorganization; a psychological state characterized by feelings of rootlessness and lack of a firm identity, often experienced by persons in cultures undergoing rapid change.

anthropoid: Resembling man.

anthropologist: One who makes comparative studies of the chief characteristics of humans, including somatic characteristics, social habits and customs, and language.

anthropometric: Pertaining to measurements of the weight and proportions of the human body.

anticipatory socialization: The process of engaging in activities that prepare one for later roles in society.

arteriosclerosis: A condition distinguished by thickening, hardening, and diminished elasticity of the arteries.

artifact: Any article made by humans.

asynchrony: A lack of concurrence in timing.

atrophy: Wasting away, especially of body tissue or an organ.

autonomous: Independent.

biculturalism: Possession of the characteristics of two cultures.

biofeedback: The employment of instrumentation to increase the control and awareness of one's own bodily processes.

bohemian: An individual who lives in an "arty," unconventional fashion.

butch: A lesbian who behaves in a somewhat masculine manner.

calcify: To harden; to change into a very hard substance.

calisthenics: Athletic exercises.

cardiovascular: Pertaining to the heart and blood vessels.

cataclysnic: Characterized by great upheaval.

catharsis: A cleansing or purgation; in Freudian terms, the patient purges the mind of repressed material (catharsis) by telling whatever occurs to her or him (free association).

chromosome: One of the minute bodies in the nucleus of a cell believed to carry genes and to constitute the mechanism of heredity.

chronic: Lasting, persistent, or recurring.

climacteric: The syndrome or pattern of symptoms (somatic, hormonal, and psychic) that characterizes the termination of the reproductive period in the female or the normal diminution of sexual activity in the male.

cognitive: Pertaining to the process of knowing and thinking.

cohabitation: The state of living together, most commonly applied to unmarried couples.

cohort: Category of persons who share some characteristic, such as age or period in history.

commune: A close-knit community of people who share common interests and activities, as in childrearing.

Confucianism: Ethical teachings introduced in the Chinese religion by Confucius; they stressed devotion to family and friends, ancestor worship, and justice and peace.

congenital: Anomaly marked by physical deviation present at, or usually before, birth.

cortical insult: Any condition that results in damage to the gray matter that covers most of the brain.

cosmology: The philosophy or theory of the principles and nature of the cosmos, or universe.

critical period: Time during which particular experiences may have especially profound and enduring effects.

cross-sectional research: The description of a number of persons in terms of one or more variables as they appear at a given time.

cult: Devoted attachment to a person, principle, or whatever, particularly when perceived as a fad.

culture: The way of life—material and behavioral—of a society, including its customs, knowledges, beliefs and morals.

cunnilingus: A sexual behavior that involves using the tongue on the clitoris or vulva.

decrement: Decrease or loss.

defense mechanism: In Freudian theory any behavior employed to achieve adjustment and ward off anxiety.

degenerative: Having the effect of causing deterioration, as in the change of tissue to a less functional form.

delusion: A false belief maintained in the face of contrary evidence.

dementia: A general term for mental deterioration.

demographic: Pertaining to the study of human populations, with reference to population trends, distribution, and differential birth rates in subcultural groupings.

de rigeur: According to proper form.

development: A process involving all the many changes, both qualitative and quantitative, that occur during progress toward maturity. It embraces both changes inherent in the maturing process and those resulting from interaction between the individual and the environment.

developmental approach: The frame of reference for studying the life span in which each phase of life is viewed in terms of both antecedent and anticipated phases.

developmental psychology: The branch of psychology concerned with characteristic behaviors at successive stages of development and the processes involved in moving from one state to another.

developmental task: Skill or accomplishment that should be satisfactorily mastered at a particular age-stage if an individual is to be ready for the next stage.

diabetes mellitus: A metabolic disorder characterized by loss, or almost complete loss, of ability to oxidize carbohydrates because of faulty pancreatic activity and consequent disturbance of normal insulin mechanism.

dichotomize: To separate into two mutually exclusive parts or categories.

dichotomous: Divided into two mutually exclusive categories.

dichotomy: Division into two discrete parts.

discrete: Distinct and separate; unrelated.

disengagement: The mutual withdrawal by aging persons and those in their social environment from each other.

divergent: Contrasting; varying from the norm.

DNA: (deoxyribonucleic acid) and RNA (ribonucleic acid): Two key chemicals in the genes that determine whether substances causing particular characteristics (for example, blue or brown eyes) will be produced. DNA is believed to contain the chemical blueprint for the cells.

dogmatism: Stubborn assertion of opinion, regardless of evidence.

Don Quixote: The hero of a seventeenth-century satirical romance who attempted in a chivalrous but unrealistic manner to help the oppressed and attack evil.

double sex standard: Code of morality that involves different codes for judging the behaviors of each sex.

dyad: A two-person combination.

dyadic: Pertaining to a relationship in which two persons or objects are involved.

ecological: Pertaining to that branch of biology that concerns the relationship between living organisms and their environment.

ego: Self, as distinguished from other; the aspect of the psyche (general psychological function) that is conscious and most in touch with reality.

egocentric: Self-centered.

electrocardiograph: An instrument for making electrocardiograms, or tracings of electric currents produced by the contraction of the heart muscles.

emasculated: Deprived of virility or manhood.

emphysema: A swelling caused by the presence of air in the interstices of connective tissues of the lungs.

empirical: Based on experience, careful experiment, and/or observation.

encounter group: A group characterized by frank, intimate, often emotional interaction.

environmental engineering: Conscious planning and manipulation of the environment to achieve certain desired effects.

enzyme: An organic compound, often a protein, capable of producing or accelerating some change in its substrate, for which it is often specific.

epiphenomenon: A secondary occurrence that results from another.

equity: Fairness.

Erikson, Erik: A psychoanalyst who is well-known for his theories and writings relating to human development.

estrogen: Any of several estrus-producing compounds, estrus being the sexual excitement, or heat, of female mammals.

ethic: Moral code.

ethical: Conforming to standards of conduct.

euphoric: Possessive of a feeling of well-being.

euthanasia, active: The deliberate killing of persons presumed to be hopelessly disabled or ill, with no prospect of meaningful life in the future.

euthanasia, passive: The practice of simply permitting a patient to die naturally instead of exerting special efforts to maintain life, when such life would, in all likelihood, consist in a vegetative existence or involve much suffering.

existential: Of, or based on, existence.

experimental method: The procedure in which specific conditions are arranged under which a phenomenon is to be observed to determine the influences of these conditions. The observed phenomenon is called the dependent variable; the arranged conditions are called independent, or experimental, variables.

extended family: A family unit that includes the parents, children, and assorted kin, usually grandparents.

extrapolate: To estimate or infer on the basis of variables within the known range.

extrovert: One whose predominant interest is in the external environment and in others and who has a correspondingly reduced concern for reflection and introspection.

fem: The individual who assumes a feminine role in lesbian pair relationships.

flexitime: The practice of allowing employees considerable flexibility and autonomy in determining their work schedules.

formal operations: (Piaget) The period (between ages 11 and 15) when truly logical thinking begins and the final step is taken toward abstract thinking and conceptualization.

functional age: Aging status based on what an individual is capable of doing, as distinct from number of years lived.

futurism: The science of anticipating and planning for years to come.

gay: Homosexual.

generation gap: Discrepancy in understanding or values between one age cohort and another (see cohort).

generation unit: A grouping within the same generation that organizes its common experience in distinctive ways.

generations effect: The differential impact on successive age cohorts, not merely because of age difference, but because they have experienced different historical events.

generativity: The impulse for procreation, or interest in establishing and guiding the next generation.

gerontocracy: A governing group composed of old men.

gerontology: Study of the elderly.

global: Assuming a broad, holistic view.

gregariousness: Sociability; fondness for associating with others.

gynecological: Relating to the study and treatment of women's diseases, especially of the rectal and genito-urinary tracts.

Hall, G. Stanley: A distinguished American psychologist and educator who pioneered in research with adolescents and authored certain classic works concerning them, including *The Contents of Children's Minds* (1883) and *Adolescence* (1904).

hemophilia: A condition inherited by males through the mother, such as a sex-linked character characterized by slow clotting of the blood and consequent difficulty in checking hemorrhage.

heterogeneous: Composed of dissimilar ingredients or elements.

hippie: A contemporary version of the Bohemian, who believes in liberty, living for the moment, and completely free self-expression.

homogeneous: Uniform; composed of like or identical parts; the same throughout in structure.

homosexual: One who is sexually attracted towards others of the same sex.

humanist: One who is philosophically concerned with the ideas and ideals of human beings.

humanistic: Concerned with the ideas and ideals of human beings.

hypothesis: An admittedly tentative explanation of a body of data.

hypothetical: Characterized by an admittedly tentative explanation of a body of data.

hysterectomy: Surgical removal of all, or part of, the uterus.

identity: A sense of uniqueness as a person, equivalent to answering the question, "Who am I?"

identity crisis: A psychological state caused by the need to make several significant decisions within a relatively short length of time.

ideology: The doctrines, opinions, or philosophy of an individual or group.

idiosyncratic: Relating to temperament or characteristic peculiar to a person or a group.

incest: Marriage between close blood relatives, especially within immediate family.

infanticide: The murder of a baby.

instrumental: Characterized by goal-directed activity.

intelligence quotient (IQ): A score derived from an intelligence test indicating how the individual's demonstrated mental ability compares with that of others at the same developmental stage.

intrapsychic: Originating within the human mind or soul.

Jung, Carl Gustaf: A Swiss psychologist (1875–1961) who made significant contributions to personality theory.

kibbutz (plural, kibbutzim): A collective farm settlement in Israel.

latency children: Individuals at the stage in psychosexual development (usually from ages 5 or 6 until puberty) when infantile sexual urges are dormant.

latency period: A stage in psychosexual development, usually from ages 5 or 6 until puberty, when infantile sexual urges are dormant.

leisure: Time spent doing what one desires to do at one's own pace.

lesbian: A female whose sexual preference is for another of her own sex.

lesion: Injury; damage.

life cycle: The complete set of phenomena and events that comprise the total life span.

life style: The overall pattern of motives, coping techniques, and behaviors that generally characterize an individual's behavior.

living will: An individual's expression of desire regarding such matters as whether or not life will be maintained by extraordinary efforts or life-maintaining machines when that individual's condition may no longer allow making such a decision.

longitudinal research: Study involving repeated observations of or measurements on.

lost adolescent syndrome: Pattern of symptoms caused by short-circuiting adolescence, before a satisfactory identity is established by premature marriage and parenthood.

Lothario: A rake or seducer of women (after the name of a gay blade in Nicholas Rowe's play, *The Fair Penitent* [1703]).

machismo: Delusion of power and strength, often associated with excessive pride in one's own masculinity or a false sense of superiority.

macro: Prefix meaning large-scale, enlarged, or elongated (Opposite: micro).

mammography: Roentgen photography of the mammary gland for diagnosing and localizing pathologic conditions of the breast.

masochistic: Tending to inflict pain on oneself.

mastectomy: Surgical removal of the breast.

metabolic: Characterized by, or resulting from, metabolism, the physical and chemical processes that proceed continuously in living organisms and cells, by which assimilated food is built into protoplasm (anabolism) and broken down into waste and simpler substances (catabolism), as energy is released for vital processes.

mid-life crisis: A critical period, during middle age, when an individual is induced by the culmination of personal, physical, and social factors to examine his or her life; it may result in important modifications of life style and philosophy.

molecular: Pertaining to a molecule, the smallest particle of an element or compound that can exist in the free state while retaining the characteristics of that element or compound.

mongolism: A congenital mental condition characterized by slanting eyes, large tongue, flat skull, stubby fingers, and other physical abnormalities.

monolithic: Massively single, solid, and uniform.

moratorium: Delay, usually for a specified period of time.

narcissistic: Self-loving.

neurites: An axon, or core, that constitutes the essential conducting part of a nerve fiber.

neuron: A nerve cell, or structural unit of the nervous system.

neurosis: A somewhat poorly defined mental disorder, less serious than psychosis, and leaving the personality relatively intact.

neurotic: (Also psychoneurotic) Tending to behave in predominantly emotional rather than rational ways.

nostalgic: Having, or causing, nostalgia (longing for home, homeland, or something of long ago).

nuclear family: The family composed only of the father, mother, and children, as opposed to the extended family, which also includes all the descendants of a common grandparent and all their relatives.

nurturant: Characterized by warmth and involvement (personal love and compassion).

obese: Very stout.

obsolescence: The process or state of becoming out of date or going out of use.

octogenarian: An individual between 80 and 90 years of age.

ontogeny: Biological development of the individual as distinguished from phylogeny, or racial (evolutionary), development of any plant or animal species.

open marriage: The practice in which two or three couples live together and share sex partners.

organic: Constitutional; inborn.

ovulation: The physiological process by which a mature ovum (female germ cell) escapes from a ruptured follicle (sac or cavity).

paranoia: A functional psychosis characterized by delusions of persecution or grandeur.

parochial: Narrow; provincial.

pathogenic: Tending to cause disease.

pathological: Pertaining to a diseased or abnormal condition of the organism or its parts.

patriarchy: A sociocultural grouping, such as a family or tribe, in which the father or oldest male is recognized as head, and descent is traced through the male line.

penis envy: In psychoanalytic theory, the female's desire for the male sexual organ, or penis.

peripheral: Secondary; remote; tangential.

phase-specific task: Responsibility that it is critical to perform at a particular period in life.

phenomenologic: Expressive of primary concern for how others subjectively experience reality.

phylogenetic: Pertaining to phylogeny or the evolutionary development of a species.

phylogeny: Evolutionary development of the species.

pluralism: The concept of stressing multiple components instead of unity, as in social or cultural pluralism, which stresses the variety of groups composing a society.

pluralistic: Embracing or representing more than one unit.

pluralistic society: A group of groups forming a single community, overall composed of more than one relatively distinct subculture.

polarized sex roles: Division of persons or objects into two mutually exclusive, opposite categories.

postpartum: After child birth.

primal therapy: Under the guidance of a therapist, the psychic pain of certain childhood experiences is experienced again in order to unlock pain lodged since early years in the brain.

projective technique: A procedure for discovering an individual's characteristic modes of behavior by analyzing his or her responses to relatively ambiguous, unstructured stimuli or situations.

prostheses: Artificial body parts such as eyes and legs.

psychiatric: Pertaining to the branch of medicine concerned with mental disorders.

psychiatrist: A physician who specializes in the diagnosis and treatment of mental disease.

psychoanalytic: Relating to a body of doctrine associated with Freud and modified by his followers; a special technique for discovering hidden motivation.

psychogenic: Of mental or emotional origin.

psychoneurosis: A somewhat poorly defined class of mental disorder, less serious than psychosis, and leaving the personality relatively intact.

psychosis: The scientific name for severe mental disturbances; commonly called insanity.

psychosomatic: Pertaining to the mind-body relationship; having bodily symptoms of mental or emotional origin.

psychosynthesis: The process of integrating individual components of the mind into a whole; the opposite of psychoanalysis.

psychotic: Having or relating to severe mental disturbance.

pubertal rites: A program of precepts and rituals by which an individual, on reaching sexual maturity, is initiated into the adult life of the community.

pubescence: The period of about two years preceding puberty, or the time span of physiological development during which the reproductive system matures.

recapitulates: To repeat, at least in broad outline.

reference group: The group of persons with which an individual identifies, and determines for that individual standards of behavior, values, and status aspirations.

reinforcement: Increase in strength of a response when the response produces a reduction in drive.

relational identity crisis: The critical emotional and psychological status precipitated by the need of individuals to redefine their identities within the context of their relationship to each other, as in the case of marital partners.

remission: Spontaneous abatement or cessation of symptoms through some automatic self-healing process.

replication: Repetition.

rite of passage: Ritual associated with induction into the adult society.

role: A pattern of behavior associated with functions in various groups.

sadistic: Tending to inflict pain or injury on another.

saliency: The quality of being prominent or conspicuous.

self-actualization: The process of moving through sequentially higher stages of motivation and organization to adequate achievement of one's potential.

senescence: The process of growing old.

senile dementia: A condition associated with later years, characterized by memory gaps filled in with imagined memories, frequent disorientation, preoccupation with personal needs and, at times, feelings of persecution and suspiciousness.

senility: Old age, ordinarily with the connotation of mental and physical degeneration.

sex role: The pattern of behaviors characteristic of male or female in a particular society.

socialization: The process by which an individual learns to behave in ways approved by the society.

sodomy: Sexual intercourse between persons of the same sex or between a person and an animal.

somatic: Pertaining to body structure or framework of the body, distinctive from the viscera.

spartan: Highly disciplined; frugal; hardy; stoical.

stage theory: The conceptualization of human development as involving several relatively discrete stages that can be identified physiologically, psychologically, and sociologically.

stereotype: A preconceived, prejudiced picture of the members of some particular group.

stress: A condition created by abnormal tension, especially when no ready solution is available for a crucial problem.

substrate: Basis or foundation.

swinging: The consensual and occasional exchange of sex partners by married couples.

synapses: Points of contact between adjacent neurons where nerve impulses are transmitted from one to another.

synaptic: Pertaining to synapse, or point of contact between adjacent neurons.

synchrony: Condition of internal harmony.

syndrome: Pattern.

tactile: Pertaining to touch.

terminal drop: Accelerated decline in cognitive development within the years just preceding death.

testosterone: Male sex hormone.

therapeutic: Healing; curative.

therapy: Treatment.

trajectory: Path of some object through space, the direction of which is determined by whatever acts as the propellant.

transactional analysis: A process of cross-communication of each member of a relationship or group by the other member or members; or the dynamic two-way interaction between a therapist and patient.

transcendental meditation: A procedure for inducing complete relaxation, ordinarily followed about 20 minutes each time twice a day, in which one sits with eyes closed, focusing on the rhythm of his or her breathing, and saying some word or number in rhythm with the breathing.

transsexual: An individual who feels like a member of the opposite sex.

trauma: Experience that inflicts serious physical or psychological shock on the organism.

value: In the ethical sense, the worth an individual ascribes to various activities, ideas, and objects.

vascular: Having vessels or ducts for conveying blood or lymph.

vas deferens: The duct that conveys sperm from the testicle to the ejaculatory duct of the penis.

vasectomy: Surgical removal of the vas deferens, or duct that conveys sperm from the testicle to the ejaculatory duct of the penis.

vicarious: Characterized by imagined instead of actual participation in an experience.

vivisectionist: One who performs surgical operations on a living animal in order to investigate the structure and function of living parts and organs.

walkabout: A half-year long endurance test during which the native Australian boy must survive alone in the wilderness before returning to his tribe or else die in the process.

yoga: A mystic and ascetic practice ordinarily involving intense mental and physical discipline, as of particular posture or controlled breathing.

youth culture: All those attitudes, behaviors, and material objects that characterize and set apart persons in their teens and early twenties.

INDEX